THE *Ultimate*
Horse Behavior
AND Training BOOK

Also by Linda Tellington-Jones

BOOKS

Getting in TTouch
Understand and Influence Your Horse's Personality

Improve Your Horse's Well-Being
A Step-by-Step Guide to TTouch and TTEAM Training

Let's Ride! with Linda Tellington-Jones
Fun and TTeamwork with Your Horse or Pony

The Tellington TTouch
A Breakthrough Technique to Train and Care for Your Favorite Animal

An Introduction to the Tellington-Jones Equine Awareness Method
The TEAM Approach to Problem-Free Training

Getting in TTouch with Your Dog
A Gentle Approach to Influencing Behavior, Health, and Performance

Getting in TTouch with Your Cat
A New and Gentle Way to Harmony, Behavior, and Well-Being

DVDS/VIDEOS

Hit It Off with Your Horse!
Understanding and Influencing Character and Personality (DVD)

Unleash Your Dog's Potential
Getting in TTouch with Your Canine Friend (DVD)

Solving Riding Problems with TTEAM
Tape 1: From the Ground (VHS)

Solving Riding Problems with TTEAM
Tape 2: In the Saddle (VHS)

TTouch for Dressage (VHS)

Starting a Young Horse (DVD)

Haltering Your Foal without Trauma: Developing a Horse's Full Potential with TEAM (VHS)

Riding with Awareness: Developing a Horse's Full Potential with TEAM (VHS)

TTouch of Magic Video for Horses (VHS)

THE *Ultimate* Horse Behavior AND **Training** BOOK

Enlightened and Revolutionary Solutions for the 21st Century

LINDA TELLINGTON-JONES

with Bobbie Lieberman

Foreword by John Lyons

Photos by Gabriele Boiselle

Illustrations by Beth Preston

TRAFALGAR SQUARE
North Pomfret, Vermont

First published in 2006 by
Trafalgar Square Publishing
North Pomfret, Vermont 05053

Printed in China

Library of Congress Cataloging-in-Publication Data

Tellington-Jones, Linda.
   The ultimate horse behavior and training book : enlightened and revolutionary solutions for the 21st century / Linda
Tellington-Jones with Bobbie Lieberman ; foreword by John Lyons.
     p. cm.
  Includes bibliographical references and index.
   ISBN-13: 978-1-57076-320-5 (alk. paper)
   ISBN-10: 1-57076-320-8 (alk. paper)
   1. Horses--Behavior. 2. Horses--Training. I. Lieberman, Bobbie. II. Title.
   SF281.T45 2006
   636.1'0835--dc22
                      2006008026

All photos by Gabriele Boiselle except: Linda Tellington-Jones (pp. 60, 92, 198, 205 *bottom*, 220, 249); Bobbie Lieberman (pp.
156, 195, 224 *top*); Kate Riordan (p. 185); Ellen Van Leeuwen (p. 223); Tellington TTouch Archives (p. 226); Ingrid Wild (pp.
29, 224 *bottom*, 280, 282, 288 *right top & bottom*); Akaka Photographic, Inc. (p. 231); Lothar Lenz (pp. 246, 275, 289 *bottom*,
290); Kirsten Henry (pp. 262, 265 *left*); Carol Lang (p. 265 *right*); Hilmar Pabel (p. 279); Lynne Glazer (p. 316 *top*); Ramsey
Papp (p. 316 *bottom*)

All illustrations by Beth Preston except: Jeanne Kloepfer (pp. 50 *left*, 173, 174, 193, 210); Heather Mansfield (p. 147 *top*); Laura Maestro (pp. 147 *middle*, 219); Tellington TTouch Archives (pp. 200, 223); Cornelia Koller (pp. 171, 180, 181, 195, 203,
204, 205, 213, 217, 231, 235, 236, 237, 240, 241, 244, 246, 247); Phil Pretty (p. 262)

Jacket design by Heather Mansfield
Book text design by Carrie Fradkin
Typefaces: Rotis San Serif, Minion, Trajan

10 9 8 7 6 5 4 3

Linda's Dedication

To my brilliant sister, Robyn Hood, and my beloved husband, Roland Kleger

Bobbie's Dedication

For Perle

Table of Contents

Foreword

John Lyons

Few human beings demonstrate the virtue of consistency to the degree Linda Tellington-Jones does. Linda not only displays consistency, which is absolutely essential in training a horse, but she displays it throughout her life, through herself as a person. This consistency is manifested as an open, caring heart. She is the same way through her whole soul. Her energy and her heart come out of her face and her smile.

I have seen many people using flowery words about being kind to horses, but I have not always seen their actions back it up, either with horses or people. If you are rude to another person, you will most likely be rude to a horse. My knowledge of Linda and what I have observed over the last 20 years is her consistency of caring with people and horses.

Her training techniques are some of the most humane ever developed. Pain is never the solution to a training problem; it is only a distraction to what we want the horse to focus on. I am always amazed at how horses keep trying to learn in spite of pain; Linda's work clearly demonstrates how pain gets in the way of learning. Her light hand on horses gets results.

I'll never forget the night Linda worked on my stallion Zip when he had an unexpected health crisis during an equine expo in the mid-1990s. In a moment that night, Zip was certainly more peaceful. Horses immediately respond to kindness. You can't lie to a horse and tell him you like him when you don't.

They pick up on all the little things you do. How you touch them can put them at peace. It can be a surface-level feeling or a heartfelt feeling—horses can tell how you feel about them by the way your hands feel when you touch them. It's the same with people; someone can give you a hug and you get a cold feeling; with another person's hug you are drawn to them and feel safe. I don't think it's a mystical thing, but it's something that reflects everything we do—it lets everybody else know who we are.

I first met Linda in 1987 in Scottsdale, Arizona. Both of us were asked to be speakers at a one-day demonstration. I watched her work on a head-shy horse and a horse with wobbles. She worked well with the horses and the audience, answering their questions in a direct manner. She was serious about her work and helping people with their horses.

The horse world is always changing, with new people coming on board all the time. That is why the problems we are all working on are the same ones we faced 25 years ago: barn sour, sore backs, buddy-bound, spooky horses, fear of losing control, moving horses beyond past abuse, dealing with fear.

It takes an immense amount of dedication to put together a work like this. It is one thing to have the knowledge needed, but to stay focused and bring that knowledge to book form takes a tremendous commitment. This is a book destined to be on every horseperson's bookshelf. Congratulations, Linda.

John Lyons
October 2006

Introduction

Susan M. Harding

In 1989, shortly after joining *EQUUS* magazine as Publishing Director, I attended an industry meeting in Jackson Hole, Wyoming. Not yet knowing many of the people there, I stood at the doorway of the hotel watching a group clearly captivated by a woman at its table. I joined them and spent the next two hours listening to Linda Tellington-Jones share her recent experiences with some very difficult horses. If I had not already been aware of Linda from a cover story written by Bobbie Lieberman in *EQUUS* magazine in 1983, I would have been incredulous. Knowing a little bit about "the touch that teaches," as Linda's method was then known, I was fascinated to watch her communicate her experiences. I quickly realized that Linda, more than just another "horse whisperer," was also a superb teacher and horseman. Her ability to connect with those people that day, based on her understanding of and sensitivity to feelings, is what makes Linda so effective in dealing with a wide range of animals, be it humans or horses, cats, dogs and other mammals.

The Tellington Method, developed over many years, also has been verified by scientific research done around the world with both animals and people. That fact, together with Linda's remarkable ability to share information, is what makes the Tellington Method of such value to horse owners. The elements can be learned and used by all who are willing to be patient, "listen" to what their horse is telling them and be consistent in their interactions with the animal. Hence, while there is no doubt that Linda is an extraordinary horsewoman unparalleled in her ability to communicate and work with horses, what makes her and her methods truly special is that they can be learned and used by anyone. And, as verified by the research, they really work.

As I have watched Linda teach people how to work with their animals, I've always been amazed at the progress that is made in a relatively short period of time. The most exciting results are witnessed when watching those owners who are truly afraid of a horse that has become very aggressive, and consequently are unable to perform even the most basic horse-handling activities. By the end of a single day, these same individuals develop a relationship with their horse, are able to lead him through an obstacle course, and smile while doing it! Less dramatic perhaps, but just as important, are similar successes seen with people whose horses are frightened, timid or generally unresponsive.

Over the almost 20 years that I have known Linda, I have been proud to publish articles in *EQUUS, Dressage Today* and *Practical Horseman* bringing her methods to horse owners across America. Experienced and new horse owners, dressage competitors and trail riders, Thoroughbred and Quarter Horse owners all have welcomed her methods.

The Tellington Method truly is a wonderful tool for all, and this book is a superb compendium of what you need to know to understand the techniques and apply them to your horses. Co-written with Bobbie Lieberman, a renowned equine journalist and a student of Linda's work for more than 20 years, this book not only teaches the method, but also puts it in the perspective of today's horse world. Working together, Linda and Bobbie have created the ultimate guide to the Tellington Method's complete body of work.

This volume will bring you understanding of why your horse does what he does, and teach you how to work with him effectively while maximizing his performance and your enjoyment. I can't imagine asking for anything more from a book!

Susan M. Harding
Vice President, Group Publishing Director
Primedia Equine Group
October 2006

Preface
What is the Tellington Method®?

The Tellington Method® is a special system of training for horses and riders developed by Linda Tellington-Jones over three decades. Its roots are in Linda's discovery in the mid-1970s that working on a horse's body releases fear, tension, discomfort and pain in a way that changes behavior, influences personality, and enhances overall health and well-being.

The Tellington Method has three components. Tellington TTouch (known as TTouch and pronounced tee-touch), is a form of bodywork comprised of a variety of circles, lifts and slides done with the hands and fingertips. Coupled with carefully orchestrated Ground Exercises and Ridden Work, the Tellington Method dramatically expands and improves a horse's capacity for learning and cooperation, improves horse and rider balance and coordination, and deepens the horse-human bond.

What is the Tellington Method?

Evolution of the Tellington Method

Doing "bodywork" on animals is generally thought to be a modern trend. However, in 1905, my grandfather Will Caywood, a racehorse trainer, having secured 87 wins at the Moscow Hippodrome, was awarded the title of leading trainer and received a prize of a jeweled cane from Czar Nicolas II. He attributed his success to the fact that all the horses in his stable were "rubbed" over every inch of their bodies for 30 minutes each day.

My grandfather's influence has had a lifelong effect on me. In 1965, my then husband, Wentworth Tellington, and I published a manual entitled *Massage and Physical Therapy for the Athletic Horse*. It was based on the bodywork done on our horses after 100-mile endurance rides, steeplechases, three-day events and horse shows, in which I competed extensively. Our horses recovered much more quickly with bodywork.

However, it never crossed my mind at the time that the behavior and character of an animal—and his willingness and ability to learn—could be influenced by bodywork. That thinking changed in 1975 when I enrolled at the Humanistic Psychology Institute in San Francisco for a four-year training course taught by Dr. Moshe Feldenkrais. My enrollment in this study was an unlikely move on my part. This was a method of mind-body integration for the human nervous system, and I came from the world of horses. I had been teaching riding and training horses for over 20 years at that time, and for the past 10 years had co-owned and directed the Pacific Coast Equestrian Research Farm School of Horsemanship dedicated to the education of riding instructors and horse trainers.

I signed up for this training hoping I could adapt Dr. Feldenkrais' method for humans to enhance my riding instruction. As it turned out, I was able to adapt the Feldenkrais system, known for increasing athletic ability, alleviating pain, improving neurological function and increasing potential for learning, to a highly effective method of improving the performance, learning ability and well-being of horses.

I worked on hundreds of horses over the next eight years, developing ways of moving them from the ground and working them through obstacles in ways that would develop new neural pathways to the brain, thereby increasing their willingness and ability to learn. I saw remarkable improvements in behavior and balance and ability to perform. The work became known as the Tellington Touch Equine Awareness Method, or TTEAM.

Tellington TTouch: The "Aha Moment"

In 1983, my work with horses made another major shift. I was working with a Thoroughbred mare who was extremely resistant to grooming and saddling, pinning her ears, swishing her tail, and sometimes kicking. I began to work on her with subtle Feldenkrais movements of my hands on her body that you could barely see. Much to the surprise of Wendy, the mare's owner, she began to relax—lowering her head, softening her eyes, and standing quietly.

Wendy could hardly believe her eyes, and asked, "What are you doing? Are you using energy or what? What is your secret?" Without thinking, I replied, "Don't worry about what I'm doing, just put your hands on the horse and push the skin in a circle." I was as surprised at my words as she was, but many years before I had learned to trust my intuition. I watched in amazement as this normally aggressive mare stood quietly with soft, introspective eyes as Wendy gently pushed her skin in small circles and the mare became as quiet under her hands as she had with mine.

Circles were not a part of the Tellington Method, yet they seemed so easy and natural. Today, I'm certain TTouch was a divine gift. I realized in a flash of knowing that something special had happened and that I needed to explore these circular touches. Over the ensuing months and years, I experimented with various pressures, sizes, and tempo of circles. I practiced allowing my hands to move in many different ways, responding to what the animals liked. My sister, Robyn Hood, is as observant as an owl, and she combined her logical approach with my intuitive sense to clarify exactly how I was holding and moving my hands.

By the mid-1980s, I had developed a simple method now known as the Tellington TTouch. Unlike the Feldenkrais Functional Integration I had used for years, TTouch was easier to learn and had a profound effect on behavior, health and performance while deepening the human-animal bond.

Using this discovery, anyone could work on a horse's body with the gentle, circular touches described by *EQUUS* magazine in 1983 as "The Touch That Teaches." Since that time, we have developed over 30 specific TTouches, each having a slightly different effect. I realized that with so much choice, we needed creative names for each movement that could be easily remembered, so I named the TTouches for different animals I had worked on—the ones who evoked special memories.

Science to Match the Miracles

When I began to see major changes in the traumatized animals that I was working with 20 years ago, there was little understanding, and no research, to support my intuitive feeling that the TTouches released fear and memory of pain at the cellular level. However, neuroscientist Candice Pert, Ph.D., in her book, *Molecules of Emotion* (Scribner, 1997), demonstrated that emotions are held in the cells and transported to our brains by neuropeptides, complex structures that serve as "messenger molecules" to integrate the mind and body. Pert notes "the power of touch to stimulate and regulate our natural chemicals." She also acknowledges the phenomenon of cellular intelligence, further validating my grasp of the cell's role in TTouch. In addition, Nobel Laureate Charles Sherrington, a medical doctor and nervous system researcher, influenced me greatly when he wrote, "Every cell in the body knows its function within the body and its function within the universe." I believe that is why the Tellington Method has had such success in transforming animals who have been abused or are timid.

In 1987–88, I worked with Anna Wise of the Biofeedback Institute of Boulder, Colorado, measuring activation of brain wave patterns in both hemispheres of the brain. She had worked as a research assistant in England for 11 years with psychobiologist and biophysicist Maxwell Cade, who had discovered that a consistent pattern of alpha, beta, theta and delta waves were apparent in both hemispheres of the brain when a person was in the most effective state of mental functioning. Cade called this the "Awakened Mind State."

Anna was curious to know if I could match those brain waves when working with TTouch. When she discovered that I did indeed consistently operate with these brain waves while working on a person, she wanted to know if my students could display the same ability. While they were doing the circular TTouches on each other, brain waves were activated in both hemispheres. Even more remarkable, the *people* being worked on exhibited the same distinct brain wave patterns.

A BREAKTHROUGH IN EDUCATING HORSES

A research project at the German Reken Equine Test Center was designed to see if the average rider could successfully retrain "problem" horses using the Tellington Method. We accepted 20 horses—two for three weeks, and eight for two weeks. Five novice riders were also chosen to test the method's effectiveness when used by average riders. Test horses, enrolled by their riders and veterinarians, had documented behavioral and neurological problems. Several were given no chance of improvement by their trainers. The results were remarkable and became the foundation for my first book, *An Introduction to the Tellington Equine Awareness Method.*

A second research project to test stress reduction in sport horses was launched in Russia at the Bitsa Olympic Equestrian Center in 1984. There I presented a 10-day training seminar to a group of eight Russian veterinarians.

We did TTouch and worked horses through the *Playground for Higher Learning* with 10 horses in dressage or jumping training. The horses were tested daily for the stress hormone cortisol along with 10 other "control" horses in training who were not worked with the Tellington Method. The results, published by the Bitsa Veterinary Center, showed a marked lowering of stress levels in the horses worked with our methods.

That's when Anna decided to attach the headband to a horse. As soon as we began doing small circular TTouches on the horse's body, the screen lit up in both hemispheres of the brain, sometimes close to the specific pattern that mirrored those of the person touching. We stood in stunned silence, first in surprise that the "thinking" beta brain waves were activated, and secondly, that the pattern in both hemispheres so often reflected that of the humans—a process called *entrainment*.*

All 20 practitioners began talking at once. "Would this pattern appear no matter how a horse was touched?" was our first thought. We proceeded to stroke, pet, rub and do repetitive circles on one spot, but we could not reproduce the brain waves in that special pattern. It was only when the skin was pushed in one-and-one-quarter circles, but not more than two circles, that we saw activation of the beta brain waves that are associated with logical thinking or the activity in both hemispheres.

A Special Learning State

A greater epiphany was yet to come. The following year, during a weeklong training in England, Anna had a remote headband fashioned so we could measure brain wave patterns while a horse was moving. Once more, we had that "aha feeling" that produces goose bumps. Whenever a horse took the shortened steps around the turns in the ground exercise we call the *Labyrinth* (p. 259), the special learning state reappeared as beta brain waves were activated.

The experience was mind-altering. To think that horses could produce brain wave activity mirroring our own gave us a whole new perspective on equine learning and indeed, gave rise to a new consideration of equine consciousness. And the fact that the human doing the TTouches had the same patterns meant that doing the TTouch could be as beneficial for the human as it was for the horse!

During the training in which this study occurred, we had a two-year-old Thoroughbred filly who was so explosive and hysterical the owner had decided to put her down. My clinic was a last chance to see if she could be brought around. When she was

---

* Anna Wise is the author of *The High-Performance Mind* (Tarcher, Putnam Publishing Group, 1996; for further information, see *Resources,* p. 311).

GRADUATE
PROGRAM IN TTOUCH

In 2001, the Center for Spirituality and Healing at the University of Minnesota developed the Center for Tellington TTouch Research and Education. The Center for Spirituality and Healing is an umbrella organization that houses the only program in the country to offer a graduate minor in alternative healing modalities.

Graduate students from any discipline may enroll, and the course entitled "Tellington TTouch for Humans" is offered as a two-credit elective course in that program. Graduate students from many disciplines and all over the world have attended this introductory course, and students may complete a research focus in Tellington TTouch at the Center for Spirituality and Healing. Further information is available at www.csh.umn.edu.

hooked up to the brain wave monitor, it showed a clear indication of a scattered mind—one might describe it as "blown." No wonder she could not focus or learn in a normal way!

When we began TTouching her body, the patterns on the brain wave monitor immediately shifted. Here was evidence that TTouch was producing measur-

able shifts in the brain. Over the next week, the filly turned around completely and became cooperative, focused and obviously capable of learning. The formerly intractable young mare had a bright future, and we had strong evidence that TTouch had the grounding of science to match the miracles.

The Tellington Method Today

The Tellington Method continues to spread around the world, inspired by 14 books in 12 languages, 23 videos, countless magazine articles, a quarterly newsletter in English and German and numerous television documentaries and radio programs in Europe, Asia, South America, Africa, and Australia as well as the United States. We have over 1,200 certified TTouch practitioners for horses and companion animals in 26 countries teaching workshops and working with individuals (see the *Resources*, p. 311, to learn how to find the name of a practitioner near you). Tellington TTouch has taken me to nearly every corner of the globe, and I'm constantly learning from my experiences. You, too, can achieve permanent changes in the health, attitude and learning ability in your horse with only a few minutes of TTouch a day.

Linda Tellington-Jones
October 2006

Note to the Reader

How to Use This Book

For the first time in my many decades of working with horses, as well as publishing books and videos about my experiences, I am including the complete compendium of techniques used in the Tellington Method in one volume   whether bodywork, ground exercises, or ridden work.

The book is arranged in three parts:

Part One: An overview of the Tellington Method where I briefly explain the background and history, and discuss reasons for unwanted behavior and poor attitude in horses.

Part Two: This contains a detailed discussion of 73 common behavioral, training and health issues (including bad habits), many of which horse people face on a daily basis. Presented in an A to Z format—from "Aggressive to Other Horses" to "Weaving" —the section describes conventional fixes to solving each of these challenges as well as offering training solutions using the Tellington Method. In order to provide easy, instant access to the step-by-step process of these training solutions, all solutions are carefully referenced to the page number in Part Three where the Tellington Method is presented in its entirety.

Part Three: This large section contains the complete body of work that makes up the Tellington Method. The section is highly illustrated with step-by-step instruction. It is divided into three parts:

1. The Tellington TTouches

2. Ground Exercises

3. Ridden Work

At the end of this part, there is a detailed case study, "The Story of Thor: Overcoming Fear of the Trailer," which includes 49 photographs showing every step along the way to successfully teaching your horse to load.

An Overview of the Tellington Method®

PART ONE

Classical Horsemanship
Meets the New Millennium

Since horses were domesticated on the central Asian steppes about 6,000 years ago, they have been an essential partner of the human race. In fact, the union of horse and human into a single, centaur-like creature is now thought to be responsible for propelling humans into an astonishing run of creativity and productivity that ultimately led to the digital era and the space age. Think about it: the horse was the impetus that transformed *Homo sapiens* from pedestrian hunter-gatherers to equestrian armies on the march, conquering and reshaping the world and its nations, cultures, languages and commerce.

I invite you and your horse on an intriguing journey, one that can become a lifelong adventure in learning for you and your equine companion. We will learn to look at personality, attitude and behavior with new eyes, and give you the problem-solving tools and techniques to meet the challenges and reap the satisfaction and joy of working with your horse to become "all you can be."

We are living in the first century in which horses are no longer essential for transportation, trade or war; in our industrialized society, we now keep horses mainly for recreation, sport and pleasure. The horse industry is changing, with many adults now having the time and resources to pursue their lifelong passion for horses. Many of these people are "returnees," who have been attracted to horses since childhood and who have a strong affinity for all the gifts these wonderful animals bring to us—adventure, freedom, an opportunity for learning and growth. However, these dreams often encounter a hard landing when the reality of riding and working with horses isn't as easy as they imagined

or remembered it to be. And when they seek advice, they often discover that rather than the trust and partnership they were hoping for, they are told that the horse must submit or obey, and to "show him who's the boss."

Successful trainers of the past and present have intuitively known that a horse must *want* to work for you to perform his or her best. For a racehorse to give everything in the last dash to the wire, for a cutting horse to dig deep to turn the cow, for a jumper to give that last bit of brilliant effort to clear the final fence, for the Olympic dressage competitor to meld with his rider, it takes more than just a horse going about his work in a mechanistic, obedient fashion.

In training discussion groups and chat rooms on the Internet, you frequently hear the word "respect" as in, "The horse must *respect* the rider." This strikes me as incomplete, as if respect only goes one way. I believe we should also treat the horse respectfully, and recognize his or her individuality. I've been strongly influenced by the African Zulu greeting, "I see you," meaning "I see your soul." I believe it is time we recognize the individuality of horses (and other animals) and acknowledge and honor their souls and intrinsic value as well as those of our own species.

Recently, while co-teaching a clinic, my sister and fellow instructor Robyn Hood observed, "Everybody's talking about the 'horse whisperers,' but I feel it's time *we* began to listen to the whispers of our horses." I couldn't agree more. When we tune out our horse's whispers, they often escalate into "shouts" that indicate something is wrong, and we often miss the message. The Tellington Method embodies a compassionate approach to training and begins with the recognition that:

- When a horse is uncooperative there is always a reason, whether it is physical, mental or emotional.

- When a horse is overstressed, he cannot learn.

- When a horse is fearful, he cannot listen.

- When a horse is uncomfortable or in pain from an ill-fitting saddle or bit, or improper shoeing, he cannot respond to your requests.

- When a horse does not get enough exercise or is undernourished or overfed, he cannot be cooperative.

More than a quarter of a century ago, I began looking more deeply into the reasons that horses behave the way they do. Using biological and neurological principles, I developed solutions that any person—from raw beginner to professional trainer—could safely and successfully use. I began looking for ways to get the horse's attention so that he accepts our leadership and, in the process, we develop a relationship that leads to a safe and mutually enjoyable partnership.

As noted earlier, common advice for eliminating undesirable equine behavior is to be dominant, as if a shout, smack or whack will solve every problem of misbehavior. This may work in the case of the very experienced horseperson. But what about someone who doesn't have the timing, skill, strength—or the desire—to dominate the horse? And what about the horse that doesn't respond to intimidation?

It's time to go beyond outmoded models of dominance and submission and the centuries-old precept of "man's dominion over the beasts." In this new century, there is exploding recognition in the scientific community that animals are far more intelligent and sensitive, and capable of more complex emotions and feelings, than we ever thought possible.

As scientific efforts combine with an increasing public appreciation for the diversity and sacredness of all life on our planet, it's no longer culturally acceptable to treat animals as if they have no feelings, emotions or ability to think. How sensible is it to run a horse for hours in a round pen to teach him to come to you when he doesn't understand what you want? Or to leave him tied up in the hot sun all day, hoping he'll eventually "just get it" and stop "digging a hole to China"? How else can we explain the standard techniques of working horses until they submit from sheer exhaustion, tying the head back to the stirrup or tail for hours to "supple" them, or longeing with a front leg tied up to learn "obedience"?

In view of what we now know about the damaging effects of stress on health, learning and longevity, it's time we developed a new approach to educating the horse. The Tellington Method takes the horse beyond instinct, overriding the fight-or-flight reflex, and expands not only his ability to learn but also his desire to cooperate with you. Our approach gives you a way to engage your horse's interest and fine-tune his focus so that he likes and respects you. The result is both you and your horse gain self-confidence and can feel safe in any situation. My motto: it's easier to influence a few pounds of brains than 1,000 pounds of horseflesh. You will find that the relationship you develop when your horse likes you and takes pleasure from working with you will be much richer and more rewarding.

Results You Can Achieve with the Tellington Method

- Overcome behavioral, training and conformation challenges without force.

- Enhance your horse's trust, cooperation and willingness to learn.

- Build confidence in horse and rider.

- Increase your safety both on the ground and in the saddle.

- Improve your enjoyment of your horse and your mutual performance.

- Improve your horse's balance, soundness and longevity.

- Experience the joy of riding at a new level.

- Enrich your horse's environment.

- Expand your capacity to be an effective horseman.

Through the years, my organization, Tellington TTouch Training, has received countless case studies of people giving their horses a fresh start and, in a relatively short time, having that horse completely change his attitude. Throughout the book, you'll find their first-hand reports, mini case histories that will inspire you to try the Tellington Method yourself.

Typical horse training approaches are linear, with each step mastered before moving to the next. In contrast, the Tellington Method is a three-dimensional set of relationships—like a hologram—capable of being approached at any point. Such a rich sphere of choices might seem daunting, but the beauty of the work is that you can jump in anywhere and be successful. No matter which area you choose to work on, you will affect the whole horse. And even though you may not have thought a lesson was as effective as you might have liked, you are likely to discover the next day that your horse learned more than you imagined.

THE SEVEN PILLARS OF THE TELLINGTON METHOD

❶ Based on cooperation and compassion, the Tellington Method enhances learning, reduces stress and makes training and performance pleasurable for both horse and rider.

❷ The Tellington Method takes the horse beyond reflexive, fight-or-flight instincts (see p. 22) and teaches him to think—to overcome fear, feel safe and cooperate willingly and trust the rider.

❸ Horses learn easier and faster when in the company of another horse or horses, or watching other horses being calmly worked. Whenever possible, teach your horse in a group situation. This prepares your horse, from the beginning, for the "real world" of working around other horses on the trail or in the arena.

❹ Pain, tension and discomfort, often undetected, all limit learning, restrict performance and lead to resistance and common behavior problems. When a horse resists, we believe this behavior stems from pain, fear, frustration as well as unfair or unclear communication.

❺ When you reduce one fear, you reduce fear in all situations. The Tellington Method gives you the tools to help your horse become more confident and less reactive in the arena and on the trail.

❻ Every horse is a teacher. Over the past five decades, my best teachers have been so-called "problem" horses brought to me in frustration after all other avenues had been tried.

❼ We recognize that horses have different emotions and individuality. With the Tellington Method, we aim to work with kindness rather than force, and apply the TTouch Golden Rule of Horsemanship: *Treat your horse as you would like to be treated.*

A Closer Look at the Roots

of Unwanted Behavior
and Poor Attitude

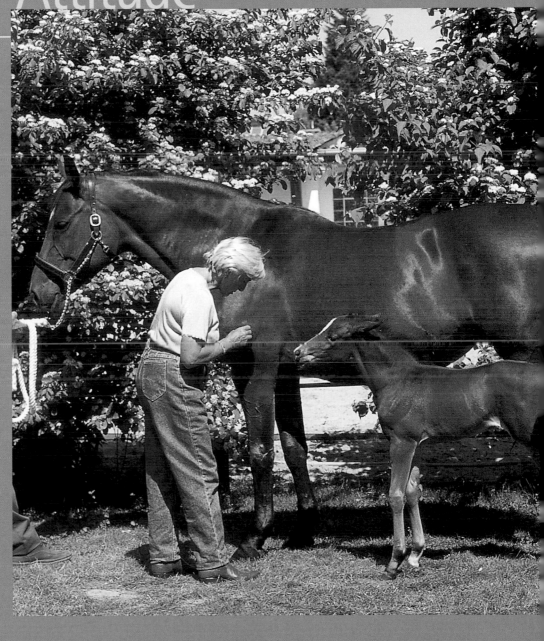

B efore you assume your horse has a "bad attitude" or behavioral problem...before you reach for a stronger bit or sharper spurs...even before you try any of the exercises explained and illustrated in this book... consider the following 14 common contributors to resistance, poor performance or difficult behavior in horses.

Saddle Fit

Possibly the most often overlooked cause of spook-iness, unexplained bucking, bolting and a sour atti-tude is poor saddle fit. Many common behavior problems are caused by pain or restriction as a result of an incorrectly fitting saddle. A pinching saddle restricts freedom of movement from the poll to the pelvis, creating discomfort and shortening stride. A saddle can be too narrow or set too far forward, jamming the shoulders and withers and inhibiting movement. Painful pressure points, such as from the pommel crowding the withers can be exacer-bated when the horse is high headed, dropped in the back or traveling downhill.

I've seen horses wearing expensive, custom-made saddles that no longer fit properly when the horse gains or loses condition or weight. Most saddle makers take their measurements without considering the weight or balance of the rider, which completely changes the way the pressure points apply. The common method of placing a saddle on a towel and checking the points without the rider on board becomes a useless exercise.

Some saddles do not have enough gullet clearance and compress the horse's withers, causing soreness. A saddle that is too big for the horse will not be stable, so the rider is always trying to "catch up" with the horse. "Bridging," in which the front and back of the saddle make contact with the horse but the midsection does not, is a common cause of discomfort. A saddle that is too long may jab into the loins. Even some of the so-called "flexible" trees end up being too narrow or too long.

Some horses are a challenge to fit, especially those with "dippy" or dropped backs or asymmetrical shoulders. Some of the behaviors that have their roots in poor saddle fit include irritability, going crooked, overreacting (or not responding at all) to the aids, restricted range of motion, holding the breath and high levels of tension.

New choices in alternative saddles—including adjustable/flexible panels, treeless models and those with adjustable shimming systems—are heralding a new age in saddle fitting. (For a listing of saddle companies and pads, see Resources, p. 311.)

Shoeing and Hoof Issues

Refusal or inability to move freely forward may appear to be stubbornness, unwillingness or lazi-ness, but in fact may be caused by a variety of foot issues. These include long-toe, low-heel syndrome, contracted heels, quarter cracks, sore heels, ten-der soles, hoof abscess, chronic laminitis, imbal-anced trimming and/or shoeing, close or quicked nail, corns, leaving the shoes on too long, and sub-solar bruising. Any of these issues can prevent the horse from performing at his best. If his feet are uncomfortable or hurting, the horse will respond with a choppy or unwilling gait, frequent stum-bling or refusal to move forward. More serious manifestations will result in outright lameness, but subtle shifts in balance over time may go unnoticed and be interpreted as a behavior issue.

Soreness

I believe that body soreness, from back to feet, has been missed or misread more than any other reason for problem behavior. A quarter century ago, when I first discovered that soreness or pain was a primary cause of resistance or bad behavior, it was then a completely unrecognized concept. Soreness can result either from a single episode of work that overwhelms the system (acute), or from continuous work without sufficient attention to rest and recovery (chronic).

For as long as I can remember, the accepted way to check a horse's back for soreness has been to run the fingers down the sides of the spine. However, I have seen many sore horses checked this way that show no reaction. Using the TTouch method of pressure and comparison (see *Body Exploration*, p. 151), you can "tune in" to any horse's back, but you must get your hands on many horses to be able to judge what is "normal." Without experience, it's difficult to tell whether a horse is simply sensitive or truly sore.

Your horse can be sore virtually anywhere on the body, but there are some common "hot spots": back, hips, girth area, shoulder/neck junction, behind the poll (atlas/axis), legs and feet, including stiffness or tightness of muscles in the gluteals, gaskins, or forearm muscles. All can limit a horse's ability to move, causing the rider to think the horse is lazy, stubborn, unwilling or uncooperative. Soreness and stiffness can be caused by a multitude of factors, including overwork or working in footing or conditions to which the horse is unaccustomed, such as deep sand, rocky going, irregular footing or hill work. In addition, too much jumping, too many hours in the saddle, longeing in small circles, driving or work under saddle without adequate preparation, over-collection and too much sitting trot

with inadequate padding or conditioning can lead to soreness and sourness. Be alert for heat, swelling or tenderness (especially in the legs and ankles) as well as a loss of enthusiasm for work.

A horse can be sore in both shoulders or front feet and appear to be just a little "off"—manifesting as short-strided, unwilling or stiff; this may be mistakenly attributed to the horse's attitude or dismissed with "He'll warm out of it." Watch for filling or heat in the ankles, a dull hair coat and sour attitude. If you are uncertain, back off on your training and check for a pounding digital pulse in the ankles.

Teeth and Dental Issues

Dental problems are one of the most overlooked causes of behavior problems, especially in younger and older equines. Problems such as head tossing, rooting at the bit, sticking the tongue out, hanging the mouth open, stargazing, unwillingness to accept the bit, fidgeting, nervousness or inability to stand still, clumped or dropped food, and lack of focus are among the behaviors that can be caused by problematic teeth. The practice of floating (rasping) teeth without a speculum or sedation can often miss an abscess, wolf teeth that may or may not be embedded, or a broken tooth or baby teeth (caps) that don't fall out as adult teeth emerge. (Watch for the telltale bulges in the cheeks, or evidence of infected or swollen gums or tongue.) Raw areas in the mouth can be traced to jagged hooks, ridges or uneven back molars.

When dealing with equine behavior and training problems, one of my first recommendations is to have your horse checked by a competent equine dentist. The new thinking and methods of equine dentistry involve sedation, speculum and power tools that enable the veterinarian or equine dental technician to do a more thorough job. According to Alexander Zingher, DVM, whose practice is devoted to equine dentistry, you should look for a dentist who charts the entire mouth, like a human dentist; has a lighting source that illuminates the entire mouth and all the teeth; avoids thermal damage and preserves as much of each molar's crown as possible.

Dietary Considerations

Nutritional imbalances and feed allergies can cause behavior and attitude issues. Overfeeding protein or supplements coupled with under-exercising can lead to excess energy and bucking, head flinging and a horse who is difficult to rate or straighten. Under-feeding can cause loss of energy and impulsion and lack of spirit and willingness. Nutrient deficiencies such as vitamin E and selenium can lead to short, stilty strides and even "tying up." Today's horses, especially those who live on the fringes of metropolitan areas or whose grazing opportunities are limited, may benefit from supplementation with antioxidant vitamins and minerals to prevent free-radical stress from air and water pollution (just like humans).

Good quality forage is the foundation of the equine diet. If you have concerns about your horse's diet, consult an equine nutritionist and have your hay and feed analyzed. Allergies to grain can cause resistance and uncontrollable temperament and inconsistent performance. Studies show that grain puts horses at high metabolic risk for colic and founder. Beet pulp (high fiber) and rice bran (high fat) have proven to be excellent, safer alternatives to grain-based diets. I have seen many horses become unmanageable when fed sweet feed, and seen many behavior problems disappear when the feed program is adjusted.

Conformational Clues

You can prevent many undesirable behaviors or resistances by choosing a horse whose conformation is suitable for the discipline or style of riding that interests you. Conformation faults may cause a horse to be resistant and lead to behavioral issues when doing manoeuvers that are difficult.

For example, a dressage horse with a very tight crest may have a tendency to explode when asked for higher levels of collection. Similarly, a wasp-waisted, narrow-chested jumper may be limited for eventing because the challenge of galloping and jumping fences with a breast collar tight enough to keep the saddle from slipping may restrict the stride and freedom of movement. A ewe-necked horse will have a tendency to be unbalanced and flighty because of discomfort in the back as well as restricted breathing.

It's common for narrow-chested, long-legged horses to be flighty, a problem I attribute to a sense of insecurity caused by poor balance. Long backed, wasp-waisted horses generally have limited weight-carrying capacity and a tendency to be strung out. Steep-shouldered, straight-pasterned horses won't be able to produce the long floating stride prized in many disciplines. A horse with extremely straight or bent (sickle) hocks may have difficulty going down-hill. However, you can avoid many common behavior problems caused by conformation weaknesses by choosing a horse that is physically suited to the discipline you choose.

Hormonal Havoc

Some mares are more sensitive to the fluctuations of the estrous cycle than others, and their empathetic companions have learned to respect the five to seven days out of the month that their mares are in heat. However, occasionally something more serious may be brewing beneath the surface. When a mare kicks or squeals to even light pressure almost anywhere on her body, or if she is constantly difficult to control under saddle, it's time for a vet check and hormone blood panel to be sure she doesn't have an ovarian cyst, persistent corpus luteum or some other endocrine anomaly that is responsible for her behavior. Ten minutes a day of TTouches during the rest of the month have been helpful in

MYTH: *Once you get into a fight with your horse (such as a horse that won't cross a bridge or stream), you must never give in or your horse has "won."*

Horses aren't keeping score or holding grudges. And, if you are too tired, impatient, angry or concerned about your safety to work with your horse, *walk away.* A subset of this myth is: Never get off your horse, or you've "lost." Oftentimes, all it takes to get a horse over his fear of water is for the rider to dismount and show him how to walk across it. (Endurance rider Julie Suhr shares her remarkable story on p. 40.)

MYTH: *If your horse is aggressive, kicks or bites, you need to really "get after him."*

Horses who kick or bite are doing so because we haven't heeded their "whispers." They have raised the volume to get our attention. Learn to tune in to the whispers, and your horse will never need to "shout."

MYTH: *Horses learn only through repetition.*

If a horse can learn a "bad" habit in one session, why can he not learn a "good" one? In fact, Dr. Moshe Feldenkrais proposed 40 years ago that the human nervous system can learn in a single session, using gentle nonhabitual movements. While some repetition is useful to lay down the neural pathways for learning, I do not believe that hundreds of repetitions are necessary. Actually, I believe mindless repetition creates boredom and resistance and can stress a horse to the point of unsoundness.

MYTH: *Horses will take advantage of you if you let them.*

Horses are simply responding to your requests, cues and visual pictures. Your horse's response perfectly mirrors what you put out there for him. We get back exactly what we ask for.

MYTH: *Never give your horse treats because they will spoil him and make him nip.*

Using small crunchies or treats during training can encourage your horse to breathe, promote relaxation and encourage him to lower his head. Besides, it's a nice reward.

MYTH: *Never pet your horse.*

Horses are emotional beings who need to make connections with other horses as well as humans. If we deny them this essential desire, they will find another outlet (such as nipping, wood-chewing, stall walking or kicking the stall). The Tellington Method provides a way of connecting with your horse that transcends "petting." Through mindful, circular TTouches, you can produce relaxation as well as awaken the mind and body of the horse to learning and being cooperative.

MYTH: *Personality defects are usually permanent character flaws in horses.*

In my experience, attitude problems in horses are often misunderstood and misinterpreted, and the horse is labeled with the negative assessment forever. However, upon closer examination, most behavioral issues can be traced to one or more factors, including pain, fear, conformation, breed and management.

MYTH: *Once a biter, always a biter.*

You can change this habit along with many other unwanted behaviors—like the horse snapping the air while the girth is tightened. Instead of assuming malicious intent, reframe your approach to realize that the horse is trying to let you know that what is being done is uncomfortable. It may be his only way of getting you to listen. You can change your approach so he doesn't have a reason to bite, using *Mouth TTouches* (p. 182) and *Abalone TTouches* (p. 171) in the girth area.

MYTH: *Horses are stupid.*

If this were true, this book wouldn't need to be written; and we would never say that horses "outsmarted" us. All creatures evolved with an innate intelligence appropriate for their species, or they wouldn't have survived. Intelligence was defined by Darwin as *the ability to adapt to one's environment.*

reducing the intensity of these hormone imbalances and mood swings during the heat cycle. Herbs and oral progestins can sometimes be helpful.

Training Techniques and Riding Style

A heavy or unyielding hand and a driving seat leading to over-collection can contribute to tension and soreness over the horse's body, especially in the poll, shoulders, back, loins and pelvis. Any training technique used excessively can cause repetitive-motion stress. This risk is most apparent in sports such as dressage, reining, cutting and barrel-racing, which emphasize repeated drilling of patterns and lateral movements. Be on the alert for body soreness, uneven gait, tight neck, sour attitude, explosive and resistant behavior, filling in the ankles and pinned ears. To avoid these problems alternate your training schedule with trail rides, ground driving or other types of cross-training.

Rider Attitude

I feel strongly that a rider's attitude is more important than his or her raw skill. The best technical rider in the world will limit a horse's potential if his or her attitude doesn't recognize and honor the horse's individuality or isn't flexible enough to work with the horse. On the other hand, if you have a compassionate attitude toward your horse that allows him the freedom to be comfortable and express his side of the story, you're well on your way to a rewarding relationship.

The Stress Factor

Many common equine activities are stressful. We now know, thanks to extensive research, that many mental, emotional and physical problems are the direct result of stress. Leading "stress-producers" include confinement, training, shipping, competition, and surgery. Give your horse a chance to adapt gradually to new situations or training and watch carefully for signs of stress.

Stomach ulcers are frequently found in horses in training, perhaps because of the long hours spent confined when they often develop a tendency to fret, lack the company of other horses, and eat too much concentrated food for too little activity. A horse needs as much socialization, turnout and free exercise as possible. Use TTouch, which has been proven in studies to reduce the stress levels in horses in training and trailering. It can also help relax stall-bound horses and substitute for social contact in situations where horses cannot be turned out with others.

Be especially careful when shipping long distances that your horse remains well hydrated (give electrolytes before shipping and every day of the journey) and, en route, is able to put his head down to clear his airways. Vitamins C and E can help his system ward off the debilitating effects of stress.

Neurological Dysfunction

A change in your horse's behavior or way of going can signal a neurological disorder such as EPM, herpesvirus, Lyme disease or Wobbler's syndrome. Typically, an afflicted horse will stumble frequently, be lame, have difficulty circling and turning and appear uncoordinated. (See p. 134 for a more detailed discussion of these disorders.)

Exercise and Stabling Practices

For horses to be healthy, sound and willing, they need daily exercise and plenty of it. As open space dwindles, many horses have to spend much of their day confined to a stall or small corral. Such confinement can lead to laziness and lethargy, or becoming difficult and explosive when they first come out of the stable. Stabled horses are at much higher risk of metabolic diseases such as colic and founder. In one study, colic was virtually unreported in horses kept on pasture full-time.

If your horse isn't turned out at least eight to 12 hours per day (or night, depending on the season), it is up to you to provide organized activities and exercise every day. Stabled horses are prone to developing behaviors such as stall walking/weaving, kicking the walls and biting at passersby. Many horses are lucky to get out two hours a day. In such instances, it's unrealistic to think you can jump on your horse and fully collect him, or take off at a gallop down the trail, without his becoming stiff, sore and resistant.

Depending on your schedule, your time to work with your horse may be limited so you are tempted to simply run him around a round pen or longe him to release excess energy. If you work your horse 30 minutes a day on the longe line, for instance, he will build up condition and take longer and longer to work down—plus it takes 30 minutes out of the time you could be riding. Because it may also become boring or physically uncomfortable, the horse can start to get the idea 20 feet out that you can't control him and make up his own games to amuse himself and challenge you. This may mean bolting and running, kicking out at you, turning back, or even coming at you and attacking.

The Tellington Method gives you an alternative to longeing or the round pen to "work a horse down." With 10 minutes of TTouches for Trust (p. 168) before riding—particularly *Ear TTouches*—you can relax your horse as much as 30 minutes of longeing ever can.

Environmental Impact

If horses had an "Equine Bill of Rights," it would include clean bedding with no ammonia fumes, no standing manure, limited numbers of flies and other biting pests, daily turnout and grazing, clean fresh food and water, clean water buckets, safely constructed facilities with no sharp edges, halters off, safe fencing, shade in the summer and a windbreak in the winter, contact with other equines and humans daily, and kind handling.

When a horse goes to a new home, adjustment to the new surroundings can take time. The horse may have left buddies behind, adding to the stresses of shipping and arriving at a strange new stable with different horses, smells, feed, handlers…and even the invisible microbes in the earth provide a different antigenic challenge for the horse's immune system, which must adapt to all of these changes quickly. And, we wonder why horses go off feed, become lethargic or depressed or even have a nervous breakdown when they are moved! I've known two horses who had nervous breakdowns and lost their hair from what I believe was simply homesickness.

Eyesight

I've seen horses be overly tense, skittish and high headed if their depth perception or eyesight was not 100 percent. One horse labeled "unwilling," "unresponsive" and "dumb" turned out to see very little and had followed his pasturemate closely—almost with his nose on his friend's rump—for years, and no one paid much attention. There was also the Warmblood who spun around when another horse passed him head on. His eyes were set so far to the sides that when his head was perpendicular to the ground—as when he was collected and you were facing him from the front—you could barely see his eyes. I believe the horse could not see forward when he was on a collected rein, which was almost all the time. Have your veterinarian check your horse's eyesight.

Learn to Read the Language of Your Horse

Taking the time to learn your horse's language can bring you to a new level of trust in your relationship and enhance mutual progress. A great many behaviors and attitudes are really *the horse trying to tell you that he is not comfortable in some way.* For example, a reflexive kick while grooming in cross-ties may indicate that your horse is ticklish or sore somewhere on the body and that the style of grooming is too vigorous or harsh. At other times, the behavior can stem from lack of adequate training or the horse has never learned patience. As you begin to tune in to your horse, you might see that his "bad attitude" is the result of soreness in the neck, back or croup.

The next time you go to a horse show or trail ride, or are simply hanging out at a barn, put on your "detective's cap" and see if you can pick out which horses are enjoying their jobs and which are distressed. Carefully observe the ears, eyes, nostrils, mouth, chin and tail—the visible emotional "transmitters" that can tip you off to a horse's state of mind. As you tune in to equine conversation, your horse will no longer have to "shout" to get your attention. In the next chapter, I'll delve more deeply into the horse-human dialogue.

The Personality Paradox

What's Behind the Behavior?

n the study of behavior in humans and equines, it has been widely assumed that one's personality is, on the whole, permanent and unchangeable. But, even a cursory glance at the latest thinking in fields as diverse as business, psychoneuroimmunology (PNI) and linguistics reveals that each of us indeed possesses the capacity to reinvent the self. And, when it comes to the horse-human dynamic, your attitude toward yourself and your horse and the world at large can further influence your horse's behavior and attitude.

Personality has long been considered the sum total of an individual's physical, mental, social, and emotional characteristics, which I believe applies to horses as well as humans. *The Random House Dictionary* defines personality as "the embodiment of a collection of qualities; the organized behavioral characteristics of an individual."

I'm not talking about Skinnerian, "conditioned-response" behavior that would reduce our horses to mechanistic automatons responding to stimuli like so many rats in a maze. Instead, I'm bringing forth a new language for educating the horse—one that allows for the possibility of awakening intelligence, overriding the flight instinct and increasing willingness, balance and athletic potential in both members of the partnership. I seek nothing less than a new language that leads to new practices that go beyond dominance, submission, force and alpha training.

Don't worry, we won't get bogged down in the muck of socio-babble. First, a few major distinctions I need to go over, and then we'll all get to the fun part: becoming ready to explore your horse's behavior, attitude and personality in a whole new way. Change is indeed possible, and it may be easier than you think!

PERSONALITY + ATTITUDE = BEHAVIOR

Your horse's personality can be modified by his attitude. Attitude is influenced by health, environment, diet and training. The resulting personality and attitude affects his behavior. And, of course:

Behavior Directs Performance

Does Your Horse Have an Attitude?

Of course he does. And so do you! Who doesn't?

One dictionary defines attitude as a "mood or state of mind regarding a particular matter." How often have you heard statements like this:

"This horse is a brat."

"She's a nasty witch."

"My horse is stubborn and lazy."

Many horse people see their horses through a fixed lens of inevitability. They perceive the attitude or behavior as "the way the horse is," as if it were an intrinsic character flaw of the horse. Unfortunately, such assessments often become self-fulfilling prophecies, as the human partner unwittingly reinforces the unwanted behaviors.

My own way of thinking about attitude shifted in the summer of 1975 when I was asked to look at a Thoroughbred gelding for a client. This became a defining situation for me as I watched the horse being ridden around the arena with his ears pinned and his body stiff and tense, obviously unhappy and unwilling to move forward.

I asked the owner if the horse was always like this. It turned out that the horse was indeed sore from a trail ride two days before when he had been ridden out with a group and his rider had to pull his head to one side for most of the ride to slow him down. As a result, he had a hot spot on his neck that was very sore to my touch. In those days, pain or soreness simply wasn't considered a cause of resistance in horses.

I intuitively thought, "Hmmm…let me check out his body." This discovery—that unwanted behavior or attitude might stem from discomfort or pain on the body—was one of my first "aha moments" on the path to the development of the Tellington Method. In retrospect, this turned out to be a landmark in my understanding of the often-concealed roots of behavior in horses and, ultimately, other animals and even our own species.

In the ensuing quarter century, we have recognized dozens more factors that often underlie and precipitate a horse's undesirable attitude and resulting behavior. As we discussed in chapter 2, not only soreness and pain, but also diet, exercise, teeth, saddle fit, shoeing, stress, hormonal imbalance or neurological dysfunction from injury, EPM, herpesvirus or Lyme disease can trigger attitude and behavior that is frequently perplexing and sometimes dangerous. Riding style, such as an unyielding hand or punishing seat—regardless of the discipline or rider experience—can also cause common resistance and behavior problems.

Not only do we have to consider the horse's attitude in the behavior equation, it is also essential to realize that the *rider's opinion* about the horse matters as well. Consider the story of the legendary racehorse Seabiscuit, who was branded an untrainable outlaw until he had the good fortune to fall into the hands of appreciative owner Charles Howard, the brilliant and kind trainer Tom Smith, and the empathetic rider Red Pollard. This compassionate trio of horsemen, recognizing their charge's keen intelligence and competitive fire, brought out the best in the "Biscuit" to give the world one of the most spectacular performers in sporting history.

Instinct or Learning?

Many training methods today claim to manipulate the horse's instinct in order to establish dominance. But what is instinct? Is it the equine propensity for flight? Is it fighting back and resisting? Or, is it simply shutting down and going into "freeze" mode? When you look more closely, you'll find that the "instinctive" behaviors I've identified here are most often triggered by lack of understanding, stress/anxiety, nerves or fear. In the Tellington Method, these instinctive behaviors are identified as the "Five Fs."

• **Flight** Perhaps the most pervasive tendency of horses is to flee in the face of perceived danger. In preparation for flight, the head goes up, the neck becomes rigid, the back drops, circulation is shunted away from the extremities, the heart rate quickens, and the horse's gaze becomes fixed on a faraway point. Flight was the escape of choice in the wild; however, domesticated horses may also display any of the following reactions to a fearful situation:

• **Fight** When a horse is prevented from fleeing a threatening situation, or forced to do something that is painful, frightening or physically impossible, kicking, biting, or rearing are common modes of resisting.

• **Freeze** Rather than fight or flee, some horses in certain circumstances will simply freeze in place as if rooted to the ground. This is often seen during trailer loading or when a young horse is mounted for the first time without first learning, from being ground-driven, how to go forward from a signal. These horses may stand stock-still, holding their breath, and often the only way they can move is to "break in two" with a big buck.

• **Faint** In extreme cases, a horse under intense pressure will simply collapse onto the ground rather than fight. This is nervous system reaction that often follows the freeze reflex. This reaction can occur in the following situations: when a horse

- **Fidgeting or Fooling Around** A fifth behavior has recently been recognized at Texas A & M University as stress-related and not simply an "attitude" as so many horse people had previously believed. It describes the horse who nips or "lips" the lead rope or chain, and fidgets as you work with him. Although many consider it bad behavior, it's actually a *displacement activity* for the horse to release anxiety and deal with stress. Obviously it's more subtle than the other "F" responses, and usually not dangerous, but it also requires understanding in order to solve. An insightful perspective is offered by Tom Beckett, DVM, who has studied the effects of the Tellington Method on animals for over 20 years (see sidebar).

The Five Fs are, in my experience, instinctive responses to lack of understanding or fear. As a result, using force or domination is counterproductive. Our goal is to help you learn to take your horse *beyond instinct*—beyond the Five Fs—and in the process, enhance your horse's intelligence—his willingness and ability to adapt to new situations.

One of the principles of the Tellington Method is that if a horse is having trouble understanding or accepting a step in training, you have choices other than simply repeating the exercise over and over and hoping the horse will figure it out. Nor should you subscribe to the common notion that the horse is "getting away with" something if you start an exercise and don't finish it. Instead, pause and think about how you can "chunk down" the exercise to make it easier for you and your horse to succeed. When we can divide the lesson into smaller parts, we learn to be more flexible and, in many cases, create a smoother training process.

How Responsive Is Your Horse's Nervous System?

I'm sure you're familiar with the sight of a horse in freeze or flight mode—his head and neck high and rigid, his back dropped, he stops eating, holds his

has been forced or beaten in an attempt to load him onto a trailer; when restrained in a bitting rig with tight side-reins and an overcheck, and even sometimes when cinched up too tightly or too quickly.

breath, his limbs become stiff and unresponsive to your bidding.

Fear, pain and anxiety release stress hormones, such as cortisol, as the sympathetic nervous system (SNS) kicks into gear. Some stress is unavoidable, but at a certain threshold it blocks awareness and learning. In this state, blood is drawn away from the extremities as a reflexive response of the horse going into the flight, fight or freeze mode.

When a horse can't feel his legs or feet, he becomes unpredictable and is likely to hold his breath, buck or bolt. Peggy Cummings, a Tellington Training and Centered Riding practitioner and developer of the Connected Riding® technique, says that such a horse is "out of his body." (The Tellington technique of stroking a horse with the wand brings a horse back into his body and overrides the flight, fight or freeze instinct.) This ancient biological response was critical for survival of horses and other mammals of the short-grass plains—those who didn't mount a proper stress-response would soon be eaten by a predator.

The stress-response was designed to get horses, humans and other creatures through brief, intensive periods of life-threatening risk—most often by fleeing, but occasionally by taking a stand and fighting. In his fascinating book, *Why Zebras Don't Get Ulcers*, author Robert M. Sapolsky states that the fight-or-flight reflex can be deadly in modern society. Long-term, modern-day stressors, such as fear of losing one's job, or sitting in traffic for hours at a time, keep the chemicals of flight circulating in the bloodstream far longer than is healthy or wise. This can set us up for chronic disorders such as cardiovascular disease.

Likewise, I believe that the fight-or-flight reflex is no longer warranted in our equine companions. Although it occasionally can get you both out of trouble, its frequent or long-running expression is more likely to harm than help. This book, while dealing with very specific behaviors, is really

THE FOUR MODALITIES OF LEARNING

Recognizing that horses are unique and sentient beings with different learning styles, the Tellington Method incorporates four modalities of learning to give our equine friends the opportunity for stress-free learning. You have at your fingertips a comprehensive body of information, which can be learned logically and applied intuitively. As you progress through the range of TTouches, Ground Exercises and Ridden Work, you will connect with your horse all the way from the surface of his skin to the deepest levels of cellular intelligence, activating all four learning modalities:

KINESTHETIC When you move your body and "dance" with your horse in ways he can mirror you, such as exaggerating your steps as you step over *The Fan* (p. 253), you encourage your horse to similarly pick up his feet. Such movements improve both your and your horse's awareness of your body in space, known as *proprioception* and *spatial awareness*.

AUDITORY By using your voice in long, low sounds ("*Eeeasssyyy…..*" and "*Whoaaaaaaaa…..*") that we call "toning" rather than using short, clipped commands ("Whoa!" or "Quit!") you quiet the horse's autonomic nervous system and override the flight reflex.

VISUAL Use a white four-foot-long stiff whip we call a "wand" three to four feet in front of your horse's nose to give him a visual guide to refine his direction and to maintain his distance from you.

TACTILE With TTouch, you explore, soothe, awaken, relax, release, comfort, inform and focus, manifesting the magic of the method for both you and your horse!

ACKNOWLEDGING FEAR

Unchecked fear can trigger a potentially dangerous reaction. For example, when a horse spins, bucks or bolts, a rider's reaction might be to clutch with the hands and legs, which sends a signal to the horse to flee even faster. By "chunking down" the learning experience for both horse and human, the Tellington Method supports the process of being safe and confident around horses—including knowing when to back off. By using TTouch on your horse, you also reap the benefits of reducing fear and tension in your own body.

Are you sometimes uncertain, tentative or a little timid around horses? Or, are you perhaps a normally bold rider who has met up with a new horse who is unpredictable and reactive? You need to trust that feeling of fear as a safety valve. Rather than being pressured into taking a chance, take a few steps back and proceed with the knowledge that there is a safer way to train your equine partner.

If you decide your horse is too much for you to handle, listen to your inner wisdom. No matter how much you love him, it's not worth the risk of getting hurt. Your life and your limbs are very precious. Therefore, if you're dealing with a horse who scares you and you feel you are "in over your head," consider getting professional help. If such training doesn't achieve the results you were hoping for, you might think about finding someone else for that horse, and find yourself another one that will give you pleasure and keep you safe. A horse who is a serious problem for you can be the perfect partner for another person.

about teaching your horse—and you—to override the fight-or-flight reflex and replace it with new responses that eventually become a part of your nervous system's repertoire so they almost become automatic. For example, you can often override the flight reflex by feeding your horse when he's tense or nervous because the parasympathetic nervous system (PNS) is activated when a horse eats. That is one of the reasons we find feeding a frightened horse to be so effective.

The Tellington Method takes the horse beyond instinct, overrides the flight reflex and opens new possibilities for learning and performance. Our approach develops the horse's mind, so that the animal gains self-confidence and will no longer need the herd to sustain a sense of security. The result is an all-around safer, happier, more responsive horse.

Ready to "Team Up" with Your Horse?

With the Tellington Method, I have discovered a way for any rider—regardless of age—to successfully work with a horse in a way that is safe, easy to learn, and from the heart. When we start a horse with the Ground Exercises (see p. 227), the horse will *want* to work with you once you are on his back. And, starting from the ground lets you get to know your horse in a way that you feel in control. Using these exercises, you will also see improvement in balance and flexibility on the ground and in the saddle, for both your horse and you.

Many riders have come to the magical world of horses not only for recreation but also for *re-creation*. I believe horses are our teachers, and it may be that the challenge you have with your horse, so long as it's not dangerous, is an opportunity to develop a new level of understanding and skill. Many people come to the Tellington Method because of problems they haven't been able to solve, and then realize that a whole new level of relationship and rapport with their horses becomes possible.

PART TWO

Behavior and Training Issues A to Z

AND SELECTED HEALTH TOPICS

Over a span of years, a horse owner or rider can expect to face a long list of behavioral, training, and health issues. Nearly all horses can someday develop a prejudice toward another resulting in aggressive activity; be frightened by something that may (or may not) pose a danger; fall into bad habits caused by boredom or lack of human attention; or succumb to various ailments or maladies relating to climate, living conditions, athletic pursuits, or ill-fitting tack and equipment.

Behavior and Training Issues A to Z: In this first alphabetical listing, p. 29 through p. 126, I address 65 common problematic behavioral, living and training issues and situations. I discuss each one in detail with suggestions as to its root or cause, and I offer a wide variety of solutions, which include commonsense "fixes," as well as applicable techniques from the Tellington Method's huge collection of TTouches, Ground Exercises and Ridden Work.

Health Topics: In this second section, p. 127 through p. 138, I present some commonly encountered horse health problems and their diagnoses, and I suggest solutions for recovery and tell you what you can do while waiting for a veterinarian to arrive. I also discuss the link between a horse's undesirable behavior and pain, distress and discomfort, and demonstrate how the Tellington Method techniques can help ease chronic pain and consequent day-to-day difficulties, as well as actually help to save a horse's life in an emergency situation.

Behavior
& Training Issues A to Z

BEHAVIOR AND TRAINING ISSUES A TO Z

O n the following pages you'll find discussions and recommendations for solving 65 common behavioral and training issues. The problems are listed below alphabetically with their page numbers. This list includes multiple entries cross-referenced to related problems and different terminology.

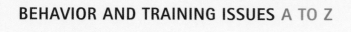

BEHAVIOR AND TRAINING ISSUES A TO Z

Accident-Prone

see also *Balance or Coordination Issues*

Does your horse often show up for breakfast with little nicks, scrapes and cuts? Does he bump into doorways with his hips, bang his head on the fencepost, and generally seem to lack a sense of where his body parts are in space?

Check your horse's environment for safety. Are there sharp, protruding edges anywhere in his stall, paddock, pasture or trailer? Is the stable area or pasture cluttered with machinery, tools, rakes or forks? You can reduce risk by making sure your horse doesn't have to navigate a gauntlet of hazards as he goes about his daily life. In addition, be sure to rule out a medical condition that affects stability and motor control, such as Wobbler's Syndrome or EPM (see *Neurological Dysfunction*, p. 134).

Some accident-prone horses lack coordination and don't seem to know where their borders are; others are quite coordinated and athletic and perhaps *too* bold. Using the Tellington Method, you can give your horse a new sense of his boundaries and teach him more refined responses to your signals. Think of it as an inexpensive insurance policy; by increasing his awareness, your horse will be better equipped to deal with the "real world" and take better care of himself and you, both at home and away.

Training Solutions

TTouches

- Begin with *Lowering the Head*, stroking the wand (for description of the wand, see p. 157) downward with a sweeping motion on all four legs, under the neck and belly, and over the topline. Finish with *Hoof Tapping*.

- To help your horse develop trust in his own body, do *Connected Circles* with *Lying Leopard TTouches* over the whole body. In another session, do *Coiled Python Lifts* with *Abalone TTouches* wherever your horse is touchy about contact. If your horse is wary of contact, use a sheepskin mitt to do the circles the first few times.

- If your horse has poor balance, do a series of *Tarantulas Pulling the Plow* on the body and *Octopus TTouches* on all four legs.

Ground Exercises

- Put your horse in the *Body Wrap* and take him through the *Labyrinth*, *Pick-Up Sticks* and *Tires*. Over time, add other Playground for Higher Learning exercises such as *Neckline and Ground Driving*.

Ridden Work

- Improve your horse's spatial awareness with the addition of a *Balance Rein* and *Promise Wrap*. After first working on the ground, you can ride your horse through Playground obstacles like the *Platform and Work with Plastic Sheets*.

Solutions at a Glance: *Accident-Prone*

Lowering the Head 163 ~ Hoof Tapping 196 ~ Connected Circles 173 ~ Lying Leopard TTouch 181 ~ Coiled Python Lift 172 ~ Abalone TTouch 171 ~ Tarantulas Pulling the Plow 203 Octopus TTouch 200 ~ Body Wrap 160 ~ Labyrinth 259 ~ Pick-Up Sticks 253 ~ Tires 274 Neckline and Ground Driving 261 ~ Balance Rein 279 ~ Promise Wrap 288 ~ Platform 269 Work with Plastic Sheets 265

Aggressive to Other Horses

see also *Low on Pecking Order*

In an established herd, each horse knows his place, and it takes only a flick of an ear or a swish of the tail to maintain peaceful boundaries. Occasionally, one horse will constantly "bully" the others or pick on a horse at the bottom of the heap.

Although you might associate such aggressive behavior with the so-called "alpha" horse or herd leader, most aggression actually comes from a state of fear. This might be fear of not getting enough food or not having enough space. People often describe such a horse as "mean," "nasty" or a "bully"; however, in many cases you can change such behavior.

You may have hoped to give your horse a companion, and they seemed compatible enough when you rode together. However, once they began sharing feeding time, your mare took over and kept her companion well away from the feed with just a switch of her tail, flashing teeth and pinned ears. It's a challenging situation, but you may be able to smooth out the relationship.

Sometimes it helps to give horses more space, making sure the pasture or corral is large enough to allow one horse to escape another's aggression. It is also important to make sure the enclosure has no square corners where a timid horse could be trapped. Perhaps moving the aggressive horse to a different pasture or turning the horses out at different times during the day will be necessary.

At feeding time, put the hay in several places instead of just two, or consider building two standing stalls or pens with mangers so horses are separated when eating. Make the stalls narrow enough so your horse cannot hassle his companion when he's in the stall. If your horse is aggressive, it's your responsibility to keep your horse at a safe distance whether in the pasture or on the trail.

Training Solutions

TTouches

• Start with flat-hand *Body Exploration* to identify those areas where your horse is especially sensitive to contact. Aggressive horses are often anxious about their legs below the knees and hocks, the insides of the hind legs, the head and the flanks. They also have a tendency to tighten or clamp the tail.

• Over a period of time, you can bring a safe feeling anywhere in the body using TTouches for Trust and Awareness on pages 168 and 190. Spend several sessions relaxing your horse with *Ear TTouches*, *Mouth TTouches* and *Tail TTouches* before you ride. Add slow *Lick of the Cow's Tongue* and connected *Abalone TTouches* with *Coiled Python Lifts* all over the body and on the legs. It's ideal to do these TTouches in sight of another horse.

Ground Exercises

• Invite a friend over and work your horses through the *Labyrinth, Teeter-Totter, Platform, The Fan,* and *Work with Plastic Sheets.*

Ridden Work

• With another horse being worked in hand in the arena, ride with a *Liberty Neck Ring* to help your horse tune in to you rather than focus on another horse. If your horse pins his ears at another on the trail or in the arena, instead of reprimanding him, have him turn his head back and take a small carrot or crunchie out of your hand so that he associates another horse with a pleasant experience.

Back Problems (long, hollow, stiff, dropped, sore)

How a horse carries his back is central to his ability to carry a rider and perform his job, whether it's cutting cows, jumping fences, dressage or trail riding. One of the keys to developing a strong, supple back is the ability of the belly muscles (*rectus abdominus*) to contract effectively and provide strength so that the horse can move in self-carriage.

A horse's early experiences under saddle can have long-lasting effects on his behavior, willingness and posture. Be especially mindful of the young horse's still-maturing back*. Introduce the weight of a rider progressively and carefully so the core muscles can properly develop to carry the rider.

Ewe necked, long backed and some high-headed horses are candidates for tight, stiff, weak, hollow or "dippy" backs—which usually means sore. Leading causes of sore backs are ill-fitting saddles and unbalanced or tense riders. Another cause can be habitual bracing against a standing martingale or tie down. If your horse's back is sore, review the sections on saddle fit and rider style (pp. 11 and 15).

Horses that are trained and shown with extreme collection and elevation of the head and neck, such as Warmbloods, Arabians, Morgans, National Show Horses and American Saddlebreds, often suffer from back problems and will especially benefit from the following exercises.

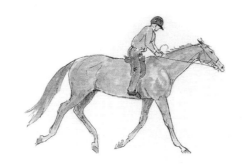

Training Solutions

TTouches

• Every horse, and especially those with back issues, can benefit from a few minutes of *Lick of the Cow's Tongue* and *Back Lifts* before and after riding. Making these TTouches a part of your routine can help prevent back problems or solve existing ones.

• *Belly Lifts* and *Pelvic Tilt* can help horses with low backs whose hips tend to keep the back "locked down."

• A series of connected *Lying Leopard TTouches* along the back, *Neck Releases*, *Inch Worm* on the crest, and *Tail TTouches* will help encourage the head to lower.

Ridden Work

• Ride your horse with the *Tellington Training Bit* and elastic *Promise Wrap*, a great combination to bring the back up and increase suppleness under saddle. In many cases, this duo will also reduce back soreness.

---

* According to equine biomechanics expert Deb Bennett, Ph.D, vertebral closure of the horse's back typically does not occur until age seven.

CHECKLIST FOR A HEALTHY BACK

- *Do* check saddle fit, dental health, and riding style to ferret out causes of a sore back. Learn how to assess saddle fit and consider using a tool such as a Port Lewis Impression Pad or EquiMeasure that will reveal pressure points. Read *The Horse's Pain-Free Back and Saddle-Fit Book* by Joyce Harman, DVM, MRCVS (see *Resources*, p. 311).

- *Don't* tie or cross-tie your horse's head higher than he normally holds it at rest. Beware of mechanical hot walkers that crank the horse's head sideways and up. High-headed and hollow-backed often go hand in hand, and each can contribute to and reinforce the other.

- *Do* be sure to have sufficient saddle padding of a type that allows your horse to engage the back muscles without his back dropping away from the pressure of the saddle.

Note: Avoid gel pads, which tend to accentuate pressure points (see *Resources*, p. 311).

Solutions at a Glance: *Back Problems*

Lick of the Cow's Tongue 177 ~ Back Lift 193 ~ Belly Lift 209 ~ Pelvic Tilt 222 ~ Lying Leopard TTouch 181 ~ Neck Release 221 ~ Inch Worm 197 ~ Tail TTouch 185 ~ Tellington Training Bit 290 ~ Promise Wrap 288

Backing Up (rein back)

Teaching a horse to back up properly is a stumbling block for a lot of people and horses. Even the Olympic gold-medal-winning dressage horse Goldstern, who I worked with in Germany, had problems backing up. Fortunately, this essential step in the education of any horse can be very simply taught from the ground. Even if your horse has been ridden for years and doesn't back up as well as you would like, you can improve and refine this ability with just a few sessions of Ground Work.

Training Solutions

- Lay out two 10-foot ground poles about five feet apart. Lead your horse forward until his front feet are inside the space between the poles. Hold the chain lead about two inches from the side ring of the halter, and take your thumb and softly press-and-release on the point of the shoulder with the *Rhino TTouch*—on the bone, not the muscle—and ask the horse to step one step back, with the drawn-out word "*baaaack.*" Then *Dingo* him forward two or three steps and back up a couple of steps. This is a good place to stop and give your horse a chance to think about it overnight.

- *Cha Cha* with your horse! Ask with the chain lead (or Zephyr lead—see p. 157) and voice to back, tapping with your wand lightly on the chest. As above, ask for just two steps back. Then *Dingo* him forward two steps and stop. Repeat two or three times until he gets into the motion.

- Using the same light signals and your voice, touch the front foot that is the most forward with the wand and ask the horse to back up one step. Reach back to stroke and tap the diagonal hind foot, paying attention that your horse doesn't take too big a step; if the front step is too long, he might lose his balance. You're looking for only a few short steps both front and hind.

- From the saddle, lighten your seat, tap the chest with the wand and invite him to move back with a light ask-and-release motion with your *Balance Rein*. It's not a pull, just an "invitation." Remember to breathe and visualize what you want. It can be very effective to ask your horse to take one step back at a time using one rein, and take the next step with a little ask-and-release with the other rein.

___

Tellington Tip

If the horse will not back up no matter what you do, do Hind Leg Circles and make sure he can step both hind legs back. One year I had a horse at EquiFest of Kansas who would get "stuck"—his front feet went back, but his back feet wouldn't budge. I picked up his back feet and circled them a few times, and he quickly got the idea of stepping back.

___

Solutions at a Glance: *Backing Up*

Rhino TTouch 224 ~ Dingo 235 ~ Cha Cha 232 ~ Balance Rein 279 ~ Hind Leg Circles 175

Balance or Coordination Issues

see also *Accident-Prone*

I'm often surprised just how little attention is paid to balance. Quite frequently, it's simply ignored, or the horse is written off as a hopeless oaf. Sometimes the horse is push-pulled in an effort to compensate for lack of balance. Other times, the horse is described as too young or clumsy to be in training, and is turned back out to pasture to "mature" for another year.

Warmbloods and draft breeds are especially slow to mature, and their lack of responsiveness and balance is often mistaken for mental slowness. In my experience, it does take longer for the signal from the handler to reach the brain and generate a response in some of the larger breeds, especially when they are younger than five or six years old.

Good horsemanship ultimately flows from both horse and rider being in balance. My mentor, Moshe Feldenkrais, who held a black belt in the martial arts, often spoke to his students about the importance of balance. He showed how "awareness through movement"—activating new neural pathways to the brain—could enhance  balance and therefore our ability to be efficient and stay safe in any situation. Sally Swift, in her classic text *Centered Riding*, devotes an entire chapter to balance and body freedom (see *Resources*, p. 311).

Balance is not just physical but also emotional and mental. Without this foundation, you can easily be knocked off center physically, and any little stimulus can set your horse off. The horse who is not balanced cannot respond effectively to your requests.

For the equestrian, balance is about having the posture or carriage that allows you to shift your position at any moment in order to make a clear request to your horse for a change in speed or direction. For the horse, balance is about being able to respond to your requests promptly and smoothly, without resistance or difficulty.

Training Solutions

TTouches

• *Connected Circles* bring a new awareness by covering all of the horse's body. *Leg Circles* and *Hoof Tapping* improve the horse's awareness of where he puts his feet. *Tail TTouches* give a connection through the whole body.

Ground Exercises

• Work in the *Labyrinth*. Observe how the horse steps around on the turns: Do the hind feet follow the track of the front feet, following the bend of the nose around the corner? Does the horse truly "track up" around those corners? Some horses either have to speed up around the corners, or when you stop, take two steps with one leg before moving the next one. To improve balance around the turns, put your horse into the *Body Wrap*; then stroke the back and tap with the wand as you move him around the corner. Stop on each straightaway before proceeding.

• *Dingo, Cueing the Camel, Cha Cha* and *Half-Walk* represent different stages of collection and extension as they activate new possibilities for movement. Try them progressively in the *Labyrinth*, then over the *The Fan* and the *Teeter-Totter*, then eventually *Freework* without any tack at all. You can train your horse to respond to an "invisible" wand and chain.

TIPS FOR IMPROVING YOUR HORSE'S BALANCE

• Make sure the saddle fits and has sufficient padding, and the farrier has balanced the feet correctly.

• Using the *Liberty Neck Ring* high on the neck will help your balance automatically, because you have to move your body in a different way in order to use it.

• Ride with one hand on the reins instead of two to loosen up your shoulders. Western riding offers a light, open hand with very little contact.

Ridden Work

• Rather than using your leg as a constant reminder to bring the horse into your hand, use the *Promise Rope* and *Balance Rein* to bring your horse into balance. Often, we find that the novice rider has an easier time of this than some advanced riders, because the novice has not been schooled to hold the horse in balance at every moment. These two simple tools work directly with the horse's nervous system to help him find his own balance and rhythm—to shift his center of gravity back toward the hindquarters and to achieve self-carriage.

• Riding with a *Liberty Neck Ring* without a bridle helps the horse find his balance, especially with the *Balance Rein* and *Promise Wrap*. You can also ride with a *Tellington Training Bit*, which is like having a secret weapon for quickly rebalancing any horse.

Evaluate Your Horse's Balance

• *Does your horse stand in hand with all four legs squarely under him, weight proportionately distributed, or does he more often stand with a front leg splayed out and a hind leg resting?*

- *Can your horse move a single step backward or forward using diagonal sets of legs (i.e., left fore, right hind), or does he respond in random fashion to your cues to take a step back and come forward?*

- *When you ask for a gait transition, does he respond promptly, or is there is a lag time? Keep in mind that a green horse may not respond at all, or may stumble or trip.*

- *Does your horse cross-canter under saddle or at liberty?*

- *Does your horse "fall on his nose" going downhill?*

- *Does your horse trip or stumble often?*

If you answered "yes" to one or more of these questions, your horse will benefit from the balance exercises in this section. In addition, severe disturbances of balance may indicate a neurological problem such as Wobbler's syndrome or EPM. If you have this concern, or your horse appears to be getting worse, consult your veterinarian.

Solutions at a Glance: *Balance or Coordination Issues*

Connected Circles 173 ~ Front Leg Circles 174 ~ Hind Leg Circles 175 ~ Hoof Tapping 196 Tail TTouch 185 ~ Body Wrap 160 ~ Dingo and Cueing the Camel 235 ~ Cha Cha 232 ~ Half-Walk 280 ~ Labyrinth 259 ~ Freework 257 ~ Pick-Up Sticks 253 ~ Teeter-Totter 273 ~ Balance Rein 279 ~ Liberty Neck Ring 282 ~ Promise Wrap 288 ~ Tellington Training Bit 290

"Balky" (refusal to move forward)

see also *Walk, too slow*

Your horse refuses to move forward, or seems to get "stuck" in one or more situations, either in hand or under saddle.

Such horses are often described as "having an attitude." The conventional wisdom is to sit hard and deep in the saddle, apply the aids with vigor and, if necessary, "get after" the horse with whip and spurs. This may work with some horses, but in many instances, their next move is to dig in, tense the neck muscles and run backward, often kicking out behind. Further pressure may cause the horse to rear and spin, putting the average rider in a compromising if not dangerous position. In the case of a young horse, you may deepen the resistance and erode willingness and trust. With a more mature horse, you will often hear the rider say, "He knows better!"

If he won't cross water, consider that maybe the horse can't judge the depth, or is concerned about reflection in the water; or the footing may be uncertain. I recommend that you get off and lead the way, carefully, making sure you hold the horse to the side so he doesn't jump on top of you. Hold the reins with both hands, with one arm extended and holding the reins close to the bit to keep your horse on his own path beside you.

The Tellington approach to the balky horse is to teach him to move forward to a light signal on the croup, with *you* leading the dance.

Training Solutions

- Instead of sitting hard and deep in the saddle and pushing with your legs or seat, sit quietly for a few moments, breathe deeply from your core (center), and lighten your seat. Now reach forward and do a few *Clouded Leopard TTouches* behind the ears, which will encourage your horse to lower his head.

• Still in the saddle, stroke your horse across the top of the croup with the wand and then tap lightly. Alternate tapping the wand on the shoulder and hindquarters. This technique has three benefits: it gives the horse a rhythm to go forward; the movement breaks the freeze pattern; and, because the taps are light, horses do not become agitated and tense the back. If he still will not move forward, hop off and lead him, tapping the croup with your wand in the *Dingo* leading position.

• To produce a deeper attitude shift, work your horse through various exercises of the Playground for Higher Learning, especially the *Work with Plastic Sheets* and the *Platform*, in which your horse will build self-confidence for any situation. Coupled with the *Dingo*, with its precise start, stop and back signals, you can quickly get your horse to pay attention and be obedient as you teach him to come forward and stop to the lightest of cues.

• Check your horse's chin. If it's tight and hard, a few minutes of *Mouth TTouches* will address his emotional blocks, soften his resistance and reawaken his ability to learn. *Ear TTouches* and *Forelock Slides* will foster a new level of trust and cooperation that can make your horse *want* to work *with* you, instead of "having" to work *for* you.

• Ride your horse in a *Liberty Neck Ring, Balance Rein* and *Promise Rope*.

Julie Suhr's Story

Julie Suhr, legendary endurance rider and author of Ten Feet Tall, Still, *writes about her experience on the trail with a "balky" horse:*

"…Along the edge of a jeep trail there was water dripping about six inches on to maple leaves caught in some rocks. It made a strange sound and for the first time Carolana planted her feet and said, 'No, I am not going to go!' It was obvious we were about to have a real test of wills. My urging and the resultant spinning, rearing and backing off a bank certainly would have made a liar of me if witnessed by the many people I had told that my young horse would go past anything. Her uncharacteristic behavior took me by surprise, and without thinking I responded with force. When a total impasse was reached, I realized I had to win the battle or be sorry in the future.

"I decided to try jumping off and leading her. I really did not think it would work, but it did. After passing back and forth several times, I mounted, and she walked by with little concern. In retrospect, knowing of her past willingness, I should have realized that she was seriously upset by a sound she did not recognize and did not understand. She probably interpreted it as dangerous, although to me it seemed so insignificant. I learned a lesson. If you know your horse is honest, and its behavior suddenly takes an uncharacteristic turn, think the situation through before you act. Carolana had been frightened by this situation, and I should have reassured her with gentleness rather than reacting with the physical punishment appropriate for a disobedient, balky horse. Because she trusted me, she was quite willing to follow me past the obstacle. All that unpleasantness could have been avoided so easily.

"Another thing that bothered her was puddles. It is hard to understand why, after coming through a Santa Cruz Mountain winter in which her feet were not dry for months at a time, a horse feels she has to avoid water in the trail. However, this was the case. She jumped the smaller puddles, side-stepped the larger ones and scared me by walking the thin line between a puddle and a canyon drop-off on several occasions. By the end of most rides she had tired of the game and would go through the center of a puddle without much thought. However, I had my second balking incident with her when we came to a puddle that stretched the entire width of the trail. She refused to enter it. Re-

membering my earlier experience, I tried leading her by wading through the puddle ahead of her. When I had muddied the waters, she entered willingly. I have *to believe that the reflections of the sky and trees were visually deceptive to her. There have been no further problems in this regard."*

Barn Sour (nappy)

see also *Herdbound, Rearing*

The scenario is familiar: the rider tacks up, mounts and starts down the road. Just as the barn or stable slips out of sight around the corner, the horse suddenly stops and freezes. His head comes up, his neck tenses, his nostrils flare and his eyes flash as he whirls to face the direction from which he came.

You'll often see a flailing of arms and legs, or crops and spurs, as the rider tries to persuade the horse to head down the trail. The horse may take a few steps, then balk, freeze, whirl, back up or even rear. Such horses have not been educated to go out solo or have never been taken out of the arena or round pen. Their behavior can become habitual, even dangerous, if the rider repeatedly capitulates. You can re-educate your horse to travel calmly away from the barn, stable or trailer alone by using a combination of Ground Exercises and Ridden Work.

Training Solutions

Ground Exercises

• In the arena, practice *Dingo* in the *Labyrinth* without the saddle, so that when you stroke and tap the croup, the horse comes forward without anticipating punishment. This is important, so that when the horse starts to turn back out on the trail, you can redirect and refocus the horse without a fight by stroking him with the wand on the shoulder and sides.

Ridden Work

• Swap your snaffle or hackamore for the *Tellington Training Bit*. In my experience with many horses, just putting this bit on can produce a major change in a horse's focus and willingness to listen to you. Teaming up the bit with a *Liberty Neck Ring* can help you signal your horse through the body and keep him on a straight track. When you get out of sight of the barn, from the saddle, reward your horse with a bite-sized treat. You may want to lead your horse away from the barn and give him treats as you go. With TTouches like *Lowering the Head, Ear TTouches* and *Lying Leopard TTouches* all over the body, your horse will bond with you and not feel the need for the "safety" of the barn or other horses.

• *Visualize!* Before you get to that place where your horse refuses, sit quietly in the saddle and make a clear picture in your mind of the spot where your horse has a tendency to turn back. Then replay the film and imagine you and your horse going right past that place, singing and smiling, your horse's ears pricked forward. Then, when you start down the road, keep breathing and hold that picture. Your *intention* can make the difference. Horses "read" our mental pictures!

If your horse still turns back at one particular point, be prepared by already having a halter over the bridle, and bringing your chain and wand along—then get off and lead the horse. You may also need to go back and do more homework with the Ground Exercises, particularly the ones in the Playground for Higher Learning, but in the meantime, lead your horse past that place a little further down the trail, and then remount.

Solutions at a Glance: *Barn Sour*

Dingo 235 ~ Labyrinth 259 ~ Lowering the Head 163 ~ Ear TTouches 210 ~ Lying Leopard TTouch 181 ~ Tellington Training Bit 290 ~ Liberty Neck Ring 282

Biting, Nipping, "Lipping," Snapping the Air

see also *Grooming Sensitivity and Mare, moody*

When your horse tries to bite, nip, lip, pinch or even nibble on you, he is giving you an important piece of communication. When simply "lipping" or licking you, I believe he is transmitting friendliness and a desire for attention; if you are a horse with four feet on the ground, what do you have? Your mouth! Then there are the playful nips, such as when foals think they can treat you like another horse; they haven't yet learned the distinction between foals and people.

A horse who snaps at the air is trying to tell you that he is nervous about the way he is groomed or the girth is tightened, or his back is sore; or he is exceedingly sensitive, and can't take what you are doing. His whispers have failed and the biting is the "shout." Then you get the extreme biter, whose behavior signals a level of intense pain in the body. It could be terror from being hurt or abusive punishment; or rage syndrome from a hormonal imbalance caused by a tumor.

There is no way for such horses to release high levels of energy or tension when kept in a stall, with no chance to jump, run, buck or roll. They kick the stall, they paw—and they get punished. Their teeth and hooves become their only outlet for frustration.

People often label a biter: "The horse has an attitude," or "Once a biter, always a biter." This is not my experience. Instead, if you understand that "mouthiness" is his way of being social, of connecting with you, you will realize the futility (and abusiveness) of simply try to beat the behavior out of him. I have never found such methods to be effective and, in fact, they can drive a horse to retaliate, creating much worse and more aggressive behavior.

We are told when a horse bites, you must retaliate instantly, but most of the time, he just goes into freeze mode, which only deepens the stress and tension, and destroys trust. Such a reaction is often based on the belief that if you do nothing, you are letting the horse "get away with" something.

Some trainers advocate punishing your horse by retaliating immediately, as though "getting even" will change his behavior. I believe that striking a horse sends a mixed message and fails to look at the core of what's causing this behavior. If this technique is used on a stallion, it will only make him dangerous: next time, he will really be out to get you! Other horses will just wait until you turn your back before striking again. With some horses, punishment only drives the reaction deeper. *Reacting with aggression against aggression rarely brings lasting change.*

Your goal is to go beyond reaction—to *act* and not *react*. First, determine the cause of your horse's biting, nipping, lipping, or snapping the air because therein lies the solution. Your goal, of course, is to not have your horse want to bite or nip you when you are working around him. As you will see, part of the solution will be to provide more, not less, contact with his mouth, since most "biters" are reaching out to make a connection.

Training Solutions

- Put your adult horse in *Taming the Tiger* position in the stall, or a safe corner in a paddock, and work quietly over his whole head with an emphasis on the mouth. Hold the side of the halter firmly so there is no possibility of him getting his lips or teeth on you.

We have found over many years that putting a horse in this position so he cannot bite, and then working the whole head, particularly the mouth, nostrils and ears, can make a major shift in behavior over several sessions.

I don't whack horses away from me when they lick or nip, nor do I ignore the behavior. Instead, I hold the side of the halter and do quiet work on the side of the mouth to give the contact. Many horses are missing the social contact in the herd: *you* are their social contact. It's normal for them to want to nip you. For horses who have been rescued or abused, start with light *Abalone TTouches* using a sheepskin mitt or a heat pack.

- *Mouth* and *Ear TTouches* are particularly effective because they influence the limbic system, the brain's control center for the emotions and learning. With *Mouth TTouches* you can give your horse the attention he is seeking—but *you* are leading the dance.

- **Foals or young horses:** Here's how to prevent nipping, or nip it in the bud. Young horses will often try to catch your skin, as if you were another horse. The way to avoid this is to make sure that when they are growing up, do not put your fingers in their mouth or think it's cute that they suck on you; this almost guarantees they will nip and pinch as they grow. Here's a solution: Holding the side of the halter, do *Chimp TTouches,* circling with the back of your folded fingers on the soft area on the side of the muzzle. Then slip your fingers into the mouth and slide them back and forth over the gums above the teeth. If the gums are dry, wet your fingers. I have seen amazing turnarounds in weanlings, yearlings and stallions using this method.

- **Stallions** are often nippy—it's part of their biological wiring to nip, bite and roughhouse with other stallions in a bachelor herd. You may have noticed that a stallion will try to bite another horse's shoulders. When they are isolated and lack social contact, their tendency to lip and nip intensifies. Work stallions in *Taming the Tiger*; lead them in *Journey of the Homing Pigeon* through the *Labyrinth*.

- **Snapping and biting the air while being groomed or saddled** is very clear language saying, "Whoa, this is too much for me! This is not comfortable!" First, check saddle fit and take up the girth slowly. Use *Taming the Tiger* with sheepskin mitt TTouches until the horse learns to trust that you will groom or saddle him in a way that is comfortable. Such horses are often also very reactive to girthing up, and will swing their heads around to bite as they are cinched.

Solutions at a Glance: *Biting, Nipping, "Lipping," Snapping the Air*

Taming the Tiger 166 ~ Abalone TTouch 171 ~ Mouth TTouch 182 ~ Chimp TTouch 194
Ear TTouches 210 ~ Journey of the Homing Pigeon 243 ~ Labyrinth 259

Bridling, difficulty with (won't accept bit)

see also *Ear Shy*

Refusal to take the bit can take many forms. Some horses clamp their teeth tightly; others evade the bit by raising the head out of reach or won't let you slip the headstall over the ears.

If your horse refuses to take the bit, first check the teeth and make sure his dental work is up to date. If your horse is two years or younger, he might have caps that haven't shed. Mature horses may have a painful, jagged tooth or an infection that you cannot see. Telltale signs of tooth troubles include grain falling out of the mouth at mealtime, weight loss, resistance to the aids in one direction or head tossing.

Once you've ruled out physical problems, check your bridling technique. Does your horse keep his head at an even level, or does he suddenly get as tall as a giraffe? Are you guiding the bit so it actually fits between the teeth, or is it slipping down under the lower lip? When you unbridle, is your horse raising his head and catching the bit on his teeth? Are you bending the ear in an uncomfortable manner with the crownpiece of the bridle? All of these details can make a difference!

In a few sessions, you can educate your horse to keep his head still and at an ideal level for bridling, about even with his withers. As you go through the steps on p. 45, don't try to force the bit into the mouth if your horse doesn't open his mouth or raises his head. For a while, when you ask the horse to open his mouth, give him a little bit of grain.

Training Solutions

• Teach your horse *Lowering the Head* to approximately withers level from your light signal. This is an essential component of trust and will probably help you overcome many behavior and training issues, both on the ground and in the saddle.

• *Mouth* and *Ear TTouches* will help prepare your horse to accept the bit. With a flat hand, do *Abalone TTouches* on the outside of the mouth and the chin. Especially with a young or green horse, insert your thumb in the corner of the mouth and wiggle it around until your horse opens the mouth. If you are comfortable doing so, tap the roof of the mouth and the tongue with your fingers, as if you're playing the piano.

Introducing the Bit

❶ Take a stripped-down bridle with only a headstall and bit—remove the reins and browband. (Make sure it's not adjusted too tightly, so you can easily slip it over the ears.)

❷ Hold the bridle with the two cheekpieces together in your right hand, snug against the forehead in front of the ears.

❸ Cradle the bit's mouthpiece with the forefinger and middle finger of your left hand, holding it steady in a "V" formation.

❹ As you lift the headstall and bit with your right hand, wiggle the side of the mouth with your left hand to open it and slip the bit in precisely between

IF YOUR HORSE CLAMPS HIS TEETH...

If your horse still keeps his teeth closed or raises his head every time to try to bridle him, follow these steps: take a half- or three-quarter-inch rope. Attach the snap to the upper ring on the off side of the halter, run the end through the lower ring, bringing the rope under the chin and back up through the lower ring on the left side. Snug the rope up against the chin.

Offer a little bit of grain from your hand or a shallow tray. When the horse begins to nibble at the grain, take up the tension on the rope so it goes between the teeth. *Make sure it's really going into the mouth and not just tightening against the gums.* Tickle the corner of the mouth at the same time.

Once your horse keeps his head still while the bit goes in and out of the mouth, remove the rope, and quietly bridle him one or two times with grain in the hand and tickling the corner of the mouth with your thumb just going in.

the upper and lower rows of teeth. Give a bite of grain the first few times. Be careful not to hit the teeth with the bit going in. Take your time, breathe, and hold a clear picture of your horse taking the bit willingly.

When you unbridle your horse, be sure your horse's head remains perpendicular to the ground, so the bit does not catch on the upper teeth if he raises his nose. Do this by pressing firmly down on the forehead as you bring the headstall down and off the ears, keeping contact down the bridge of the nose.

Solutions at a Glance: *Bridling, difficulty with*

Lowering the Head 163 ~ Mouth TTouch 182 ~ Ear TTouches 210 ~ Abalone TTouch 171

Bucking

Bucking is an instinctive movement that horses often do at liberty. As exhilarating as it may be to watch, however, when we are on their back, bucking is rarely good news. When your horse makes a single high kick with the back legs you may be able to stay on board, but if he seriously wants to unload you and goes to "crow-hopping" with his head down taking repeated leaps into the air and landing with jaw-jolting stops, you may find yourself on the ground.

Horses buck for many reasons, so the first step is to sleuth out the reason. Here are a few scenarios to consider:

• Trace the behavior backward to determine when the bucking started. Did he unexplainably start bucking whenever you first mount? Does your horse buck every time he's ridden? Does he buck in the pasture, on the longe line, bareback, with a saddle, with a rider?

• Is your horse bucking simply because he's feeling good and playful, such as horses sometimes do in cold weather or after a lay-off or unaccustomed confinement? Crow-hopping may be no more than a few playful bucks when you first get on a horse who is fresh and cool.

• Perhaps you're on a trail ride, and your horse is afraid he'll be left behind. The tendency of many riders is to restrain the horse even further, intensifying the reaction to buck because he's mad or frustrated.

• Bucking, especially that of sudden onset in a previously tractable mount, is often the result of pain or discomfort on the body or in the mouth. Two common causes of such bucking are an improperly fitting saddle or a girth that is too tight. A third factor might be the weight of the rider, especially if he or she is too heavy or unbalanced for the horse's age and level of fitness. The horse will tense up, hold his breath and brace himself; the only way he can release his tension is to explode into a buck.

If your normally well-behaved horse suddenly starts bucking and you've ruled out saddle fit or dental problems, it's possible that the horse has been injured in some way. I have seen really nice horses suddenly start to buck hard enough to get you off. Perhaps they have fallen in the pasture. Here, I recommend veterinary, chiropractic or a neurological check-up. You could also be looking to rule out Lyme disease, herpesvirus or EPM.

Once you have identified the source of the bucking, you can move on to the appropriate steps to remove its cause. Let's take a closer look at three common causes of bucking and discuss a plan of action for each one:

Training Solutions

Scenario 1: Your horse bucks on the trail

Many horses buck when they think they are being left behind or held back, because they are afraid to be left alone and desperate to catch up with their buddies. When the rider attempts to hold the horse back, he may coil like a spring ready to explode; bucking finally becomes the only way left to release the pent-up energy. Both horse and rider will benefit from exercises to increase their confidence together.

• Begin with *Ear TTouches, Lick of the Cow's Tongue* and *Tail TTouches* to foster a new connection with your horse. Your goal is to stimulate and engage learning centers of his brain to override an explosive, fear-based response. Your horse will enjoy being with you and learn to think before he leaps, replacing reactivity with a more intimate connection.

- Take your horse through the *Labyrinth*, both from the ground and mounted, for 10 minutes before you ride. Both you and your horse will begin to focus, relax and breathe, reducing tension when trail-riding with other horses.

- *Work with Plastic Sheets*, preferably in the company of another horse, will help your horse learn to listen to you on the ground before you get on his back. *Neckline and Ground Driving* will also teach patience. *Platform* and *Teeter-Totter* will help ground your horse.

- The *Tellington Training Bit, Balance Rein* and the *Body Wrap* under saddle can help you to steady your horse without overcollection; it's getting behind the bit that sets up the buck.

- Horses often get excited when they see other horses go into a canter, so ask your riding buddies to give you some warning and not just take off. Stay in the middle of the pack or up front until you and your horse feel comfortable in the group. Add an elastic *Promise Wrap* for a couple of rides to give your horse a sense of being secure.

- Ask one of your riding buddies to walk beside you, and then ask her to go on ahead in an easy trot about 30 feet before waiting for you to catch up. The idea is to get your horse used to transitions and learn to stay calm when other horses are ahead.

- Have your friend and her horse trot toward and past you, then you trot toward her and circle around her. Reward the horse for good behavior with a horse cookie or carrot. If your horse tenses up when other horses go ahead at the trot, use the *Balance Rein* to steady him. Keep breathing and stay soft through your joints. This prevents the coiled-up response that can lead to bucking.

POOR SADDLE FIT

This is a common cause of bucking. Maybe the horse has lost weight, or his body has changed shape due to training so that the saddle no longer fits and is causing pain; such horses are most often high-headed or tight-backed from the discomfort. When horses are in pain, they really want you off their back— and with good reason!

Scenario 2: Your horse bucks during transitions to canter

What makes a horse buck when cued to canter? Resentment from an overzealous cue from the rider can be one cause. It's usually from the use of spurs or the rider's heel being dug into the ribs. In this case, connected *Lying Leopard TTouches* with *Coiled Python Lifts* around the sensitive area can help overcome the reactivity. In addition, the rider has to lighten the signal from the leg and most likely eliminate the spurs.

I've known two Grand Prix dressage horses who bucked violently when cued to canter. Both were tight in the neck and back from much collection and extremely sensitive in the back under the cantle area of the saddle. When the riders sat a little deeper and applied more weight on one seat bone to cue the canter, the horses responded by tightening their backs, holding the breath and giving a really big buck.

- Relieving the back pain is the first necessity in such cases. *Lying Leopard* and *Clouded Leopard TTouches* on the back, *Belly Lifts* and light *Lick of the Cow's Tongue* can help relieve the back soreness, in addition to hind leg circles, *Tail Pulls* and *Pelvic Tilt*. I also recommend using a protective saddle pad (see *Resources,* p. 311).

Scenario 3: Your horse bucks when the weather is cold, windy or he is fresh.

• Begin with three to four minutes of *Ear TTouches* before you mount to help warm the whole horse. Follow with the warm-up exercises: *Zig-Zag TTouches* on the back under the saddle pad and finish with a few strokes of *Lick of the Cow's Tongue*. If your horse is tensing up, do a little more; repeat the circles and slides with a small, hand-held heat pack along the back before you get on. Ride with a wool quarter sheet when it's really cold.

• For extra security, ride in the *Tellington Training Bit* to keep your horse's head from plunging between his knees. When a horse takes a jump and a buck in a snaffle, he can more easily get his head down, or if you take a hold of him, he can throw up his head and make things even worse. Longeing is fine if that is what keeps your horse from bucking and makes him safe, but in some cases, the horse may bolt on the longe and become even more worked up.

• *Front* and *Hind Leg Circles* can help warm up and ground your horse before you mount.

• One more tip: just before mounting, lead your horse through the *Labyrinth* in *Half-Walk*, then ride him once or twice through it, to encourage him to focus on you and think. Adding a few *Tail TTouches* can relax the back so your horse walks off calmly from the beginning of your ride.

WARNING

For safety, I advise that you work with a professional trainer if your horse is bucking hard enough to unseat you. If you have the misfortune to buy a horse who turns out to be a chronic bucker, your best bet may be to return the horse. If the horse was fine when you tried him, but now consistently tries to buck you off, he may have been tranquilized earlier. I don't believe it's worth the risk keeping a horse who bucks in a way that endangers a rider.

Solutions at a Glance: *Bucking*

Ear TTouches 210 ~ Lick of the Cow's Tongue 177 ~ Tail TTouch 185 ~ Labyrinth 259 ~ Work with Plastic Sheets 265 ~ Neckline and Ground Driving 261 ~ Platform 269 ~ Teeter-Totter 273 ~ Tellington Training Bit 290 ~ Balance Rein 279 ~ Body Wrap 160 ~ Promise Wrap 288 ~ Lying Leopard TTouch 181 ~ Clouded Leopard TTouch 195 ~ Coiled Python Lift 172 Belly Lift 209 ~ Pelvic Tilt 222 ~ Zig-Zag TTouch 206 ~ Front Leg Circles 174 ~ Hind Leg Circles 175 ~ Half-Walk 280 ~ Tail TTouch 185

Cinchy/Girthy

see also *Biting*

It's Saturday morning at the stable. You watch as the new boarder tacks up her horse. As she takes up the girth another notch, you notice

that her horse is tensing his body, holding his breath, stretching his front legs forward like a cat and sinking toward the ground.

It's a classic case of cinching a horse up too fast or too tight. Some horses respond by snapping at the air, trying to bite, or pinning the ears as the girth comes up. Or, when the horse is asked to move off, he may travel with a stiffened, shortened gait. In extreme cases, he may stand frozen like a statue, then explode backward or forward when asked to take a step.

Perhaps the horse was girthed up too tight or too fast in the past—it only takes a few times to leave a lasting impression—or his saddle didn't fit. (When you approach with a saddle, your horse may already be showing his concern by tensing the body, raising the head, moving to the side or pinning the ears.)

People often "get after" a cinchy horse by reprimanding him verbally or kicking or kneeing him in the belly, simply ignoring or not realizing the extent of his discomfort. It is widely believed that you must girth up a horse extra tight to keep the saddle from slipping, and there are even leverage devices to get the girth tighter than you can get with your own power. I consider these approaches inhumane.

In addition, tightening a girth too much or too fast can limit the movement of the ribs and diaphragm, which limits breathing and inhibits the stride. If your horse is of normal weight, and not rolling in fat without withers, you may be able to ride with the girth a notch or two looser than you have been. Find out what's really comfortable and safe for you and your horse. Consider adding a breastplate and/or crupper to help keep the saddle from slipping back or forward on a low-withered horse.

I find it much more useful to fasten the girth comfortably snug but not tight. Lead the horse out for a few steps and take it up again before or just after mounting. Check again after riding for five to 10 minutes.

Fortunately, it is possible to erase the girthy horse's anticipation of discomfort during the saddling process by allowing him to breathe and release his tight back and barrel muscles. In addition, over just a few sessions, these exercises will improve a horse's length of stride and willingness under saddle.

Tellington Tip

Riders who habitually mount from the ground from the left side may be pulling their horse off balance and twisting the saddle tree. See "Mounting, won't stand for" (p. 87) for an alternative way of mounting.

Training Solutions

•   Start with slow, deliberate *Abalone TTouches* and *Coiled Python Lifts* using a flat hand over the entire girth and barrel area to release tense muscles. Your goal is to encourage the horse to lower his head, breathe and release tight muscles when he feels contact there. Continue onto the flank area, because the sensitivity often extends a way back, and the entire area needs your attention. In extreme cases of snapping or biting, encourage your horse to breathe and lower his head by letting him eat either hay or grain so that the neck remains parallel to the ground.

•   If your horse is "ticklish" in the girth area, he may benefit from *Belly Lifts* with a towel or unattached girth. You want him to learn to feel secure with contact around the sensitive area.

•   When your horse is feeling safer about contact there, you will be able to do very light *Lick of the Cow's Tongue* without eliciting objections from your horse such as pinned ears and snapping. This may take several sessions.

•   After your horse accepts you using the towel or unattached girth to do the lifts, put the saddle on without girthing it up. Try working from the right side of the horse—it's nonhabitual and will bypass the area with which he associates the most sensitivity. While your horse eats at chest level, stabilize the saddle with one hand and *slowly* lift the girth and do light *Belly Lifts* with the girth attached to the left side of the saddle only.

• From now on, do the girth up loosely when you first tack up. Put on the bridle, take the girth up another hole, even lead your horse out for a bit, return and take it up another notch. Lead a few steps and take it up another notch. After you mount, preferably from a mounting block, check your girth again in a few minutes. The settling of the rider into the saddle, the compression of the pad (and, in some instances, the saddle itself, as in the case of treeless saddles) will loosen the girth somewhat.

Tellington Tip

While the traditional method of stretching the front legs does prevent wrinkles and folds from gathering in front of the girth, we find it even more useful to do a minute of Leg Circles on all four legs before mounting. This will enhance the flexibility of the limbs, encourage breathing and help the horse release tension in the back. Pick up the foot and circle it around where the hoofprint is, moving the knee as you are circling the hoof.

Check the placement and comfort of your girth or cinch, and perhaps try some different materials, such as a girth with elastic ends or a string or mohair girth. Some leather girths develop sharp edges that may irritate tender skin. Make sure your girth is just as clean as your other tack. Consider a sheepskin or fleece girth cover, and make sure the ends are shielded. Your girth should not crowd or jam the elbow.

For Western riders, if your cinch is riding too far forward, as it may be with a double-rigging, consider switching your saddle to a three-quarter rigging. If you don't know how to do this, you may need the help of your local tack shop or saddle maker. If your horse has been "galling" behind the elbows, in addition to moving the cinch back you may find it effective to add a crupper.

Once a horse has the habit of tensing up, you may have to continue being careful when saddling; you can no longer be casual about it. Saddle fit may also be an issue. For more information on this, see chapter 2, A Closer Look at the Roots of Unwanted Behavior and Poor Attitude, p. 9.

Solutions at a Glance: *Cinchy/Girthy*

*Abalone TTouch 171 ~ Coiled Python Lift 172 ~ Belly Lift 209 ~ Lick of the Cow's Tongue 177
Front Leg Circles 174 ~ Hind Leg Circles 175*

Claustrophobia

Many horses become fearful and nervous when asked to go into a small space, such as through a narrow door into a stall, through a gate, or into a horse trailer. Others are reluctant to enter stalls and pipe corrals with low overhangs. For most, these are instinctive, automatic responses to protect the horse from becoming cornered. Others may have once caught a hip on a stall door or latch, or bumped their head going under a low overhang. As a result, they may refuse to go forward and if they do, they may bolt through the opening.

The problem may also arise when there is high contrast between light and shadow in the area you are working, typically at a stable door or stall entrance. The problem may be amplified if the horse is asked to take a step down or across an area that's difficult to see or unfamiliar to him. If you observe closely, you may see him showing his concern by holding the breath, tightening the back, raising the head or tensing the neck muscles.

Claustrophia is manifested in several ways:

- refusal to go forward through a narrow space
- rushing forward through a narrow space
- refusing to go forward due to low overhead
- fear of being in tight quarters with other horses

Forcing an obviously uncomfortable animal to go through a tight space may only intensify the fear. The horse may relent, but next time the behavior may be repeated. We need to acknowledge such fear in a horse rather than imposing our expectations that he shouldn't be afraid.

Your horse must learn to trust you and wait for your signal, so that when you ask him to come forward, he will do so calmly and confidently. Instead of responding fearfully—by freezing, rearing or spinning back—you can teach him to stop, consider the situation calmly and await your guidance.

WARNING

If your horse unexpectedly refuses to go forward out on the trail, be certain that there is not some underlying danger that you can't see or sense. I had this happen trotting down the road in the pitch black practicing for moonless endurance riding when my horse threw on the brakes. I turned on my flashlight and saw to my surprise that the road had washed out and a three-foot ditch had opened up six inches ahead of us!

Remember to "chunk down" the steps to teach the horse to trust you. Be patient while your horse is learning. If possible, take the horse away from the problem area he is refusing to enter, such as a stall, stable, pipe corral, or trailer.

Training Solutions

TTouches

Ask the horse to *Lower the Head* so his nose is just slightly lower than level. Bring the head down and do *Ear TTouches.* You can give your horse a more confident and clear sense of how much space he has around him by putting him into a *Body Wrap* while doing some *Clouded Leopard TTouches* over his face and neck.

Ground Exercises

If your horse stands at the entrance of the stall and is afraid to go through the door, or rushes through, get his attention and calm him using the four steps of *Dingo:*

❶ Get his attention with a *steadying* cue on the lead that tells him to listen to you.

❷ Quietly *stroke* the back two or three times from withers to croup to calm him.

❸ *Signal* him to come forward with the lead.

❹ Follow immediately with a *scooping* circular tapping motion of the wand on the croup to activate forward motion.

If possible, practice *Dingo* first away from the door so that your horse is listening to the signal of the lead and wand at a time when he is not stressed from the fear of going through a small space.

For horses who may have once "hooked" a hip on a sliding door or stall latch, be sure to allow plenty of clearance when leading in or out of tight quarters. If you don't have the luxury of time and the floor is level, you can back the horse into the stall. For a more lasting solution, review the basic *Elegant*

Elephant leading position. Add a light tap on the chest as you ask your horse to "stay back."

• Teach your horse to slow down, pay attention and wait for your signal with the *Labyrinth* in *Half-Walk*. These Ground Exercises make it easy for your horse to learn to listen to your signals on the chain and wand.

• *Work with Plastic Sheets,* and especially *Work under Wands,* are some of the most effective confidence-builders, especially if your horse ducks away from or refuses to go under things overhead. This work is a real opportunity for your horse to go beyond instinct and learn how to learn.

Turnaround Tale

An off-the-track Thoroughbred with difficulty trailer-loading was taken to a horse exposition in Wichita, Kansas. It took three hours to load him, and the horse finally had to be tranquilized just to get him to the fairgrounds.

When I went to look at the horse the day before the demo, the owner was trying to put him back in his stall. *He was clearly frightened, and "stuck." His head was up, and he was braced—mentally and physically. He wasn't going in! First, I tried the conventional approach of backing him into the stall. I could not even get his hindquarters into the doorway.*

So I took him about 20 feet away, into a more open stall aisle. First, I Lowered the Head and worked his ears for a couple of minutes. Then I did Dingo, tapping him on the croup and chest so he would wait and listen for my signals. When I took him back to his stall, his head went back up, and the fearful look returned to his eye. Four stalls away, I found one that had a light in it and was even more open. After a slight hesitation, he responded to the tap-tap on the croup, lowering his head and walking right in. I rewarded him with a few nibbles of grain, took him back out, and repeated the process.

Then I took him back to his original, darker stall, and this time, with his increased trust in me, he readily came in. The next day, when we did the trailer-loading demo, he loaded calmly and without incident.

Solutions at a Glance: *Claustrophobia*

Lowering the Head 163 ~ Ear TTouches 210 ~ Body Wrap 160 ~ Clouded Leopard TTouch 195 ~ Dingo 235 ~ Elegant Elephant 237 ~ Labyrinth 259 ~ Half-Walk 280 ~ Work with Plastic Sheets 265 ~ Work under Wands 267 ~ Body Wrap 160

Clipper-Phobic (fear of clipping)

see also *Grooming Sensitivity*

Today's the day. You've decided to clip your horse. You've assembled your clippers, oil and lubricating spray, extension cords, and you've bathed your horse to help the blades glide over the coat. You bring your horse out, cross-tie him, switch on the clippers—and he wants nothing to do with the procedure.

Some horses are fine until you reach a certain part of the body, such as the ears, neck or belly. I've known many horses who become sensitive when the clippers get near the head.

Many clipper-phobic horses are also sensitive to grooming and have a tendency to throw their head up and hold their breath when they are uncomfortable. Many also resist treatment by the veterinarian.

Unfortunately, many clipper-averse horses are simply twitched or tranquilized in order to "get the job done." While this is better than getting into a battle and risking injury, we have found that a little bit of education can quickly accustom even sensitive horses to the clippers.

Many people use cross-ties for clipping; however, we have seen many injuries, even with well-trained horses who startle or become entangled in the power cord. In addition, cross-ties encourage the horse to raise the head and neck and tighten the back.

To make it easy and comfortable for the horse to be clipped, boundaries can be useful. A closed wash rack can make clipping your horse easier than working out in the middle of a stall aisle where the horse can run backward. It can be useful to clip another horse where your horse can watch and see (and hear) that it's no big deal. Or, bring a buddy up for moral support when you get ready to clip. Shoe, clip or vet the easiest horse in the barn first.

Training Solutions

❶ If your horse dances around, do *Taming the Tiger*. This position is extremely effective for horses with any type of fear or phobia on the ground, or who have difficulty standing for the farrier, veterinarian, or even for saddling.

❷ Before you can safely clip your horse, you will need to teach him *Lowering the Head* from a signal on the chain. If the horse will not stand still or is trying to barge through you, put the chain over the nose (see p. 157) and stroke the wand on the underside of the neck and down the chest and front legs to calm and ground him. Do *Ear TTouches* to fur-

> ## CLIPPING TIPS
>
> • Put a feedbag on your horse and let him eat while you are clipping, or place hay at chest level where your horse doesn't have to reach too far.
>
> • Pack your horse's ears with cotton if your horse is noise sensitive.
>
> • Check out some of the quieter, lightweight, cordless clippers on the market.

ther calm your horse and encourage *Lowering the Head*, and *Inch Worm* to relax the crest.

❸ Before clipping, do *Clouded Leopard TTouches*, *Lick of the Cow's Tongue* and *Tarantulas Pulling the Plow* on any sensitive or ticklish areas. *Tarantulas* are especially useful to accustom the horse to the sensation of the clippers and *Lick* is especially good for the ticklish belly hairs.

❹ Do a few circles with the clippers turned off, each time asking him to turn back to look at you and take a treat out of your hand. With the clippers held away from him to reduce effects of the sound, turn the clippers on and off several times until the horse will turn and take a treat from a flat pan with the clippers running.

Caution: Clippers may get very hot, so be sure to take breaks to let them cool down. If your horse does not stand quietly, have a helper hold the horse with the chain up the side of the halter (see p. 159) and stroke the body and legs with the wand. If he tries to run backward, tap his croup with the wand as in *Dingo*.

Solutions at a Glance: *Clipper-Phobic*

Taming the Tiger 166 ~ Lowering the Head 163 ~ Ear TTouches 210 ~ Inch Worm 197 Clouded Leopard TTouch 195 ~ Lick of the Cow's Tongue 177 ~ Tarantulas Pulling the Plow 203 ~ Dingo 235

"Cold-Backed"

see also Cinchy/Girthy

You swing the saddle over your horse's back, and he suddenly sinks down. He appears to regain his composure and balance, so you continue taking up the girth. When you mount, he may sink again, and he moves off stiffly as if he's walking on eggshells, but you "ride him out of it" in a few minutes.

In some instances, such horses may pull back when first girthed or cinched and actually fall or lie down when they feel the weight of the saddle or the rider. I've also seen the horse who humps his back and "minces" along, feeling as if he's going to buck.

Whatever the manifestation, "cold-backed" horses often have a tense or tight back that may go unnoticed. In most instances, I've found that such horses may not have had their backs properly prepared before they were first saddled and ridden as youngsters. This should be done with a few sessions of TTouch on the back and girth before introducing the pad and saddle—doing so can stay with a horse for his entire life.

Over the years, "cold-backed" has been thought to be the horse's first reaction to the saddle being put on. The conventional thinking was, "It's all in his head; he'll work out of it." People didn't think anything could be done about it.

Twenty-five years ago, I realized how common it was for horses to have a sore back and how seldom their pain was recognized. Today, thanks to the disciplines of endurance riding and eventing, we know that a "cold back" is often more physiological than attitudinal. Often, saddle fit can be the culprit, even in the cases where horses have had professional fitting. This is usually because saddles are rarely fitted with the rider sitting in the saddle.

Training Solutions

TTouches

• *Lying Leopard TTouches* with *Coiled Python Lifts* all over the back, barrel, girth and belly, followed by *Lick of the Cow's Tongue*, help relax and take the tension out of the back and girth area.

• *Back Lifts* raise the topline and help fill in those little hollows behind the withers so that the horse can carry the saddle and the rider with a rounded instead of hollowed back.

• Do *Belly Lifts* with a towel, and *Abalone TTouches* with *Coiled Python Lifts* on the girth area. Feed the horse at withers level while saddling. Place the pad and saddle onto the back gently, and mount from a mounting block.

Ridden Work

Use the *Balance Rein* and *Promise Rope* to round and lift the back. Have someone observe you or perhaps videotape you in the saddle at different gaits to see if the horse's back stays up. If needed, use shims (small pieces of high-density foam) to help make sure the saddle is comfortable until your horse redevelops his balance and symmetry under saddle. You can also try a different saddle pad. Remember, saddle fit is a dynamic process as your horse's back may change shape as he develops fitness.

Solutions at a Glance: "Cold-Backed"

Lying Leopard TTouch 181 ~ Coiled Python Lift 172 ~ Lick of the Cow's Tongue 177 ~ Back Lift 193 ~ Belly Lift 209 ~ Abalone TTouch 171 ~ Balance Rein 279 ~ Promise Rope 288

Cribbing (windsucking)

Most horse people are familiar with the unsettling sights and sounds of a cribber. The horse seems utterly devoted to grasping a rail or other object with his front teeth, then arching and tightening the neck and back muscles as he rocks back, gulping air with a grunting sound. Some studies have shown that cribbers become addicted to the feel-good endorphin "rush" that accompanies the activity. Horses may begin to crib out of boredom, stress, stall confinement, dental problems or lack of roughage.

There is some controversy over the health effects of cribbing. Recent research shows that the habit increases the risk of digestive difficulties and colic. However, of greater concern is loss of weight because the horse spends so much time cribbing and not enough time eating. There is also the likelihood of uneven or excessive wear on teeth. Overdevelopment of the muscles on the underside of the neck is also common (see *Ewe-Neck*, p. 61).

It is common to place a snugly fitting strap around the throatlatch of cribbers to discourage the behavior. While this is effective in some instances, many established cribbers are not discouraged. The success of such devices is variable. However, you must be careful with any such device so that is does not interfere with the horse's airways. One that we recommend is the Miracle Collar, available from tack suppliers, which appears to control the problem more effectively and humanely (see *Resources*, p. 311).

Training Solutions

Bring the head down and work the ears, poll, throat and jaw with the TTouches listed below. Do *Back Lifts* and *Lick of the Cow's Tongue* to relieve the back muscles.

While you may not be able to eliminate the habit, you may be able to reduce its incidence and prevent a build up of stress-related problems in training or health. Make sure your horse has plenty of roughage, fed on the ground, at all times, and maximize the amount of turnout. If you have a choice, an electric fence is preferable to a wood-rail fence, giving the animal fewer places to crib on.

Solutions at a Glance: *Cribbing*

Lowering the Head 163 ~ Ear TTouches 210 ~ Neck Rocking 199 ~ Back Lift 193 ~ Lick of the Cow's Tongue 177~ Lying Leopard TTouch 181 ~ Coiled Python Lift 172 ~ Inch Worm 197

Cross-Cantering (disunited canter)

Your horse, when asked for a transition to canter, picks up a different lead with his front and back legs. You'll know this instantly as it is very jerky and uncomfortable. Cross-cantering (also called cross-firing) is not uncommon in young horses just beginning saddle training who haven't found their balance. We also see it in horses who have suffered muscle damage from a recent episode of tying up. However, you'll see horses cross-cantering at liberty as well. The under-saddle type of cross-canter is usually due to lack or loss of balance or an injury; the at-liberty type is usually simply uncoordination. I'll discuss solutions for both.

The conventional method of dealing with cross-cantering under saddle is to bring the horse back down to a trot and pick up the canter again. Often, the rider sits deeper in the saddle to push the horse forward; however, in my experience, this often doesn't help if the problem is caused by poor balance. Instead, it may be useful to get your weight up and out of the saddle to free the hindquarters. A thicker, high-density foam saddle pad may also help.

Training Solutions

TTouches

• Since most horses who cross-canter are imbalanced or uncoordinated, do a *Body Exploration*. You may find tightness, stiffness or soreness in the back and loin area.

• To improve balance and coordination, first increase the horse's awareness of his own body. "Connect the dots" using connected *Clouded Leopard TTouches* all over the body. A stiff horse will be slower to respond to your aids under saddle, and may not step away when you give him a cue to move sideways in hand. For this type, do connected *Clouded Leopard TTouches* with a number 3 or 4 pressure (see p. 148) with two-inch slides. With a sensitive horse use 2 to 3 pressure. Work the head one day, the neck and shoulder the next, and so on. Bring it all together with *Lick of the Cow's Tongue*.

• Another balancing and coordinating exercise is *Front* and *Hind Leg Circles* in both directions, along with *Coiled Python Lifts* and *Octopus TTouches*. Begin at the top of the leg and work down to the hoof.

Ground Exercises

• For horses who cross-canter at liberty, first work from the ground with *Half-Walk*, *Cha Cha* and *Dancing Cobra*. Use the elastic *Body Wrap* for these exercises.

• Do single step/stops in the *Labyrinth* for two or three steps, with the horse's head at whatever level feels comfortable for him. Then teach him different ranges: bring the head up higher holding the chain two inches from the side ring of the halter. This shifts the center of gravity back. Use two taps on the croup with a little circular motion forward, and two taps on the chest to stop (*Dingo* and *Cueing the Camel*). Then, bring the head lower, so that the poll comes slightly below the withers, and finally return to the center position. Challenge yourself to show the horse three different levels. These exercises practiced together can help to improve coordination and balance.

Ridden Work

• Under saddle, ride in the *Promise Wrap*; if your horse is strung out and slow to respond to the leg, ride with the *Promise Rope*. Add a *Tellington Training Bit* to help your horse engage his hindquarters, shift his balance toward his hind end, and improve coordination.

Tellington Tip

Wear a small waistpack filled with thinly sliced carrots or other bite-sized horse treats as you work your horse both on the ground and mounted.

Solutions at a Glance: *Cross-Cantering*

Body Exploration 151 ~ Clouded Leopard TTouch 195 ~ Lick of the Cow's Tongue 177 Half-Walk 280 ~ Cha Cha 232 ~ Dancing Cobra 234 ~ Front Leg Circles 174 ~ Hind Leg Circles 175 ~ Coiled Python Lift 172 ~ Octopus TTouch 200 ~ Body Wrap 160 ~ Labyrinth 259 ~ Dingo and Cueing the Camel 235 ~ Promise Wrap 288 ~ Tellington Training Bit 290

Crowding/Pulling on Lead

see also *Balance or Coordination Issues*

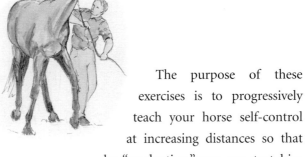

I'll never forget the sight of an experienced horsewoman I'll call "Sigrid," as she proudly led her prize-winning dressage mare into the arena to show her off. As the mare came in, she barged through the door, brushing Sigrid to the side. Sigrid attempted to slow the mare down by bracing her back against the mare's shoulder. The mare ignored her, knocking her to the ground as she blasted free and raced to the end of the arena. Sigrid got up and brushed herself off with a sheepish grin, excusing her mare's "enthusiastic" behavior.

It turned out that this mare's habit of pulling free was not new. Since Sigrid had expressed an interest in the Tellington Method, I offered to show her some of the basics. It only took a 10-minute session in the *Labyrinth* with the wand and the chain to get the mare's attention and focus.

Crowding and pulling on the lead are common problems, yet they are widely ignored. Such behavior represents a fundamental lack of training in basic manners. A fresh look at leading can help you to mold your "bull in a China shop" into a safer, more cooperative and responsive partner.

If a horse is pulling, or barging into your space in such a way that you are at risk of being stepped on or even knocked down, you're dealing with a potentially dangerous habit, especially if you should ever find yourself attempting to lead your horse over a ditch or along a narrow, hazardous spot on the trail.

Training your horse to stand and lead in a calm, obedient manner is fundamental to good horsemanship, but the rewards don't stop there. As a bonus, you'll find that once your horse learns to respond to your light signals on the chain and with the wand, he will be more balanced and listen more readily to your rein aids when you are in the saddle or driving in harness.

The purpose of these exercises is to progressively teach your horse self-control at increasing distances so that by "graduation," you can trot him over a series of ground poles as if by remote control. Another reward from practicing these leading Ground Exercises will be the enhancement of your own coordination, learning and balance, both from on the ground and later, from the saddle.

Tellington Tip

If you are leading your frisky horse to the paddock and don't want to put the chain over the nose, you may find that just attaching your regular lead to the side ring of the halter gives you more control than the normal ring under the chin. The side ring gives a more direct connection to the nose and dampens his pulling power; when you snap to the side, you have a lighter, finer control. Just be sure to fit the halter correctly—if it's too big or adjusted too loosely, the halter will twist too much.

Training Solutions

• Use the classic *Elegant Elephant* leading position to teach the horse to start and stop on a straight line and to stay in his own space. Get your wand out, thread the chain over the halter noseband and step forward so your shoulder is even with your horse's nose. Start out holding the chain about six inches from the halter ring with your shoulder about two-and-a-half feet away. Rotate your body one-quarter turn toward your horse as you ask him to stop.

It's the combination of your signal on the chain and your wand about two feet in front of his nose that will get his attention enough to slow him down and keep him from crowding. You may have to tap him lightly on the bridge of the nose or the side of the neck with the thicker end of the wand to keep him over. If he still tries to crowd, hold the chain against his jawbone and gently reposition his head.

- To further help your horse focus, slow down and listen to your subtle signals with the chain and wand, take him through the *Labyrinth*.

- Over the course of a few sessions, move out to the side about four feet and practice *Joyful Dolphin*. Ask your horse to stop or slow down from this distance from the lightest possible touch on the nose or chest with the tip of the wand combined with a light connection on the lead. Use a drawn-out, low "toning" sound: "*Whoaaaaa*" or "*Slowwwww.*" Place two lines of parallel ground poles two to three feet apart, so they form an open channel between you and your horse as you lead him. You will be amazed at the quality of attention your horse will give you once you both have mastered this exercise.

- If your horse is quite pushy, he may benefit from having two people lead him in *Journey of the Homing Pigeon*. This exercise will quickly teach him to stay in his own space. Tap him lightly on the nose bone the first time you ask for the stop.

- *Dancing Cobra* in the *Labyrinth* (see Photo 6 on p. 260): in this unusual exercise, you stand in front of your horse and teach him to stay back from your lightest signals from the wand and your body language. This is a remarkable way to teach your horse self-control and feather-light response. Or, sweep your wand like a windshield wiper back and forth between you and the horse, slowly and rhythmically, in *Peacock*.

- Once you've mastered the basics of leading, you can have all sorts of fun with your horse. For example, walk your horse over four ground poles set about four feet apart, with your horse going straight down the middle of the row and you on the outside (see p. 255). Once you've got this down pat, the next step is to trot your horse through the poles in this position. Try *The Fan, Cavalletti, and Pick-Up Sticks*.

Turnaround Tale

A horse trailer pulled in to a clinic in Ojai, California, driven by a father with his 13-year-old son. In the trailer was a three-year-old Tennessee Walker mare, brought to the clinic because of an extreme habit of crowding and frequently almost running the boy down when something scared her, which was often. I first asked both of them to show me how they'd been leading the horse.

The father took hold of the lead rope directly under the snap, with the mare almost wrapped around his body, with full contact of her neck against his shoulder.

It was clear that he had inadvertently taught her this behavior—not only to crowd but to be dependent upon him. She became very nervous whenever she felt she was on her own. When I asked him why he was leading her so closely, it became apparent that it gave him a good feeling to have the mare so dependent upon him, that he liked having her so close and in his space.

Although this closeness was desirable to the father, the son felt he was constantly in danger of being run over. It only took two 15-minute sessions over two days using the Elegant Elephant to teach the mare to stop and stand in her own space, away from both handlers.

Once the mare learned to keep her distance, the father realized that they could still be connected even when she wasn't in such close physical contact. The mare gained confidence and overcame her spookiness so that the son could safely handle her.

Solutions at a Glance: *Crowding/Pulling on Lead*

Elegant Elephant 237 ~ Labyrinth 259 ~ Joyful Dolphin 244 ~ Journey of the Homing Pigeon 241 ~ Dancing Cobra 234 ~ Peacock 247 ~ The Fan, Cavalletti, and Pick-Up Sticks 253

Ear Shy (head shy)

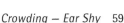

An ear-shy horse is reluctant to let you touch one or both ears, whether putting the bridle on, the reins over the head or handling the ears. He could be a model citizen in every way—until you get close to his ears. Then, he might toss or lift his head high to avoid contact, or twist his head away from you—whatever it takes to keep your hands away from his ears.

Horses become ear shy for a variety of reasons. There could be infection or inflammation (past or present), within the ear, or an extreme sensitivity to insects or light. An old practice called "earing," in which the ear is used like a twitch to control a horse, is notorious for producing ear-shy horses. There may even be a genetic propensity—I've known some lines of Arabians who were sensitive on the right ear.

Many horse people deal with the situation by simply avoiding handling the ears or taking the bridle apart every time they want to go for a ride. The smallest gesture can become a dodging match, and treatment or inspection of the ears can only be accomplished by twitching the upper lip. Specific TTouches can help your horse learn to accept and enjoy contact all over his head, working up to the ears.

Replace anticipation of pain or discomfort with pleasure. You'll find these exercises to be quite enjoyable for your horse. In just a few sessions, you'll be able to shift his attitude about having his ears handled.

Training Solutions

• Since most ear-shy horses raise their heads out of reach to evade contact, first check his willingness to *Lower the Head*. Use small bites of carrots or horse treats to encourage your horse to keep his head in a position level with his withers, and begin TTouching on an area where your horse is comfortable, then progress toward the more sensitive areas.

• Do *Lying Leopard TTouches* over every inch of the head, especially the forehead, but not the ears

- If your horse seems more sensitive on one side, have a chiropractor check the poll area for out-of-alignment vertebrae, and check the temperomandibular joint (TMJ).

- If your horse is sensitive to ear flies, do *Ear TTouches* and *Raccoon TTouches* over every inch of the ear, pressing the insides of the ear together to make them less reactive to contact; then put on a fly bonnet to protect the ears.

- If your horse is also head shy or afraid of the veterinarian, you may find it useful to place him in the *Body Wrap* while following the above steps, or try this unusual approach:

Place an elastic bandage across the forehead with a helper holding both ends as you put on the bridle, or try a miniature variation on the *Body Wrap* around the forehead and ears as shown in the photo.

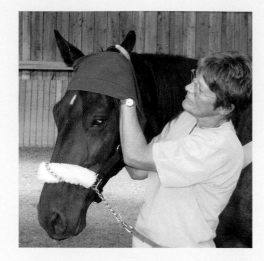

Practitioner Bettina Weidle-Loris demonstrated this brilliant idea at a Tellington training in Germany. This mare was very resistant to having her ears touched, and by using the wrap in this way, within minutes Bettina could touch the ears with ease.

just yet. Using a sheepskin mitt or the back of your hand to do the circles shortens the time needed to win his trust.

- *Forelock Slides:* Take a hold of the forelock near its base, and slide your hand slowly down to its end as you hold it against the forehead. Repeat. Horses seem to like this soothing motion, which encourages acceptance and head-lowering.

- *Llama TTouches* with the back of the hand help you approach the ears in a non-threatening manner. If you still can't get near the ears, do *Mouth TTouches* first.

- After practicing the above TTouches, stroke the ear back *flat against the neck* with long, sweeping strokes. At first, you may want to use a sheepskin mitt or your wrist and forearm instead of your hand, which are less threatening. Many horses accept this

type of contact when they're not yet ready to accept you taking hold of the ear.

- Now you're ready to do *Ear TTouches.* Hold one side of the noseband of the halter to keep the horse balanced as you work. In a continuous motion, stroke from the middle of the poll over the base of the ear, and lightly but confidently stroke your fingers out to the very tip. Work with one ear at a time, being sure to do a little press on the base as you cup your hand around it and continue the motion. If your horse is more ear shy on one side, start on the more accepting side.

Benchmark of Success

You can slide a rein over the forehead and ears and place the headstall over both ears quietly.

Some horses prefer a light stroke; others accept firmer pressure. Your goal is to have your horse *accept* and *enjoy* the contact.

Within a session or two, your horse should "change his mind" about having his ears handled. Most horses find these new and unusual sensations to be pleasurable. Stroke the ears for a few minutes each day (in time, you should be able to do both ears at the same time), and visualize success.

Solutions at a Glance: *Ear Shy*

Lowering the Head 163 ~ Lying Leopard TTouch 181 ~ Forelock Slides 198 ~ Llama TTouch 180 ~ Mouth TTouch 182 ~ Ear TTouches 210 ~ Raccoon TTouch 213 ~ Body Wrap 160

Ewe-Neck

When the muscles on the underside of the neck are overdeveloped, a horse is considered ewe-necked. Typically, the horse also loses the muscling over the crest and topline. Many ewe-necked horses wind up as problem horses—high-headed, stiff- or hollow-backed, uncoordinated, strung-out or spooky. I am sure such horses are uncomfortable in the back and put out of balance by this upside-down posture—they seldom look happy. Their breathing may be restricted and they appear disconnected, as if they were in three different pieces.

A tie-down or martingale may keep the horse's ears out of your face but rarely overcomes the problem and often makes it worse. In my many years of dealing with ewe-necked horses, I did not think that ewe-neck could be changed. However, we've had tremendous success over the years in changing this conformation with a combination of Ground Exercises, reshaping the back with *Back Lifts* and using specific equipment.

When you begin to shift a horse's posture, his behavior also changes. The success of transforming a ewe-neck in this way seems to come from the horse learning to use himself through the back and hindquarters.

Training Solutions

TTouches

- *Back Lifts* daily—especially before and after tacking up—will encourage your horse to engage the belly muscles, lift the back and release the muscles in the neck. Add *Lick of the Cow's Tongue* on the barrel, *Inch Worm* on the crest and lines of *Connected Circles* from poll to hindquarters to bring a new awareness throughout the body. *Tail TTouches* reconnect the horse from the tail to the ears.

Ground Exercises

- Lead your horse in *Dingo* to help him give the head, flex at the poll and step up from behind and step under himself. *Neckline and Ground Driving* with a *Body Rope* also helps bring the horse's back up and lift the root of the neck to reshape the topline.

- Under saddle, combine the *Tellington Training Bit, Balance Rein* and *Promise Wrap.* Experiment to see which is most effective. These tools will encourage the horse to step under himself and round the back. The *Balance Rein* has the effect, according to Dr. Deb Bennett, of activating the chest muscles that run between the front legs and cause the horse to lift the back, and at the same time, trigger the "seeking" reflex that encourages the horse to extend the neck and activate the ring of muscles. It has been our experience that within a week under saddle with the *Tellington Training Bit* alone, the horse will dramatically change his posture and no longer display a ewe neck under saddle. They may still have it when you are not riding them, however.

Solutions at a Glance: *Ewe-Neck*

Back Lift 193 ~ Lick of the Cow's Tongue 177 ~ Inch Worm 197 ~ Connected Circles 173 ~ Tail TTouch 185 ~ Dingo 235 ~ Neckline and Ground Driving 261 ~ Body Rope 160 ~ Tellington Training Bit 290 ~ Balance Rein 279 ~ Promise Wrap 288

Fear of Movement or Objects Behind

see also *Shying ("spooky"), High-Headed, Tail Clamping*

Ever notice how the horse on the "tail end" of a trail ride often scoots forward as he keeps a wary eye on what's behind him? Horses are designed by nature to be animals of flight, and running away from perceived danger has long been hard-wired in the equine nervous system.

When horses are afraid, they clamp the tail and tighten the muscles of the hindquarters, intensifying the feeling of fear and scaring themselves. Look for these clues:

- Tense or tight in the neck or back
- High-headed or nervous
- Spooky or hyper-reactive
- Kicking when other horses come up behind
- Clamping tail or not accepting a crupper
- Not wanting to be left behind

Overriding this innate fear is one of the cheapest insurance policies riders can have. "Desensitizing" or "sacking out" has been a common solution to spooky horses in the past and does work for some horses, but it can have the negative effect of making a sensitive horse more spooky and nervous. By adding TTouches for Trust, such as the *Troika TTouch* and a variety of other TTouches, you can give your horse a new sense of self that will allow him to override the fear.

Training Solutions

- *Tail TTouches* give confidence by relaxing the buttock muscles, bringing awareness to the hindquarters and creating a connection through the whole body from back to front. Add a *Body Wrap* to further improve confidence and a sense of security while *Lowering the Head.*

- Ride with the *Balance Rein* and *Promise Wrap* so you don't "choke up" on the reins and scare your horse more when he begins to tense up. From the saddle, teach your horse to turn his head back to take a horse cookie from your hand whenever he is concerned about anything behind him. Remember, chewing overrides the flight reflex by activating the parasympathetic nervous system.

• Do *Work with Plastic Sheets, Teeter-Totter* and other Playground for Higher Learning (p. 250) exercises both on the ground and under saddle. *Neckline and Ground Driving* really help a horse overcome fear of contact from behind.

Solutions at a Glance: *Fear of Movement or Objects Behind*

Tail TTouch 185 ~ Body Wrap 160 ~ Lowering the Head 163 ~ Balance Rein 279 ~ Promise Wrap 288 ~ Work with Plastic Sheets 265 ~ Teeter-Totter 273 ~ Neckline and Ground Driving 261 ~ Troika TTouch 188

Feet, won't pick up/leave down, snatches away

Do any of these situations sound familiar?

• Your horse picks his foot up when you ask but just as quickly slams it back down to the ground.

• Your horse reluctantly picks up his foot but then leans on you.

• Your horse's hoof seems to be full of lead weight, rooted to the ground.

• Your horse snaps his foot up when you are brushing his legs or putting on leg wraps.

While the technique of leaning against a horse's shoulder and pressing the fingers into the tendon region of the lower leg often works, I don't recommend it because I believe it encourages a horse to lean back into you. What follows are the basic steps for teaching or retraining any horse to readily pick up his feet.

Training Solutions

❶ Encourage *Lowering the Head* by stroking the neck, chest and legs with the wand and follow with *Hoof Tapping*. Use *Coiled Python Lifts* and *Octopus TTouches* on the legs from elbow to hoof and on the

insides of the hind legs. You may need several sessions until the horse stands quietly and is completely calm about having these areas touched before proceeding to pick up the hind legs.

Horses who are nervous about contact on the belly, ticklish in the flanks, sensitive on the inside of the back legs or nervous about their tail being handled will benefit from *Tarantulas Pulling the Plow, Belly Lifts* from elbow to flank, quiet, light *Lick of the Cow's Tongue* and *Tail TTouches* in addition to work on the legs.

❷ With a light, upward, scraping motion of your fingernails along the inside or outside of the cannon bone, without leaning against his shoulder, signal your horse to shift his weight and pick up a foot. When your horse gives the foot, catch the fetlock and hoof with both hands, do a quick, small circle in both directions and let it go. (These are known as *Leg Circles*.) Don't hold the leg up for the beginning sessions. Begin with the easiest leg—usually the left front, and work your way around all four legs.

As your horse becomes more willing with the circles, slow them down and spiral the hoof to the ground until you can set the tip of the foot on the ground. Once your horse can stand in balance and has no fear of contact with the lower legs, you will be able to pick up each hoof from only a light voice cue and touch signal. As soon as your horse is comfortable holding up his feet, do *Front* and *Hind Leg Circles* every time you pick up the feet to clean them.

Some horses are good with three legs but the right hind is a problem. Add *Journey of the Homing Pigeon* and work from the right side. If your horse is nervous about his hind legs being picked up, add *Neckline and Ground Driving* to help him get used to activity around his hind legs. If the horse is concerned about either hind foot being picked up, hold the tail with one hand while picking up a hind leg to keep a connection and let the horse know where you are.

Placing a horse in *Taming the Tiger* can enable you to pick up a foot if you are under time constraints. In addition, *Cha Cha* can help improve a horse's balance, coordination and ability to move the legs to a light signal from the handler.

Troubleshooting Techniques

Scenario: Your horse's hoof seems glued to the ground

Do a light upward scraping with your fingernails on the inside of the forearm. The moment the horse lifts the leg, catch the hoof, do a quick circle in each direction and let the foot go to the ground. Repeat and reward your horse.

Scenario: Your horse slams the front hoof down

Take a soft, 10-foot-long driving rope and hold it behind the knee. Stand a little ahead of the leg and pull the leg forward in one hand, and as the horse picks it up, catch the fetlock joint with the other hand. Remove the rope and take the leg in both hands, circle lightly and put it down quickly so the tendency to struggle or pull away is lessened (*Front Leg Circles*).

Note: Horses who won't pick up the hoof or slam it down are afraid for their balance—they are not just being stubborn. Feeding them a little helps them breathe and override the fear response. Clicker training can also be very helpful.

Scenario: Your horse lifts and coils a back leg as if to kick

This is not the time to punish your horse, which will only drive the fear and defensiveness deeper. Go back to *TTouches for Trust* and *Awareness* to make a connection with the horse, starting with the head and ears until he feels confident. Then do *Abalone TTouches* from head to tail, *Belly Lifts* and *Tarantulas Pulling the Plow* along parallel lines from girth to flank. It's all about getting the horse to feel good and safe in his body.

Stroke the body with a pair of wands, working your way to the hind legs. Stroke down over the croup and back legs, speaking to your horse in a soothing voice. Let the horse turn back and take a treat from your hand. As he turns and chews, he sees what you are doing, releasing any tension being held. As you *tone* your voice, keep a clear picture of the horse keeping the foot on the ground until you ask him to lift it, and then doing so easily.

Now go down one hind leg and lightly scrape your thumbnail on the tendon. As the foot comes off the ground, catch it with one hand on the inside and your other hand under the hoof and circle quickly a couple of times in both directions. Put the hoof down with the tip of the hoof resting on the ground.

Solutions at a Glance: *Feet, won't pick up/leave down, snatches away*

Lowering the Head 163 ~ Hoof Tapping 196 ~ Coiled Python Lift 172 ~ Octopus TTouch 200 ~ Belly Lift 209 ~ Lick of the Cow's Tongue 177 ~ Tail TTouch 185 ~ Front Leg Circles 174 ~ Hind Leg Circles 175 ~ Journey of the Homing Pigeon 241 ~ Abalone TTouch 171 Tarantulas Pulling the Plow 203 ~ Taming the Tiger 166 ~ Cha Cha 232~ Neckline and Ground Driving 261

Gaits, too fast (rushing, flighty, high-strung)

Your horse rushes ahead at the trot or canter; you are often heard to say, "My horse has no brakes." You feel like you are sitting on a powder keg that might explode at any time.

Body Exploration of such horses often reveals extreme tension. They are tense, nervous and flighty; wary of any contact with the mouth, flanks or hindquarters; and over-reactive to leg aids. They may be "touchy" all over the body and tight in the abdominal muscles. The tail is often clamped tightly. You will frequently see this pattern this in young horses who have been started too quickly or have pain somewhere on the body, especially from poor saddle fit, dental issues or chiropractic problems (see chapter 2, *A Closer Look at the Roots of Unwanted Behavior and Poor Attitude*, p. 9).

Such horses are often restrained with leverage bits, mechanical hackamores or various types of martingales. Or, they are longed or run in a round pen until they tire out. However, such approaches often lead to an opposite and equal reaction—the horse becomes even more explosive, pent-up and frustrated. The horse might go into "freeze" mode and slow down or stop, but the tension remains.

It may take some time to retrain such a horse to release the fear and tension and replace it with self-confidence. These exercises recap the same steps we use to start the young horse. Virtually any TTouch or exercise in this book will be useful. If you take your horse through this program, he will begin to slow down and think rather than simply react. You'll also find that you will develop a relationship with your horse that's based on mutual trust and cooperation rather than coercion and domination.

Training Solutions

TTouches

•   Do *Lowering the Head* and TTouches for Trust, especially *Abalone TTouches* with *Coiled Python Lifts* over every inch of your horse, particularly the rib, barrel and girth area, so your horse will accept leg aids when you get back in the saddle. *Ear TTouches* and *Mouth TTouches* encourage emotional release. *Leg Circles* and *Octopus TTouches* help ground your horse. *Tarantulas Pulling the Plow* releases tension through the body. *Tail TTouches, Belly Lifts* and very soft *Lick of the Cow's Tongue* help release tight abdominal muscles.

Ground Exercises

•   Take your horse through the *Labyrinth*. More than any other Ground Exercise, working slowly through a maze of ground poles shifts a horse's attention, focus and attitude from "off in the clouds" directly to you. Research in the *Labyrinth* has shown that a horse's brain waves actually slow down to patterns associated with thinking rather than flight. After a few sessions, try *Dancing Cobra* and *Freework* in and out of the *Labyrinth* to further hone your horse's balance, concentration and self-control.

•   Continue in the exercises in the Playground for Higher Learning (see p. 250). *Neckline and Ground Driving* with the *Body Wrap* through obstacles (*Labyrinth, The Fan, Pick-Up Sticks*) can help bring a horse off the forehand. Teach him to move forward to a touch on the croup (*Dingo*) and stop with a signal to the chest (*Cueing the Camel*). *Work with Plastic Sheets* and over the *Platform* will replace fear of the unfamiliar with self-confidence. Once your horse accepts all of this work, add the saddle—

taking care to girth up slowly and mindfully—and repeat each exercise from the ground over a couple of sessions.

Ridden Work

•   As you mount quietly from a mounting block, invite your horse to reach back and take a small piece of carrot or other treat from your hand. You or a helper can stroke the horse slowly with the wand on the neck, shoulders, sides and croup. Have your helper lead your horse while you hold the reins lightly and sit quietly. Ask your friend to signal the halt and walk with *Dingo* and *Cueing the Camel*.

•   Ride in the *Tellington Training Bit* or a short-shanked, mullen-mouthed Pelham. Use a *Balance Rein* or *Liberty Neck Ring* and give a low, guttural "*whoaaaaaaa*" to teach your horse to stop and stand quietly from a light signal from the saddle. Reward your horse each time with a treat from a small waistpack, so that your horse turns his head back and really has his attention on you. Stay light in the saddle. It's a good idea not to sit down too hard in the saddle, as some horses will tense the back and get scared when they step forward. Now you can ride around and through the same Playground for Higher Learning obstacles you did on the ground and under tack. Spread the *Labyrinth* out twice as wide at first to make the turns easy to navigate.

_____

Tellington Tip

Pay special attention to the fit of your saddle and pad. Consider extra padding so your horse's back is well protected. When a horse is nervous, tense back muscles will create discomfort and actually scare the horse and propel him forward. Make sure your saddle isn't too long for the back and hitting your horse in the loins. For Western riders, make sure the skirt doesn't bump into the loins as your horse moves forward.

_____

- If your horse is ultrasensitive to the leg, quietly let your horse feel your leg one side at a time. Do a very light, feathery press-and-release with the inside of the lower leg with just a light touch-and-release with the inside of the heel *so your horse does not move forward until you ask.* Observe the level of pressure that your horse is responding to—it's better to ask twice than have your horse instantly take off. After a few sessions he should be responding to an acknowledged pressure signal from the leg instead of just rushing forward to *any* signal.

- Practice a variety of tempos at the walk, from the saddle and on the ground. Your horse will benefit from learning to transition from *Half-Walk* (see p. 280) to ordinary walk to extended walk on a loose rein.

Scenario: Your horse travels too fast at the canter

Use the *Tellington Training Bit* and *Promise Wrap.* If your horse is also strung-out, first do *Lick of the Cow's Tongue* and *Zig-Zag TTouches* over the croup and *Hind Leg Circles* to differentiate movement of the hind legs. *Tail TTouches* are the finishing TTouches to connect the horse through the whole body. Then ride with an elastic *Promise Wrap* to instantly encourage your horse to step under and bring the back up.

Benchmark of Success

Your horse becomes soft in the eye; the nostrils flare slightly; the head and neck become lower as he waits for your signal to go forward.

Solutions at a Glance: *Gaits, too fast*

Body Exploration 151 ~ Labyrinth 259 ~ Dancing Cobra 234 ~ Freework 257 ~ Neckline and Ground Driving 261 ~ Body Wrap 160 ~ The Fan, Cavalletti and Pick-Up Sticks 253 ~ Dingo and Cueing the Camel 235 ~ Work with Plastic Sheets 265 ~ Platform 269 ~ Lowering the Head 163 ~ Abalone TTouch 171 ~ Coiled Python Lift 172 ~ Ear TTouches 210 ~ Mouth TTouch 182 ~ Front Leg Circles 174 ~ Hind Leg Circles 175 ~ Octopus TTouch 200 ~ Tarantulas Pulling the Plow 203 ~ Tail TTouch 185 ~ Belly Lift 209 ~ Lick of the Cow's Tongue 177 Tellington Training Bit 290 ~ Balance Rein 279 ~ Liberty Neck Ring 282 ~ Half-Walk 280 Zig-Zag TTouch 206 ~ Promise Wrap 288

Grooming Sensitivity

see also *Biting, Hard to Catch*

Does your horse stand quietly, without being tied—whether in the stall, stable aisle, or in the middle of the arena—while you groom him? Or, does he toss his head, kick, snap at you or the air, switch his tail or dance around when you bring out the brushes?

Many handlers "brush off" such behavior by thinking, "Oh, that's just the way he is," or "He's such a grump when we groom him!" But, before you reach for that currycomb, stop to think about how resistance to grooming might affect your horse's work under saddle. Such a horse will be tense and stiff before you ever put the saddle on, and you are activating stress hormones. He'll be more resistant to everything you are going to ask.

Many horses are groomed too hastily, too roughly or with too stiff brushes. Thoroughbreds, in particular are often thin-skinned and extremely sensitive and ticklish to grooming. Lack of awareness during grooming can create a reactive, fearful and resentful animal. Some horses carry pain in the body, or anticipation of pain, from old traumas. Their discomfort and resistance can be intensified when they are groomed in cross-ties or tied in a way that holds the head unnaturally high, causing the back to drop and the body to tense.

A horse who enjoys grooming will have a more cheerful attitude under saddle. With TTouch, you'll reduce tension and stress and induce relaxation and cooperation. Best of all, you'll enhance your horse's ultimate response to *whatever* you ask him to do, whether from the ground or under saddle. TTouches also develop that kinesthetic feeling that gives him a sense of trust in his whole body—and the ability to *feel* the body. This is one of the keys to safety in all situations, whether you are riding, leading or driving a horse.

Training Solutions

Put away your stiff brushes and currycombs, and take your horse out of the cross-ties! You'll need a sheepskin mitt or wool sock instead. First, go over your whole horse with your flat hand and see where he is ticklish, reactive or pulls away. Then, mindfully return to those areas with your mitt or even a warm hand. Breathe and go slowly to release the fear of contact in your horse's body.

Keep both hands on your horse, and support his sensitive areas with *Abalone TTouches* or *Coiled Python Lifts*. If your horse is especially sensitive, you may find it useful to put him in the *Body Wrap* in the stall. Ask him to stand, and if he moves around, put him into *Taming the Tiger*.

Stay away from stiff, synthetic bristles, and replace them with soft horsehair brushes. For knocking off dried sweat and dirt, use a wet "scrubby" cloth instead of a stiff brush. Trade your metal currycomb for a soft rubber Grooma brush or nubby Epona Jelly scrubber (see *Resources*, p. 311). Experiment to find what your horse likes best.

As you groom your horse before riding or Ground Exercises, you are setting the mood for that day's session. Grooming is an opportunity to develop a positive relationship with your horse and an important part of "re-creation." If you groom your horse in a way that is pleasurable, both of you reap the benefits.

Turnaround Tale

A 12-year-old dressage mare came to my three-week research training in Germany in 1978. This mare was stiff under saddle (she'd been diagnosed with arthritis) and hated to be groomed. If she came within six feet of the grooming bucket, she'd respond by snapping her teeth and pinning her ears. What we discovered was that she was groomed two hours a day with an iron hand, following the groom's instructions for circulation, but not paying attention to what the horse was feeling. With TTouch, including gentle circles with a sheepskin mitt, not only did the mare learn to accept a soft brush but she became much more supple.

Solutions at a Glance: *Grooming Sensitivity*

Coiled Python Lift 172 ~ Abalone TTouch 171 ~ Connected Circles 173 ~ Body Wrap 160 Taming the Tiger 166

Hard to Catch

see also *Grooming Sensitivity*

For many horses, playing hard to catch is a game—and a very frustrating one indeed. Many horse people consider this the result of a "dominant" attitude; however, I believe it is because these horses have never really learned to trust people, or can be sour or overtrained. Their message is clear: "I don't want to be with you."

A common solution is to run the horse around a small area until he's tired out, and the "reward" is rest when he comes to you. I taught this method for years, and it works—*if the horse knows you're serious, and you don't give up.* However, most horses will test each new person who comes to catch him, and every day you have to go through the same process. Another method is to "walk the horse down," which means walking after the horse persistently until he gives up, but that could take hours and may not result in the horse coming willingly to you in the future.

Sensitivity to grooming, tail switching, restlessness or fear of touch are common behaviors in hard-to-catch horses. The sensitivity or ticklishness may be on the belly, lower legs, inside the thighs or on the tail. Check your horse for a sore back, tight neck and back muscles, dental problems or other clues to why that horse may not want to be handled.

Training Solutions

The solution to these capers is to develop trust and bring your horse to the point where he is totally accepting and enjoys being TTouched over every part of his body. Begin by *Lowering the Head* and using *Mouth TTouches, Ear TTouches, Troika TTouch* and *Connected Circles* over the body and down all four legs. *Tarantulas Pulling the Plow* from head to tail and *Tail TTouches* will intrigue your horse. Try *Freework* and *The Statue* to engage your horse's interest in a new way.

Turnaround Tale

At a Tellington Training clinic in Farmington, New Mexico, in 1983, a very experienced cowboy came to my demonstration. The day after the clinic, he called the ranch where I was staying and told my host—who happened to be a friend of his—that he had been very skeptical about going to a clinic taught by a woman with "a new method," but had been surprised and impressed by what I had to say about horses who were hard to catch. It turned out that he had a 16-year-old buckskin gelding who was one of his best cow horses but from the first time he was ridden he had to be roped to be caught.

So after the clinic, he went home and decided to try out some of the work. He roped the gelding as usual, and set to work with Ear TTouches. The buckskin stood quietly with his head lowered, seeming to enjoy the work. He didn't do much more than five minutes of Ear TTouches but he could hardly believe what happened next. When he quit working the ears and went to leave the corral, the horse came behind him to the gate and he had to close the gate to keep him from following. He was so amazed by the change in the horse that he called the ranch to tell his friend.

Solutions at a Glance: *Hard to Catch*

Lowering the Head 163 ~ Mouth TTouch 182 ~ Ear TTouches 210 ~ Connected Circles 173 Tarantulas Pulling the Plow 203 ~ Tail TTouch 185 ~ Freework 257 ~ The Statue 248 ~ Troika TTouch 188

Head-Tossing/Flinging

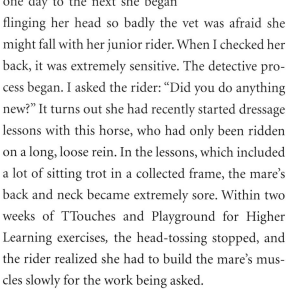

Horses who habitually toss their heads are no fun to ride and can be dangerous, as they tend to lose track of where their feet are when they are in this mode and can lose their balance, or smack you in the chin with their head. I've actually seen a horse fall down from violent head-tossing.

However, I've had a number of desert-bred Arabian mares who flung their heads out of sheer joy or exuberance, most often at liberty but occasionally under saddle. This tendency was made famous by Arabian historian Carl Raswan, who coined the term "Drinker of the Wind" as the title of one of his many books about his travels to the Arabian peninsula. I had dinner with him in the early 1960s, when he regaled us with stories of his adventures in the desert and noted that head-tossing is characteristic of certain lines of desert-bred Arabs. Although I don't consider such behavior to be a fault, it carries with it the possibility of flipping a rein over the head, so you want to take steps to prevent it.

Training Solutions

If your horse tosses or flings his head when you ride, consider the following:

• **Check the neck and withers for soreness.** Begin with *Body Exploration*: check the neck and withers with *Bear TTouch,* followed by *Clouded Leopard* circles with a moderate (number 5) pressure on both sides (see p. 148). I remember a show hunter whose muscles began to spasm when I held two spots with my fingers opposing each other, for about five seconds, every quarter inch along the withers. Within a few minutes, the spasms stopped. Then I did *Back Lifts* and changed the saddle pad, and he stopped the head-tossing. We were able to release long-held soreness in the withers in 15 minutes of TTouch.

• **Check the back and saddle fit.** One of the mares sent to me by a vet in Germany during a research project in 1978 was thought to have a neurological problem. The horse had been a fine pleasure horse, but from one day to the next she began flinging her head so badly the vet was afraid she might fall with her junior rider. When I checked her back, it was extremely sensitive. The detective process began. I asked the rider: "Did you do anything new?" It turns out she had recently started dressage lessons with this horse, who had only been ridden on a long, loose rein. In the lessons, which included a lot of sitting trot in a collected frame, the mare's back and neck became extremely sore. Within two weeks of TTouches and Playground for Higher Learning exercises, the head-tossing stopped, and the rider realized she had to build the mare's muscles slowly for the work being asked.

• **Check the teeth!** A four-year-old gray Arab gelding in England threw his head constantly despite three months of training. The horse was brought to a clinic, and the first thing we did was check his teeth. Sure enough, an impacted wolf tooth was hitting the bit. When we put on the *Lindell Sidepull,* he stopped throwing his head. And, of course, they fixed his teeth—the simplest solution.

TTouches

• Do *Abalone TTouches* with *Coiled Python Lifts* on the back and neck. If your horse is sensitive to touch, begin on the neck and back with *Lying Leopard TTouches.* Once your horse relaxes to contact, do some gentle (number 2 or 3 pressures) connected *Bear TTouches* with *Sponge TTouches* on the neck. Follow with *Lick of the Cow's Tongue* from belly to back over the entire barrel of your horse. *Ear* and *Tail TTouches* can help relax back and neck muscles.

- Horses who habitually toss their heads not only have tight back muscles but also tight abdominal muscles. Release tight belly muscles with *Back Lifts* and *Belly Lifts.*

- If your horse is sensitive and reacts by throwing the head, switching the tail, pinning the ears or kicking, use *Abalone TTouches* along the midline of the belly to prepare your horse to bring the back up with pressure from your fingertips without reacting.

- Introduce the *Balance Rein* to free up the neck and encourage your horse to raise the back. An elastic *Promise Wrap* can help to give your horse a sense of connection through the body and also bring the back up to relieve tight back muscles. Using the *Tellington Training Bit,* or a short-shanked, mullen-mouth Pelham may also be helpful in preventing head-tossing. Many horses stop tossing their heads and fretting when the rider switches from a bit to a *Lindell Sidepull.*

Solutions at a Glance: *Head-Tossing/Flinging*

Body Exploration 151 ~ Bear TTouch 217 ~ Clouded Leopard TTouch 195 ~ Abalone TTouch 171 ~ Coiled Python Lift 172 ~ Lying Leopard TTouch 181~ Sponge TTouch 203 ~ Lick of the Cow's Tongue 177 ~ Ear TTouches 210 ~ Tail TTouch 185 ~ Back Lift 193 ~ Belly Lift 209 Balance Rein 279 ~ Promise Wrap 288 ~ Tellington Training Bit 290 ~ Lindell Sidepull 286

Heavy on the Forehand

Often described as the horse lying "heavy in the hand," this tendency can be a result of conformation (the horse is built downhill, with his withers lower than his croup). In most cases, however, the horse has not learned to carry himself in balance (known as self-carriage).

The rider is often advised to use a crop and "more leg" to drive the horse forward into the bit. While this can be effective, the result is that the horse doesn't learn self-carriage. He must constantly be "propped up" by the aids or fall back into his heavy way of going. Of course, some horses, by virtue of their conformation, are always going to have a difficult time being light, but fortunately, there is much you can do to improve any horse.

For your horse to lighten in the forehand, he must be able to lift his head and neck from the withers

and base of the neck and engage his hindquarters by stepping under himself further. It's remarkably easy to teach your horse how to shift his center of gravity back so he is working off his hindquarters in a way that you will no longer have to physically drive the horse into position and support him there.

Training Solutions

- To shift the center of balance toward the back, try the *Promise Wrap* and *Balance Rein* together. This combination often helps the horse lift the back and engage the hindquarters—lightening the forehand—without you having to work so hard.

• Alternate using your regular bit with a *Tellington Training Bit*. Its copper roller encourages flexion through the jaw, poll and neck, and the soft curve of the shanks encourages the horse to carry himself in balance on light contact. The horse will become more elastic through the body, with increased elevation, shortened frame and swinging back.

The combination of these tools brings the back up and activates the pelvis so the horse can flex at the poll without having to be "driven" into the hand on the bit. This technique works on both Western horses ridden on a loose rein as well as English horses ridden on contact.

You will generally see change in a single session. However, you must practice over a period of time because the horse needs to habituate himself to this new way of going. What we suggest is that you switch back and forth between bits. If you ride with a Western curb, take the top rein off the *Tellington Training Bit* for a few minutes near the end of your training session. With an English horse, snap off the bottom rein so that you are effectively riding in a snaffle. Eventually you can transition to your bit of choice, using the bit for training touch-ups as needed.

To further lighten the forehand, try these TTouches and Ground Exercises:

• While grooming and tacking up your horse, do some *Back Lifts*, to contract the abdominal muscles and raise the back.

• *Lick of the Cow's Tongue* will bring awareness through the barrel area, from belly to back, connecting the forehand to the back.

• *Dancing Cobra* and *Half-Walk* will lift the head, shorten the frame slightly and shift the center of gravity back.

• Put your horse into a *Liberty Neck Ring* and ask him to turn with the ring high up on the neck. This will enable him to be much more flexible through the body and carry himself in a more balanced way.

Solutions at a Glance: *Heavy on the Forehand*

Promise Wrap 288 ~ Balance Rein 279 ~ Tellington Training Bit 290 ~ Back Lift 193 ~ Lick of the Cow's Tongue 177 ~ Dancing Cobra 234 ~ Half-Walk 280 ~ Liberty Neck Ring 282

Herdbound (reluctant to leave companion)

Common Scenarios

❶ You're out on the trail with a group of friends, and you've decided to head back to the barn. You turn your horse to go down the fork in the trail. But your horse won't budge. It's as if he is rooted to the ground.

❷ You're on an endurance ride with your young horse. It's her first ride, and you're trotting along on your own, nice and steady. Suddenly, a group comes up on your heels and races by, and you have a fight on your hands.

❸ Your two horses, who live, eat, hang out and train together, travel to a competition in the same trailer. All is calm and stress-free until it's time for one horse to go into his class, leaving the other behind. Your normally quiet, impeccably mannered horse starts screaming at the top of his lungs as though he was just weaned.

These scenes all represent types of separation anxiety and are generally regarded as difficult behaviors to overcome. In each instance, the attached horse is really being fearful and insecure as he seeks the safety of a buddy.

While all these strategies may be useful, at Tellington Training we've found through the years that there is no single "magic bullet" to cure this behavior. The surest way to overcome separation anxiety is through a combination of TTouches for Trust (p. 168), TTouches for Awareness (p. 190) and work in the Playground for Higher Learning (p. 250). By taking the time to work with many of these exercises, you'll develop your horse's self-confidence and override his herd instinct. As a result, your horse will learn to trust and connect to *you* instead of relying upon another horse for security.

Herdbound behavior is very stressful—for both horses and humans. Investing the time to overcome it will result in a happier, safer horse.

Training Solutions

TTouches

- *Lowering the Head* by teaching your horse to respond to a signal downward on the halter and press-and-release circles from your other hand on the crest behind the ears. Doing this for 10 minutes a day will start to shift your horse's behavior.

- Add *Connected Circles* over every inch of the horse.

- *Ear TTouches* and *Troika TTouch* will gain trust and relax your horse.

- *Mouth TTouches* and *Tail TTouches* address emotional insecurities.

- Connect with your horse so that he enjoys *your* company with *Tarantulas Pulling the Plow, Lick of the Cow's Tongue* and *Octopus TTouches.*

Ground Exercises

- *Labyrinth* will teach focus and emotional balance. *Work with Plastic Sheets* will deal with all kinds of fears—herdbound is the fear of being alone. These and other Playground for Higher Learning exercises will instill self-confidence, activate your horse's mind and take him beyond herd instinct. For additional exercises, see *Bucking* on p. 46.

Tellington Tip

Give your horse a reason to want to be with you. Make being in your company more interesting than being with the other horse. Start carrying a small pouch or waistpack with thinly sliced carrots or small crunchies. Reward small steps of attentiveness with a snack from your pack, both when on the ground and while mounted. You may find that giving you and your horse a few drops of a combination Bach Flower remedy called "Rescue Remedy" (see Resources, p. 311) might help to reduce anxiety in both of you.

Ridden Work

- Try the *Tellington Training Bit* and *Balance Rein*—this combo has helped many horses get over being herdbound.

- Practice *Lowering the Head* from the saddle when your horse is calm until the response becomes automatic. Then, when your horse begins to get riled up on the trail, you have a means of lowering his head and controlling the situation.

- Reach around from the saddle and do a few *Clouded Leopard TTouches* over the croup and base of the tail.

- Ride with a *Liberty Neck Ring* to keep your horse's interest and develop balance. Working with a friend, ride together and apart while working through these "play stations" so the horses begin to get focused on what they are doing and not only their friend. When your horse's buddy rides to the other end of the arena, give your horse a treat from your hand.

You can ride your horses through the *Labyrinth*, over the *Platform* and *Teeter-Totter*, or around the *Barrels* to make ring work fun and even more interesting for the horse.

• Make up your own lesson! Weave in and out of the various obstacles, playing follow the leader, changing places, varying the distances between your horses, trotting on by, weaving your way through the cones and tires. Grab a friend and "leapfrog" each other, adding more distance with each exchange. Your horse will learn to listen to you rather than worrying about his buddy.

After you practice in the arena, head for the trail (see *Overcompetitive*, p. 90). As the buddy disappears around the bend, have your horse turn around and take a crunchie from your hand. "Chunking" the separation from a few seconds to longer periods is essential to successfully retraining the herdbound horse.

***

Tellington Tip

If you have two horses and your second horse becomes hysterical when left home alone, consider a third companion, such as a retired pony, a donkey or goat.

***

Solutions at a Glance: *Herdbound*

Lowering the Head 163 ~ Connected Circles 173 ~ Ear TTouches 210 ~ Mouth TTouch 182 Tail TTouch 185 ~ Tarantulas Pulling the Plow 203 ~ Lick of the Cow's Tongue 177 ~ Octopus TTouch 200 ~ Labyrinth 259 ~ Work with Plastic Sheets 265 ~ Tellington Training Bit 290 Balance Rein 279 ~ Clouded Leopard TTouch 195 ~ Liberty Neck Ring 282 ~ Platform 269 Teeter-Totter 273 ~ Troika TTouch 188 ~ Barrels 253

High-Headed (above the bit)

see also *Back Problems, Ewe-Neck, Shying ("spooky")*

"High-headed equals high-strung and often triggers the flight reflex," to quote my sister and fellow practitioner, Robyn Hood. These horses are often spooky, tight and sore in the neck and back. Their tails are often clamped down. They may paw when tied and are easily stressed, often blowing up when asked to go out of their comfort zone. In short, they are a challenge.

Before you take the advice of your riding buddies or Internet message boards to "unload that horse before he hurts you," try the Tellington approach. This is not an overnight fix. But, I'll give you some of the most important steps to get you started.

Note: Before proceeding, make sure your saddle is not pinching the withers or shoulders, is well-padded, and is not only comfortable over the withers area but does not interfere with the movement of the hindquarters. Be aware that a girth or noseband that is too tight can also prevent a horse from lowering the head. If you want to be successful, consider these tack issues and their effect on your horse's comfort and ability to move.

Training Solutions

TTouches

• Begin by doing a few sessions of *Back Lifts, Lick of the Cow's Tongue, Front Leg Circles* with *Toe Rests* and *Shoulder Releases* to release habitually tight and tense muscles through the shoulders and back. Without these exercises, it may be impossible for your horse to lower the head.

• *Tail TTouches* are an essential step to retraining the high-headed horse, who is invariably afraid of movement behind him. All will contribute to a new feeling of confidence, and the *Tail Pull* in particular will intensify the connection from poll to tail.

Ground Exercises

• Teach *Lowering the Head* from a signal on the chain attached up the side of the halter rather than over the nose, then teach your horse to lower the head from circles just behind the poll. Once he begins giving his head from the ground, you'll be able to reach forward and ask him to lower the head from the saddle anytime he begins to fall into old patterns. To get a head start on *Lowering the Head*, take your horse through the *Labyrinth* in the *Half-Walk*, pausing before each turn.

• Reinforce the head-lowering gesture at the walk and trot in-hand with the poll slightly lower than the withers. You can progress to trotting over poles in-hand whenever you're ready.

• *Neckline and Ground Driving* is an excellent reinforcement of head lowering and gives the horse a chance to feel the new posture without the weight of the rider on the back.

Ridden Work

• Now you're ready to ride! You'll find that the *Balance Rein* triggers the neck-telescoping reflex to lengthen the neck and lower the head.

• Adding the *Promise Wrap* will help bring the back up, and give the horse confidence from creating a boundary behind him. The *Tellington Training Bit* relaxes the tongue, jaw and poll, allowing the rider to give the horse a freer rein so that he can lower and steady his head. This bit replaces the need for martingales, tie-downs, and other artificial aids.

Tellington Tip

Although it may send shivers up your spine to consider taking the bridle off, I've rarely seen a horse who didn't lower the head and lengthen the neck within minutes. To start, tie a knot in the reins, lay them on the neck, and use the Liberty Neck Ring to practice turns and halts. Pick up the reins if you need to reinforce a turn or halt. If you decide to go on to riding without a bridle, see Bridleless Riding (p. 282).

Solutions at a Glance: *High-Headed*

Back Lift 193 ~ Lick of the Cow's Tongue 177 ~ Front Leg Circles 174 ~ Shoulder Release 225 Tail TTouch 185 ~ Lowering the Head 163 ~ Labyrinth 259 ~ Half-Walk 280 ~ Neckline and Ground Driving 261 ~ Balance Rein 279 ~ Promise Wrap 288 ~ Tellington Training Bit 290 Liberty Neck Ring and Bridleless Riding 282

Injury, difficulty treating

Your horse has an injury somewhere on his legs, body or head. It's either bleeding, contaminated or infected—it may even have a foreign object embedded in it. You can't find out the extent of the injury, or help your horse, until you can get close enough to him to have a good look.

In most cases, an injured horse will be "twitched" or tranquilized in order to examine and treat the wound. However, perhaps no veterinarian is available, or your horse is bleeding and there is no time to wait.

Training Solutions

• Immediately, call your veterinarian. While you are waiting, to keep the horse from going into a state of frenzy or fight, your first goal is to calm him, and at the same time, reduce bleeding, prevent shock and give you a chance to examine the injury more closely. Even if the horse is bleeding, don't panic; bring the head down and work the ears to overcome the fear, lower the pulse and stanch the bleeding. Gaining the horse's trust and letting him know that you are going to help him can make all the difference.

• If the horse won't let you near the injured area or is beginning to become "shocky," first lower the head and do some quiet, slow *Ear TTouches* to make a connection with the horse, help ease pain,

lower the pulse and reduce the chance of shock. You might also do a few *Belly Lifts* while waiting for the vet. Give the horse—and yourself—a few drops of Rescue Remedy (see *Resources*, p. 311).

• Put the horse into *Taming the Tiger*. With a helper steadying the horse in this position, you can often move in to treat the injury. This can be done even if you are alone. If the horse won't let you touch the injured leg, stroke the wand on the opposite leg first.

Turnaround Tale

A horse I shipped cross-country came off a van three-legged lame. He'd sustained a puncture wound on the inside of the left hind coronary band from a caulk. I worked on the opposite hind leg with small, light circles and lifts, so that the horse's body gained trust in my hands. Then I quietly moved to the other side and started at the croup with slow circles and lifts, working my way down the back leg and finally right over the puncture wound. There I worked with light pressure, doing Raccoon TTouches with my hand cupped over the injured area, to take away the fear as much as the pain. In 45 minutes, when the vet arrived, the horse walked off, putting weight on the foot, barely lame and not in shock.

Solutions at a Glance: *Injury, difficulty treating*

Ear TTouches 210 ~ Belly Lift 209 ~ Taming the Tiger 166 ~ Raccoon TTouch 213

Jiggy/Joggy

see also *Ewe-Neck, Overcompetitive*

A jiggy horse behaves as if he has overdosed on caffeine! He simply won't relax and walk, but insists on doing a bouncy little jog-trot the whole time

you are riding him. Jigging occurs most frequently when riding in a group or when heading back to the barn. It's no fun riding a horse who travels with his chin to his chest or who flips his nose in the air.

Jigginess generally springs from tension and habitual bracing patterns in horse and rider. As a jiggy horse is held back, his neck muscles and circulation are inhibited. As a result, the horse can't think as clearly or easily respond to your requests. Many jiggers are restrained with long-shanked curb bits or hackamores, which only causes them to overbend and tighten even more through the poll, neck and back. A ewe-neck and dropped back are telltale signs of a chronic jigger.

Our Ground Exercises and TTouches will release the tension and shift the habitual patterns that often make this behavior a challenge to shift. Be sure to run a "reality check" for saddle fit, bit and teeth issues first!

Training Solutions

TTouches

• Release tension in the neck, back and hindquarters with *Ear TTouches, Neck Releases, Neck Rocking, Front* and *Hind Leg Circles, Abalone TTouches* with *Coiled Python Lifts* on the neck, back and legs, and *Inch Worm. Bear TTouch* with a *Sponge TTouch* release can help restore circulation in the neck.

• Because jiggy horses are almost always high-headed under saddle, *Lowering the Head* from the ground as well as from the saddle and *Back Lifts* can help release tight abdominal muscles.

Ground Exercises

• Chronic jiggers benefit from *Neckline and Ground Driving* with other horses present, to give them boundaries and overcome their fear of movement and other horses behind. This is an excellent way to show the horse how to extend the head, neck and stride.

• With a friend, lead your horse in *Journey of the Homing Pigeon* while wearing the *Body Wrap* with other horses working around him.

• As a prelude to riding, teach the *Half-Walk* from the ground (later, mounted) to encourage your horse to shorten his steps with a new awareness that allows for release of tight muscles and lengthening of stride.

Ridden Work

• Ride for a few sessions in the *Lindell Sidepull* with a *Balance Rein*. Practice in an arena or in a place close to home before venturing out on the trails with your friends, and review the information on *Herdbound* (p. 72). Consider riding in the full *Body Wrap*.

• *Tail TTouches* can give the horse a sense of confidence through his body and riding with the *Promise Wrap* will help overcome any fears that the horse may have from behind.

• A few exercises in the arena can work wonders. Invite your friends over, and take turns passing each other, leading and going behind.

Solutions at a Glance: *Jiggy/Joggy*

Ear TTouches 210 ~ Neck Release 221 ~ Neck Rocking 199 ~ Front Leg Circles 174 ~ Hind Leg Circles 174 ~ Abalone TTouch 171 ~ Coiled Python Lift 172 ~ Inch Worm 197 ~ Bear TTouch 217 ~ Sponge TTouch 203 ~ Lowering the Head 163 ~ Back Lift 193 ~ Neckline and Ground Driving 261 ~ Half-Walk 280 ~ Lindell Sidepull 286 ~ Balance Rein 279 ~ Body Wrap 160 ~ Tail TTouch 185 ~ Promise Wrap 288 ~ Journey of the Homing Pigeon 241

Kicking

see also *Fear of Movement or Objects Behind*

Horses who kick at other horses while being ridden, ponied or turned out can cause serious injury to another horse, a rider or handler. Most often, this behavior stems from basic fear and sometimes claustrophobia. It is usually defensive, and is typical of horses who haven't been exposed to other horses or who have had bad experiences in the pasture.

Horses who kick or threaten to kick other horses are often whacked with a crop to let them know that this behavior is unacceptable. While this may work with some, if your horse is actually fearful of other horses, it may only worsen the behavior, adding to anxiety when other horses come up behind and reinforcing the attitude that other horses are dangerous.

It's up to you to make sure your horse is well mannered and under control in all situations. In addition, the responsible trail rider needs to prepare her horse for a situation when another horse might surprise her mount from behind. The key is to re-educate such horses at home and on the trail, in a controlled situation. Until you feel completely confident that your horse won't kick, remember to warn others to keep their distance by tying a red ribbon onto your horse's tail.

Training Solutions

TTouches

•   In preparation for getting your horse to feel safe around strange horses, make sure you can TTouch the horse over every inch of the body—and particularly the hindquarters—without him being nervous about contact. Begin with *Body Exploration* to identify sensitive or tense areas.

•   *Tail TTouches* bring awareness to the hindquarters, so that any kind of contact of closeness is not seen as a threat by the horse. This is especially important in young or maiden fillies, who are often nervous about protecting their rear quarters.

Ground Exercises

•   *Neckline and Ground Driving* in a *Body Wrap* is one of the best ways to help a horse overcome fear of movement or contact behind, which can trigger the kicking reflex. Doing this ground exercise around other horses gives the horse a sense of being connected when another is brought up behind or past him.

•   Set up four ground poles at a comfortable distance to walk across. Keeping your horse in the *Body Wrap*, start by leading (or continue to ground drive) your horse over the poles in one direction. At the same time, your friend's horse (ideally, a well-mannered, seasoned, quiet horse) goes by outside the poles in the opposite direction.

When he can be led past the other horse without tensing the neck, pinning the ears or making any other gesture indicative of fear or aggression, move on to the next step: Lead your horse through the poles while the other passes at closer range, first on one side, then the other. Then take the two in the same direction, with your horse behind the other horse to start, keeping a safe distance out of kicking range. The idea is to progressively move the horses closer together while staying within your horse's comfort zone.

If your horse is still nervous or tries to kick, put more distance between you and the other horse, and find the range where you can reward the horse rather than pushing him to the point that you have to punish him for negative behavior.

Know how to anticipate the warning signs that a kick may be coming: the neck tenses, the head comes up, the ears flatten back against the neck. When you are riding with another horse, keep the wand moving back and forth between you to create a border. Stroking your horse with the wand gives a reassuring signal that you are going to keep your horse safe from another horse. Visualization is important throughout any of these exercises: keep a clear picture that you know you'll make it safe for your horse instead of fearing what could happen.

Ridden Work

• Once your horse accepts the presence of another during in-hand work, it's time to graduate to under-saddle work. Again, you'll need your friend and a quiet horse. (This technique will also work if you are ponying your horse.) As you're riding along, stroke your horse's hindquarters with the wand, reach back to do *Clouded Leopard TTouches* on the hindquarters, then allow your horse to turn his head to take a goodie from your hand when another horse comes up from behind. Ride with a *Promise Wrap* so that the horse really feels the hindquarters, and ask your helper to move closer and closer, being careful not to come too close too fast. "Chunk" it down over one or several sessions, in the arena and on the trail, until your horse is truly confident.

• If you should find yourself out on a narrow trail faced with this situation without adequate preparation, take one rein and pull it in, turning the horse a little to shift his balance, allowing the horse to see behind him and preventing him from gathering himself to kick out. In addition, riding in a *Tellington Training Bit* will give you much more influence over your horse's response.

An exception to this advice is a horse, usually a gelding or stallion, who is *not* reacting out of fear but is competitively blocking another horse from passing. This is where you need to take the upper hand, and there certainly may be a time that a swift reminder with your crop to this dominant type of horse will be effective and necessary. As before, prepare with a friend at home. Start slowly, with the other horse passing at a distance that your horse politely allows. Show your horse the behavior you desire instead of having to correct him in a competitive situation. Ask your horse to move to the right and then to the left, using the *Balance Rein* or a *Liberty Neck Ring* as an indirect rein. As your horse becomes more accepting, have the other horse pass at progressively closer distances and faster speeds.

Turnaround Tale

Years ago, I had a three-year-old mare in a week-long training who would run back 15 feet to kick out at another horse behind her. With the mare in Journey of the Homing Pigeon and a third helper Neckline and Ground Driving and rewarding her for standing still and turning back to take grain from a flat pan while the other horses moved around her, she overrode her fear and shifted her behavior. We showed her what we wanted her to do instead of simply trying to punish her for undesirable behavior. Working in an arena full of horses was also a key to of her success.

By having the horse turn and take grain while keeping her still with the lines, she had a positive experience of other horses being close. In less than a week, she was completely over her fear and habit of kicking on the ground and under saddle. Similarly, you can reward positive behavior of standing quietly as opposed to deepening the fear and tension by punishing undesirable behavior.

Solutions at a Glance: *Kicking*

Body Exploration 151 ~ Tail TTouch 185 ~ Neckline and Ground Driving 261 ~ Body Wrap 160 ~ Clouded Leopard TTouch 195 ~ Promise Wrap 288 ~ Tellington Training Bit 290 Balance Rein 279 ~ Liberty Neck Ring 282

Lazy

see also *Stubborn*

Oftentimes, horse people think that "lazy" is an attitude. But before you brand your horse a sluggard, check out the following scenarios:

• **Is the horse taking in enough fuel?** Some horses simply aren't ingesting enough energy, fats, protein or minerals for the work they are doing. Or perhaps they have a low red cell count or other blood value. First, make sure your horse is getting the right type of fuel and sufficient energy for his stage of life and performance style.

• **Does your horse have a physical problem?** A metabolic problem such as hypothyroidism will cause a horse to be extremely lethargic. Such horses display cresty necks and other fat deposits on their bodies, even when fed small amounts of food. If your horse suddenly becomes lazy, you may also want to rule out Wobbler's syndrome and Cushing's disease, two disorders that can also make horses quite sluggish.

• **Is your horse sufficiently challenged?** Horses who are only ridden in an arena and never asked to do anything interesting beyond going round and round are often bored and unresponsive to the aids. (School horses are a classic example.) If this is the case, broaden your equine horizons—mix up your ring work with some trail riding, engage your horse's mind with some Ground Exercises, or try *Bridleless Riding* with the *Liberty Neck Ring.*

• **Is your horse ridden in a way that slows him down?** For example, say you are riding dressage, and holding the horse back on the front end while simultaneously pushing with your seat and legs. It's like applying the brakes and gas pedal at the same time. Some horses ridden this way eventually just give up on going forward with any energy. This behavior is very common in young horses who are asked for collection too often or too soon. Such horses are often uncoordinated and stumbly, or suffer from a lack of clear signals from the rider.

• **Has your horse learned *how* to move forward?** Perhaps he seems lazy because he is a young, immature horse who hasn't developed sufficient strength in the hindquarters to carry himself (self-carriage). Such a horse may also lack the neural connections to carry the signals from your leg and seat to his brain. It's as if the horse isn't yet "connected" through the body. Such a horse may appear "dull-sided," as if there is not enough feeling in his body.

Try this little test from the ground to see if your horse has learned to go forward from a signal: tap him on the croup with the wand in *Dingo* while holding the halter. If the horse just stands there, he has never really learned to go forward.

Training Solutions

Like putting together the pieces of a puzzle, you may choose Ground Work with TTouches on the body or ride with training tools that will awaken and energize your horse.

• Since all movement originates in the hindquarters, ride with a *Promise Rope* to help the horse engage the hindquarters and tap the forequarters and hindquarters in rhythm with each stride with your wand to lengthen stride. Like the movement of a metronome, the *Tellington Training Bit* often improves balance, suppleness and willingness to move forward.

• Here are some TTouches to energize and increase body awareness. *Flick of the Bear's Paw, Tarantulas Pulling the Plow, Lick of the Cow's Tongue, Zig-Zag TTouches, Connected Circles,* and *Tail TTouches.*

• Teach your horse from the ground to go forward in *Dingo*, first at a slow and fast walk, then at a slow and fast trot.

• Ride with or without a bridle through Playground for Higher Learning obstacles such as *The Fan, Pick-Up Sticks* and *Labyrinth*, which will challenge and engage his mind.

• *Bridleless Riding* with the *Liberty Neck Ring* gives a horse a new sense of freedom and joy, especially if he has become bored or sour in one or more areas of the body, giving a dull horse a new lease on life.

Solutions at a Glance: *Lazy*

Promise Rope 288 ~ Tellington Training Bit 290 ~ Flick of the Bear's Paw 219 ~ Tarantulas Pulling the Plow 203 ~ Lick of the Cow's Tongue 177 ~ Zig-Zag TTouch 206 ~ Connected Circles 173 ~ Tail TTouch 185 ~ Dingo 235 ~ The Fan, Cavalletti and Pick-Up Sticks 253 ~ Labyrinth 259 Liberty Neck Ring and Bridleless Riding 282

Leads, favors one

see also *Balance or Coordination Issues*

You cue your horse for a canter, but he consistently picks up the "wrong" lead. You notice that he tends to pick up either the right or the left lead, no matter how many times you bring him back down to a trot and try again.

Riders often assume that the horse is being resistant and simply apply the aids with more insistence, sitting deeper into the saddle and driving harder with the seat and legs. Unfortunately, if the horse's back is already sensitive, this approach will not be effective.

Many trainers will ask you to trot over a pole and pick up a canter on the other side, which is often helpful, but if there is an asymmetry in your horse's "drive train" or pain somewhere on the body, this exercise won't be effective. Riding such a horse is like driving a car that is out of alignment. Leaning forward can also discourage a horse from picking up a lead at the canter. If you have the tendency to sit a little deeper to ask for the canter or the lope from the walk, lighten your seat in the saddle, and consider more protective padding under the saddle.

Asymmetry is often a major issue with horses who favor one lead. If a horse is consistently resistant to one leg, there is usually something physical going on. Before you begin mounted and Ground Exercises, do

Body Exploration to see if you can find any reaction or sensitivity in the poll, neck, shoulders or back. Typical "hot spots" include the atlas/axis junction behind the poll, across the middle of the shoulder, along the back, along the rib area on either side and over the loin area, and where your leg aids would be. Following our suggestions will help to alleviate those imbalances or tight areas in the body. You can begin on either the body or the legs.

Be sure to use sufficient padding and make sure the saddle isn't pinching or jamming into the withers or loins, either of which will cause the horse to habitually tighten the shoulder on one side. If the horse is muscled differently on one side, especially over the shoulder, the pressure of the saddle, whether English (too narrow) or Western (too far forward) can prevent the horse from comfortably picking up the lead. If the skirt of the saddle is too long for the horse, and the back is a little dropped, the saddle may be jamming the loins and discouraging the horse from picking up the lead. He may be twisting his back in one direction to avoid the discomfort.

If your horse still sticks with one lead after you've given it a good try, you may be dealing with chronic pain or asymmetry. In such instances, it can be really useful to use the services of a competent chiropractor in conjunction with the exercises described here. And, remember, any asymmetry in your own body, especially the back or the pelvis, can lead to asymmetry in your horse. Remember to check the saddle, and do an exploration of the back for sensitivity or overreaction anywhere in the back.

Training Solutions

TTouches

• Start with the leg that the horse picks up most easily. Do *Coiled Python Lifts, Octopus TTouches* and circles on that leg, then bring it slightly forward, and do *Front Leg Circles.*

• Next, think in terms of joining the body to the legs. Start on the neck with *Inch Worm*, then do connected *Abalone TTouches* and lifts to release neck and shoulder muscles, because often you may have tightness in one side of the neck, which is affecting movement all the way down the leg and shoulder. Then do a few *Neck Releases, Lick of the Cow's Tongue* and *Zig-Zag TTouches* over the croup, activating the hindquarters and pelvis.

• *Hoof Tapping:* if the horse is oblivious, tap more firmly; if sensitive, tap lightly. Tap all around the hoof wall, on three different rows of the hoof, six or seven taps on each row.

Ground Exercises

• *Cha Cha* and *Half-Walk* give the horse a different experience of moving his shoulders, legs and body.

Ridden Work

• With your horse tacked up, do *Hind Leg Circles* and *Tail TTouches*; then mount and have a helper repeat the exercises with you in the saddle.

• The *Balance Rein* will help to lighten the forehand and keep the horse from falling in on the shoulder; if the horse is stiff through the back, add the *Tellington Training Bit* to further help the horse rebalance and more easily take the other lead. Ask for the canter from the trot as you go into a corner of the arena, staying light in the saddle, sitting back and using your outside leg. Add the elastic *Promise Wrap* on alternating days.

• If you're starting a young horse or are a novice rider, start on a big circle and just ease the horse into the canter from the trot. Sometimes simply heading out of the arena for the trail can solve the problem. The varying terrain, curves and hills will naturally encourage your horse to use both sides of his body and you may find that he picks up both leads on a more equal basis.

Often, we find that simply adding the *Tellington Training Bit*, *Promise Wrap* and *Balance Rein* will instantly give your horse new awareness through his body and make it easy for him to pick up either lead.

Solutions at a Glance: *Leads, favors one*

Body Exploration 151 ~ Hind Leg Circles 175 ~ Tail TTouch 185 ~ Balance Rein 279 Tellington Training Bit 290 ~ Promise Wrap 288 ~ Coiled Python Lift 172 ~ Octopus TTouch 200 ~ Front Leg Circles 174 ~ Inch Worm 197 ~ Abalone TTouch 171 ~ Neck Release 221 Lick of the Cow's Tongue 177 ~ Zig-Zag TTouch 206 ~ Hoof Tapping 196 ~ Chu Chu 232 Half-Walk 280

Longeing/Lungeing Problems

Longeing is a classical method of putting the horse out on the end of a line and sending him around you in a circle. The diameter of this area may vary from 20 to 30 feet or more.

Why do people longe horses?

• To teach the horse obedience, to respond to the commands for walk, trot and canter from the ground

• To work a horse to release any excess energy or bucks before riding

• To exercise if you don't have time to ride

• To get the horse moving in balance with head low, back round, and hindquarters engaged

It takes a lot of skill and practice to longe a horse correctly and safely. One of the difficulties of longeing is the necessity of precise positioning and subtle body signals. If your signals are unclear, or your horse becomes bored and resistant, a number of problems can arise:

• The horse may turn in to you and refuse to go forward.

• The horse may refuse to go in one direction, almost always to the right.

• The horse may charge, rear or otherwise threaten the handler.

Incorrect longeing can also put the horse at risk:

• The horse can get out on the end of the longe line and run, buck, twist or bolt. I've seen horses fall down and hurt themselves, tie up and colic as a result of the handler being unable to stop them.

• Frequent longeing can lead to repetitive motion injuries, and even a slow trot can exacerbate musculoskeletal problems.

• Longeing with side reins or other devices can contribute to soreness.

• Longeing young horses can lead to splints and other injuries, and when done incorrectly with side reins, can cause dropped backs and ewe-necks.

For these reasons, I don't often recommend longeing, unless you are experienced or have competent instruction.

There is a trend to move away from classical concepts of longeing to "chasing" the horse out on the end of a short line at a trot and canter. These small circles often torque the head to the inside and swing the quarters to the outside, causing the horse to fall in on the shoulder. This type of habitual training is a common cause of lameness.

As an alternative to repetitive longeing, we recommend a few basic sessions designed to teach the horse to walk, trot, stop and stand straight on a circle (not facing you). At Tellington Training, we prefer to longe horses on an oval rather than a circle. In addition, we use a regular lead line and wand so the handler walks with the horse, rather than standing still in the middle of a circle. This helps the horse keep his balance and makes him mindful of his distance from the handler and where he is going.

Training Solutions

• *Joyful Dolphin* will help you teach your horse to move at a slow walk, fast walk, jog in a straight line and stop in a straight line while listening to subtle signals.

• To prepare your horse to longe, use *Dingo* to teach him to go forward from a signal. I remember a mare I had as a six-year-old in training. She would longe to the left and not the right no matter what

you did. We put her into the *Journey of the Homing Pigeon*, worked her from both sides and had her longeing in both directions in one session.

• Longe your horse in a *Body Wrap* while he is wearing a *Tellington Training Bit* (twist the reins under the neck so they can't be stepped on, and attach your longe line to a halter fitted over the bridle). This pair of tools improves balance without putting your horse into a static frame that inhibits freedom of motion and causes soreness from jamming the poll, withers and shoulders.

The *Tellington Training Bit* encourages a horse to soften in the jaw, poll and pelvis and to lengthen and round the topline from withers to poll without restriction from side reins, which limit forward stretching of the head and neck. The *Body Wrap* encourages engagement of the hind end while lifting the back. Horses who have difficulty moving in balance on the longe—rushing forward, racing at the canter—are easily able to come into balance, coming more up than forward and cantering in a very connected way.

Solutions at a Glance: *Longeing/Lungeing*

Joyful Dolphin 244 ~ Dingo 235 ~ Journey of the Homing Pigeon 241 ~ Tellington Training Bit 290 ~ Body Wrap 160

Low on Pecking Order

see also *Aggressive to Other Horses, Claustrophobia*

In most groups of horses, there develops a more or less established hierarchy or "pecking order," which determines the order in which horses can claim the best food, access to water, shade, escape from the elements and biting insects, pasture companions and other "perks."

However, in a large herd with as many as 30 horses running together, this order appears to shift through-

out the day; it's fluid, not fixed. In her experience of over 20 years, my sister and fellow instructor Robyn

SPECIAL SITUATION

Some horses that stay away from other horses, appearing to be low in the pecking order, are really claustrophobic. They are tense and reactive and will flinch or move away from hand contact or *Body Exploration*. They do not have a good feeling about their body—they don't feel safe around other horses and they don't feel safe with any contact with their body. Such horses often have a fear of being touched on the inside of their hind legs, the flank area, point of buttock and the tail. See *Claustrophobia,* p. 50, for guidelines on how to help such horses over ride these concerns.

Hood has observed in her herd of over 120 Icelandic horses that horse "A" may push away horse "B" and "B" may push away "C," but "C" and "A" may eat together. In addition, the order isn't necessarily static. The equine totem pole is not linear.

It is erroneously believed that a horse's status within a stable herd does not change. The surprising fact is that in many cases you can change the horse's standing among his equine peers by fostering a new self-image and awareness of his body. I've seen many horses rise several notches on the totem pole when they go out into the world and become performance horses. It's almost as though they come home with a "tale to tell."

If your horse is at the bottom of the totem pole, you can improve his confidence and rank with TTouches. In addition, confidence and herd status often change with training and competition: one endurance rider reported that her once-wimpy mare came home from competitions bold and proud. Returning from the ride, she raced into the pasture and flung her head, asserting her newfound self-assurance.

On the other hand, it is our responsibility to protect the horse who remains low on the pecking order. This might mean separation from the herd so he or she doesn't get beat up or lose weight due to being kept away from food, water or shade. Good horsekeepers make every effort to arrange horses in complementary groups, of like sex, age and status.

Training Solutions

• *Mouth TTouches, Front* and *Hind Leg Circles, Coiled Python Lifts, Octopus TTouches* and *Clouded Leopard TTouches* over the entire body will help give the horse a new self-image and confidence. I've seen *Tail TTouches* make a change in status in one session, so try them all.

• Teach your horse something new by taking him through the *Labyrinth*. Have your horse follow you through the maze without a halter on; you'll be amazed how he will begin to feel good about himself. Remember to visualize the shift you want to take place.

Your horse may go through a period of being somewhat aggressive to other horses. Continue the work on the body to even out the temperament and do *Tarantulas Pulling the Plow* to give your horse a new and pleasant sensation. If your horse is a loner or doesn't have the advantage of being a part of the herd, TTouch can provide that much-needed physical contact.

Solutions at a Glance: *Low on Pecking Order*

Mouth TTouch 182 ~ Front Leg Circles 174 ~ Hind Leg Circles 175 ~ Coiled Python Lift 172 Octopus TTouch 200 ~ Clouded Leopard TTouch 195 ~ Tail TTouch 185 ~ Labyrinth 259 Tarantulas Pulling the Plow 203 ~ Body Exploration 151

Mare, moody ("mareish")

Many mares become overreactive during estrus—squealing, squatting, squirting, striking, pinning their ears when other horses approach, and often resisting the aids when ridden. Such mares are often described as moody or even "witchy." Mare mood swings can interfere with performance, especially when precision is required.

A common solution is to keep such mares out of estrus with an oral progesterone product such as Regumate® during an equestrian competition. The idea is similar to a woman taking birth control bills so she will not menstruate during an athletic contest.

A medical examination may be warranted when a mare's mood changes become extreme, persistent or limit her performance. You want to be sure you are not dealing with an ovarian cyst or tumor, retained corpus luteum or other physiological factor. Your veterinarian can order a hormone panel to check levels of progesterone, estrogen and other reproductive hormones.

TTouches can be a big help to mares who naturally cycle for about five days every month for much of the year by providing a sense of overall relaxation and well-being.

Training Solutions

•   Start with slow, deliberate *Ear TTouches* from the center of the poll over the base of the ear, stroking out to the tip and feeling every inch of the ear as you slide. Fold the ear together, if the horse will allow it, so the insides are touching, and on each stroke, put the emphasis on a slightly different line. Do one ear at time while firmly holding and opposing the stroke with a little pull on the noseband of the halter in the opposite direction. The ear strokes will relax your mare and help to reduce any discomfort or pain that some mares experience during estrus. This TTouch activates acupressure points over the entire ear that correspond with specific parts of the body.

•   *Raccoon TTouches* at the base of the ears can influence the triple heater meridian, an acupuncture site said to activate energy and help balance temperature in the respiratory, digestive and reproductive organs. Excess heat or dampness in these organ systems creates an imbalance along the meridian and can affect behavior. *Raccoon TTouches* around the base of the ears can help to balance the triple heater meridian.

•   As your mare comes into estrus, do *Clouded Leopard TTouches* with *Connected Circles* over every inch of her body. Some mares experience pain in the flank area during ovulation, so consider doing gentle *Abalone Lifts* in this area through a warm towel. A supportive *Body Wrap* can bring comfort to a mare at this phase of her cycle.

•   Supplement your mare's diet with herbs. There are a number of herbal blends that appear to help mares who have irregular cycles, irritability and mood swings. One product, Vitex, includes Monks pepper, raspberry leaf, vervain and other herbs. Hilton Herbs and Wendals Herbs are two recommended producers of such products (see *Resources*, p. 311).

•   Finally, give the mare some time off during the most intensive days of her cycle. If you're a woman, you can surely identify with the mood swings characteristic of cyclical changes. If you ride, make the effort less demanding, and keep your distance from other horses.

Solutions at a Glance: *Mare, moody*

Ear TTouches 210 ~ Raccoon TTouch 213 ~ Clouded Leopard TTouch 195 ~ Connected Circles 173 ~ Abalone TTouch 171 ~ Body Wrap 160

Mounting, won't stand for

You're tacked up and ready to ride. But when you take up the reins and prepare to put your foot in the stirrup, your horse skittles forward or swings away from you before you can swing on. Or, he won't stand next to the mounting block long enough for you to hop aboard.

I'm amazed at how many people simply put up with this behavior or jerk the reins and yell at the horse. Others patiently wait until the horse stands, which is much more humane, but continues to reinforce the unwanted behavior. In many instances, the horse is fidgeting in anticipation of discomfort from a poorly fitting saddle or bit, or he may be due for dental work.

Many horses don't stand still for mounting because they are tensing the back or holding the breath. Often they do this because they are anticipating being pulled off balance as the rider mounts. They may have never learned to balance themselves properly, and the weight of the rider throws them even more off balance. A horse has to learn to balance the weight of the rider by standing squarely and keeping a "leg on each corner." At the same time, check your own technique to help your horse remain balanced and comfortable—hanging on the side of the horse in one direction is not conducive to balanced mounting. The steps that follow are the ones I use when mounting a horse for the first time, and can be used to retrain any horse to stand quietly and balanced for mounting.

Training Solutions

• A few sessions of *Dingo* and *Cueing the Camel* will teach your horse to wait for a signal to go forward and stop from a light tap on the chest. When you are ready to mount, ask a helper to steady the horse from the ground. However, your helper should not restrain the horse with a tight grip on the reins that could scare him and make him pull back.

• Position the horse between two straw, hay or shavings bales or against a fence and a single bale to create boundaries. Stand on the bale and do some *Connected Circles* on both sides of the body, from crest to croup. Invite the horse to turn back the head and take a crunchy treat, so he will learn to stand without nervousness.

• Take up the reins in your right hand along with a piece of mane, and with your left hand pick up your foot and place it in the stirrup. Then transfer your reins to the left hand and reach over to the far side of the pommel (not the cantle) of the saddle with your right hand. Keep the inside of your knee against the saddle and pointed forward so your foot is not digging into the horse's barrel.

• As you mount, instead of going straight up, direct your body diagonally over the saddle. Keep your stomach low and your head on the far side as you smoothly swing your leg over the cantle. This technique keeps you from pulling the saddle over. After you settle lightly into the saddle, invite your horse to reach around for a small carrot piece or another treat. Practice from both sides. Use a safe, solid mounting block to reduce the amount of sideways pull.

If you have a difficult horse or are starting a youngster, begin in a box stall in the *Taming the Tiger* position. Then, accustom your horse to being led through the bales (as described on p. 87), and slowly introduce him to your stepping up on the bale next to him. Then set up four-sided boundaries and stand on a bale to do TTouches until he is completely relaxed. If your horse is uncomfortable with this process, you may need to go to *Work under Wands*.

Solutions at a Glance: *Mounting, won't stand for*

Dingo and Cueing the Camel 235 ~ Connected Circles 173 ~ Taming the Tiger 166 ~ Work under Wands 267

Overcollected/Overbent (behind the bit/behind the vertical)

Riding a horse in an overcollected posture, with the nose tipped back behind the vertical, can cause pain in the neck from tight or contracted muscles. The result can be a shortened stride, front leg lameness (called "bridle lame") and sore neck and back muscles. Besides the pain caused from such overbending, it must be really boring, and sometimes frightening, for a horse to be so overcollected that he cannot clearly see where he is going.

I see this fault in all "walks" of equine life, from jigging trail horses to zombie-like "peanut-rolling" pleasure horses to Grand Prix dressage horses. Habitually traveling in this manner leads to stiffness and imbalance through the body.

In clinics, I am frequently asked to work with horses who have been ridden in an overcollected frame for many years. Sometimes their muscles have become so tight they cannot extend their necks! They are typically tight and sore on the top of the neck over the first two cervical vertebrae as well as along the crest, on the withers and often in the back and loins. Such horses often have not been schooled to come "through" from behind, where true engagement and collection begin.

Training Solutions

TTouches

• Combined TTouches on the body; especially *Clouded Leopard* with a number 3 to 4 pressure (see p. 148) followed by *Bear TTouch* with *Sponge TTouch* into the neck, from the neck to the shoulder and *Inch Worm*. Start with *Abalone TTouches* with *Coiled Python Lifts* following two parallel lines along the neck, back and loins. Continue with *Coiled Python Lifts* on the shoulders and on the front legs. *Lower the Head,* and do *Ear TTouches* followed by a *Neck Release.*

Ground Exercises

• Work over *The Fan* or through the *Labyrinth* with your horse's head at various levels.

• *Neckline and Ground Driving* is useful for horses who go behind the vertical when you take up contact with the mouth, and you can't get them to stretch out. You'll need a helper, so you can have one person at the head to lead and a second person to handle the driving lines from behind. This Ground Exercise frees the head and neck and encourages the horse to reach forward.

Ridden Work

- While riding, encourage your horse to stretch the neck out and down from *Lying Leopard TTouches* and slides along the neck and poll.

- For horses who work in a collected frame much of the time due to their discipline, it is worthwhile to do releasing and stretching exercises a couple times a week with the *Lindell Sidepull* and *Balance Rein* to free up the neck, back and hindquarters. Riding with a *Liberty Neck Ring* without a bridle can be a miracle for such horses who often will instantly stretch and lengthen.

Turnaround Tale

Justin Thyme, a Thoroughbred gelding ridden by Olympic medal winner Claus Erhorn, was an excellent event horse, having been on the German gold-medal winning team. However, at 13, his stride was not as free and fluid as it had been, and Claus wondered if Tellington TTouch could help. Justin was a brilliant cross-country jumper but his dressage was never the best—typical of event horses.

When I watched the horse move under saddle, he was overbent and behind the vertical. No matter how loose a rein he was given, he would not stretch his neck out. His stride was restricted by his tight neck and back muscles.

I began with a 30-minute session of TTouch all over the body, and then asked Claus to remount. Justin was moving a little more freely, but still behind the verti-

cal with shorter strides at the trot. First I loosened the noseband, thinking that would allow him more freedom to stretch out. But even when the reins were hanging loosely he still kept his head behind the vertical. I took the noseband off completely—still no change.

When I saw that these tactics were not working, I asked if I could ride Justin to see how Bridleless Riding would help. After riding a few minutes with the neck ring and the reins hanging on the neck until Justin understood how to stop and turn, I took the bridle off completely. The horse immediately dropped his nose to the level of his knees and stretched into a lovely, long-strided trot when I asked him. Claus was astounded. I rode Justin for five minutes or so at the walk, trot and canter and popped him over a few low jumps before reluctantly giving him back to Claus, because it was so much fun riding him.

After Claus had his moment of delight at the bridleless jumping and newfound freedom of movement, I put the Tellington Training Bit on Justin. Typical of the effects of this bit, the horse became even more fluid and supple through the back and began moving correctly without being overbent. When we added an elastic Promise Wrap, his gaits smoothed out even more. Claus continued to ride Justin in the training bit and several times in the neck ring. Five weeks later, competing in one of the most prestigious three-day events in the United Kingdom, he won the dressage phase for the first time in his career.

Solutions at a Glance: *Overcollected/Overbent*

Balance Rein 279 ~ Lindell Sidepull 286 ~ Clouded Leopard TTouch 195 ~ Bear TTouch 217 ~ Sponge TTouch 203 ~ Abalone TTouch 171 ~ Coiled Python Lift 172 ~ Lying Leopard TTouch 181 ~ Lowering the Head 163 ~ Ear TTouches 210 ~ Neck Release 221 ~ The Fan 253 Labyrinth 259 ~ Neckline and Ground Driving 261 ~ Liberty Neck Ring and Bridleless Riding 282 ~ Tellington Training Bit 290 ~ Inch Worm 197

Overcompetitive

see also *Bucking*

The overcompetitive horse is the one who can't be rated, especially at the beginning of a competition. This problem commonly occurs in endurance riding, eventing, steeplechasing and flat racing. Because of the rider having to fight the horse, both team members waste precious energy rather then settling smoothly into stride. As a result, the horse can tie up, tire out, colic or become sore in the mouth, neck and back from the restraint. Of course, the rider also suffers corresponding aches and pains in the neck, back and shoulders.

Although there are certainly experienced horses who are controllably competitive, the overcompetitive horse becomes a problem when he burns up his energy reserves long before the finish line. In many instances, the problem may arise from the adrenaline rush that triggers the flight reflex and overrides the horse's ability to listen to the rider.

You'll often see various martingales, hackamores and bits enlisted in the effort to help to slow the horse down, but these aids can create secondary problems, including tight necks and sore backs from the overproduction of lactic acid from high heart rates. In addition, they fail to address the core problem of overexcitement from adrenaline stimulation, not to mention safety concerns for anyone unlucky enough to get in the way.

In the long run, the use of strategies to preserve and improve the horse's balance while teaching him to rate may serve you better than the latest trend in tack. I've found that a combination of a few simple tools can give the horse a new sense of his body and "bring him into himself."

Training Solutions

• Use the *Tellington Training Bit* and *Balance Rein*. These tools alone will make a huge difference in your ability to rate your horse, whether in training or competition. The *Tellington Training Bit* will encourage your horse to keep his head down, soften his poll and help him stay loose in the back. The *Balance Rein* will lighten the forehand and enable you to hold your horse through the body without pulling on his mouth, especially going downhill. You'll also be able to keep him from breaking from a trot into a gallop, or from a gallop into a runaway. By using a press-and-release motion on the *Balance Rein,* you'll take the pressure off your own shoulders and arms.

• With an especially excitable, high-strung or high-headed horse, the night before the event put him into the *Body Wrap* for a couple of hours using a pair of connected, stretchy polo wraps. This will help him relax into a rounded frame. If the weather is on the cool side, put on a lightweight sheet or blanket to keep the large muscles of the back loose and warm.

• The night before and the morning of a competition, warm up your horse from the ground with some *Ear TTouches, Coiled Python Lifts, Front* and *Hind Leg Circles, Lick of the Cow's Tongue, Back Lifts* and *Tail TTouches* to prepare your horse's body for the saddle. Many overcompetitive horses are tight in the back even before the tack goes on, contributing to their reactive, flighty response. Just before mounting, make sure you are breathing from your core and centered. Use a mounting block, and tighten the girth the last few notches once you are on board. Keep a rump rug over the hindquarters to keep the large muscles from stiffening up, and, if you're on an endurance ride, be prepared to deploy it again at the first vet check.

Turnaround Tale

Endurance rider M.J. Jackson, then of Salt Lake City and now a resident of New Mexico, had a wonderful horse qualified for the Race of Champions in Montana. The horse was very competitive, didn't want other horses to get ahead of him and was nearly impossible to rate for the first 30 miles. He used up a lot of energy and would wind up with his head up and back dropped, potentially creating soreness through the neck and back.

Two days before the race, M.J. brought the horse to me for a mini-clinic. I recommended the combination of the Tellington Training Bit, Balance Rein and a different saddlepad. I then rode the horse briefly to show her how to lower his head with the bit and hold him back and rate him with the Balance Rein. She found she was able to rate him effectively from the start and by the end of the race, his back was sound and he finished in excellent condition.

Solutions at a Glance: *Overcompetitive*

Tellington Training Bit 290 ~ Balance Rein 279 ~ Ear TTouches 210 ~ Coiled Python Lift 172 Front Leg Circles 174 ~ Hind Leg Circles 175 ~ Lick of the Cow's Tongue 177 ~ Back Lift 193 Tail TTouch 185 ~ Body Wrap 160

Overreaching/Forging

When the hind hoof strikes the front hoof on the same side, your horse is said to be forging or overreaching. It can be the result of conformation, hoof imbalance or back problems; it can also begin when a horse becomes fatigued. Forging can be a minor annoyance or severe enough to pull a shoe or injure the heel bulb of a front hoof.

Training Solutions

• The problem can often be alleviated by changing the balance and breakover of the hoof, by rolling the toes in front or setting the shoe back.

• The *Tellington Training Bit* will help the elasticity and movement of the back and is sometimes all it takes to eliminate forging, especially if the horse tends to forge when fatigued.

• The *Balance Rein* and *Promise Wrap* will shift the center of gravity back and help the horse track up. *Lick of the Cow's Tongue* and *Back Lifts* will activate the back and increase flexibility.

Solutions at a Glance: *Overreaching/Forging*

Tellington Training Bit 290 ~ Balance Rein 279 ~ Promise Wrap 288 ~ Lick of the Cow's Tongue 177 ~ Back Lift 193

Paste Deworming (worming), resistance to

You need to give your horse a tube of dewormer paste, medication or electrolytes. But, soon there is paste smeared everywhere—except where it is supposed to go.

Most horses resist simply because they have never been taught to lower or raise the head when you ask them to. Or the horse may have been twitched, "eared" or otherwise restrained in a way that has only made him more resistant. You can teach the horse to stand quietly with his head at the level you ask whenever you want to introduce anything into the mouth, be it a bit or a syringe.

Training Solutions

You need a nylon or leather halter with side rings and a chain lead, adjusted as shown on p.158, or a Zephyr lead (see p. 159). (Later, you should be able to administer the dewormer with little more than a soft rope around the neck.)

- *Lower the Head* and do *Mouth TTouches* with your fingertips or hand all over the muzzle and gums.

Muzzle Wrap

- Take a lightweight cloth or thin towel, wet it and wring it out, and lay it over the halter's noseband. Then bring it under the muzzle and fit it under the chin strap of the halter, so that the nose is encased in the towel. Next, slip the syringe quietly into the corner of the mouth and administer the paste. Use something tasty the first few times, such as applesauce or flavored yogurt, so your horse will look forward to receiving it. Tip his muzzle slightly up and do a few TTouches on his throat and neck to encourage him to swallow the substance.

The nose wrap seems to have an unexplainable, quieting effect on horses, and it's never failed to work for me with the most difficult horses.

Turnaround Tale

A nine-year-old Arabian stallion was brought to me in a demo at Stoneleigh in England, home of the British Horse Society. This was an excellent endurance horse except for the fact that he refused to allow his gums to be examined by the vets at the check-in; he'd been disqualified and told not to come to another endurance ride until they got him over this.

I went through the usual Lowering the Head and Lying Leopard TTouches on the face, working in an open arena without the advantage of an enclosed space, similar to conditions at an endurance ride. I could slip my hand under the gums, but as soon I would go to lift the lips to check capillary refill and gum color, the horse would revert to rearing. This is where I discovered that using a wet towel over the horse's muzzle stopped the rearing. I pulled my towel out of my bag, wet it, wrung it out and put it over the horse's nose. His response changed immediately. He stood quietly while I opened his lips, tapped his tongue and pressed his gums—all parts of a standard endurance exam—to my heart's content. He was able to go back to endurance competition successfully.

Solutions at a Glance: *Paste deworming, resistance to*

Lowering the Head 163 ~ Mouth TTouch 182 ~ Lying Leopard TTouch 181

Pawing

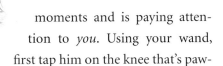

Pawing the ground with one front hoof is an expression of impatience. It also can signal an overemotional reaction to a stressful situation. You've probably seen the horse who digs himself into a hole or bangs a hoof on a stall door. Many people simply ignore the behavior, or "get after" the horse with a "No!" or "Quit!" which has little, if any, effect.

Some trainers advocate tying the horse for several hours, in the belief that he'll eventually "figure it out" and stop. Horses who bang the stall with a front foot at feeding time are often forced to wait until last to be fed. These approaches are rarely effective. I tend to feed this type of horse first, because 1) if you don't, he will teach the others to paw; 2) maybe that horse is hungrier than the others; and 3) you are only reinforcing the behavior when he has to wait.

Horses who paw may also be undisciplined or uncooperative in other ways. Some horses alternate pawing with holding up a front leg when they're impatient, thereby tightening the muscles in the shoulder, forearm and neck on that side. This can affect a horse's performance by shortening the stride and tightening the back.

Dealing with a pawing problem provides an ideal model of how we can change a horse's behavior. By affecting the horse's nervous system via the TTouches and Ground Exercises, we create the possibility for new patterns of behavior.

Training Solutions

• When your horse paws or holds a leg up, put him in *Taming the Tiger*. Keep a little extra tension on both lead lines so the horse is held still for a few moments and is paying attention to *you*. Using your wand, first tap him on the knee that's pawing. Then, using two wands, stroke down the front and back of both front legs at the same time. As you work, keep a clear visualization of both feet remaining on the ground. Your expectations can have a major influence on the outcome!

When a horse is pawing out of separation anxiety, or is in a state of fear, the brain sends a message to the body to prepare for flight. Such horses don't feel their legs—they're ungrounded, which intensifies their sense of anxiety. By stroking the legs with a wand, you can restore awareness, reground the horse and reduce anxiety.

• When your horse is relaxed and not pawing, do a few minutes of *Front Leg Circles* and *Abalone TTouches*. If he's nervous at feeding time, give him a small bite while holding him in *Taming the Tiger* with light pressure on both leads.

• Combine *Labyrinth* and *Cha Cha* to bring awareness to the legs and connect the horse to the ground. Stroke the legs with the wand, and ask the horse to stand absolutely still, even for 10 seconds, and then ask him to move on.

• If your horse begins pawing with one leg, use your wand to stroke and tap the *other* leg, or stroke down the front of both legs. Add *Octopus TTouches* to ground the horse.

• With some horses, you may first need to release overall tension with TTouches for Trust (p. 168), including *Ear TTouches*, *Mouth TTouches* and *Connected Circles* with *Coiled Python Lifts*.

Solutions at a Glance: *Pawing*

Taming the Tiger 166 ~ Front Leg Circles 174 ~ Abalone TTouch 171 ~ Labyrinth 259 ~ Cha Cha 232 ~ Octopus TTouch 200 ~ Ear TTouches 210 ~ Mouth TTouch 182 ~ Connected Circles 173 ~ Coiled Python Lift 172

Pulling Back when Tied

Your horse is standing quietly, tied to the hitching rail as you groom him. You walk into the barn for the saddle; when you return moments later, you find your horse locked in mortal combat with the lead rope and hitching rail. What happened?

Many horses have an instinctive fear of being restrained—not surprising when one considers that flight is their principal means of defense. I have observed two types of pulling back. First, there is the horse who has learned to test the line. Such horses have typically discovered that they can break their lead rope, so they will try it again and again. Then there is the horse who panics, flips out and tries to escape by violently pulling back until something gives. This type of puller is much more dangerous, because the horse can actually flip over backward and seriously injure himself.

There are differing schools of thought on tying. The British Pony Club, citing safety concerns, advises against tying horses hard and fast, and Pony Clubbers in England learn to tie with breakaway twine. Better to break the twine than hurt the horse, the thinking goes, and I agree. The further west you travels, the more likely you will encounter the philosophy that when a horse is tied, he shouldn't have an opportunity to break free.

A common approach is to "tie him up hard and fast, and let him pull until he gets it." Or place a rope around the animal's middle and up through the halter ring so that the horse pulls against himself. Other techniques involve tying to walls and inner tubes. Although some of these methods can work some of the time, I think the danger with such unforgiving approaches is twofold: first, these methods trigger the horse's fight-or-flight instinct rather than educate him; and secondly, a horse can sustain serious damage to the cervical vertebrae. The horse can flip over and break the withers or, in a number of cases,

break his neck. Considerable skill and strength on the part of the handler is required, given the risks of such methods.

Tying with a stretchy bungee-type cord can work for some horses who "test the line," but there is always the danger of the rope's hardware snapping under extreme pressure, resulting in a dangerous whiplash to any horse or person in the flight path. So-called panic snaps have their drawbacks as well. If the horse is flailing about when you are trying to reach the snap, the situation is potentially dangerous.

A better option is the Blocker (also called the Aussie) Tie Ring (see *Resources*, p. 311), which resembles a half-snaffle bit. It works by allowing a small amount of slippage on the lead rope if the horse pulls back but not so much that the horse breaks free. Horses seem less claustrophobic with this device, which can also be used as a trailer tie. A mare I'd worked with who'd broken several halters, leads and hardware never pulled again from the first time she was tied with this simple (and portable) device.

Over two or three sessions, you can teach your horse to lower his head from a signal from the wand and lead until he is absolutely reliable in response. The following guidelines work for training a horse to tie for the first time as well as retraining a confirmed puller. This is how we start our young horses who have never been tied in their lives.

Training Solutions

❶ Start by teaching your horse to *Lower the Head* to light pressure. Do *Ear TTouches*, and *Inch Worm* on the poll and neck to release any tension and encourage the horse to lengthen and lower the head and neck. If your horse is tense, do *Connected Circles* all over the body so the horse begins to get a new awareness of his body to prepare him for being restrained, or to release his fear of being restrained.

❷ Using a chain or Zephyr lead (see p. 157) placed up the side of the halter rather than over the nose or under the chin, which often triggers the horse to pull even harder, ask the horse to *Lower the Head* from light pressure-and-release on the lead. Lead the horse forward a few steps and ask him to *Lower the Head* from a slow walk or standing.

Some horses respond by lowering the head immediately, while standing still, to a light pressure on the side of the halter. Others respond once they have moved a few steps forward. Once your horse has the idea of coming forward one or two steps in response to your request, add a little pressure on the head and noseband of the halter with one hand lightly on top of the halter.

❸ The goal is that when the horse feels any pressure on the head, he steps forward rather than pulls back. *Dancing Cobra* is an excellent way of teaching your horse to come forward from a light signal on the Zephyr or chain. *Dingo* will further encourage him to step forward from pressure on the lead as you tap the croup. You're giving him an impulse from behind to step forward as you simultaneously ask from the head and the croup.

I used this technique in a weeklong clinic with a Norwegian Fjord mare who had a tendency to pull back. When her rider, Eleanor, went to bridle and saddle her, the mare caught her bit on a hook. Eleanor thought she was going to explode backward, but the mare simply put her head down and waited for help. Once a horse learns to step forward from a light signal behind, you have "insurance" she'll often respond by coming forward on her own rather than struggling to escape.

WHAT ABOUT CROSS-TIES?

Our reliable *Taming the Tiger*, which we often call the "half cross-tie," can also be used to teach your horse. Pay attention to the height at which the cross-ties are set and to the weight of the lines. Many cross-ties are set so high that the horse can't lower the head. Your horse should be able to bring his head and neck level with his withers while you are grooming him.

When a horse has to hold his head up as you are brushing and saddling him, tension builds up in the back and can carry over to under-saddle work. If you are in a stable where the community cross ties are set too high for your horse, hook them to the top rings of the halter. Or make two foot-long extension lines using lightweight rope, twine or clothesline and place snaps on both ends (stay away from heavy chains, because you don't want too much weight on the horse's head). Keep these extenders handy in your grooming kit. (Be sure there is a breakaway device on any cross-ties that you use.)

If your horse is stomping or tossing his head in the cross-ties, he may be trying to tell you that he is sensitive or is being groomed too hard or too fast. If he is also switching his tail, he may be sore or tight in the back (see *Grooming Sensitivity*, p. 67).

❹ In *Taming the Tiger*, steady the head with the halter, then turn the head back so he can see you while you release any tightness on that side. Do slow *Connected Circles* and *Coiled Python Lifts* with a sheepskin mitt all over the horse's body. Alternately tighten and release pressure on the lead lines, releasing as he relaxes. Groom your horse with a soft brush or a glove like a Grooma, available in tack shops (see *Resources*, p. 311), using slow, steady circles.

TEACH YOUR FOAL TO TIE

You can teach foals from the first or second time you halter them not to pull by attaching the rope to the side of the halter, and asking and giving a little until they learn to come forward between the movement of the wand and the rope. The idea is never to put them in a position where they learn to pull back. Using the ring at the side of the halter is very different than the bottom ring, because they can easily give the head and follow rather than reflexively pull back when they feel pressure under the chin. If you have many foals, another possibility is to borrow this method from the stud farms throughout Poland, where foals are brought in and tied during the dams' feeding time, staying with their mothers all the time.

With the chain or soft Zephyr lead up the side of the halter, and boundaries on the off side and behind, you have the horse in a position where you can challenge him a little with pressure. If your horse has learned to lower the head from the hand and the soft lead up the side, he will accept this sim-ulation of being tied. Give and take with varying degrees of pressure.

Snap the lead *to the side of the halter instead of to the chin,* so you won't trigger the pullback reflex. Tie the horse at approximately the same level as the head. Use judgment and common sense when tying any horse. If you have any concerns about your horse's ability to remain tied, I would not tie him hard and fast. I would leave such a horse in the stall or the trailer where he is safe and secure, tie to a breakable leather thong and not leave him alone at any time.

When you do tie your horse, do so in a safe place, to minimize the possibility of the horse getting hurt. If you are traveling to a show or trail ride, keep your trailer attached to your vehicle, and keep the area clear of freestanding items like wheelbarrows and manure forks. Tie your horse to something that's not going to move if he does.

Advanced Work

Teach your horse to *stand absolutely still* without being tied at all—a position we call *The Statue.* It's a great way for a horse to learn obedience and learn to listen. It takes patience, but ultimately the reward is a more relaxed, cooperative horse.

Solutions at a Glance: *Pulling Back when Tied*

Lowering the Head 163 ~ Ear TTouches 210 ~ Inch Worm 197 ~ Connected Circles 173
Taming the Tiger 166 ~ Dingo 235 ~ Dancing Cobra 234 ~ Coiled Python Lift 172 ~ The Statue 248

Rearing

When some people think of a rearing horse, they conjure up the image of Roy Rogers and superstar Trigger rearing majestically on command. However, the horses we get in Tellington Training clinics don't rear on command. They use rearing as a way of resisting. You'll sometimes see this behavior in horses who don't want to leave the stable area to head down the trail alone or are reluctant to enter an arena for an event like barrel racing or jumping. Stallions and young horses will sometimes try this tactic to escape control while being lead.

Rearing may arise from a variety of sources, including:

- Fear resulting in resistance
- Lack of clear direction from the rider
- Lack of basic ground manners
- Tightness in the horse's neck, shoulders and back
- Ill-fitting saddle
- Pain in the mouth from dental issues or bit

Rearing is commonly seen as manifestation of a "dominant attitude." "Cures" for rearing horses historically range from breaking a water-filled balloon over the horse's head while they are rearing to pulling them over backward. The problem is that it takes a lot of skill and perfect timing to manage these methods and even then there is danger of serious injury to both horse and rider. And secondly, since the development of the Tellington Method, I've found we can lay a foundation so that a horse is not afraid and wants to cooperate—in other words, a safe, willing partner.

If horses discover that rearing works to scare their rider or they get away with rearing in-hand, they quickly learn to use this vice. And, once a horse has learned to rear, punishing him can drive the habit even deeper.

Horses who are training alone, either in a round pen or small area, or who are not given enough preparation from the ground, tend more toward this vice. We find that working two horses together, and preferably more, develops confidence and focus.

It's commonly thought the horse must be punished from the saddle to be effective. Even if you are a strong enough rider to convince the horse he'd better keep four feet on the ground, if he's obeying under pressure he may test you at moments when your choices are limited, such as on an icy road or narrow trail with barbed wire on one side and a deep ditch on the other.

So we go back to the beginning and retrain the horse to cooperate without going into resistance mode. Rearing is a serious habit, and safety is paramount when dealing with such a horse. Spend enough sessions with Ground Exercises until you are absolutely confident that your horse will not rear when you mount. If you are out riding and your horse refuses to go forward, be safe: dismount and go back to your basic ground exercises in the arena.

Don't be afraid of being called a "chicken"—it's not worth getting hurt or "losing the battle" and setting up a pattern. You make up the rules for the game of riding, so if your horse has to go forward with you in the saddle or on the ground, he's still going forward. If you're inexperienced or have any concerns, contact the Tellington TTouch Training office (see *Resources*, p. 311).

Training Solutions

❶ A rearing horse has taken high-headed posture to its extreme, putting himself and his rider at risk of serious injury. So your first step is to teach your horse *Lowering the Head* from your light signal on the lead or poll using the chain or Zephyr lead up the side of the halter. If your horse is tense through the body, particularly the neck and shoulders or back and withers, a full bodywork session emphasizing *Ear TTouches, Lick of the Cow's Tongue, Front* and *Hind Leg Circles* and *Tail TTouches* will also be in order.

❷ Horses who rear in hand often haven't learned to come forward from a signal on the head and back. Work your horse from the ground in the *Dingo*, stroking the back and tapping it with the wand while asking the horse to come forward from a light signal on the chain or Zephyr lead. Spend as many sessions as necessary on this until your horse comes forward readily and stops easily.

❸ Take your horse through the *Labyrinth*. This exercise will awaken the horse's capacity to think and respond in a new way, and will encourage him to keep his head low as he follows your signals through the maze of ground poles. Continue stroking the back lightly with the wand as the horse comes through the poles.

❹ The first time you mount after the Ground Exercises, have a helper lead the horse in *Elegant Elephant,* with a wand and chain lead (or Zephyr lead) placed on a halter that you can fit over your bridle. Introduce the situation that triggered rearing in the past, such as leaving the barn alone. "Chunk" every step until you have moved past the obstacle (physical or mental) that produced the rearing behavior.

If your horse rears in hand, *Journey of the Homing Pigeon* often works to create control from two sides. With young horses, we often use the chain up one side and the Zephyr lead up the other instead of over the nose. (Caution: Although *Homing Pigeon* can stop or prevent rearing in some horses, it can also cause a horse to rear if they feel under too much pressure.)

Remember, rearing, like bucking, balking or other behavior, is often a horse's way of "training" the rider to stop the session or otherwise change the direction of the ride. It may reflect a lack of confidence on the rider's part. Or, the horse may be "too much horse" for the rider. If this is the case, think carefully about whether it's prudent to continue your partnership with this horse.

Turnaround Tale

In a two-day clinic in Atlanta, I worked a mare who was said to fight and rear for as long as a half hour at a time when asked to go out on the trail, whether alone or to lead a group of horses. This nicely conformed Quarter Horse mare had been perfectly trained at the walk, trot and canter when she was in the round pen. However, venturing out alone or at the head of the group had not been part of her training program. On the first day of the demo, when I worked this mare in Dingo, she refused to move, having absolutely no concept that a tap was a request to move forward. By the end of our first session, she had learned clearly that the tap on the croup, following a slight signal on the lead shank, was a signal to move forward without hesitation.

Next we worked in straight lines through the Labyrinth using the Half-Walk, encouraging her to pay close attention to the signal from the wand and the chain lead (or Zephyr lead). On the second day, I worked her again on the ground, and we did a full bodywork session before I asked to see her under saddle. The mare was very cooperative, moving forward even when her stablemate was led through the arena and out the other end, a time when she would normally have blown up and gone into her rearing act. By the end of the session, I had taken the bridle off. I first rode her with a Liberty Neck Ring between, through and away from other horses under saddle. Her owner then rode the mare away from the group, in both directions, with no resistance or inclination to rear.

Solutions at a Glance: *Rearing*

Lowering the Head 163 ~ Ear TTouches 210 ~ Lick of the Cow's Tongue 177 ~ Front Leg Circles 174 ~ Hind Leg Circles 175 ~ Tail TTouch 185 ~ Dingo 235 ~ Labyrinth 259 ~Elegant Elephant 237 ~ Journey of the Homing Pigeon 241 ~ Half-Walk 280 ~ Liberty Neck Ring 282

Resistant to the Leg

When you give a squeeze or a kick, your horse won't go forward or pick up speed, or he even sucks back and "bunches up." If you give a bigger squeeze and a harder kick, the horse either doesn't move any faster or actually slows down. If you "get after him" with your crop, his response is often a buck or a kick. In extreme cases, if you continue to push, the horse will stop and simply refuse to go forward or even rear.

Horses who are resistant to the leg are often described as "balky," lazy or worse. Unfortunately, more vigorous application of the aids—crop, spurs, kicking with the heels—is most often counterproductive. Such horses are often holding their breath along with tension through the barrel. If your horse is "dead to the leg" and you just try squeezing more, it's exhausting to the rider and only dulls the horse's response to the leg even further.

There are many reasons horses may not move forward willingly from your leg aids. A few include diet, overwork, being sour from being held back by the reins and pushed forward from the legs, or because they haven't actually been taught how to go forward. A chiropractic evaluation may be in order.

If you've checked out all the health issues and they are not a cause, take heart, because you can change this behavior by retraining your horse from the ground.

Training Solutions

TTouches

• Complement leading exercises with some sessions of TTouch work on the body, especially around the barrel area where your leg connects with the horse. For example, do *Tiger TTouches* with one-second circles where the leg goes so your horse will be more responsive. Add *Lick of the Cow's Tongue*.

On the other hand, if the horse balks when you squeeze harder, he may be hypersensitive to the leg.

If this is the case, do gentle *Abalone TTouches* with *Coiled Python Lifts* to bring more awareness to the area.

Ground Exercises

• Stroke the back and tap the croup with your wand in *Dingo*. As your horse moves forward, he will learn to respond to your signals, slowing the walk and shortening the frame between two hands, then lengthening the frame at the walk, and then the trot. This gives your horse more gears and transitions and helps him respond more readily to lighter signals.

Ridden Work

• I've had much success with a combination of *Promise Rope* and *Tellington Training Bit*. Do make sure that you release the reins and try little "flutters" of the heel and calf instead of a kick or poke. Another very successful option is riding with a *Liberty Neck Ring* with nothing on your horses head.

Having the freedom this brings can change the attitude of a sour, unresponsive, or "pokey" horse.

• If your horse is reactive against any type of leg pressure or does not respond at all, lightly tap your wand right behind the saddle on the loin. This will activate the hindquarters—a completely different result than whacking with a whip. Preparing your horse from the ground to step forward with *Dingo* will pay off with responsiveness under saddle.

Solutions at a Glance: *Resistant to the Leg*

Dingo 235 ~ Tiger TTouch 205 ~ Lick of the Cow's Tongue 177 ~ Abalone TTouch 171 ~ Coiled Python Lift 172 ~ Promise Rope 288 ~ Tellington Training Bit 290 ~ Liberty Neck Ring 282

Ring Sour

As your instructor calls out *"Trrrrot!"* your horse refuses to go to the end of the ring. You apply the aids, your horse stands as if rooted to the ground. You flail away with legs, heels and crop, to no avail. Your horse kicks out with a hind leg, pins his ears and rears, refusing to go forward.

Why is this horse refusing to go forward? I've commonly seen two scenarios. The horse may be mentally or physically fatigued from overtraining, he may not be convinced of your equestrian expertise, or some basic training has been left out.

What should you do? "Getting after" the horse can create more resistance and set off a battle you may lose. Plus it rarely addresses the core issue. This is the time to stop, take a deep breath, and think before you act. Those who tell you you have to "win this battle" are not considering the fact that we humans are making up the rules of this game, and we don't have to engage in a battle.

Training Solutions

A very effective, safe solution can be to dismount and work from the ground. It can be effective no matter whether your horse is undertrained, over-worked or not convinced of your ability to "lead the dance" in your partnership. You'll be amazed at the payoff when you invest time out of the saddle. Starting with TTouches for Trust (p. 168), followed by exercises from Dancing with Your Horse (p. 228), and more from Playground for Higher Learning (p. 250), can sweeten the attitude of your ring-sour buddy and put you back on a positive track.

Dismount and remove all your tack and bring out the trio of Tellington Training Tools: halter, lead chain (or Zephyr lead) and wand.

• Begin with a few minutes of *Ear TTouches* to calm and ground you both. Take more deep breaths.

• Follow with three sets of slow *Lick of the Cow's Tongue*, working your way over the entire barrel from girth to flank, on both sides of your horse. As you work, release any animosity, anger or frustration that you may be experiencing.

• Now do a few minutes of *Dingo* so your horse learns to move forward when you ask from a tap on the croup with your wand for a step or two and then stop and stand perfectly still. Many horses have never been taught to go forward from a specific signal. The goal is to get your horse moving forward from a clear signal from the wand and chain. First, do this from the ground, and once your horse is listening, tack up and have a helper lead you around the arena, using a halter over the bridle, so you still have control. For further benefits, add work in the *Labyrinth* from the ground and from the saddle.

• Whether your horse is afraid of something at the far end of the arena or is simply sour, give him a reward for going where he would rather not go. Place feed pans or stations in the arena with a few bites of grain, as described on page 108.

• Riding with a *Liberty Neck Ring* (with your reins hanging loose on the neck), will often change your horse's attitude. If you're dealing with an experienced competitive horse sour from overwork, taking the bridle off completely (beginning with a helper on the ground with a long line serving as a safety net—see p. 284 for specific instructions) and riding with the *Liberty Neck Rein* can give your horse a new lease on life. Riding without a bridle releases and lengthens the neck, shoulders, back and hindquarters—pleasurable for horse and rider.

see p. 284 for specific instructions

TIME OUT FOR TTOUCH

If your horse won't let you touch his ears or is "goosey" on the barrel or flank, I suggest you take some time out from your under-saddle training or lessons until your horse willingly lowers the head from a light signal and enjoys a selection of TTouches and Ground Exercises. It may sound like a lot of work, but imagine the results: shifting your relationship from adversarial and dominating to a true partnership—safe, successful, joyous and mutually pleasurable.

Begin with what's possible. It could be *Coiled Python Lifts* and circles on the legs from the elbows to the hoofs to override the freeze and fight reflex, and re-ground. You can also do *Inch Worm* along the crest of the neck; *Ear TTouches* and *Lick of the Cow's Tongue* will relax you both and renew your relationship.

Solutions at a Glance: *Ring Sour*

Ear TTouches 210 ~ Lick of the Cow's Tongue 177 ~ Dingo 235 ~ Labyrinth 259 ~ Liberty Neck Ring 282 ~ Coiled Python Lift 172 ~ Inch Worm 197

"Rooting"/Snatching at the Bit

Rooting at the bit is an annoying equine habit of snatching the reins through the rider's hands with an abrupt movement of the head, most commonly seen with snaffle bits. It's generally caused by uneducated or hard hands, or from a horse constantly being constrained on too tight a rein. Ponies can develop the habit to overpower a young or inexperienced rider.

Training Solutions

• This problem can be solved from the saddle. Sometimes simply riding with the *Balance Rein* will overcome it for adult riders, because it allows them to signal their horse to slow down or stop with less contact and pressure on the horse's mouth.

- In cases where the horse has rooted for years, using the double-reined *Tellington Training Bit* can stop the habit overnight as long as the rider consciously allows the horse more rein than with a snaffle. This bit allows the horse more freedom to lengthen the neck while giving the rider control without constant contact.

For Ponies Only

The *Balance Rein* alone will rarely work in these cases. When the pony has the habit of snatching the reins from the rider to grab a mouthful of grass or lower the head to take off, I suggest rigging up a type of check rein. Run light lines or reins from a D-ring on each side of the pommel of saddle through rings attached to the sides of the browband and fastened to the top of the bit. This arrangement automatically prevents the pony's nose from going to the ground, and the child holds the bridle reins as usual. In this case, I suggest a pony-sized Kimberwick bit instead of a snaffle.

Solutions at a Glance: *"Rooting"/Snatching at the Bit*

Balance Rein 279 ~ Tellington Training Bit 290

Rough-Gaited

Your horse has a jarring trot or a rough canter. Is there any hope for smoothing him out? While inherent conformation can be a limiting factor, there is much you can do to improve almost any horse's way of going.

Training Solutions

TTouches

Start by bringing the back up with *Back Lifts* and *Lowering the Head.* Increase movement and flexibility through the shoulders and back with *Lick of the Cow's Tongue, Tail TTouches, Shoulder Releases* and *Front* and *Hind Leg Circles.*

Ridden Work

- Riding with the elastic *Promise Wrap* around the haunches will encourage softening movement through the back.

- The *Balance Rein* can also work wonders. Use a light alternating contact to smooth out the trot. The *Balance Rein* activates the muscles that run over the chest and between the front legs and ultimately engages the back muscles. These, along with *Shoulder Releases,* trigger the seeking reflex on the chest, causing a horse to lengthen the neck and open the shoulders.

- The *Tellington Training Bit* is another excellent tool to smooth out a rough-gaited horse, having the effect of making the back more flexible and the movement more fluid.

Be sure to check shoeing and hoof balance and consider a chiropractic evaluation before coming to any conclusions about a rough-gaited horse.

Solutions at a Glance: *Rough-Gaited*

Back Lift 193 ~ Lowering the Head 163 ~ Lick of the Cow's Tongue 177 ~ Tail TTouch 185 Shoulder Release 225 ~ Front Leg Circles 174 ~ Hind Leg Circles 175 ~ Promise Wrap 288 Balance Rein 279 ~ Tellington Training Bit 290

Rubbing against Handler

You come back from a good workout, and your horse is hot and sweaty. You dismount and before you can even loosen the girth, your horse annoyingly shoves you with his head or tries to use you as a rubbing post.

Some riders enjoy having their horse rub on them, perhaps thinking it's a sign of trust and bonding. There's nothing wrong with this as long as you enjoy it (there's little doubt that the horse enjoys it!) and the horse does it in a polite way.

However, many people don't the like the idea of being their horse's tree, especially when the horse is hot and sweaty, or pushy. I prefer to have my horse stand still while I rub or scratch him.

Training Solutions

If your horse is a "rubber" and you want to teach him to stand quietly while you do the honors, you can keep out of rubbing range by holding him by the cheekpiece of the bridle or halter. Then take a damp sponge or towel and clean up that sweaty face. You can also use your hands to seek out the itchiest spots and assuage the horse's desire to itch.

Teach him to give you space and keep his distance with *The Statue* and *Joyful Dolphin*. For extreme cases, put him in *Taming the Tiger* and do *Lick of the Cow's Tongue*, *Troika TTouches* and *Zig-Zag TTouches* under the saddle blanket before you pull it off. Once he has the idea of politely keeping his head still, *you* can give a nice rub with a damp towel on the face and around the ears. If your horse is sweaty all over, and the weather is reasonable, spray him off and let him roll.

Solutions at a Glance: *Rubbing against Handler*

*The Statue 248 ~ Joyful Dolphin 244 ~ Taming the Tiger 166 ~ Lick of the Cow's Tongue 177
Troika TTouch 188 ~ Zig-Zag TTouch 206*

Running Away and Bolting

Few things are more frightening to a rider than a runaway horse, whose awareness of his surroundings is often shut down during his mad dash. Running off, which may be preceded by bolting, usually has a basis in fear or pain.

Fear of this sort, in my experience, stems from a horse being inadequately prepared to accept a rider on his back, so that the horse tenses every time the rider shifts in the saddle, raises an arm, or allows a leg to carelessly brush the horse's sides. Pain is a less frequent cause, but I have known horses to bolt or run off from pain in the back caused by an ill-fitting saddle or a pinched nerve.

Advice for stopping or slowing a horse who is running away is to take him in a circle. Unfortunately, this technique doesn't work every time or with all horses, since first, you have to be in a field in order to turn him around and second, you've got to be pretty skillful (or strong!) to pull it off. While this may be your only option at the time, our interest is in preventing the horse from running off in the first place. Runaways are a serious issue, one that can get you badly hurt, so start from the ground.

Training Solutions

TTouches

• Determine first whether you are dealing with a case of *inadequate training and fear response* or *pain on the body. Body Exploration* can help you to determine where a horse is reactive to contact. Sensitivity to contact in the rib area or girth area can set a tense horse off just from a brush of your leg. (How often have you heard, "Don't put your leg on him!") Normally these horses lack confidence in people and don't enjoy being handled. Often, they're reluctant to be groomed and respond by moving around, switching their tail, and grinding their teeth. Common reactive areas in runaways include a painful back, or sensitivity in the neck, ribs, shoulders and hindquarters. (Paying attention to saddle fit, providing dental and chiropractic care can often prevent the behavior.)

• Go over the whole horse to reduce reactivity to contact, whether from tensing, holding the breath or tightening the muscles. Start with connected *Clouded Leopard TTouches* parallel to the topline and down the legs. Then do slow *Tarantulas Pulling the Plow* and *Abalone* circles with *Coiled Python Lifts* and *Lick of the Cow's Tongue* until the horse accepts contact on every inch of the body. These TTouches release fear at the cellular level and activate new neural pathways, teaching the horse to think instead of react.

• Do *Lowering the Head*, then *Ear TTouches* and *Mouth TTouches* where the horse is tense or reactive to release pain or fear.

• Teach the horse to turn his head back to accept food from you, both from the ground and from the saddle. Chewing activates the parasympathetic nervous system and overrides the flight reflex. This is the cheapest insurance you can buy—preparation to take the horse beyond flight, fight, freeze and faint.

Turnaround Tale

A very experienced, skillful trainer sent me a seven-year-old Icelandic considered too dangerous to get on. The horse would run off and could not be stopped. When you mounted him, he would tense his body, stiffen and raise his neck and hold his breath. You could not put your leg on him at all. This is a horse who had been pulled out of a herd at five, and with no preparation was tied between two horses and ridden for an hour. As an eight-year-old he was still terrified of any movement that you made on his back. My solution was to teach him to lower his head and to accept touch over his whole body. I did Mouth TTouches to release fear, and lots of relaxing Ear TTouches. I ground drove him without, and then with the saddle, had him led with me on his back, and taught him to turn his head back toward me and take grain out of my hand. I also taught him to accept careful contact with my legs on his sides, and my shifting in the saddle—movements that had previously caused him to bolt. He completely got over his tendency to run away within a month-long clinic.

Stroking the legs with the wand, *Coiled Python Lifts* on the legs, *Octopus* and *Front* and *Hind Leg Circles* can restore awareness and bring the circulation back into the legs of a nervous horse.

• Try *Tail TTouches* and *Pelvic Tilt. Neckline* and *Ground Driving* can be particularly beneficial for horses who are tense with a tendency to bolt from noise or movement behind.

Ridden Work

• The first few times that you get back on, have a helper on the ground with chain and wand lead the horse through the *Labyrinth.* Sometimes riding with the *Lindell Sidepull* instead of a bit may be the key to change. On the other hand, if the horse's habit is to throw the head up, then the *Tellington Training*

Bit can be an important aid. With a *Promise Wrap*, you keep the horse feeling his boundaries so he is less afraid of his surroundings. The end result: self-confidence, safety and cooperation.

Caution: We don't recommend that amateur riders attempt to retrain runaways—there is too great a danger of being hurt. I don't believe that you're a "chicken" if you decide that such a horse is too much for you. Listen to that inner voice! Get competent professional help or contact the Tellington TTouch Training office (see *Resources*, p.311, for contact information) for referral to a practitioner in your area.

Solutions at a Glance: *Running Away and Bolting*

Body Exploration 151 ~ Clouded Leopard TTouch 195 ~ Tarantulas Pulling the Plow 203 Abalone TTouch 171 ~ Coiled Python Lift 172 ~ Lowering the Head 163 ~ Ear TTouches 210 Labyrinth 259 ~ Lindell Sidepull 286 ~ Tellington Training Bit 290 ~ Promise Wrap 288 ~ Lick of the Cow's Tongue 177 ~ Mouth TTouch 182 ~ Octopus TTouch 200 ~ Front Leg Circles 174 Hind Leg Circles 175 ~ Tail TTouch 185 ~ Pelvic Tilt 222 ~ Neckline and Ground Driving 261

Short-Striding (not tracking up)

Most horses are considered to be "tracking up" if the hind foot travels a little farther than the print left by the front foot. The amount of overstride is influenced by breed and conformation as well as tempo and gait. At some gaits, such as a Western pleasure jog or the shortened, animated walk of a show American Saddlebred, you won't see an overstride at all. Nor would you expect the average Quarter Horse to have the same amount of overstride as the average Warmblood. And, an overstep is not part of the normal gait pattern at all for many gaited horse breeds.

However, most horses are considered to be short-striding when the hind footprint fails to overstep the front hoofprint at the ordinary walk and trot. Causes of short-striding include:

- Overcollection over long periods of time that shortens the muscles

- Tight muscles in the neck, shoulders, forearms, back, loins or gaskins

- A saddle that pinches and jams into the shoulders

- Too-tight girth or abrupt tightening of the cinch

- Undiagnosed lameness or chronic stiffness

- Medical condition, such as tying up, laminitis or navicular syndrome

If your horse has a medical condition that's affecting his stride or soundness, consult your veterinarian. TTouch can be helpful during recovery; see individual health listings starting on p. 127. If your horse has saddle or girth issues, these must first be addressed before TTouches can be effective.

Here we will focus on solutions for short-striding caused by tight muscles in the neck, shoulders, forearms, back, loins or gaskins.

Training Solutions

TTouches

• Do *Inch Worm* on the crest and loins and *Lying Leopard TTouches* with *Coiled Python Lifts* on the forearm and gaskin muscles. Doing these TTouches through hot towels in these areas will enhance their effects. If the shoulder muscles are sore, a cold towel may be more effective. Observe your horse to see if he seems to prefer heat or cold.

• If the crest of the neck is tight, add *Mane Slides*, *Neck Rocking* and *Shoulder Release* to free up the neck and lengthen the stride. Do *Front* and *Hind Leg Circles* to encourage tight muscles to release.

Ground Exercises

• Practice *Half-Walk* from the ground, then mounted, with the horse's head up slightly, then give the horse a free head and let him stretch out. Measure the length of overstride before and after doing the *Half-Walk*. You are looking for how far the hind hoofprint oversteps the print of the front foot. The best way to see the prints clearly is to rake an area of level footing in your arena.

• The *Tellington Training Bit* can be an effective tool for lengthening stride on a longe line without a rider. Tie the reins around the neck, put your horse on the longe with a halter over the bridle and observe any difference in tracking. In many cases, simply wearing the bit frees up the joints and lengthens stride. This counters the commonly held belief that the rider must drive the horse with the seat to lengthen the stride.

Ridden Work

• *Promise Wrap* or *Promise Rope*—experiment to see which is more effective in influencing the horse to round the back, allowing him to engage his hindquarters and lengthen the stride. For best results, do this after the TTouches and *Leg Circles* have done their job.

Solutions at a Glance: *Short-Striding*

Inch Worm 197 ~ Lying Leopard TTouch 181 ~ Coiled Python Lift 172 ~ Mane and Forelock Slides 198 ~ Neck Rocking 199 ~ Shoulder Release 225 ~ Half-Walk 280 ~ Front Leg Circles 174 Hind Leg Circles 175 ~ Tellington Training Bit 290 ~ Promise Wrap and Rope 288 ~ Abalone TTouch 171

Shying ("spooky")

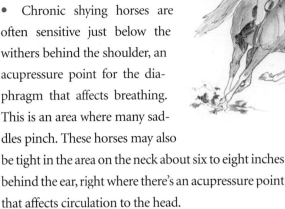

You and your horse are trotting smoothly down a familiar trail, leading a group of riders. You're feeling at one with your horse, nature and the world when *BOOM!* your horse leaps violently to the side with no warning. You're not sure whether to reprimand or soothe him, so for now you simply trot forward. But, your hands take up a little more rein this time, and your legs stay a little closer to the barrel.

Many horses habitually spook from certain objects—barking dogs, mailboxes, bicycles, flapping plastic, the invisible "tiger" in the corner of the arena. Sometimes shying comes out of the blue, such as when a plastic bag blows in front of your horse on a windy day, a rabbit jumps out from the tree line or a hot-air balloon flies overhead. Some horses spook at things that other horses walk right by. Other horses shy only at specific items—a plant with broad, shiny leaves; the freshly fallen log.

Shying can spring from fear and tension; it can also be the result of playfulness or habit. In the case of some lines of Arabians, it might even be genetic. Lady Wentworth, the famous Arabian breeder, once wrote: "If they don't shy from a butterfly, they should be shot." For many generations in the desert, Arab horses needed to be extremely aware, as their rider's life was dependent on detecting any movement of an enemy on the horizon.

Since the horse's principal means of survival in the wild has been his vigilance and speed, his flight reflex has been fine-tuned for millennia to be prepared to escape at the first suggestion of a threat. *Horses who shy are often simply displaying a well-preserved flight reflex.* It is our job to teach our equine companions to override this ancient impulse by listening to the rider or simply stopping when he is unsure rather than running off.

Regardless of why horses shy, I have often found that they share one or more of these characteristics:

- Chronic shying horses are often sensitive just below the withers behind the shoulder, an acupressure point for the diaphragm that affects breathing. This is an area where many saddles pinch. These horses may also be tight in the area on the neck about six to eight inches behind the ear, right where there's an acupressure point that affects circulation to the head.

- Horses who habitually shy are often nervous about things around their feet. The more connected they get to the ground, the more confidence they gain.

SECRET TO SUCCESS: VISUALIZE!

As you work with your horse, be sure to picture what you want your horse to do—*change the image in your mind.* If there is a particular place that your horse shies, make a clear picture of your horse walking or trotting quietly on by.

Training Solutions

TTouches

Spooky horses are often tense in the neck and back so begin with *Lowering the Head* and some TTouches for Trust: *Ear TTouches, Troika TTouch* and *Lick of the Cow's Tongue.* To ground your horse and develop confidence, stroke the front legs with the wand and do *Coiled Python Lifts, Octopus TTouches* and *Front* and *Hind Leg Circles. Hoof Tapping* is a good way to end a TTouch session.

Ground Exercises

Exercises from Playground for Higher Learning, especially *Work with Plastic Sheets, Tires, Pick-Up Sticks* and the *Platform,* will reduce tension and develop trust, making your horse safer and more confident.

Set up a situation using different surfaces—such as *plastic*, *plywood* and *cardboard*—in a controlled environment in which your horse can learn to trust and be obedient (not just putting up with doing things). For example, if your horse believes there are unseen monsters in a corner of the indoor arena, set a shallow rubber tub there with grain at chest level to your horse. The eating will help to override the fear. Setting up the *Labyrinth* in these parts of the arena can also be helpful.

Ridden Work

If you're the type who prefers to solve problems from the horse's back, or who enjoys the thrill of the spook and just wants to take the edge off, or your horse is one who shies mainly from playful exuberance, you will find the following under-saddle tips to be effective.

• Introduce your horse to a variety of troublesome objects in a controlled situation. By first leading him through the various obstacles of the

Playground for Higher Learning (p. 250)—from the ground, you'll find that his spookiness will subside and his confidence will soar. Then, ride through the Playground obstacles.

• Ride with the *Balance Rein*. Horses who shy often become even more reactive if the rider tightens the reins to try and prevent or control the shy. Using the *Balance Rein*, you don't have to take a hold on the mouth. The *Tellington Training Bit* will steady your horse (and yourself) while keeping his back up and head down.

• Use a *Promise Wrap*, tied from the cinch ring or latigo on a Western saddle or the back billet strap on an English saddle. Fit the wrap just below the point of the buttocks under the horse's tail with enough stretch so that it won't slide up or down. Be careful not to make it too snug. Before mounting with the wrap in place, lead your horse in hand, without a rider, at a walk and trot to make sure he's comfortable with the wrap. The *Promise Wrap* helps keep a horse connected from front end to back, encouraging engagement from behind, and is very useful for horses who are nervous about movement behind them. You may get a few strange looks from passersby, but the difference in your horse's confidence can be significant.

Turnaround Tale

Rex, a five-year-old Haflinger, was brought to one of my two-week courses in Germany in 1978. The horse was described as too dangerous to ride in the woods because he would shy and bolt at any flapping object. We put him through the whole Playground course and his greatest challenge was the exercise over, between and under plastic sheets. By the end of the two weeks he had gained so much confidence that we could ride him with plastic hanging over his hindquarters with no fear. Years later, I received a letter from the owner that Rex was 24, still going strong and completely safe.

- It may be hard to imagine, but working in a safe environment with the *Liberty Neck Ring*—at first, with your bridle reins hanging on the neck for security—can work wonders, but of course, only after you've done your homework from the ground. I've ridden many horses in clinics who were extremely spooky with a bridle on, and totally steady once everything was removed from their head.

Solutions at a Glance: *Shying*

Lowering the Head 163 ~ Ear TTouches 210 ~ Troika TTouch 188 ~ Lick of the Cow's Tongue 177 ~ Coiled Python Lift 172 ~ Octopus TTouch 200 ~ Front Leg Circles 174 ~ Hind Leg Circles 175 ~ Hoof Tapping 196 ~ Work with Plastic Sheets 265 ~ Tires 274 ~ Pick-Up Sticks 253 ~ Platform 269 ~ Labyrinth 259 ~ Balance Rein 279 ~ Tellington Training Bit 290 Promise Wrap 288 ~ Liberty Neck Ring 282

"Spray-Phobic"

Many horses respond to unfamiliar situations by attempting flight. When they can't flee, they fight. As a result, these horses throw up their heads and tighten the back when "attacked" by a spray bottle or hose. Adding to their panic is the fact that they are usually restrained, either by cross-ties or in a wash rack.

The conventional approach is often to jerk on the lead shank, tie the horse tightly or simply yell at the horse. More often than not, this results in more resistance and body tension. In addition, if the horse is on a slick surface like cement, there is a great risk of the horse slipping and falling.

The Tellington approach is to educate the horse to trust you and expect a positive experience when he sees a spray bottle or hose appear. You can teach him to override the fear response using secure boundaries and a small amount of food. As the act of chewing releases calming hormones from the parasympathetic nervous system, helping the horse to override the flight-or-fight reflex.

Training Solutions

❶ *Taming the Tiger* provides an effective and safe means of overriding the fight-or-flight reflex. The

secret to success is that the horse is contained—he can't go back, sideways or forward—yet you can "give" to him. Hold the ends of the two leads in your left hand near the shoulder (if the horse is really reactive about this, have someone hold him during the first session). If necessary, have your helper hold a rubber feed tub at the horse's chest level with a little grain or hay, as eating will encourage him to breathe and keep his head lower.

❷ Turning your body slightly so the sound is muffled, spray a cloth lightly with plain water and wipe the horse on the neck with the dampened cloth. Next, invite him to turn his head back and take a little nibble from your hand. Then stroke the horse with the bottle on the neck, followed by a light spray on the least-threatened part of his body, most likely the neck. (Pay attention to what's in the bottle; start with plain water or even add a few drops of Rescue Remedy or other flower essence to help the horse overcome his fear—see *Resources*, p. 311.)

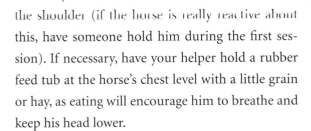

❸ If it's the hose your horse is fearful of, stay in *Taming the Tiger*, making sure you have a wall or safe fence on one side and behind the horse. Holding the leads in your left hand as before, turn the hose on lightly and run some water on the ground away from your horse so that you are between the horse and the hose. Let it run for a short time on the ground, then turn it off and bring it up to the shoulder or chest. Don't hose the feet or ankles at first; this may scare or tickle him. Turn the water back on and run the hose down the shoulder, while giving him a small treat.

If your horse doesn't like the sensation of water dripping down the legs—many mares especially are ticklish between their hind legs—take a few moments to prepare him with *Lying Leopard TTouches* with *Coiled Python Lifts* all down the legs. Wipe the legs down with a sponge so the water doesn't drip and tickle them. You can also place a wet towel on a leg and then run water from the hose through the towel.

If you teach your horse to turn around each time for a small horse cookie or carrot bite, it won't take long before he knows that something good will happen each time you spray or hose. Your horse gets a reward, and the action of chewing is overriding the flight reflex. It's amazing how little time it really takes to shift this behavior from reaction to acceptance.

Solutions at a Glance: "Spray-Phobic"

Taming the Tiger 166 ~ Lying Leopard TTouch 181 ~ Coiled Python Lift 172

Stallion Behavior, inappropriate ("studdy")

You've just settled in to the campground, picket-lined your mare and are filling her hay net when you notice your neighbor's horse. A muscular bay, he has his eye on your mare. He is making some noise and pawing the ground, and as you size up the situation, there is no question that he is a stallion. You wonder what to do: Should you pack up and move to another part of the campground, or say something to the stallion's handler?

What's going on? In a nutshell, testosterone, which produces behavior natural to a stallion in a breeding situation—erection, vocalizing, and striking out. Sometimes people simply ignore the behavior or run the horse in a small circle; more often you'll see the handler whipping the penis, kicking the horse in the belly or sharply reprimanding him for dropping, vocalizing or striking. While some of these human responses are, in my opinion, abusive, allowing these behaviors around other horses and people is potentially dangerous, and at the very least, bad mannered.

Any stallion that appears in public, such as at a show or trail ride, should be well-mannered and obedient. This means not trumpeting or even nickering while under saddle or in hand, not dropping the penis or acting "studlike." The key to attaining this behavior starts with good ground manners and a *lot* of handling—not just locking the horse in an isolated stall away from other horses and activity to be brought out just for breeding.

Training Solutions

• Place the stallion into *Taming the Tiger* (which we originally developed for handling dangerous, aggressive stallions). This position gives you control without force, while keeping you safe. Then, do *Lying Leopard TTouches* with *Coiled Python Lifts* all over the body. These will release instinctive responses triggered by contact, reduce tension, and increase the horse's ability to listen and learn. *Raccoon TTouches* on a tight chin will release tension and a tendency to resistance. These and other TTouches for Trust (p. 168) on the head, neck, shoulders, legs, back, girth, barrel and hindquarters can result in a more calm, confident, obedient and cooperative stallion.

Note: If you do the TTouches slowly, a stallion may relax too much and drop his penis, getting an erection that will excite him. So make your circles faster, a little deeper and move crisply from area to area.

- It's important for a young stallion to have the experience of socialization with other colts as a yearling and two-year-old, even if only for a few months in a bachelor herd pasture environment. In many cases in our modern way of keeping horses, however, this is simply not possible. Working young stallions in hand over the Playground for Higher Learning (p. 250), ideally in the presence of other horses, can lay the groundwork for a safe, well-adjusted, well-mannered adult. The youngster learns to concentrate while he works beside, past and around other horses who are also paying attention to the various obstacles. The *Half-Walk* in the *Labyrinth* gives boundaries and teaches focus, especially an easily distracted stallion. Working over the *Platform* and through *Pick-Up Sticks* and *Plastic Sheets* will teach manners and develop a good working relationship.

- *Journey of the Homing Pigeon* is effective with the horse who crowds his handler, or nips at the chain. By keeping a four-foot distance between two handlers and the horse, you avoid the potentially dangerous situation when a lone handler has to elbow a stallion in the shoulder to keep him from crowding him. This action can trigger a stallion's reflexes to bite or strike when provoked in this way.

- Preparing a stallion with *Mouth TTouches* before you take him to his first show will help avoid unwanted behavior like dropping the penis, which leads to overstimulation and control issues. At home, teach him to *Lower the Head*, give you his attention, and allow you to tap the roof of his mouth while you hold his head steady with one hand on the halter. Almost like magic, this technique will encourage most stallions to retract the penis.

Turnaround Tale

An Arab stallion who would bite, kick and squeal while being groomed was brought to a seven-day training. He had lived in a stall isolated at the end of the stable and was only brought out for breeding. No wonder he developed these habits! Within a couple of days of bodywork in Taming the Tiger, he started connecting with us and getting over his fear and oversensitivity in the body.

Next, we brought him into the arena in Journey of the Homing Pigeon. At first, he could not step over even a single pole because he was so high-headed and tight in the body. After four days with creative obstacle work, making a "V" for him to walk between with only a six-inch separation where the poles came together, he could step over a series of poles relaxed enough to stand quietly while other horses were worked around him.

Solutions at a Glance: *Stallion Behavior, inappropriate*

Taming the Tiger 166 ~ Lying Leopard TTouch 181 ~ Coiled Python Lift 172 ~ Mouth TTouch 182 ~ Raccoon TTouch 213 ~ Journey of the Homing Pigeon 241 ~ Labyrinth 259 ~ Half-Walk 280 ~ Pick-Up Sticks 253 ~ Work with Plastic Sheets 265 ~ Lowering the Head 163

Stiff Laterally (doesn't bend well in one direction)

Just like humans, horses are often less flexible in one direction, most often to the right since we tend to lead and handle and mount them more from the left side. In hopes of improving lateral flexion, it's common for a rider to turn the horse's nose back repeatedly to touch the stirrup, and many Western trainers tie the head back to the stirrup. Repetitive head-turning, however, can cause muscle soreness and stiffness through the poll, neck and back and does not necessarily increase flexibility.

These methods can lead to a "bad attitude" and a sour, uncooperative mount. Some horses even begin to look for ways to resist tipping the nose back while in motion by "popping" a shoulder. How often have you seen a nonplussed rider, her horse heading off in one direction with the nose tipped back toward the stirrup? These horses don't know how to move forward in a straight line.

You can increase lateral flexion or teach a horse to bend evenly in both directions, often in a single five-minute session if your horse already has TTouch preparation, without the risk of creating the undesirable habits that can accompany conventional approaches.

I adapted this exercise from the teachings of a nineteenth century dressage master, James Fillis, who was known for his amazing ability to influence a horse's balance in order to do such exercises as canter on three legs and trot backward. I learned this head-turning technique, which Fillis did using a double bridle (curb bit and bradoon), from his book when I was 12 years old and have been using it ever since in a much simpler form.

Training Solutions

• Your horse should already know about *Lowering the Head,* and accept *Lying Leopard TTouches* over the entire face and *Inch Worm* over the crest.

If the neck is extremely tight or your horse reacts to being touched on the face, prepare for *Neck Bending* with *Lowering the Head, Lying Leopard TTouches* all over the face, *Inch Worm, Neck Release, Neck Rocking* and *Shoulder Release.*

• As you stand to one side of the head, place your fingers in *Bear TTouch* in the middle of the neck about eight inches behind the ears. Press into the neck with one hand as you use the noseband to signal him to turn his head back toward you.

• Begin by asking for a *very small movement* in the direction that's easiest for your horse, then return the head to the centerline. Do this two or three times in the easy direction, then ask in the other direction. Keep the centerline of the nose perpendicular to the ground if you can.

Turnaround Tale

At the Paralympics in Atlanta in the early 1990s, we had a group of 11 practitioners working on all of the horses of 16 countries represented. The horses were donated and not all were well trained for the dressage competition. The Irish team could find only three horses suitable for their riders, giving them the minimal number eligible for the team competition. Unfortunately one of those horses was impossibly stiff to the left. It's at times like this that the Tellington Method can work miracles. Practitioner Kirsten Henry saved the day with one 30-minute session on the horse, using Neck Bending, Rib Release, Shoulder Release and Back Lifts combined with Lick of the Cow's Tongue. With only this one session the horse could bend correctly to the left and the Irish won a team award.

• These small movements help release muscles in the upper neck and prepare your horse to turn the head back easily. If you turn too far at first, the neck will come off the centerline, putting more weight over one front leg, causing your horse to move or brace himself.

• Be sure you are standing balanced with your feet slightly apart, and keep a clear visual image as you ask your horse to bring his head back with a light signal. Your horse may surprise you by turning his head and looking back toward his tail almost on his own. As long as you are clear and balanced, most horses "get it" within minutes.

To increase your horse's lateral flexion and overall suppleness, add the following Ground Exercises and TTouches to your daily routine for two weeks:

• *Back Lifts:* to release the neck muscles

• *Journey of the Homing Pigeon*: to reduce one-sidedness

• *Rib Releases:* to allow suppleness and flexion throughout the body rather than just in the neck

• *Leading and mounting from the right side*: to increase awareness and awaken neural connections on the right side

Solutions at a Glance: *Stiff Laterally*

Lowering the Head 163 ~ Lying Leopard TTouch 181 ~ Inch Worm 197 ~ Bear TTouch 217 Neck Release 221 ~ Neck Rocking 199 ~ Rib Release 224 ~ Neck Bending 219 ~ Shoulder Release 225 ~ Back Lift 193 ~ Lick of the Cow's Tongue 177 ~ Journey of the Homing Pigeon 241

Stubborn

Definition of "stubborn": *obstinate; difficult to handle or work; resistant; contrary.*

A horse may be labeled as "stubborn" if he is ring or barn sour, "balky," hard to catch or load on a trailer, or won't pick up his feet—basically, any situation in which the horse resists doing what you ask him to do. There are numerous causes for stubborn behavior: inadequate training, overwork, pain, unclear aids and inadequate riding skills, to name a few.

Rather than "getting after him," try to look at things from the animal's perspective. In my experience, these are the major reasons for a stubborn horse:

❶ The rider is not giving the horse clear signals.

❷ The horse has learned that certain behaviors elicit desired responses; for example, going back to

the barn. Such behavior may be caused by the horse or rider's lack of experience or confidence.

❸ The horse has pain, soreness or discomfort.

If you approach your horse's stubbornness with equal obstinacy, you'll often create more resistance. You have a choice of getting in a fight and thinking that you're going to be able to overpower him, or you can decide to use your brains instead of your limited brawn, and find ways to influence the horse's mind.

You have a choice: attempting to overpower the horse; or finding a way of relating to him in a way he wants to work with you and trusts you, and accepts your leadership role. This is the essence of the Tellington Method.

When working with a stubborn horse, we often have to confront our own inflexibility. Are you willing to try new solutions, to take a step back and think? When you reach a point of resistance, instead of pushing hard, are you willing to stop and ask yourself, "How can I make this easier for the horse and myself?"

One of the core messages of the Tellington Method is learning to be flexible and look for new solutions that are safe and that will carry through in other parts of your life.

Training Solutions

TTouches

Do *Mouth TTouches,* sliding your fingers back and forth on the gums to soften resistance and shut-down emotions. *Lowering the Head, Ear TTouches* and connected *Coiled Python Lifts* all over the body will establish a connection between you that leads to trust and willingness to work.

Ground Exercises

Head for the Playground for Higher Learning (p. 250) and its variety of brain-stimulating Ground Exercises to give your horse more behavioral choices, so he'll be willing to follow your lead instead of having his own agenda. Just getting out the whip and spurs can often cause a bigger battle, and you could lose. Using your brain instead of your brawn is safer and more effective in so many cases, and you and your horse will both feel good in the end.

Teaching the Ground Exercises will show your horse how to learn and cooperate. When you set up the situation in a controlled manner, where both you and your horse can be successful, you really change the expectation, for you both. The more you can expand your horse's ability to cooperate in a controlled situation, the more he will cooperate in all situations.

COULD IT BE SOMETHING PHYSICAL?

If your horse's behavior changes unexpectedly, consider the possibility of trouble spots, such as a sore back in a jumper or bruised soles in an endurance horse.

A typical example was a very attractive Icelandic gelding I was asked to evaluate in Germany, recently purchased by a student. The horse had wonderful gaits, but would rear or bolt when asked for a turn to the right. He was labeled "stubborn" by his frustrated owner. An exploration of his body with my fingertips failed to find any sensitive areas in the back or neck that could have triggered this behavior. I then checked his mouth and found sharp hooks on his back teeth. An equine veterinary dentist found raw open sores in his cheeks from chewing with razor-sharp back molars. Once the gelding's teeth were floated, he became the cooperative, brilliant saddle horse my student thought she had purchased. To rule out other causes of stubborn behavior, see chapter 2, *A Closer Look at the Roots of Unwanted Behavior and Poor Attitude.*

With exercises such as *Work with Plastic Sheets* and the *Platform,* you can set up situations you can control from the ground and orchestrate the learning so that it's "chunked" into baby steps. Working your horse through the *Labyrinth, Teeter-Totter, Pick-Up Sticks* and the *Cavalletti* in leading positions like the *Joyful Dolphin,* along with a variety of TTouches for Trust and Awareness (pp. 168 and 190), for a period of 10 minutes a day will generally produce a change in attitude. Be sure you are clear with your cues and your intention, and visualize your success.

Stumbling

Your horse is trotting along nicely on even ground when, without warning, he trips and almost falls to his knees. Fortunately, he catches himself and goes on. My own Arabs would never miss a step in the rocks, but on the flat they often tended to look off into the distance and sometimes stumble.

Stumbling is not uncommon in young horses still finding their balance, horses whose toes are too long or feet not correctly trimmed, and horses who have a touch of osteoarthritis. Horses can trip when they are not paying attention to where they are putting their feet or if they travel heavy on the forehand. Conformation and carriage can play a role; for example, long or dropped backs and ewe necks can contribute to stumbling.

Horses who aren't yet strong enough to carry the rider in self-carriage are more likely to stumble, especially where the footing changes. Other frequent stumblers include horses who are high-headed, nervous or flighty.

First, rule out foot, saddle-fit and medical issues. Have your farrier and veterinarian collaborate to be sure your horse's feet are balanced both medial-laterally and longitudinally. Rolling or "rockering" the toes can help the horse break over more easily. In addition, shortening the toe can take the pressure off the coffin bone and equalize the concussive forces. Saddles that pinch or are set too far forward often cause stumbling.

Some horses who chronically stumble or who have trouble turning in small circles may have a neurological disorder such as Wobbler's syndrome or EPM. If you suspect your horse may have a medical reason for his lack of coordination, consult your veterinarian.

Horses with upright or tight shoulders, long backs, or heavy forearm muscling may be more prone to stumbling. I've seen exceptionally heavily muscled, hardworking older Quarter Horses with tight muscles in the forearm and gaskin who were particularly prone to stumbling. They simply could not pick up their feet cleanly due to the limitation of their tight, heavy muscles.

The following exercises can be very effective in helping a horse who stumbles to move in a more balanced manner and become a safer, more pleasurable mount.

Training Solutions

TTouches

- *Hoof Tapping* and stroking the legs with the wand increases a horse's awareness of his feet and lower legs.

- *Coiled Python Lifts* and *Octopus TTouches* increase circulation to the lower extremities, improving coordination and balance.

- *Lowering the Head* can help a high-headed, tense horse watch where he is going and improve his proprioceptive ability.

Ground Exercises

- *The Fan* will improve your horse's temporal-spatial ability and encourage him to lower his head and pick up his feet cleanly.

- *Pick-Up Sticks* will help your horse pay careful attention to where he places his feet. He'll be better able to handle uneven terrain by learning to places each foot with precision.

Ridden Work

- The *Tellington Training Bit* and *Balance Rein* help to shift the horse's center of gravity back to keep him off the forehand and prevent stumbling.

- The *Promise Wrap* helps your horse engage the hindquarters and be more balanced on uneven terrain.

- *Pick-Up Sticks* helps him put it all together as you ride him through the jumbled poles.

Note: Most important in the event of a stumble is to take up the reins instantly and keep your weight back. This rein support can prevent a devastating somersault that could seriously injure both horse and rider.

Solutions at a Glance: *Stumbling*

Tellington Training Bit 290 ~ Balance Rein 279 ~ Promise Wrap 288 ~ Hoof Tapping 196 Coiled Python Lift 172 ~ Octopus TTouch 200 ~ Lowering the Head 163 ~ The Fan, Cavalletti and Pick-Up Sticks 253

Tail Clamping

see also *Fear of Movement or Objects Behind*

Many horses are fearful of movement or contact around their hindquarters and respond by tightening the tail and tensing their bodies. The result, if the unexpected occurs—such as catching a rope under the tail—can provoke bucking or bolting.

You can educate your horse so he won't clamp his tail should something become caught in or under it. It takes very little time to train your horse to accept handling the entire tail, including its underside. Your goal is to teach your horse to lift the tail quietly rather than clamp it in response to any stimulus. He'll then be able to override a tendency to flight or freeze, and to *stop and think* about the situation, rather than just react.

Preparing the horse to accept handling or touching the tail is useful in the following situations:

- Taking the temperature

- Wrapping the tail prior to shipping, breeding or foaling

- Accepting natural breeding, artificial insemination or rectal palpation

- Accepting a crupper

- Preventing your horse from scooting or bolting when he gets a branch caught in his tail

- Preventing your horse from clamping his tail over a rope while ground driving, longeing or ponying another horse

Oftentimes, however, people just ignore a clamped tail or force the tail up to set the crupper on. But, a horse might be eliminated from an endurance ride or event if the vets can't take his temperature, and for vets doing a rectal palpation, a clamped tail can be very uncomfortable for the vet and the mare, who is very tense and often unpredictable in such a situation.

Over the years, I've found that horses who habitually clamp their tails usually lack self-confidence; they're often low in the pecking order. It often takes only a few sessions to give such horses a new awareness, which seems to "reconnect" the horse's hindquarters and tail to the rest of his body. In the process, not only will your horse become more accepting of the above situations, but often his or her attitude will shift for the better. You can expect your horse's self-confidence—and standing in the pecking order—to go up markedly. And you can feel more secure knowing your horse will not be rattled by unexpected "snags" that arise on the trail.

Training Solutions

• If your horse is nervous around the hindquarters, spend time doing TTouches for Trust and Awareness (pp. 168 and 190) so that he accepts and enjoys being touched all over before doing *Tail TTouches*. Do connected *Clouded Leopard TTouches* over the buttocks area before working directly with the tail.

• Because horses who clamp their tails are often tense and nervous, they will benefit from *Ear TTouches,* connected *Lying Leopard TTouches, Lick of the Cow's Tongue, Zig-Zag TTouches* and *Tarantulas Pulling the Plow.*

• Do quiet, slow *Hair Slides* (see Photo 1 on p. 187) on the tail to relax a nervous horse. Start by taking a small clump of hair at the top of the tail and slide your fingers lightly down to the end of the tail. Continue doing the slides in a random fashion. Do the *Hair Slides* as lightly on your horse as you would like on yourself. It's commonly said that horses have no nerve endings in their manes and tails; however, it was once explained to me by a neurologist in one of my trainings that the horse's hair is actually an extension of the nervous system. So we are really affecting the whole horse when we do *Hair Slides.* Be sure to stand to the side where you are safe until your horse begins to relax and enjoy the slides. If

you have any sense that your horse might kick, work through the TTouches for Trust exercises until your horse trusts you and you feel safe.

• Using the fingertips of both hands, do a minute or so of tiny, circular *Raccoon TTouches* around the sides of the tail bone and sides of the buttocks until your horse relaxes and lifts the tail instead of clamping it. Most horses will begin to lift the tail within a few minutes; others may take a few sessions.

• Return to the top of the tail and pick up a small clump of hair. This time, lift the tail by the hair and circle the tail bone in both directions.

• Once your horse accepts the above work and voluntarily lifts the tail, lift the tail bone with both hands, curve it into an arch, and circle it slowly and gently in both directions between your two hands.

• While the tail is still raised, do a few *Clouded Leopard TTouches* on the underside of the dock to bring a new awareness to that area. As you begin working here, make sure you don't take the chance of getting your hand clamped under the tail!

Caution: If you have a horse with a tendency to kick or are working with a young horse without a lot of prior handling or an unknown history, do not stand directly behind him! Be sure to stand at a safe place where you can't be kicked, and work the horse from the side. If he is really clamping his tail, take a firm hold of the tail bone about 12 inches from the root, and pull the tail bone out of the tail groove to the side. This prevents clamping so you can begin to safely do the *Hair Slides.*

You can also put your horse into an elastic *Body Wrap,* first with stretchy polo wraps, then with a rope, to help your horse become comfortable with anything touching him.

Scenario: Wearing a Crupper

Your horse should readily lift his tail from the *Tail TTouches* you have done along with small circles under the tail. Place the unattached crupper under the lower part of the tail bone. As you work the crupper further up under the tail bone, have a helper give your horse a little bit of food. If you are working alone, have your horse turn back for the food reward.

When you put the crupper on for the first time, adjust it loosely. Do *Clouded Leopard TTouches* on the croup and walk and trot the horse in hand. If possible, take him up and down a few hills to let him feel the pressure. The first few times you ride with the crupper, reach back from the saddle while your horse is standing still and do some *Tiger TTouches* with one hand to release any tension.

Scenario: Preparing a horse to feel a rope under his tail

This training prepares a horse to "pony" another horse, as well as to being driven—both occasions when he needs to stay calm if a rope or line gets caught under his tail.

Once your horse is accustomed to the elastic *Body Wrap*, put a figure-eight rope (shown on p. 161) around the chest and hindquarters. Preferably with a helper at the head, start with the rope low just above the hocks, and bring it higher in small stages, giving your horse a little bite to eat with each step. Your helper can stroke the horse's chest and down the front legs with the wand as you work. Invite your horse to turn his head and neck back to take a little bit of food from you as he feels the rope coming up under the tail. You want him to respond by *lifting* the tail and relaxing the back muscles rather than clamping it, tightening the back and going into flight mode. This exercise, when done step-by-step slowly, is a great way to develop trust and keep you safe on the trail.

Solutions at a Glance: *Tail Clamping*

Clouded Leopard TTouch 195 ~ Tail TTouch 185 ~ Zig-Zag TTouch 206 ~ Tarantulas Pulling the Plow 203 ~ Raccoon TTouch 213 ~ Ear TTouches 210 ~ Lick of the Cow's Tongue 177 ~ Lying Leopard TTouch 181 ~ Body Wrap 160

Tail Switching/Wringing

• The dressage horse performing flying changes of leads wrings or switches his tail in an agitated fashion with each transition, thereby lowering his score.

• The jumper's tail circles like an airplane propeller as he flies over the jump, which may be viewed as humorous by unknowing spectators.

You may have seen one of the above scenarios and wondered about the cause. Back pain from an ill-fitting saddle, a too-tight cinch, sour attitude from fatigue and overdrilling, overzealous or unintentional spur or heel pressure, hypersensitivity to leg aids—all can trigger tail switching or wringing. All too often, the horse is punished for such "misbehavior" by working him even harder, tying the tail to the stirrup or even "clipping" the tail ligaments. Such misguided "solutions" fail to address the root cause of the problem.

Training Solutions

Tail switching may be the only way for a horse to express discomfort, frustration, or pain. Following are some suggestions that can reduce it if your horse is sour, sore, or overreactive to leg aids:

- **Sour attitude:** Add variety to your training routine and shorten your arena sessions; spend some time riding with the *Lindell Sidepull;* and give you and your horse some fun with *Bridleless Riding* in the *Liberty Neck Ring.*

- **Back pain:** Ten minutes a day of a combination of *Belly Lifts, Back Lifts, Lick of the Cow's Tongue, Coiled Python Lifts* and *Lying Leopard TTouches* on the back with *Tail TTouches* and *Pelvic Tilt* can help alleviate back pain. During riding sessions, include exercises to give the horse plenty of rein in order to stretch and relax the neck and back. Be sure to check the fit of your saddle and consider the tightness of your girth because this is so often an underlying source of such problems.

- **Oversensitivity to leg aids:** Do *Abalone TTouches* with *Coiled Python Lifts* over the entire belly and barrel area, using a sheepskin mitt if your horse is reactive to your hand in the beginning. When grooming, pay attention to your horse's reactions—overzealous grooming can contribute to the tail switching reaction to leg pressure. *Belly Lifts, Tarantulas Pulling the Plow* and *Tail TTouches* are also useful.

_____

Turnaround Tale

In a clinic in Toronto in 1981, I remember working with a high-headed, 12-year-old Warmblood gelding who literally scared himself when he switched his tail! He had a terrible reputation as the most difficult horse in the barn, was extremely aggressive and reactive to grooming or handling by a stranger, and only his rider could handle him. I was asked to work with the gelding for a TTouch demonstration. After observing the horse's behavior I was convinced he was aggressive out of fear, not an opinion shared by others in the stable. However, an hour of TTouches for Trust (p. 168) and work in the Labyrinth produced such a remarkable and unexpected transformation that my demonstration was still being talked about 20 years later.

_____

Solutions at a Glance: *Tail Switching/Wringing*

Lindell Sidepull 286 ~ Liberty Neck Ring 282 ~ Back Lift 193 ~ Lick of the Cow's Tongue 177
Coiled Python Lift 172 ~ Lying Leopard TTouch 181 ~ Tail TTouch 185 ~ Pelvic Tilt 222
Abalone TTouch 171 ~ Tarantulas Pulling the Plow 203 ~ Labyrinth 259 ~ Belly Lift 209

Tail, carrying to one side

This conformational quirk is most commonly seen in Arabs. Horses who carry their tail to one side are sometimes said to have tight muscles on one side of the back. While the source is unknown, it may have a genetic component that is not expressed until later in life. I don't consider crooked tails to be a health concern in Arabs or any other breed, although some may consider it to be a conformation flaw.

Training Solutions

- We've had success using all of the *Tail TTouches: Pearling, Arching, Circling, Pulling* and *Hair Slides.*

- *Lowering the Head, Neck Releases* and *Back Lifts* along with a variety of TTouches can help to release tension in the body. While it's easier to "reprogram" the nervous system of a foal (see p. 120), we've had enough successes with adult horses to encourage you to give it a go.

Turnaround Tale

I was asked to work on a three-day-old Warmblood foal who was born with his tail held distinctly to the left. His owner was concerned about his lack of energy—although not lethargic, he had yet to exhibit typical foal behavior of running and playing. She wondered whether his crooked tail might somehow be related to his lack of enthusiasm and energy.

I began with gentle Raccoon TTouches (number 2 pressure, see p. 148) all around the base of the tail, then continued with a few minutes of light Hair Slides, and Arching and Circling of the tail. I completed the first session, which lasted about five minutes, with Pearling and light Tail Pulls.

I gave the youngster a chance to integrate this session by allowing him to move freely around the stall for a few minutes. After a short break, I did another five minutes of Tail TTouches, this time with emphasis on Hair Slides. I finished by grasping the top of the tail securely with both hands, and minutely pushed it toward the spine followed by an equally tiny stretch back toward me. This gave the nervous system new information and options.

When I ended the session and released the foal, he surprised everyone present by blasting out of the stall door into his paddock, his mother excitedly following, and raced about, his tail held straight as an arrow. His "rudder" was finally working as it should, and it stayed that way.

Solutions at a Glance: *Tail, carrying to one side*

Tail TTouch 185 ~ Lowering the Head 163 ~ Neck Release 221 ~ Back Lift 193 ~ Raccoon TTouch 213

Tailgating

see also *Herdbound, Overcompetitive*

Your horse loses his cool when his buddy disappears around a bend in the trail, even for a few seconds. Suddenly, his head is in the clouds, a shrill whinny punctuates the air, and you can feel his entire body tense and tighten beneath you. You might even feel his heart pounding through the tack!

Riding such a horse can be unnerving as you're not sure whether to hold him back or let him go on and catch up. He may be ignoring your aids and reacting more off instinct than listening to you. Most horses with this behavior are perfectly happy to trot along with the group once they've caught up. (If your horse wants to pass and take the lead, see *Overcompetitive* on p. 90).

Horses afraid of being left behind are often quite insecure, tight in the neck and wary of movement behind them. Your goal is to help your horse learn to override his fear and hold back when you ask.

Training Solutions

TTouches

A combination of TTouches for Trust and the Playground for Higher Learning exercises (pp. 168 and 250) can be effective and create a bond that will reduce your mount's desperation when separated from another horse. *Ear TTouches*, connected *Clouded Leopard TTouches* all over the body, *Lick of* the Cow's Tongue and *Tail TTouches* will give you a good start.

Ground Exercises

Pick any four Playground for Higher Learning exercises that would be fun for you because they will all help to strengthen your relationship. Several sessions of *Neckline and Ground Driving* help to develop your horse's confidence and get him to focus on you.

Ridden Work

Begin with the arena exercises riding with a friend as described in *Herdbound* (p. 72), and later practice on the trail. Gradually extend the distance between you and the other horse, taking turns leading and following. Eventually, ask your friend to ride on ahead, around the bend and out of sight. Invite your horse to turn his head back for a treat so he will focus on you and not on the other horse going away.

Tellington Tip

Begin under saddle with the Balance Rein so you can hold your horse back without getting him "bunched up" and more tense by having to use a tight rein. (See Herdbound, p. 72, for details.)

Solutions at a Glance: *Tailgating*

Balance Rein 279 ~ Ear TTouches 210 ~ Clouded Leopard TTouch 195 ~ Lick of the Cow's Tongue 177 ~ Tail TTouch 185 ~ Neckline and Ground Driving 261

Tongue Biting, Sucking or "Lolling"

Tongue "lolling," sucking or biting is an unpleasant habit that is often a sign of physical or emotional stress. It can happen in a stall, in the pasture or during work. This undesirable habit can take many forms, from sticking the tongue out to pulling it way back into the mouth. Some horses bite or suck their tongues or "loll" them from side to side. Others combine this habit with pawing.

These habits might stem from overconfinement (no turnout, or not enough), and boredom from lack of socialization with other horses. Another source of stress is consistent collection with a tight rein and restrictive noseband, never allowing the horse to stretch his head, neck and back while being ridden. Rather than punishing the horse or tying the tongue in place, try to find the source of the habit and make a change, whether it's from a tight noseband or an ill-fitting bit.

Tongue lolling, sucking or biting can also come from dental problems, especially in young horses who have not shed their caps, or who have jagged teeth that have caused gum irritation. I once raised a Thoroughbred filly who started sticking her tongue out at six months of age. No other horse on the property did this. Her dam had very poor teeth, and this filly's teeth were as sharp as a shark's.

Training Solutions

TTouches

• *Mouth TTouches*, with emphasis on tapping the tongue. I once was called to work on a mare who had an extreme habit of lolling the tongue. Careful observation revealed tiny nerve and muscle tremors along the side of tongue up the side of the face all the way to the ear. The horse had been ridden with a heavy hand and tight cavesson at the upper levels of dressage. The previous owner wanted to have the tongue cut off so she would not be penalized in competition; the veterinarian refused to carry out this barbaric act, and asked me to look at her. I did several TTouch sessions on the mare, primarily *Lying Leopard TTouches* with *Coiled Python Lifts* all over the face along with *Ear TTouches* and *Inch Worm* on the crest to reduce the long-held tension she was carrying in her head, jaw, crest and neck. In addition, *Neck Releases* can also help discharge some of this tension. I believe the problem was initially caused by a very hard hand, a tight rein, and hours of overcollection on the bit.

Ridden Work

• Giving your horse a break by riding with the *Lindell Sidepull* can sometimes help, as can a *Tellington Training Bit* and *Balance Rein*. Keep the bottom rein loose and your hands soft; ride off the *Balance Rein* as much as possible.

• If your horse sticks his tongue out when you ride, tap the tongue or the side of the bit from the saddle with the wand to remind him to put it back in. The goal is not to punish but to send a reminder along with a clear visualization for the horse to change the behavior. Hold a picture in your mind of a quiet mouth instead of intensifying the habit of seeing him with his tongue out.

Solutions at a Glance: *Tongue Biting, Sucking or "Lolling"*

Mouth TTouch 182 ~ Lying Leopard TTouch 181 ~ Coiled Python Lift 172 ~ Ear TTouches 210 ~ Inch Worm 197 ~ Neck Release 221 ~ Lindell Sidepull 286 ~ Tellington Training Bit 290 Balance Rein 279

Vet, fear of the

Veterinarians (veterinary surgeons in the UK) do many things with horses that we might not adequately prepare them for during daily handling: taking the temperature, tubing, giving intramuscular and intravenous injections, performing rectal palpations, examining and treating wounds.

Although many vet visits are in the realm of "preventive maintenance," others may occur while the horse is under acute stress, as from an injury or illness. Many horses respond to the veterinarian by running backward until they hit the back of the stall or a fence. Often, their head is in the air, and neck muscles so rigid that a needle will bend and pop out. The horse may be so tense in the neck that the medication, vaccine, or nutraceutical will not be well absorbed and can create significant swelling.

Your goal is for your horse to become cooperative and trusting for the veterinarian. In some instances, the handler might grasp a few folds of loose skin at the junction of the shoulder and neck, or hold one front leg up. While these are acceptable when you "have" to get the job done, in the long run you and your horse will be better off investing in a few training sessions so that the horse will readily accept such handling. Of course, in the event of serious injury requiring deep cleaning and suturing, it may be necessary to twitch or tranquilize. (Contrary to what some horse owners believe, twitching does not hurt and can keep your vet and your horse safe.)

B-R-E-A-T-H-E

Any time you are working with your horse to change behavior, remember to *breathe* slowly. Your horses will "mirror" your breathing. Also keep a clear "picture" in your mind of how you *want* him to be, not what you *fear* him to be.

Training Solutions

• All horses who have any issues with the veterinarian or farrier will benefit from a few sessions in *Taming the Tiger*. This position works for horses with any type of fear or phobia on the ground. For best results, practice well before you have the need to call a vet out. When the vet arrives, keep your horse in *Taming the Tiger* to steady him, and stroke the neck, chest and front legs slowly and firmly with the wand. If he tries to run backward, tap his croup with the wand in the *Dingo*.

• Teach your horse to *Lower the Head* from a signal on the chain. If the horse is sensitive, hurting or afraid, run the chain up the side of the halter instead of over the nose. If the horse will not stand still, put the chain over the nose and stroke the wand on the underside of the neck, and down the chest and front legs to calm and ground him.

• In a research study done for a Ph.D. thesis by Dr. M. Cecelia Wendler at the University of Wisconsin-Eau Claire, Tellington Touch significantly reduced the level of anxiety in soldiers coming in for their "shots." Since many horses are "needle-phobic," before giving any injection in the muscle, do six or seven *Clouded Leopard TTouch* circles to give the feeling of the needle around the injection site to prepare and relax the muscles. A minute or so of *Raccoon TTouches* after the injection will improve absorption and prevent swelling at the injection site.

Continue doing *Clouded Leopard TTouches* and *Ear TTouches* with the head lowered while the vet is working in the sensitive area.

If your horse fears intramuscular (IM) shots in the neck, place the chain or Zephyr lead up the side of the halter, lower the head, and prepare him with *Inch Worm* on the crest of the neck along with upward *Mane Slides*, *Ear TTouches* and the varied pressures of *Clouded Leopard* and *Bear TTouches* with *Sponge TTouches*.

• If your vet has to do some maneuvering in a delicate area such as under the eyelid, first do some light circles behind the ears to lower the neck to level position. Then use *Ear TTouches* and *Raccoon TTouches* around the sensitive areas of the eye.

Tellington Tip

To overcome fear of a specific veterinarian, do Ear TTouches and Lowering the Head while that person is nearby. Include Lying Leopard TTouches on the face, forehead and jowl. If possible, have the veterinarian do the TTouches on the horse at the same time as you.

Solutions at a Glance: *Vet, fear of the*

Taming the Tiger 166 ~ Dingo 235 ~ Lowering the Head 163 ~ Clouded Leopard TTouch 195 Ear TTouches 210 ~ Raccoon TTouch 213 ~ Bear TTouch 217 ~ Sponge TTouch 203 Lying Leopard TTouch 181 ~ Mane and Forelock Slides 198

Walk, too slow

see also *Lazy, Stumbling*

Your horse is sluggish under saddle and he always seems to lag behind your riding companions. You're constantly being forced to trot to catch up. Typically, "lazy" horses are encouraged to go faster by intensifying the aids or using a crop or spurs. But many horses develop a slow walk because the rider is always banging on them with the legs and heels until the horse is dull to the signals. This is very common in school horses.

Tellington Tip

Here's a tip for lengthening stride and speeding up a "pokey" horse that works immediately on at least 50 percent of the horses: attach the Promise Rope about eight inches above the hocks. Tie a knot in the rope so it has more weight and swings from side to side with each stride.

Horses who are sluggish under saddle usually have not learned to respond to leg aids or have been allowed to develop a "pokey" walk. If your usually free-moving horse suddenly becomes sluggish and blocked, he may be in need of chiropractic care as well. Another consideration when he is lackluster is to make sure that the horse's health is in order—there are times when you may be dealing with a physical condition such as a low red cell count, not enough feed for the work or not the right vitamin/mineral balance. If you suspect there is a health issue, play it safe and have a blood panel run by your vet.

Training Solutions

• Begin from the ground in the *Dingo* position, teaching your horse to come forward with circular taps on the croup: starting at a slow walk, a medium

walk and then really walk on with energetic encouragement from the light, quick, circular tapping of the wand. Tapping the croup with a flick of the wrist encourages forward impulsion as opposed to tapping down, which makes the horse tense the croup muscle and further limit length of stride.

Once the horse learns to go forward with more energy and engagement from the hind legs from your ground signals, you're ready to ride. Tap the loin lightly just behind the saddle, instead of using the crop behind your leg. There is something about this area—located at the sacro-lumbar junction—that forms the coiling of the quarters and the energetic origin of each stride. To further encourage forward motion, tap the wand on the shoulder and hip in a metronomic rhythm in concert with the stride.

MEDICAL NOTE

If your horse is *dragging* his toes, *stumbling* or *tripping*, you may be dealing with a *subluxation* (partial dislocation) that should be checked by your veterinarian to rule out a more serious neurological condition such as Wobbler's Syndrome or EPM. You can supplement veterinary treatment with Tellington TTouches. For example, you can bring awareness over the back and croup and down the legs with *Connected Circles*. The *Body Wrap* and *Front* and *Hind Leg Circles* activate new neural pathways that can give the horse ability to move in a new way. For more information, contact Tellington TTouch Training for the booklet, *TTEAM as a Complement in the Rehabilitation of Horses with Neurological Deficits* (see *Resources*, p. 311).

Solutions at a Glance: *Walk, too slow*

Dingo 235 ~ Promise Rope 288 ~ Connected Circles 173 ~ Body Wrap 160 ~ Front Leg Circles 174 ~ Hind Leg Circles 175

Weaving, Pacing, Stall Walking

Horses are herd animals and have been so for millennia. This type of social structure provided stability as well as safety in the wild. However, in modern times, most horses are kept separated from each other for many reasons, including their value, scarcity of land, and sometimes, their caretakers simply not realizing the importance of maintaining social contact and interaction.

Horse people who design facilities so that their horses can live in herds—or at the very least see each other and touch noses—have happier and healthier horses. When horses are turned out together, they can groom each other, scratch and rub on trees, and roll in the dirt or sand. When we deprive them of that environment, we strip away their natural behavior and invite problems—stall weaving, nipping, casting, cribbing—collectively known as "stable vices."

Training Solutions

• You can release tension in the horse's body with the TTouches listed on p. 126. Although you can help a horse with these habits, for humane treatment of animals, you must also consider changing his surroundings. Ideally, he should get out with other horses for several hours a day to touch noses, If this isn't possible, at least have him in a paddock adjacent to another horse.

• Stallions, who are often isolated, need to be in a place where they can at least maintain visual contact with other horses. You can separate them from other horses with a double fence. Being able to see activities through a window or in an arena where there is lots going on adds important stimulation to a stabled animal. Installing a stall guard or screen in place of a solid door so that he can look out and feel part of the daily life in the barn is another possibility.

• Many stalls are made isolated by solid walls and doors. This setup results in little or no visual or tactile stimulation. Think *enrichment*. For example,

MIRROR, MIRROR IN THE STALL

Research from the Animal Behavior, Cognition and Welfare Group at the Lincolnshire School of Agriculture in England sheds (or reflects) new light on stall weavers. When researchers placed acrylic mirrors in the stalls, every one of the horses stopped weaving. Some had been chronic weavers for up to six years. The horses turned and faced the mirrors for about one quarter of the time they were in the stall.

For years I have suggested putting murals in barns with pictures of green meadows and trees. If you have a stall weaver in your barn, the mirror is worth a try, but be sure to use a non-breakable acrylic material, not glass! We'd love to hear from you if you give this a try.

when you are building a stable, design it with see-through partitions instead of solid wood extending from floor to ceiling. It is so much nicer for horses when the stalls are at least 12 by 12 feet. Make sure the footing is supportive to the health of the legs and use adequate bedding. Stall mats are really worthwhile: they prevent a horses that paces back and forth from digging a furrow along the front of the stall.

• In the stall itself, make sure there is enough light, and arrange it so your horse can see others across the aisle. If your horse is a weaver, put in a racehorse-type screen with a cut-out place for the head to come out. This is preferable to a standard stall guard, since it is harder to weave.

• Add music—studies have shown that soothing classical music lowers animals' pulse and respiration. When I placed a tiny cassette player onto the halter of a stall-walking stallion in Germany, he stopped his pacing, and you could see a change in his eyes with the music playing. You can relax or stimulate any horse as needed, and music supports the immune system.

• Flower essences have also been shown to rebalance the emotions of animals. One such product, *Essence of Nature* (see *Resources*, p. 311) was developed specifically for the animal who is confined to an artificial environment. It brings the "essence of nature" indoors.

• Ride or drive your horse more, and practice Ground Exercises to stimulate his mind and body, such as the *Labyrinth, Freework, Pick-Up Sticks, Teeter-Totter* and *Platform.* "Dance with your horse" and practice *The Statue* and *Glide of the Eagle.*

• Remember, any TTouch that you do will help take the place of contact with other horses, as in mutual grooming.

• Experiment with some of the innovative horse toys now available, such as cubes with bits of food inside or other items that can engage the horse's attention in a constructive way.

Solutions at a Glance: *Weaving, Pacing, Stall Walking*

Abalone TTouch 171 ~ Coiled Python Lift 172 ~ Octopus TTouch 200 ~ Labyrinth 259 Freework 257 ~ Pick-Up Sticks 253 ~ Teeter-Totter 273 ~ Platform 269 ~ The Statue 248 Glide of the Eagle 246

Selected Health Topics

SELECTED HEALTH TOPICS

While the Tellington Method is never intended to replace veterinary care, it gives you a way to help your horse be more comfortable until your veterinarian arrives. In many cases where emergency care was not available, using TTouch has been lifesaving—as attested to by hundreds of case reports we at Tellington Training have received over the last 25 years.

The connection between health and behavior may not always seem obvious. However, there are often underlying physical reasons for "unexplainable" behavioral changes. A suddenly "psychotic" mare may have an ovarian cyst or tumor; a horse who, out of the blue, begins bucking may have a painfully sore neck or back; a usually mild-mannered animal who becomes resentful of even the most sensitive handling and care may have a thyroid or muscle disorder.

Even when a healthy horse is exposed to new conditions—such as changes in feed, or a new barn, new trainer or new saddle—he may become nervous, "ungrounded" or flighty. Such a horse is showing you that he is stressed! Stress contributes to colic, laminitis, gastric ulcers, tying up and even shock.

With the Tellington Method in your daily routine, you will foster an emotionally and mentally sound horse able to handle stressors— such as shipping, training and competition—in stride. Owners, trainers, breeders and veterinarians worldwide have also found the Tellington Method to be helpful in many health-related situations, including:

- humane restraint making working on a horse safer for the horse and handlers

- part of emergency or chronic care

- stress reduction and injury prevention in performance and pleasure horses

On the following pages you'll find recommendations for dealing with eight acute and chronic health conditions:

Choke

Your horse is quietly eating dinner when you hear a disconcerting sound. You find him with head extended, neck rigid, and liquefied food may be spurting from the nostrils. Your horse is suffering from *choke*, a condition in which food becomes lodged in the esophagus. As the horse coughs in an effort to shift the mass, saliva and food particles exit the nostrils, since the horse is unable to swallow.

In many instances, you can help your horse dislodge the mass and overcome the problem on his own, or ease the situation while waiting for your veterinarian to arrive. Choke is usually not considered an immediate medical emergency since the horse can still breathe. However, if the situation has not resolved within an hour, or your horse is pawing or panicky, summon your veterinarian.

Solutions

• While waiting for your vet, you can reassure your horse with *Ear TTouches* to encourage him to lower his head and relax the lower part of his neck and release some of the discomfort. Then do *Coiled Python Lifts* and *Neck Rocking* all along the lower edge of the trachea/esophagus, working your way to the chest. This will acitvate peristaltic waves and encourage the horse to swallow.

• You may hear gurgling sounds as the mass of food is dislodged and begins to move. At this point, offer your horse water in a shallow bucket. Horses who choke may be prone to recurrence, so be sure that all food—especially pelleted foods and beet pulp—are thoroughly soaked before feeding.

Turnaround Tale

Ruby, a 21-year-old Thoroughbred mare, had a habit of bolting her dinner. One night she choked on her pellets. Her neck went rigid, frothy material spewed from her nostrils and the dreaded sounds of choke reverberated through the stable. With the permission of her owner, I began to work on her while we waited for the veterinarian.

Since choking horses are often very rigid, first I did Ear TTouches to relax her. I alternated with Neck Rocking to dislodge the lump of food, which could be felt at the upper end of the esophagus. Ruby did a lot of gurgling. In about 15 minutes, she wasn't any worse but still wasn't "out of the woods"—not eating or drinking, just standing with outstretched, lowered head in considerable discomfort. I did Coiled Python Lifts all the way along the underside of her neck and then continued with Belly Lifts to awaken peristaltic action. Two of us worked the rest of her body at the same time. Within 10 minutes, she dove for the feed bucket and began slurping the beet pulp water. That was the end of the choke.

Solutions at a Glance: *Choke*

Ear TTouches 210 ~ Coiled Python Lift 172 ~ Neck Rocking 199 ~ Belly Lift 209

Colic

see also Shock

Colic, a term referring to general abdominal distress, can strike when you least expect it. Invariably, it happens after veterinary office hours or on weekends. There are many other sources for you to consult that will provide you with details about medical support for this condition, but you can take an active role with TTouches while waiting for the veterinarian to arrive.

Over 30 years ago, I discovered the benefits of stroking the ears in a case of colic, and in the process, saved the life of my endurance mare, Bint Gulida, after the veterinarian said there was no hope. Since then we have found that in many cases, *Ear TTouches* and *Belly Lifts* are more effective than walking a horse. We have literally hundreds of cases of people who have read or heard about the Tellington Method for colic and have tried it with remarkable success.

Note: I recommend that you *call your veterinarian first* with information about your horse's pulse, respiration, temperature and gum color.

Solutions

• **A horse has scant or absent gut sounds.** Do *Belly Lifts* and *Ear TTouches.* There is an acupressure point beneath the root of the tail, just above the anus that can help to release gas in the case of gas colic. Do slow, deliberate press-and-release circles, one-eighth inch around, at this point. If your horse has a twisted gut, he will require surgery but there is a chance that *Ear TTouches* can keep the pain level under control long enough to get medical intervention.

• **A horse has sand colic.** You can help relieve the pain, but an accumulation of sand can build up so much weight that a horse may be irritable. We recently received a report of a horse in Finland who was getting more and more irritable under saddle and refus-

ing to go forward. At first, the rider just thought the horse was getting sour, but during a Tellington Training clinic it was suggested that the attitude could have a physical cause. Veterinary examination discovered a very large block of sand that had to be surgically removed. The "attitude" shifted immediately and the horse went back to his normal, cooperative self.

• **A horse begins to look "off" or "ain't doin' right."** Check temperature, pulse and respiration (TPR) and listen at the flank for gut sounds. Normal equine temperature ranges from 99 to 101.5 degrees Fahrenheit (37.2 to 38.6 degrees Celsius). Average resting pulse is 36 to 40 beats per minute and respiration around 8 to 16 breaths per minute, although all of these parameters can be influenced by heat, humidity and unfamiliar surroundings. By checking TPR you can often detect colic in the early stages when a horse refuses to eat and is looking uncomfortable but not yet rolling or looking back at his sides. In many colic cases, there are *limited* gut sounds, or abnormally *overactive* (hypermotile) gut gurgles. It is a good idea to listen to your horse's gut sounds on both sides and know what his pulse and respiration count is when he is feeling well and at rest (see sidebar, p. 132).

We have hundreds of cases on record where TTouch has brought horses out of colic or kept them out of shock (when veterinary care was not available) and even, in some cases, when the owner was told there was no hope. We've discovered the interesting fact that when a horse is in pain, even head-shy horses will allow you to work the ears. In the case of colic or distress, keep up the work until the pulse and respiration return to normal and the horse is feeling well.

Over many years and many horses, I have found that when a horse starts to look uncomfortable and appears to be colicky, the respiration is over 40 and the pulse usually elevated as well. This is the time to put in that call to your veterinarian, then begin *Ear TTouches* and *Belly Lifts*. The ear strokes seem to reduce pain and *Belly Lifts* activate the peristaltic movement in the gut. However, I've also seen horses who quit eating and look "off" but have pulse and respiration within reasonable ranges. These may be the early stages of discomfort and, I feel, the time to call your vet.

Solutions at a Glance: *Colic*

Ear TTouches 210 ~ Belly Lift 209 ~ Tail TTouch 185

Exhaustion

see also *Colic, Shock, Tying Up*

Horses can become exhausted in a variety of circumstances, from high-intensity sports to backcountry riding. For example:

- An eventer comes in from the cross-country phase on a day of high heat and humidity with elevated respiration and a high pulse. Despite the best efforts of his crew using ice water, misting fans and shade, 30 minutes later the horse has still not recovered.

- An endurance horse comes into a rest stop with a dull, sunken eye. He won't drink, and just picks at his food. His pulse initially recovers to the required 60 beats per minute, but 20 minutes later, one minute after a trot-out (*see footnote below), it jumps into the 70s and hangs there.

- A pleasure horse and his rider miss a turn and are lost on a hot summer day. After three hours on the trail without water or shade, the horse's hindquarters become stiff as a board, and the horse cannot move—he has become exhausted and is stricken with tying-up syndrome.

In the first two instances, the horses were both pulled from further competition that day and treated with intravenous fluids, electrolytes and other medical therapy. In the third case, the rider called for help and kept her horse's rump covered until help could arrive.

Signs of equine exhaustion may include:

- Loss of energy

- Loss of interest in eating and drinking

- Elevated pulse, respiration and temperature

- Dehydration

- Cramps, muscle tremors or tying up

Should your horse show these signs, *call your veterinarian*. While such an emergency is something you hope will never happen, you should be prepared to help your horse during the time a vet is not available. On the next page are some proven TTouches to help a horse survive a severe episode of exhaustion.

---

* A very sensitive indicator you can use to pick up impending problems is the Cardiac Recovery Index (CRI), developed by Kerry Ridgway, DVM. Take your horse's heart rate for 15 seconds. Trot him out and back 250 feet. Take his heart rate again exactly one minute from the first reading. The second heart rate should be no higher than one beat of the first using 15-second counts. In fit, healthy horses the second heart rate will be equivalent to or even lower than the first reading.

Learn your horse's normal values when he is rested and in good health:

Heart rate: at home, at rest, 28 to 44 beats per minute. Your horse should be able to recover to the low 50s within 10 minutes after finishing exercise. Slow recovery rates may suggest illness, injury or not enough conditioning for the task at hand.

Respiration: at home, at rest, 12 to 20 breaths per minute. Often, however, panting can be a normal way to dissipate body heat.

Temperature: 99 to 101.5 degrees Fahrenheit (37.2 to 38.6 degrees Celsius).

Hydration: pinch the skin on the point of the shoulder. The skin should snap back to a flat position in less than a second. If the skin "tents" for more than two to three seconds, your horse may be dehydrated.

Mucous membranes: check the color and feel of the gums. Pink and moist is normal; darker shades and a "tacky" or dry feel signal fatigue or exhaustion.

Capillary refill: press briefly on the gum until it turns white, and count the number of seconds it takes the color to return. Less than two seconds is normal.

Gut sounds: check your horse at home to familiarize yourself with the normal symphony of sounds emanating from the flank and barrel of a healthy horse. Scant gut sounds may herald fatigue.

Urination: light or straw-colored urine is normal; dark-colored urine signals overwork.

Manure: fecal balls should be moist but well formed. Hard, dry nuggets indicate dehydration.

Solutions

Recovery from Exhaustion

• Stand directly in front of your horse's head and *work the ears briskly*—from their base to the tips—with an *Ear Pull* every second, to lower pulse and respiration and reenergize the horse. Move him into the shade and fan him if there is no ventilation.

• Do *Mouth TTouches* to encourage a horse to drink. If the gums are dry to the touch, as is common with dehydration, moisten them first with a wet towel.

• Do *Belly Lifts* to help reactivate gut sounds and encourage your horse to eat. Offer soaked beet pulp or wet hay, since dehydrated horses are at greater risk of choke.

• Cool your horse by sponging cold or iced water on the inside of the front legs and on the lower neck (jugular veins) as well as the head. If the temperature and humidity are high, scrape the water off as you go so it doesn't create an insulating layer of even more heat on the body. Avoid chilling the large muscles of the shoulders and hindquarters in cool weather. In such instances, use a rump rug or wool or fleece cooler.

While veterinarians have made tremendous advances in the management of the exhausted horse, it remains difficult to predict which metabolically compromised horses will "crash" or progress to a serious condition such as colic or tying up. It can be a very helpless feeling to see a horse go down and into shock despite heroic medical care. Tellington TTouch practitioners have become involved in many such cases over the years and have been credited with saving horses who were on the verge of death.

Recovery from Performance

Whether it's the last loop of an endurance ride, the fourth chukker of a polo match, or the final day of a three-day event, you want to be sure your horse stays physically and mentally fresh for the challenge.

After a long trail ride or a full day of competition, a 30-minute session of these TTouches can refresh your horse so he will eat and drink well, sleep deeply and be ready for the next day's efforts:

- Three minutes of slow *Ear TTouches*.

- *Lick of the Cow's Tongue* from girth to flank, three times on each side.

- *Abalone TTouches* with *Coiled Python Lifts* on the inside and outside of the hind legs. Hold at the top of each lift for four to six seconds, followed by a slow release.

- *Tail Pulls* with gentle traction and slow releases to help relax tight back and neck muscles.

- *Jellyfish Jiggles* followed by counterclockwise *Lying Leopard TTouches* can help delay formation of lactic acid.

- Five minutes of soothing *Troika TTouches*.

- Finish with an enlivening series of *Flick of the Bear's Paw*.

Turnaround Tale

In 1984, I gave a two-day seminar for the French Olympic Committee to demonstrate how the Tellington Method could help recovery in performance horses. I was asked to demonstrate on a horse who had completed a three-day event the day before and was becoming excessively dehydrated. When I walked into his stall, the gelding was standing in a corner with lowered head, refusing to eat or drink. His eyes were dull, his capillary refill time was slow—in short, he was metabolically depressed. During the 60-minute TTouch session over every inch of the body, the gelding began eating and drank deeply. He became alert and interested in his surroundings. The change was dramatic. The horse looked as if he had gained 50 pounds and the effects of his hard weekend of competition no longer bothered him.

Solutions at a Glance: *Exhaustion*

Ear TTouches 210 ~ Lick of the Cow's Tongue 177 ~ Abalone TTouch 171 ~ Coiled Python Lift 172 ~ Mouth TTouch 182 ~ Tail TTouch 185 ~ Jellyfish Jiggle 197 ~ Lying Leopard TTouch 181 Troika TTouch 188 ~ Flick of the Bear's Paw 219 ~ Belly Lift 209

Gastric Ulcers

see also *Colic*

Gastric ulcers, once thought to be mainly a threat to foals, are now known to occur in 90 percent of racehorses and 60 percent of show horses. Risk factors include stall confinement, high-grain diets, insufficient roughage, infrequent feedings, strenuous exercise, administration of NSAIDs such as phenylbutazone (known as "bute") and stress caused by being turned out with different horses. To date, no infectious cause of gastric ulceration has been identified in horses as it has in humans.

The equine digestive tract is designed to process grass and hay nearly 'round the clock. As a result, "normal" levels of digestive enzymes can turn the stomach into a vat of acid if it's not kept busy all day long. The excess acid will eventually erode the stomach lining and an ulcer is the end result, especially if other risk factors are present.

Signs of gastric ulcers are often subtle and include depressed appetite, weight loss, sour attitude, abdominal discomfort (colic), unwillingness to work, dull hair coat and teeth grinding. But many seemingly healthy horses with no overt symptoms have them.

Ulcers can be diagnosed with a fiberoptic endoscope that enables the veterinarian to view the lining of the stomach for signs of erosion, thinning or bleeding. The most commonly prescribed treatment is omeprazole (GastroGard, Merial Ltd.), which decreases acid production for up to 24 hours. Drugs may ease the clinical signs, but veterinarians agree that management is the key to preventing recurrence of ulcers.

Solutions

To reduce the chance of ulcers, mimic a horse's life on the range by providing as many of the following as possible:

- Free-choice hay or grass: keep the stomach busy!

- Maximal turnout with compatible herdmates.
- Plenty of "downtime" with less demanding training.
- Frequent feedings to help buffer stomach acid.
- A diet high in roughage and low in grains.
- Stress reduction.

A horse with chronic ulcers is often extremely sensitive around the flanks and may try to bite or kick if you attempt any contact in the area. Hold such a horse in *Taming the Tiger* so he can't bite or kick you, and do *Abalone TTouches* with a sheepskin mitt using very slow (three-second) number 1 pressure circles. Working to release fear of contact can help activate the cells' natural healing ability. This can be helpful in conjunction with veterinary care and other stress-reducing steps by releasing fear of pain that often remains even after treatment.

Belly Lifts, Tail TTouches and *Neckline Driving* can further help horses who display discomfort or reactivity in the flank area.

If your horse is nervous about being handled and tends to be spooky and high-headed, *Lower the Head* with *Ear TTouches* and relaxing *Lying Leopard TTouches* all over to give the horse a way to enjoy contact on the body.

Solutions at a Glance: *Gastric Ulcers*

Taming the Tiger 166 ~ Abalone TTouch 171 ~ Belly Lift 209 ~ Tail TTouch 185 ~ Neckline and Ground Driving 261 ~ Lowering the Head 163 ~ Ear TTouches 210 ~ Lying Leopard TTouch 181

Neurological Dysfunction

A change in your horse's behavior or way of going can signal a neurological disorder such as EPM, herpes virus, Lyme disease or Wobbler's syndrome. Typically, an afflicted horse will stumble frequently, be lame, have difficulty circling and turning and appear to be uncoordinated. In cooperation with Dr. Mark Mendelson, a veterinarian in Albuquerque, New Mexico, we have developed a protocol for horses recovering from EPM or other neurological disorders.

Solutions

• Once the horse has been treated medically, follow up with many of the TTouches and Ground Exercises listed below—starting in a *Body Wrap*—can help a horse regain coordination and function. Because the neurologically compromised horse is often unaware of his limbs, *Connected Circles* in long lines all over the body give the horse kinesthetic information about his boundaries. Using our protocol, many horses with Wobbler's syndrome and other neurological deficits have overcome much of their incoordination so that they could be safely ridden.

• Read the booklet, *The Tellington Method as Complementary Therapy in the Rehabilitation of Horses with Neurological Deficits* available from Tellington TTouch Training (see *Resources*, p. 311).

Caution: We encourage you to work with your veterinarian to achieve a diagnosis and map out a treatment plan.

Solutions at a Glance: *Neurological Dysfunction*

Connected Circles 173 ~ Lowering the Head 163 ~ Ear TTouches 210 ~ Clouded Leopard TTouch 195 ~ Lying Leopard TTouch 181 ~ Neck Bending 219 ~ Inch Worm 197 ~ Octopus TTouch 200 Rainbow TTouch 222 ~ Front Leg Circles 174 ~ Hind Leg Circles 175 ~ Tail TTouch 185 Pelvic Tilt 222 ~ Cha Cha 232 ~ Labyrinth 259 ~ Hoof Tapping 196 ~ Lick of the Cow's Tongue 177 ~ Zig-Zag TTouch 206 ~ Journey of the Homing Pigeon 241 ~ The Fan 253 ~ Platform 269 Body Wrap 160

Shock

A horse has been injured, is losing blood, has a fracture, is chilled, colicking, or in extreme distress. First, in all these situations, waste no time in calling the veterinarian. These are emergency situations! However, while you are waiting, there is a great deal you can do to make a difference. In fact, you may even save your horse's life. Rather than following a step-by-step approach as I suggest in most of this book, do as many TTouches as you can at the same time.

Solutions

• *Ear TTouches* can prevent or bring a horse out of shock. Use firm, smooth strokes starting in the middle of the forehead, pressing over the base of the ear, and stroking firmly all the way to the tips with a little squeeze on the tip as you finish. Work both ears at the same time, then alternate. If the horse has a lowered body temperature as evidenced by ice-cold ear tips, work the ears vigorously; wrap a towel around the ears and poll to warm the head as you stroke under it, or wrap a blanket around the neck—warming the jugular veins helps to warm up the body more quickly.

• When the body goes in shock, the abdominal muscles contract, and you often lose gut sounds. *Belly Lifts* are important as they can reactivate peristaltic action, relax the belly, and restore gut movement. Visualize those muscles relaxing, the peristaltic action gurgling up and starting again.

- Work the extremities with *Coiled Python Lifts,* starting with the forearm and working your way down, to activate blood flow into the feet. Alternate with *Octopus TTouches* to balance the polarity.

- In addition, keep the horse warm with blankets or hot towels, even a heating pad or electric blanket. Administer Rescue Remedy (see *Resources,* p. 311) directly on the tongue, or spray near the face. If the horse has gone down, keep up the ear strokes until medical help arrives. Have one person work the ears while you do *Abalone TTouches* with upward circles and lifts. When the body is in shock, there is a shut down, or slowing of the neural connections at a cellular level. I see TTouch as jump-starting the communication network between the cells so the healing potential of the body is reactivated. You want your actions to be soothing and supporting and not add to the distress.

Solutions at a Glance: *Shock*

Ear TTouches 210 ~ Belly Lift 209 ~ Coiled Python Lift 172 ~ Octopus TTouch 200 ~ Abalone TTouch 171

Stress: Pre- and Post-Surgical Care

Equine surgery is stressful—and does carry an element of risk. Preparing your horse with a full body session of *TTouch* and *Ear TTouches* can ensure that your horse is relaxed going into surgery.

Solutions

- Immediately before surgery, it's valuable to have a horse calm; to reduce stress, bring the head down and work the ears quietly and slowly stroking from middle of the head to the tip of the ears. Combine with *Connected Circles* all over the body and down the legs.

- To help the horse wake up and reconnect the whole body, do *Tarantulas Pulling the Plow* down the neck, shoulders, and over the barrel and hindquarters. Rhythmical *Ear Slides* can help a horse come out of anesthesia cleanly, and stand without disorientation or thrashing. (Many veterinarians have reported positive results from *Ear TTouches*).

Solutions at a Glance: *Stress*

Ear TTouches 210 ~ Connected Circles 173 ~ Tarantulas Pulling the Plow 203

Tying-Up Syndrome

Tying up, medically known as myositis or exertional rhabdomyolysis, is an occupational hazard of hard-working performance horses, although it can also be caused by emotional distress, lack of condition, a high grain diet, or a combination of these factors. In its most severe form, the horse stops suddenly, becomes extremely stiff and cannot move. Tying up can frequently occur out on the trail, where you are without veterinary help and sometimes beyond the reach of a trailer.

I've encountered horses tying up many times over the years, most often on endurance rides or trail rides where someone was along for a group ride on an upset, insufficiently conditioned horse. It can certainly be a helpless feeling if you don't have some tools at hand. And, in this case, the outcome may literally be in your hands!

Solutions

• Begin with *Ear TTouches* if the horse is sweating or "shocky." Alternate between connected *Lying Leopard* and *Abalone TTouches* to soften spasms of the muscles of the back, loins, and hindquarters with the warmth of your hands. When you begin to feel a softening, shift to slow *Tiger TTouches* with about a number 5 pressure. If you have access to a source of warm water, do the TTouches through heated towels over the back and loins. The best scenario is for the horse to be able to "walk out," which may be possible with a light case of the syndrome.

Turnaround Tale

At the World Endurance Championships in France in 2001, a Dutch Warmblood tied up less than 20 miles into the ride. This was a heavy-boned mare, who had gone down on the side of the trail and could not get up. She was in shock from exhaustion and in a remote location with no chance of getting adequate help. After more than an hour of attempts, all efforts to get the mare on her feet had failed and the vet recommended the mare be euthanized.

I was working with the American endurance team, and our chef d'equip agreed to release me to help this horse from another team. When I arrived, people were standing around totally helpless. The mare was lying downhill with her legs higher than her back, wedged against a tree, and she had given up. I began working on her ears and started her rider doing Lying Leopard TTouches on the loins.

After an hour of vigorous work, the mare was still not willing to get up, but she was looking more alert and no longer gave the impression of defeat. I suggested they continue doing the Ear TTouches and working on the loins to see if she would eventually rally. They worked with determination and finally, after five hours, the mare struggled to her feet and walked the quarter mile to the road where a trailer was waiting. The following day that team's vet reported that much to their surprise, the mare had recovered and blood work indicated that there was no kidney damage, the feared side effect from tying up.

Solutions at a Glance: *Tying-Up Syndrome*

Ear TTouches 210 ~ Lying Leopard TTouch 181 ~ Abalone TTouch 171 ~ Tiger TTouch 205

PART THREE

HOW-TO GUIDE

The Tellington Method®

The Tellington Method consists of three main components: THE TELLINGTON TTOUCHES (TTouch stands for "trust touch"); GROUND EXERCISES; and RIDDEN WORK.

THE TELLINGTON TTOUCHES

TTouches for Trust (p. 168)
A collection of 12 circles, lifts and slides done with the hands and fingertips over various parts of your horse's body to enhance trust, release tension, overcome habitual holding patterns that lead to resistance, and open new possibilities for learning and cooperation.

TTouches for Awareness (p. 190)
14 additional TTouches that ease your horse's tension, increase flexibility and enhance your enjoyment of your equine companion.

TTouches for Health (p. 207)
3 special TTouches that have proven to be invaluable in certain health conditions, including colic, shock and tying up.

Performance Plus in 10 Minutes a Day (p. 214)
A group of 9 TTouches that have proven especially beneficial for performance, working and sport horses.

GROUND EXERCISES

Dancing with Your Horse (p. 228)
10 precise ground and leading exercises to enhance coordination and cooperation between horse and human.

Playground for Higher Learning (p. 250)
Includes 11 specialized exercises using obstacles such as plastic, poles and barrels to reduce spookiness and improve balance, coordination, willingness and ability to learn. These exercises are done from the ground and under saddle.

RIDDEN WORK

Joy of Riding (p. 276)
6 under saddle adventures to improve equine and rider balance, coordination and confidence; increase safety; enrich awareness and deepen the horse/human bond.

CASE STUDY: TRAILER LOADING

In addition, at the end I have included a photographic section, *The Story of Thor: Overcoming Fear of the Trailer,* (p. 295). It is one of the most common difficulties horse people encounter.

The Tellington TTouches®

Guide to TTouches by Category

Guide to TTouches by Type

Getting Started with TTouch®

Over the past 20 years, the Tellington TTouch has evolved to include almost 20 different TTouches whose animal names invoke the way in which you place your hands on your horse's body, and do other body work. Naming each TTouch after an animal was inspired by the interesting names and movements of Tai Chi. Although these names may seem a little unconventional at first, they add an element of fun and lightness, making learning easier.

The animal names have a positive effect on the person doing TTouches (as well as the horse). We frequently hear from people who use TTouch on a regular basis that they feel more creative and mentally flexible. I believe this is a result of activating both the intuitive and logical parts of the brain.

When you visualize an animal-inspired TTouch such as a *Clouded Leopard* or *Octopus,* you are activating the *intuitive* part of your brain. Whenever you think of the numbers around the face of the clock, which you need to do when learning the Circular TTouches, you are stimulating the *logical* part of the brain. So every time you TTouch your horse, you are using your whole brain, a phenomenon called "whole-brain" or "one-brain learning." This activation of the whole brain was substantiated by the studies we did with Anna Wise, founder of the Biofeedback Institute of Boulder, Colorado, in the late 1980s. (For more about Anna's work, see p. xviii.)

What makes TTouch easy to learn is the system of pressure and tempo combined with various ways of holding and using the hands. The pressure scale is from 1 to 10 and the tempo (the time it takes to push the skin in a circle) from 1 to 3 seconds. In addition to the Circular TTouches, there are Lifts, Slides and Pauses to activate circulation, enhance breathing, connect the circles, and give the body time to process the information.

Taming the Tiger (see p. 166)

THE BASIC CIRCLE

The intent of TTouch is to activate the function of the cells, enhancing cellular communication and awakening cellular intelligence—I call it "turning on the electric lights of the body"—to stimulate the body's potential for healing and learning.

TTouch may be done over the entire body, and each circular TTouch is complete within itself. It is not necessary to work the whole body in a single session as with many other modalities of bodywork. You may decide one day to work on your horse's head and neck, another day the legs and tail, another day the shoulders and back, and so forth.

The one-and-one-quarter-circle size is a hallmark and foundation of TTouch. You can practice on any handy human if your horse isn't nearby. While visualizing the face of a clock, start at the bottom of the circle at "6 o'clock" and *push the skin—do not rub your fingers over the surface*—once around the face of the clock to stop at 9 o'clock. Pay attention to the quality of the roundness of the circle, and keep the same rhythm as you push the skin around the imaginary clock.

• With your fingers slightly curved, lightly place one hand on the body of the horse. Position your thumb about two inches from your index finger, softly connected to the horse's body to establish an anchor for the movement of your fingers. As you make the contact, feel the connection between your thumb and fingers. The darkened areas of your fingers—as shown in the drawings for individual TTouches in Part Three of this book—are where contact with the horse is made.

Hold your wrist upright (as straight as possible without being rigid) so the heel of your hand does not come into contact with the horse's body. This will ensure fluid movement of the hand and fingers.

• Whenever possible, place your other hand lightly on the skin surface to hold a contact between two hands. This creates a connection between your two hands and the horse. Experiment with finding a comfortable balance between your hands. (The spacing depends on the size of the person. A child's hands would be closer together and a large adult's further apart.) When working on the shoulder, I usually place my other hand on the chest. When working on the neck, one hand could be on one side of the neck, and the other hand on the opposite side.

• Now visualize the face of a clock. Holding your fingers lightly together with the middle finger leading, start at 6 on your imaginary clock (always the point closest to the ground), then push the skin *clockwise* in a single one-and-a-quarter circle. Continue past 6 again until you reach 8 or 9 o'clock. (**Note:** If you begin at 12 going downward, your fingers will tighten the skin rather than release it.) Using an even, smoothly consistent pressure, the time taken to do one circle will vary from 1 to 3 seconds (see *Pressure, Direction* and *Tempo* on the following pages).

• As you finish each single circle, make a short connecting slide to the next circle (for more on this, see *Connected Circles*, p. 173). Think of it as "connecting the dots."

When making the circles, do only one circle and a quarter on any one spot. When learning TTouch, there is a tendency to make three or more circles on the same place. When you do more than two before moving on to the next spot, the circles just irritate and the value of the TTouch is lost on the horse.

Pressure

One of the most common questions I hear about TTouch is, "Don't you get tired while doing this work?" Because our interest is in developing awareness in the body and working at the cellular level rather than simply manipulating the muscular system, we can work with light pressure most of the time.

The TTouch pressure scale ranges from 1 to 10. For many years we taught the pressure scale by using contact with the eyelid as a measure. However, for those wearing contacts, that does not work so well, and over the years we found that touching the soft tissue directly under the eye was easier for many people. My sister, Robyn Hood, who has been instrumental in the development and the teaching of the work, discovered that a broader range of pressure was possible using the cheekbone to establish our scale.

• To learn the feeling of each pressure, begin with the lightest contact—a number 1 pressure—as a baseline: First, bring your right hand up to your face, supporting your bent right elbow snugly against your body with your other hand. (Of course, do the reverse if you are left-handed.)

• Then, placing your thumb against your cheek in order to steady your hand, put the tip of your middle finger just below your lower eyelashes on the

very soft tissue, and push the skin in a circle with the lightest possible contact—so you can feel only tissue and not the top of the cheekbone—and just enough contact so you do not slide over the skin.

• Next, on the fleshy part of the top of your forearm, between your wrist and your elbow, place your curved fingers on top of the arm with your thumb on the underside so you hold the arm between the fingers and thumb. Make a circle using the same minimal possible contact as you did below your eye. Observe how little indentation you make in the skin. This is a number 1 pressure.

• Register the feeling of this number 1 pressure in your mind. If you wonder how such a light pressure can possibly be effective, remember, in this case our intention is to affect the nervous system and the cells rather than the muscles themselves. This is the pressure we generally use to work around a sore or sensitive area to enhance healing.

• To identify a number 3 pressure, repeat the process, only this time, push the skin in a circle with enough pressure that you feel the top of the cheekbone clearly, without pushing hard. Then, retaining the sensory memory of that pressure, return to your forearm and compare this slightly increased pressure to the number 1 pressure.

• The indentation on your forearm will be twice as deep into the muscle with a number 6 pressure. If a pressure heavier than a 6 is done with the pads of the fingers, it can cause both "doer" and "do-ee" to feel discomfort (and hold their breath.) So, if you feel you need to go deeper into the muscle than a 6, try the *Bear TTouch* (see p. 217). With the *Bear TTouch*, you tip your fingers until your nails are perpendicular to the body and make the circle with your nails. You can then go into the muscle without discomfort to you or the horse.

(When working on a heavily muscled horse, make a circle with a number 3 pressure and then

TTOUCH PRESSURE SCALE

TTOUCHES FOR TRUST	Pressure
Abalone TTouch	1 – 3
Coiled Python Lift	1 – 3
Connected Circles	2 – 3
Lick of the Cow's Tongue	1 – 3
Llama TTouch	1 – 2
Lying Leopard TTouch	1 – 3
Mouth TTouch	2 – 3
Nostril TTouch	1 – 3
Troika TTouch	1 – 4

TTOUCHES FOR AWARENESS	
Back Lift	2 – 5
Chimp TTouch	2 – 3
Clouded Leopard TTouch	1 – 4
Hoof Tapping	1 – 4
Inch Worm	2 – 3
Jellyfish Jiggle	3 – 4
Mane and Forelock Slides	1 – 3
Neck Rocking	2 – 4
Noah's March	1 – 3
Octopus TTouch	2 – 3
Sponge TTouch	2 – 3
Tarantulas Pulling the Plow	2 – 4
Tiger TTouch	1 – 6
Zig-Zag TTouch	2 – 3

TTOUCHES FOR HEALTH	
Ear TTouches	1 – 5
Raccoon TTouch	1 – 3

PERFORMANCE PLUS IN 10 MINUTES A DAY	
Bear TTouch	1 – 8
Flick of the Bear's Paw	1 – 4
Rainbow TTouch	3 – 4
Rhino TTouch	2 – 10
Rib Release	3 – 4

"sponge" into the middle of the circle with a deep *Bear TTouch* (4 to 6 pressure). This helps to release tight muscles and increase circulation. I see this as "aerating" the muscles.)

Circle Direction

Most people and animals respond best to clockwise circles. However, as acupuncture techniques have verified, the clockwise direction *strengthens* or *tones* the system while the counterclockwise *releases tension*. The direction in which you make the circles usually remains the same regardless of whether you are right- or left-handed. Sometimes, if a horse objects to being TTouched, has an injury, or is in pain, the counterclockwise circle may be preferable. In many cases, you may observe the horse relax when you change direction.

Trust yourself when this happens and just continue on—your intuition is usually right. Although we have been working with the TTouch circles and their direction for over two decades now, I still don't have the final answer about when to use clockwise or counterclockwise, because I find there are always exceptions.

Refining the Finger Movements

Your fingers (not your thumb) are divided by three joints into sections called *phalanges*. We nicknamed the three joints DIP, MIP and PIP based on the anatomy of the fingers. The phalange from the tip of your finger to the first joint is called the distal interphalange (DIP). The section from the first joint to the middle joint is called the medial interphalange (MIP), and the section from the middle joint to the knuckle is called the proximal interphalange (PIP).

When most people first try the TTouch, they tend to keep the DIP, MIP and PIP joints straight and stiff with the heel of the hand in contact with the horse's body while they attempt to push the skin around in a circle. If you try this stiff finger position with light pressure, you may be able to feel how your diaphragm tightens a bit and constrains your breathing. Now, make a circle with the DIP, MIP and PIP joints lightly bent and flexible and see how much more softly and easily you can push the skin around when all three joints move with the motion.

The size of your circles will depend on the looseness or tightness of the skin. If the skin is tight, it's necessary to make the circle very small to keep the roundness. Where the skin is loose, a larger circle works well.

When you first begin to use TTouch, it helps to visualize each number on the face of your imaginary clock. As you start from 6 and move toward 7, the DIP joint curves and by the time you reach the top of the circle at 12, the fingers lengthen and flatten out. The fingers then begin to curve again as you return toward 3. As you move past 6 to finish the circle at 8 or 9, your fingers begin to extend again and the joints open.

At 9, pause and release. This sounds more complicated than it is in practice.

Tempo

The speed and rhythm of your fingers while moving around the circle should be consistent. Most beginners have a tendency to start by making a straight line from 6 to 9, speeding up and losing the rhythm as they move around to completion. Instead, pay attention as you begin and as you move the skin to 7 and 8, make sure to keep each circle round and the pressure and pace even.

To refine your technique after you've been doing TTouches on your horse for some weeks, you could find it helpful to practice the one-, two- and three-second circles with a friend actually timing you with a second hand of a watch. Or you can count, one-one-thousand, two-one-thousand,

etc, with attention on the rhythm and smoothness of the circles.

A one-second circle with a one-second connecting slide is useful for a nervous horse, for establishing contact, and for relieving acute pain (*Connected Circles*, p. 173). A two-second circle followed by a pause before a two-second slide to the next circle, creates a deeper awareness because it allows the nervous system time to register the connection. A three-second circle is rarely used on horses except perhaps on the face with *Abalone* circles to develop a rapport and deepen the trust between you.

Feedback

Stay tuned-in to your horse's response as you work. His head may lower, the eyes soften, you may sometimes get a deep sigh, and it is common for geldings to drop the penis. If your horse begins moving around or becomes agitated, try another TTouch or change the pressure and tempo. It may be that your fingers are stiff, so try the back of your hand (*Llama TTouch*, p. 180) or the flat hand (*Abalone TTouch*, p. 171) to give warmth. Sometimes switching from clockwise to counterclockwise can get a positive response.

You might give him a little hay to eat while you're working, and don't forget to give frequent breaks to process the information. If you are tense, take some long, deep breaths yourself to relax.

Breath Awareness

Breath is communication and sends a message to your horse if you are tense or relaxed. Unless you have practiced breath awareness, you may find yourself holding your breath when you concentrate on the TTouch. Holding the breath creates stiffness in your hands and tension in your body. Compare what you feel when making a circle holding your breath to when you breathe freely and rhythmically. Can you describe the difference?

Many people tend to breathe shallowly, into the upper chest area, stopping the inhalation there. Instead, take a full breath into your chest, and continue to breathe down into your belly, as if you are expanding a balloon or a bellows. I often imagine my breath going down my legs into the earth to mingle with the rhythm and breath of the earth in order to ground myself.

As you make the circles, develop an awareness of your breath, experimenting with it until it feels even, rhythmic and easy. Conscious breathing will aid in stilling and focusing your mind, relaxing your neck and shoulders and softening your hands. Your fingers will seem to be connecting with the horse effortlessly on their own.

How you stand while working affects your breathing and the connection you are creating with your horse. Keeping your feet under your hips, your knees unlocked and your weight balanced over the balls of your feet is healthier for your back. This position also keeps you in balance and ready to move in any direction should your horse suddenly startle.

BODY EXPLORATION

As you become more adept at TTouching your horse, you may find it enlightening to incorporate a *Body Exploration* to find specific areas of sensitivity, tension, soreness or resistance to being TTouched.

Here are two ways of exploring the body:

Flat Hand Exploration: Using the flat hand as an overall body check-in.

Fingertip Exploration: Using the fingertips to check for tension or soreness.

I advise having someone hold your horse (rather than tying him) while you work on him so that you can clearly observe his response.

Flat Hand Exploration

With *Flat Hand Exploration*, check the entire body using the *Abalone TTouch* (p. 171). Feel for hot or cold areas, swellings, lumps, indentations, changes in muscle tone, differences in hair quality or concern about being touched. Your horse may move away to avoid contact or threaten to kick. Ears, legs, flank, sheath or udder and tail are areas where many horses object to contact, and TTouch can be a gentle means of overcoming these objections. The *Flat Hand Exploration* is also a useful way to get acquainted with a new horse. Run your hands systematically over the entire body. Note any anomalies on a chart.

Fingertip Exploration

Fingertip Exploration is done with a *Bear TTouch* (see p. 217) to effectively pinpoint soreness and reactivity. For example, a high-strung or spooky horse will often be reactive to a light (number 3) pressure. You'll discover that these types of horses will mellow out markedly once they learn to relax with TTouch. In contrast, a horse who accepts deeper pressure will usually be the steady, unflappable type. *Fingertip Exploration* can be a valuable tool for testing and transforming temperament (see p. 156).

It takes some practice to be able to know how much pressure to apply to judge if your horse is sore and to know what is a normal reaction for that horse. Get your hands on as many horses as possible to develop a baseline for comparison. Muscle tone varies dramatically depending upon breed, age, exercise and the discipline the horse is engaged in. Make a habit of systematically checking the same areas on each horse by following the areas marked in the series of photos on p. 154.

Tellington Tip

To be successful you will need some length to your fingernails—fingertips without nails rarely achieve a meaningful response!

Neck

Hold your fingers firmly together, with the fingernails at a 90-degree angle to the horse's body. Begin at the top of the neck, in the middle of the large muscle just behind the ears. Before you press in with your fingers, stroke the area firmly with your flat hand so you don't surprise your horse, then press straight into the muscle with your fingertips and release.

For most horses, begin at the top of the neck with a 3 pressure. With a horse who is nervous, tense or spooky, begin with a 1 pressure. Increase or decrease the pressure to discover which gives you the most information about his degree of sensitivity or acceptance. Some horses react strongly to just a 2 pressure, while very calm horses may not respond until you reach a 5 pressure. Make a note of any places that are tender, sore or tense.

Sometimes a horse will be startled by the quick press-and-release and throw the head up the first time. So always repeat the pressure to be sure the resulting reaction is not from surprise. If your horse is not sore, the head will actually lower on the second press-and-release.

A really sore horse may object to you simply placing your hands on the top of the neck behind the ears. If that's the case, further pressing-and-releasing is not necessary. Simply begin with slow, soothing *Lying Leopard TTouches* (p. 181) in long connected lines from the top of the neck to the shoulder until your horse lowers his head and clearly accepts and enjoys the contact.

There are four possible responses to the *Bear TTouch* exploration of the neck. A horse may:

- Relax and lower the head
- Raise the head, tense the neck and step back
- Throw the head up abruptly
- In extreme cases, half rear

Observe your horse's response carefully. When a horse throws his head and steps back, this is his way of "talking" to you, so listen and stay alert. You can expect a healthy, calm horse with no soreness in the neck or back to show a slight response to a number 5 pressure, but display no spasm or fear.

If your horse shows little or no response to your probing, he may be the quiet, steady type, or you may be pressing-and-releasing with the pads rather than the tips of your fingernails. If the neck or back has a hard, "wooden" feeling and there is no reaction even to a 5 or 6 pressure, I recommend having your horse checked by a veterinary chiropractor.

Continue your *Body Exploration* from head to tail, checking these areas for sensitivity:

Crest

Check the crest for soreness or tightness that can cause shortened stride, stiff gaits and resistance to collected movements. An abrupt reaction to a number 2 pressure—half-rearing, throwing the head and stepping back—can indicate a hormone imbalance, subluxated vertebrae or other medical issue. Should such extreme resistance occur to even a light pressure, check with your veterinarian.

Withers

Soreness in this area almost always points to an ill-fitting saddle (see p. 11).

Back and Loins

TTouch *Body Exploration* differs from the usual mode of checking a horse's back by sliding the fingers along both sides of the spine. We check the back by applying individual *Bear TTouches* (p. 217) every few inches from the withers to the loins about four inches below the top of the spine. If your horse drops his back abruptly from only a 2 pressure from the fingertips (nails) or displays tiny muscle tremors, this is an indication of soreness. In such instances, *Lying Leopard TTouches* with little lifts and/or slides all along the back will help relieve the soreness. (See *Back Problems*, p. 35, for more information.)

Gaskin and Forearm Muscles

These upper-leg areas can feel tight as a drum, yet rarely appear sore to exploration. If your horse's stride is short, or he has difficulty stepping over very low poles or into a step-up trailer, carefully check this area on all four legs. Hot towels and TTouches help alleviate any tightness that you find. (Realize, however, that Quarter Horses have heavier muscles than most other breeds, so it takes experience and practice to know what's normal and what's too tight.)

Croup and Buttocks

This is another classic place to check for soreness. Horses who contract the buttock muscles and slightly drop the hindquarters in response to a single press-and-release on the point of the buttocks are often spooky and fear movement behind them. You can "de-spook" them with *Lying Leopard* and *Tail TTouches* (see pp. 181 and 185).

Abdominal Muscles

Tight and sore abdominal muscles go hand in hand with sore backs. *Belly Lifts* (p. 209) can be helpful.

Lack of a response to a number 5 pressure or more, usually goes along with the calmer, less sensitive type of horse, but when your horse does not respond to your initial efforts, make sure you are using your fingernails at the correct angle with sufficient pressure to elicit a response. Study the photos and captions on the following pages to gain a deeper sense of this valuable TTouch tool.

HOW TO

Fingertip Exploration using Bear TTouch

Photo 1 Bea, a 16-year-old Warmblood mare, reacts to a 4 pressure near the third cervical vertebra by tossing her head up, indicating tension and sensitivity. I am standing slightly to the side pressing evenly on each side of the neck with both hands. Pressure on only one side rarely gives you an accurate "read" on tightness or soreness. If a horse is relaxed and free in the neck, he will usually lower the head from this pressure.

Photo 2 Continuing down the neck, Bea shows no sensitivity or tightness to a 4 pressure. However, with similar pressure on the lower part of the neck, Bea tightens her muscles and shows an uncertain reaction with her eyes and ears, tilting her head as if to say, "Not quite so much pressure, thank you."

Photo 3 I check the large muscle above the forearm with a 3 pressure. Bea is still not completely comfortable; note the concerned expression in her eye and the set of her ear.

Photo 3 (inset) A close-up of the exploratory TTouch in the center of the shoulder area. I check all three points shown here, pressing from both sides at the same time. If the horse is sore in the shoulders, you'll get muscle spasms when you hold these pressure points. The horse may also step back and throw the head up.

Photo 4 Many horses are "goosey" in the ribs behind the girth area. Bea is still showing skepti-

cism, but she is not contracting the muscles, pinning her ears, snapping the air or trying to move away from the pressure. Response to pressure here is not necessarily undesirable—it indicates she will respond to leg aids. If your horse pins the ears or snaps the air to a 3 pressure or less on the ribs, he may also respond by "sucking back" under saddle, bucking, kicking out or refusing to go forward when pushed with a raised heel to canter. If a horse is completely "dead" in this area, he may be unresponsive to leg aids.

Photo 4 (inset) A close-up of number 3 pressure on the ribs. When a horse is "ticklish" or goes into spasm from direct *Bear TTouches* in this area, there could be a number of causes. If the horse has never been ridden, he could have been born this way. I have seen foals react like this. It is an important area to relax and prepare before you ever girth up a horse; otherwise, you will most likely encounter bucking the first time he is saddled or ridden. If you see this response in a mature horse, it can be a reaction from a too tight girth (see *Cinchy/Girthy*, p. 48).

Photo 5 Now I check Bea's back about four inches below the center line. Check the back every four inches or so from the withers to the loins. If your horse is sore, he will drop the back and often throw the head up, step to the side, switch the tail or spasm from a light number 1 to 3 pressure. A 5 pressure is a lot to use on the back, and if the back is strong, it will only reveal the slightest reaction. However, if the back and neck show *no* reaction to a 6 along the points shown, and the area feels like wood, either you are not pressing straight in, or your horse may be too rigid to respond. In such instances, we have often found an underlying physical cause that needed veterinary attention.

Photo 5 (inset) Points to check on the withers: if your horse is sore, he will flinch, drop or spasm from a 4 pressure on both sides of the withers. Sensitivity in this area, along with behavior such as head-tossing and short-striding, often go along with an ill-fitting saddle. We find that the conventional wisdom of "just turning the horse out" rarely solves the issue. TTouch can help relieve the soreness.

Photo 6 Checking the loin area: if the horse drops away from a 5 pressure or less, there could be many causes, from saddle fit to riding style to conformation. Here, Bea shows a more relaxed eye and she is unconcerned with a 4 pressure.

Photo 7 Over the top of the croup: Bea is relaxing even more and is strong over this croup point. If a horse drops down by collapsing through the hocks, you know you've identified a major trouble spot.

Photo 8 Now go back one more point—notice that Bea is more relaxed from the set of her ears and the lowered neck; she appears to be accepting the body work.

Photo 9 View from the top, showing pressure on both sides. Note the angle of my fingers at 90 degrees to the horse's body.

Exploring the body, both with the flat hand and the fingertips, can be helpful for assessing temperament in many situations, including pre-purchase assessment.

Temperament, as discussed in chapter 3 (see p. 19), is defined as a manner of behaving—the physical and mental characteristics that make up an individual. Which means, of course, that these characteristics can change. For example, if a horse is in pain because of saddle fit, riding style, overwork or is "hot-tempered" and overreactive because of lack of exercise, feed allergy, herpesvirus or other physical cause, the temperament will change when corrections are made or the disease is treated.

At one extreme of the *Temperament Gauge* are high-strung, reactive and usually spooky horses who throw their heads up abruptly—sometimes violently—and step back or even come off their front feet. They may react to surprisingly light fingertip pressure of number 2 or 3 below the crest over the second or third cervical vertebra. The young Percheron in the photo fit this pattern when I first explored his body.

Such horses will often react by dropping the back

The neck and poll are often windows into the temperament of horses during *Body Exploration*. This young Percheron, who was in training to be a pairs driving horse but who had a habit of bolting in the traces, reacted strongly to light fingertip pressure by tossing his head up violently and tensing the neck muscles; his concern and wariness of humans are mirrored in his eye. Fortunately the behavior of such horses can be shifted in a surprisingly short time. Within 10 minutes of *Head-Lowering* in *Half-Walk*, *Ear TTouches*, *Tail TTouches*, *Coiled Python*, *Leg Circles*, *Neck Rocking*, *Lick of the Cow's Tongue* and *Mouth TTouches*, this gelding's head came down, his stride lengthened and his eye softened.

when pressed with a 3 pressure behind the withers, or jerk away, throw the head up, or snap at the air when fingertip pressure is applied on the girth area behind the elbows and startle or have muscle "jumps" in the big muscles of the shoulders ahead of the elbow. In many cases, horses who are considered unpredictable or unreliable under saddle will be reactive to their legs being TTouched, or the udder, inside of the hind legs or tail being handled.

Checking the Neck

Mares in particular are often strongly influenced by hormonal fluctuations. They may be unpredictable or uncooperative, "squeal and squirt" or flash their teeth at even the lightest pressure anywhere on the body during estrus. (See "Mare, moody," p. 86, for solutions.)

Highly reactive horses are often a challenge, but they can make exceptional performance horses with careful attention to feed and exercise, treatment for hormonal issues and chiropractic care, as well as regular TTouch sessions. And remember, saddle fit, teeth and shoeing, among other factors, can all play a part in temperament and require careful attention. (See chapter 2, *A Closer*

Look at the Roots of Unwanted Behavior and Poor Attitude, p. 9, for a discussion of 14 common contributors to resistance, poor performance or difficult behavior in horses.)

Temperament and reactive behavior will change in any horse when the pain is relieved and the horse loses the fear of contact or pressure in those areas.

At the other end of the *Temperament Gauge* is the calm, steady, quiet horse who will usually have a higher pain tolerance than more reactive types. In contrast, these horses will usually enjoy a number 4 pressure exploration and lower their head when you "check the gauge" on the top of the neck. And, a calmer horse will tend to react not so sensitively to soreness in the back or croup and won't be "ticklish" in the girth area.

Such horses are usually safer to ride but can offer their own challenge of being less responsive to leg aids. They are sometimes labeled lazy, and some riders find such horses to be very frustrating. The good news is that with TTouch and exercises like *Cha Cha* and *Dingo* (pp. 232 and 235), you can increase a horse's responsiveness without having to get out the whip and spurs.

With TTouch, your horse's temperament "temperature" can be brought toward the middle, no matter where on the gauge he initially registers!

TELLINGTON TOOLS

Chain Lead Line, Zephyr Lead, Wand

These are the main tools you'll need to get started with the Tellington Method. They are designed to give you control without force and enable you to give your horse clear signals that will give him the understanding necessary to be responsive to the bit or hackamore.

WHAT YOU NEED

• A well-fitting leather or heavy nylon halter with smooth side rings that a chain will not catch or hang up on. A thin nylon halter or a rope halter will not give you the capability to give your horse clear signals.

• A six-foot, flat, nylon lead line with a 28-inch chain attached. When purchasing, check the length of the chain carefully because many chains sold in tack shops are too short and only work for a small horse or pony.

• A Zephyr lead, a quarter-inch thick, soft rope attached to a six-foot nylon lead line you can use in place of a chain lead with sensitive or young horses.

• Tellington Wand—a four-foot, stiff white whip, with a plastic "button" on the end. This whip, imported from Germany, is specially constructed for optimum balance and effect. We call it the "wand" for two reasons. First, if you think of it as a whip, most people are reluctant to stroke the horse and use it as much as we find useful. And secondly, the calming and communication effects work like magic.

Think of the **wand** as an extension of your hand, not as a whip. It becomes another way to clearly signal your wishes to your horse. It also can be used to calm and soothe, and focus a horse almost instantly. You can use it to calm and lower the head of a nervous horse or teach a slow or sluggish one to move forward with more energy.

The **chain lead line,** despite its reputation for harsh handling when used incorrectly, is a wonderful tool when used thoughtfully in conjunction with the wand. You can use it or a **Zephyr lead** to teach your horse to respond to clear, light signals on the halter, to walk forward, halt easily and stand quietly:

To move your horse forward in *Dingo* (p. 235) at the walk, first stroke his back firmly two or three times, then tap him on the croup with a circular motion combined with a steady voice command to "*waaaalk*" and a forward signal on the chain lead (or Zephyr lead). To stop your horse, tap his chest lightly three times (*Cueing the Camel*, p. 236) at the same time you intone a slow "*whoaaaa*" and a light backward signal-and-release on the chain.

HOW TO

Adjust the halter so that the noseband is sitting about three fingers' width below the horse's protruding cheekbones. A halter that is too big and loose will produce too much lag time between your signals and his ability to respond. If the noseband is too tight your horse will not be able to chew or yawn (both signs of relaxation) or move his jaw.

Chain over the Nose

Photos 1 and 2 Run the chain through the side ring on the left from the outside downward, then lift the chain up so that it crosses over the noseband of the halter. Take it back out through the lower right halter ring from the inside of the ring out. When properly fitted, the chain should not lie directly on the horse's nose, but across the noseband, as shown here.

Photos 3 and 4 Attach the snap at the end of the chain to the upper right ring of the halter. Be sure to attach the little knob on the snap away from the horse's face so it doesn't dig in. You want to have about four to six inches of chain left over on the side you are leading from. (All these steps assume you are working from the horse's left side; be sure to alternate left and right so that your horse learns to respond to your signals from both sides of the body.)

Photo 5 If your horse has a small head, the 28-inch chain will be too long. You can shorten it by running the snap through the top ring and attaching it back onto itself. It's also helpful to shorten the chain for exercises like *Cha Cha* (p. 232) or for backing up.

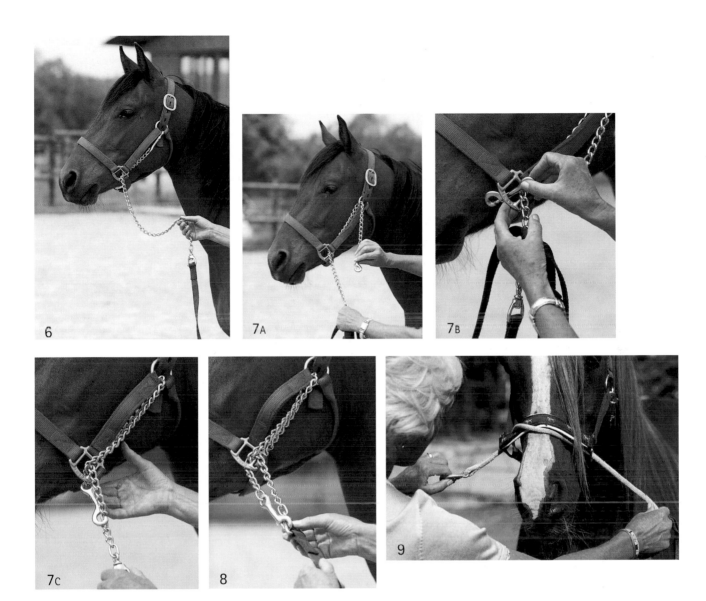

Chain up the Side

Photo 6 If your horse is high-headed, throws his head up or resists lowering it, fasten the chain up one side of the halter as shown. This configuration will encourage your horse to lower his head more readily than with the chain over the nose. Use this alternative position while retraining horses who pull back (see *Pulling Back when Tied,* p. 94). Be especially careful to wear gloves for this exercise to protect your hands in case your horse pulls back.

Photos 7A, B, and C Once your horse lowers the head from pressure up the side, you can shorten the chain by making this figure eight through the ring. Attach the snap as close to the halter ring as possible, as shown here. This holds the chain more firmly in place.

Photo 8 *Avoid the mistake* of fastening the snap to the ring at the end of the chain like this because a horse could put a foot through the loop while hand grazing and it makes the side chain shorter than ideal.

Photo 9 The Zephyr lead can be attached just like the chain lead—either over the nose to slow a horse down or up the side of the halter to lower the head.

BODY ROPE and BODY WRAP

The *Body Rope and Body Wrap* improve a horse's body awareness and his ability to move in a smooth and coordinated manner, the twin hallmarks of proprioception (see *Inside Information,* p. 163, for an explanation of the proprioceptive system). Information is relayed from the limbs to various parts of the brain, which in turn send signals back to the muscles that allow the horse to make appropriate adjustments to perform a specific movement. Such two-way neuronal input also enhances release of serotonin, a neurotransmitter that fosters a sense of safety and contentment. Ground Exercises—especially those in Dancing with Your Horse (p. 228) and Playground for Higher Learning (p. 250)—enhance a horse's potential for integrated movement.

If you ask a horse to step over ground poles and notice that he consistently hits the poles with his back feet, the *Body Wrap* or *Rope* can improve the flow of proprioceptive data going to the nervous system and thus his awareness of how he is moving. This reinforces the horse's "internal body picture," giving him a better sense of his boundaries. This ability becomes critical when the horse is moving through narrow spaces, over obstacles or being trailered.

With a Fearful Horse

A *Body Wrap* or *Rope* calms a nervous horse by providing a specific type of sensation to the nervous system known as *pressure touch*. This pressure touch—very light against the skin—results in a calming, relaxing response from the horse. This can be particularly helpful in any situation that would normally cause concern for the horse, such as a visit from the veterinarian, chiropractor or farrier.

Key Uses

- Creates boundaries to help a horse stand quietly for the veterinarian or farrier

- Calms horses who are tense, tend to shy or spook, or are nervous about objects or sounds behind them

- Helps claustrophobic horses cope with the challenge of entering confined spaces, such as trailers or narrow doorways

- Teaches a foal to lead and stand quietly without haltering or tying

- Fosters a sense of security and safety in any situation

With a Foal

The *Body Wrap* is an easy, effective and safe way to teach foals to "come-along" before haltering. It keeps the foal in balance and gives you control of his body without pulling on his head. Hold the wraps where they cross over at the withers like a suitcase handle and give signals by moving it backward or forward. You can practice with short lessons with the foal's dam alongside.

HOW TO

The *Body Rope* is formed from a 21-foot nylon rope around the shoulders and hindquarters of the horse, forming a figure eight. (This is the same lightweight rope we use for *Neckline Driving,* p. 261.) The *Body Wrap* is arranged in a similar manner using elastic bandages or wraps instead of ropes. We use either Ace-type bandages or colorful elastic leg wraps four inches wide. It takes two or three bound together depending upon the size of the horse.

The *Body Wrap* can be used over the saddle tied in a figure eight to steady a spooky horse. On an English saddle, place the center of the "8" over the saddle and run the elastic underneath the stirrup leathers and tie at the horse's side. It reduces fear or spookiness by giving a horse a sense of connection of the forehand to the hindquarters. (You can also use the *Promise Wrap*, which attaches to the saddle just around the hindquarters, to help the horse free up his back as well as overcome fear of movement or objects behind—see p. 288.)

Choosing whether to use the rope or the elastic wrap is often a toss-up. When a horse is nervous around the hindquarters, I usually prefer putting on an elastic wrap, but I think the rope gives clearer boundaries to keep a horse quiet for the veterinarian or farrier.

The Body Rope

Photo 1 To prepare your horse for the sensation of the rope touching him as he moves, do some preparation before placing it on your horse. Fold the rope in your hand and stroke the hindquarters.

Photo 2 Place the rope around the neck and put a little pressure on it. This is a cautionary measure for a horse who might be reactive to the rope around the neck because of a bad experience.

Photo 3 Twist the rope twice at the withers and lay it carefully around the hindquarters without tying it.

Photo 4 Walk a few steps with a helper leading your horse.

Photo 5 Once the horse has accepted the feel, tie the rope in a quick release bow and drop it to mid thigh. (When your horse is relaxed about the process, place the rope lower so it lays almost at gaskin level, about eight inches above the hocks, and pull the tail out from under the rope—not shown in this picture.)

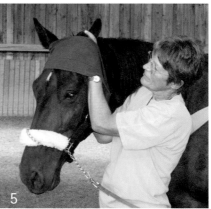

The Body Wrap

Photo 1 Wrap one elastic wrap around the horse's neck and tie it with a square knot.

Photo 2 Attach one end of the second bandage to this knot, then carefully guide it around the horse's hindquarters and under his tail (always watching your horse's reaction), and tie the other end to the first bandage about 15 inches away from the first knot to form a "bridge" of wrap, going over

the horse's back just behind the withers. It should fit around the hindquarters just below the point of the buttocks. Make sure the second bandage fits snugly enough and does not slide down or slip up under the tail when he walks.

Photo 3 Here is a cautionary measure to take with spooky horses: place the wrap over the tail so it can be slipped off easily if a horse panics.

Photo 4 A variation: here, the second wrap is

INSIDE INFORMATION

In addition to the familiar five senses of sight, sound, smell, taste and touch, you and your horse have two other sensory systems that process information from "inside" rather than external sources. The *vestibular system* responds to changes in head position and is critical to balance and postural security via receptors located in the inner ear. Anyone who has ever had an inner ear infection or vertigo knows what happens when this system is out of whack! The *proprioceptive system* gives internal awareness of where our body parts are in space, critical to spatial awareness and coordinated movement. The receptors for proprioception, located in joints and muscles, respond to compression of joints or movement. People or animals who have suffered a stroke or other head injury often experience a loss of proprioceptive function and tend to have impaired movements.

around the barrel. We use this on young horses to accustom them to the feeling of a girth, before a surcingle or saddle is carried, or for the few really reactive horses who are too skittish to have the wrap around the tail in the beginning.

Photo 5 Here's an unusual variation of the *Body Wrap*, positioned around a horse's ears and forehead to help the horse overcome ear shyness (see *Ear Shy*, p. 59).

LOWERING THE HEAD

Teaching a horse to lower his head from a signal from the halter, or from your hand on the top of the neck, may be the single most important lesson to earn your horse's trust. *Lowering the Head* overrides the flight instinct, and "de-spooks" a flighty, high-headed, unpredictable, herdbound or potentially dangerous mount. The result is a safer, more trusting and confident partner for the trail or ring.

You can teach your horse to lower his head to a variety of levels, but we recommend keeping the nose above knee level. (Taking the nose all the way to the ground may be an interesting trick, but horses tend to "shut down" if it goes too low. When the poll is about six inches below the withers, your horse will stay "present" and still relax the neck and back muscles.)

Key Uses

- Fosters relaxation, trust and cooperation
- Overrides the flight instinct
- Relieves muscle tension in the neck and back
- Encourages deeper breathing
- Relaxes an anxious horse for the veterinarian and farrier and for clipping, acupuncture or chiropractic treatments

HOW TO

Photo 1 This 12-year-old, ewe-necked Warmblood gelding was said to be stubborn and resistant to "giving his head," whether from the ground or from

THE FOUNDATIONS OF TRUST

Two valuable "tools" in Getting Started with TTouch are *Lowering the Head* and *Taming the Tiger*. They are the foundation of the Tellington Method—building trust and ensuring a base of good behavior for a lifetime. You'll want to include them in the training of every horse. They are important because both teach a horse to think and trust you rather than "spook" in scary situations, such as when a dirt bike roars up behind you or a stray plastic bag flaps in a tree above you.

The two exercises are useful for all horses, whether you are starting a youngster or retraining a mature horse; it will only take a few sessions to ensure that your favorite saddle horse is a good citizen—a safe, willing partner and companion.

the saddle. It is not unusual for horses who are tense or high-headed to raise the head—as he did when he was asked to step forward and lower it. In such cases, thread the chain up the side of the halter, as shown here, instead of over the nose. Stroke the neck, chest and legs down to the ground while asking him to lower his head with an ask-and-release signal on the chain. Once your horse understands what you want, he will release the neck and lower the head on the release, so your signal downward should be brief. Stroking the chest and neck simultaneously helps to relax your horse and keep him from stepping forward.

Photos 2, 3, and 4 It can help to bend your upper body forward and squat down. (For safety, make sure you squat slightly off to the side—not right in front of your horse.) "Milk" the lead rope downward with a light pulsating pressure. When your horse lowers his head, stand up slowly, keeping his head lowered.

Photo 5 Next stand in front of your horse and lightly place one hand on the noseband and the other on the chain, being sure to hold with slightly curved, open fingers in case he tosses his head up. When your horse lowers the head easily, you can place both hands on the noseband.

Photo 6 For the ultimate trust test, place one hand on the noseband and the other on the horse's crest near his poll. With light pressure on the noseband and using small, circular *Clouded Leopard TTouches* (p. 195) on his crest, ask your horse to lower his head. With some horses, it helps if you gently rock the head and neck from side to side a little the first time you ask for the lowering.

Photo 7 When a horse resists lowering the head, you may find it easier to achieve this by leading in the *Labyrinth* (p. 259) with the chain up the side of the halter.

Photo 8 Try calming *Forelock Slides* (see p. 198) for horses who don't appreciate having their head handled. Quietly slide from the root of the hair down to the tip. Most horses will enjoy this meditative movement after a few slides and respond by lowering the head.

Additional Tips

High-strung or spooky horses who habitually move and stand with high head and neck posture may initially resist. If you can't get the head down within a session or two, here are several additional aids:

• A tip that works like magic is to raise the back with a *Back Lift* (p. 193). Nearly 90 percent of the time, as soon as that back comes up, the head will drop. Continue doing *Back Lifts* daily to encourage the new head carriage.

• With short-striding, tight-necked horses, opening the shoulder with a *Shoulder Release* (p. 225) will also contribute to changing habitual posture.

• If success still eludes you, squat down with a little grain in your hand as you signal on the chain for the head lowering, but put the emphasis on the signal. Use the grain as a reward for lowering—not as a bribe.

Once your horse has learned to lower the head from your hand on the crest behind the ears (as in Photo 6), you can reinforce the response from the saddle by reaching forward and TTouching the crest.

TAMING THE TIGER

Taming the Tiger is a "half" cross-tie position. It is extremely effective for teaching patience and self-control and safely prepares a horse to stand quietly in regular cross-ties. Pressure on the poll or under the chin triggers many horses to pull back and struggle. Horses quickly learn to override this response when they are contained but not restrained within *Taming the Tiger*. For safety, we always place the horse where there is a barrier behind him like in a box stall, so he can't go back more than about three feet.

WHAT YOU NEED

- Safe place to work with your horse, such as a corner with one side and back

- Chain or Zephyr lead line

- 15- to 20-foot rope or lightweight line (such as a driving line)

- Extra lead rope with snap to create a temporary slot (see Photo 5)

- Wand

HOW TO

- Begin with the lead line fastened up the left side of the halter (p. 159).

- Place your horse parallel to a wall or fence. In the photos, we've created a fixed "ring" on the fence with a rope and large snap.

- Now thread your long rope through the halter ring under the horse's chin, and take it on through the ring on the fence, bringing it back to fasten to the lower ring of the halter on the off (right) side. If I'm working with a horse who has a tendency to charge forward, I sometimes put the chain over the nose.

Key Uses

- Teaches a horse to stand quietly for the veterinarian or farrier

- Deals with difficulty tying or a tendency to break halters or lead ropes struggling to escape

- Controls pawing when tied

- Prevents kicking or biting when being handled

- Helps treating an injured horse who won't stand still

- Encourages a horse to stand tied

Photos 1 and 2 Hold the rope and lead line in one hand separated by your index finger. In this way you will have the other hand free to reposition the horse or stroke him with the wand. The wand is very important to help reposition the horse if he moves. (For a larger picture of this, see p. 146.)

Photo 3 If your horse becomes restless it may help to steady him with the rope in two hands. Keep a connection with both lines and when he stands quietly, loosen the contact slowly so his head is free again. To adjust the position of the horse's head sideways in either direction, lengthen one line as you shorten the other. For this, the rope must be able to slide around the post.

Photo 4 If your horse pulls back, release the rope slightly as you tap him on the hindquarters with the wand to encourage him to come quietly forward. With no resistance on the halter, most horses stop pulling back, and for safety, be sure to have a barrier, such as a fence or stable wall, behind him.

Photo 5 Here is the rope wrapped on the rail to create a temporary slot to run the long line through.

What should you do if...

- *Your horse cannot be safely tied?*

Go back to basic *Lowering the Head* (p. 163) and combine it with *Dingo* (p. 235) and *Dancing Cobra* (p. 234). Once your horse has learned to lower the head and step forward from a light signal on the chain, then you're ready to try *Taming the Tiger*.

- *You do not have a smooth fence to put the rope around?*

The long rope must be able to move and slide, so tie it to a metal ring (in this case, a lead snap) attached to the fence, post or wall (see Photo 5).

TTouches for Trust

TTouches for Trust are at the core of forming a relationship and bond with your horse based on mutual trust.

Horses, just like humans, need to feel safe and see you as a trustworthy person whose requests will be reasonable. Your horse needs to know you will listen to and respect him. Such a high level of trust will result in a horse willing to cooperate with you.

With TTouches for Trust, horses who have become sour or are emotionally "shut down" come out of themselves; those who have lost their spirit begin to trust again. Your horse will become more involved, curious, connected and sees you as an "interesting" person. Don't be surprised when he starts following you around without tack!

In fact, this kind of trust goes beyond bonding: horses who receive TTouches for Trust actually consider people differently. Horses are happier to see you, easier to catch and handle—they want to be with you, and show a willingness to cooperate that goes beyond conditioned responses or rote learning.

TTouches for Trust begin the process of giving you and your horse more choices a win win situation for both. You're transcending the ego game into the realm of fair play.

Why should your horse learn to trust others? Isn't he your "special" horse? If your horse only trusts you, it limits your possibilities. Consider the need for cooperation with your veterinarian, farrier, dentist, caretaker or friend, if you want to share your horse with someone. In an emergency situation, such as an evacuation during a fire, your horse's life might depend upon his ability to respond quickly to another person's requests.

With TTouches for Trust, you and your horse will still have a special relationship, but not one based on codependency or coercion. Your horse will be a better partner as fear gives way to confidence.

Note: The how-to description for *Ear TTouches*, which are excellent for both fostering trust and restoring health, can be found in the *TTouches for Health* section on p. 210.

Mouth TTouch (see p. 182)

ABALONE TTOUCH

This TTouch is done with the whole hand placed softly on the horse's body. Use just enough contact with the fingers, palm and heel of the hand so that you can push the skin in a circle without sliding over the hair. The center of the circle will be in the center of the palm of your hand. Imagine your hand sticking to the hair like an abalone sticks to ocean rocks. Move the skin and tissue

Key Uses

- Prepares for saddling
- Soothes girthy/cinchy horses
- Quiets horses reactive to touch or grooming
- Lowers the head or releases tight neck muscles
- Stimulates gut sounds
- Encourages breathing

in a clockwise circle and a quarter, keeping enough contact to avoid sliding your hand across the hair.

To relax your horse, do two-second circles, pausing briefly between each circle, and slide lightly to the next circle. To increase awareness and relaxed alertness, do one-second circles with firm slides between the circles. By having two hands on the horse, the left hand completes the connection between horse and human.

Pressure: 1 to 3

Keynotes: Soothing, relaxing, comforting, whole-hand, diffused, noninvasive, warm, nonthreatening, easy to do.

Key spots: Neck, back, barrel, belly, inside the thighs.

HOW TO

Photo 1 An *Abalone TTouch* on the atlas/axis region just behind the poll: note my left hand on the side of the halter stabilizing the head. It is excellent for the horse with tight neck muscles who is high-headed and reactive to touch. Lowering the head in this way overrides the flight reflex.

Photo 2 A "push-pull" movement between the two hands deepens relaxation and release of the neck. The left hand invites the head down while the right hand continues *Abalone* circles, pushing the skin toward the withers.

Photo 3 The *Abalone TTouch* combined with the *Coiled Python Lift* (p. 172) to relax tight back muscles. The left hand steadies as the right hand circles, then pushes the skin upward toward the spine and slowly releases.

COILED PYTHON LIFT

This TTouch was inspired by my work with an 11-foot Burmese Python named Joyce who lived at the San Diego Wild Animal Park. These lifting TTouches relaxed her to the point that she enjoyed the work I was doing on her, and it helped her recover from recurring bouts of pneumonia attributed to lack of exercise. We named this touch in her honor.

The *Coiled Python* is a combination of either an *Abalone* or *Lying Leopard* circle with a lift of the skin. You can use your right or left hand to make the circle. Begin at the top of the leg, using both hands with just enough contact with the skin so your hands do not slide over the hair. Lightly push

Key Uses

- Releases muscle tension and spasms in the back

- Increases awareness in the legs so a horse feels connected to the ground

- Improves coordination

- Increases confidence

- "De-spooks" a flighty horse

- Relaxes nervous horses

- Lengthens stride

- Eases stress of late gestation in broodmares.

the skin in a circle with one hand, then push the skin upwards with both hands and hold for four seconds, supporting the skin as it returns slowly to the beginning place. Then slide several inches lower and repeat the circle and lift. Work from the top of the legs all the way down to the fetlock joints. To be effective requires only small moves. If your horse

shifts away, you're squeezing too hard or pushing the skin upward too much. Sometimes we do a simple lift without the circle; however, starting with a circle brings more awareness to the horse, and helps the person breathe before making the lift.

Pressure: 1 to 3

Key spots: Legs, back, inside thigh. On the back, it release tight muscles and increases blood flow.

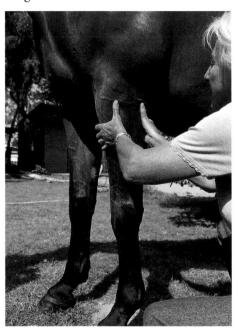

HOW TO

Photo Beginning at the top of the forearm, place both hands lightly on either side of the leg. Start the movement with a number 2 pressure. Circle with one hand and then push the skin upward with both hands with just enough contact that your hands do not slip over the skin. On most parts of the leg you'll see very little movement. It is simply a little stretch of the skin upward, increasing circulation and minimizing the effects of gravity for those few moments. If you are working on a flighty, nervous horse, and your desire is to ground him and slow him down, hold for a few seconds at the top of the lift and slowly return the skin to the starting point. Then slide a few inches downward to start your next lift. If, on the other hand, you want to energize your horse, make the circles, lifts and return in a few seconds with a swift release downward. I suggest you try out different tempos on your friends to get a sense of the potential of this TTouch.

Use before competition: Speed up the circles and *Coiled Python Lifts* on the legs to refresh and rejuvenate the horse. At the top of the lift, do not pause, but instead slide your hands down the leg lightly to the next lift point a few inches below. If you lift too slowly, you may induce relaxation, which is counterproductive just before a competition.

CONNECTED CIRCLES

Each circular TTouch is complete within itself; however, connecting the circles with a short, clear slide over the hair, with two to three inches between circles, will give the horse an enhanced sense of the body—an improved self-image.

Pressure: 2 to 3

HOW TO

• Run rows of *Connected Circles* parallel to the topline of the body (crest and spine) to give a sense of connection and continuity from forehand to hindquarters. You can also connect any basic circle TTouch from the forearm to the hooves and down the back legs. Think of it as "connecting the dots."

Key Uses

- Develops confidence, coordination and balance
- Gives your horse a sense of connection

• If your horse is concerned about being TTouched, you may find it helpful to begin with five or six random circles on the neck with a one-second tempo, done several inches apart. Then switch to the connected circles.

FRONT LEG CIRCLES

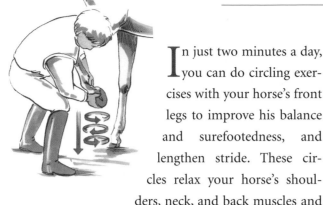

In just two minutes a day, you can do circling exercises with your horse's front legs to improve his balance and surefootedness, and lengthen stride. These circles relax your horse's shoulders, neck, and back muscles and

Key Uses

- Teaches your horse to easily balance on three legs for hoof cleaning, trimming or shoeing
- Prepares a horse to stand still on the trailer without kicking, scrambling or leaning on the divider
- Improves suppleness, reduces stumbling
- Relaxes and releases tension from tight shoulders, neck and back muscles
- Warms-up before riding, conditioning or competition
- Detects back or leg stiffness before it shows up as lameness under saddle
- Helps keep a stall-bound horse limber and flexible

improve balance. It can save you warm-up time if your horse tends to be stiff for the first minutes under saddle, and I find it more useful than the act of pulling the leg forward to smooth out the hair under the girth before mounting.

HOW TO

Position yourself facing the hindquarters and prepare to pick up your horse's foot by stroking down the leg with the back of your hand. Then, scrape lightly upward on the tendon above the fetlock or just above the inside of the knee with the fingernails. This signal teaches the horse to take his weight onto his other three legs and rebalance to lift his foot. It is clearer for the horse, and easier for you, than the normal method of pinching the leg and leaning on the shoulder. When you finish a leg exercise (or cleaning out a hoof), avoid dropping the foot—guide it down and *place* it on the ground.

Photo 1 Support the fetlock joint with your hand closest to your horse.

- Support the hoof, with your thumb on the side of the bars and your fingers around the front of the hoof.

- Keep the sole of the foot perpendicular to the ground, and the pastern and fetlock joint aligned instead of allowing the fetlock joint to collapse downward—a common cause of horses dropping a shoulder and leaning on you.

- Circle the leg by moving your pelvis, knees and feet rather than your arms. To avoid strain, keep your back straight, and rest your outside elbow on your outside knee to protect your back if the leg is heavy.

Photo 2 Circle the hoof in both directions around the point where it had initially rested on the ground. Use a horizontal motion like a helicopter propeller: toward the other leg, forward, to the outside, and then back. Do two circles in both directions at different heights from the ground, spiraling down until you are just above the ground. Instead of putting the hoof down, do another circle as close to the ground as possible and tap the toe on the ground at several points on the circle.

Photo 3 Place the toe on the ground about six to eight inches behind his other hoof so the shoul-

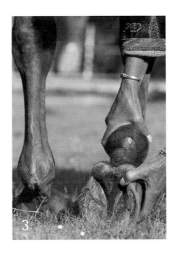

der releases. Support the hoof firmly with one hand over the back of the fetlock joint and one on the side of the hoof for a few seconds to give your horse the idea of balancing without weight on the foot. If your horse is tight in the shoulder or low in the heels, resting the toe may be difficult; your horse may rest the toe for only a moment at first. This position can markedly improve balance.

What should you do if…

• *Your horse has a tendency to pull his leg away?*

Don't get into a struggle. Remember, it takes two to fight. Instead of hanging on for dear life, give the leg a little shake, or vibration. You can also let the horse put his foot down to regain his balance. Then try again, and this time ask for only one or two small, fast circles before letting the leg down. Do this a few times until he seems more secure standing on three legs. Add some *Coiled Python Lifts* (p. 172) from elbow to hoof to improve his awareness of the area and take away any fear he might have of being handled there.

• *He leans on you when you pick up his leg?*

Support the leg at the fetlock joint and under the cannon bone. Fold the leg at the knee, keeping the lower leg parallel to the ground, and raise it high enough so that your horse cannot lean on you. Horses often lose their balance and lean when the handler holds the hoof higher than the knee and allows the fetlock joint to collapse downward. Give the leg a little shake to encourage him to be responsible for his own balance. Steady yourself and don't lean into the horse.

HIND LEG CIRCLES

Moving a horse's hind legs in small circles is an exercise to help your horse overcome nervousness about having the hind feet picked up and handled. It can also ease the discomfort of stiffness or arthritis in the hindquarters and increase mobility. I'm often amazed at how many horses are reprimanded (or even tranquilized!) for failing to hold a leg up for the farrier for long periods of time when the only time they're asked to do so is during these sessions. A few minutes of *Front* and *Hind Leg*

Key Uses

- Ensures picking up hind feet quietly
- Lengthens stride
- Improves suppleness and engagement
- Evens out short and choppy gaits
- Helps the horse stand balanced and quietly for your farrier
- Teaches a foal to hold up a leg and remain balanced and relaxed
- Releases tight back muscles

Circles each day as you're cleaning out the feet can make a major difference in your horse's ability to cooperate.

If your horse kicks or pulls away when you first pick up a hind leg, you can safely stroke him quietly with the wand. Start the stroking on the chest and front legs and then proceed along the belly and down the hind legs. This will help him gain confidence about being touched and will improve his balance by "reminding" him of his connection to the ground. Follow the wand work with connected *Lying Leopard TTouches* (p. 181) all over the body and from the hindquarters to the ground until your horse becomes confident and unafraid of your contact. I believe horses kick out of fear or previous aggressive handling and can be soothed by quiet TTouches rather than punishment.

HOW TO

Position yourself facing the hindquarters and prepare to pick up your horse's foot by stroking down the leg with the back of your hand. Scrape lightly upward on the tendon above the fetlock with the fingernails. This is clearer for the horse than the normal method of pinching the leg and leaning against on him to put him off balance.

I've worked on high-level performance horses who could not make a six-inch circle due to incredibly tight, sore back muscles. Don't attempt to stretch or force the horse but continue to just make small circles. After a few sessions, the muscles of his hindquarters and his back should relax. When they do, you will be able to gradually make larger circles that will help increase his range of motion and improve his way of going.

Caution: With arthritic horses, or those with stifle problems, be conservative and make very small circles low to the ground.

Photo 1 Hold the hoof with your thumb on the bar and your fingers on the outside of the hoof using your hand that's farthest away from your horse.

- If the leg is heavy, rest your outside elbow on your outside knee.

- Bring your inside hand around the front of the leg and grasp the back of the leg above the fetlock joint.

- Start with small circles at the height offered to you by the horse. If he pulls the leg up high and tight, make a few tiny, fast circles at the height he offers until he relaxes and lowers the leg.

- Begin with small circles and expand the circle as large as the horse allows without resistance.

Photo 2 Circle the leg in both directions and at different heights, working your way down to the ground. Rest the toe of the hoof six to eight inches behind the other hind foot. This position helps the horse relax the muscles in his hindquarters.

Photo 3 Draw the hind leg forward with your inside hand on the back of the fetlock joint and your outside hand drawing the hoof forward toward the front leg. Move the hoof in an oval pattern, keeping it under the belly and as level as possible. Do this several times in both directions. Take the leg only as far forward as is comfortable for the horse.

What should you do if...

• *Your horse will not hold his leg up for long?*

Do only one or two fast, small circles, then lower the leg. Place the toe on the ground slightly behind the other hoof. With one hand on his hock, jiggle the leg. This will help relax the hindquarters and make it easier to pick the leg up again.

• *Your horse has trouble performing lateral work (such as side-passes or half-passes)?*

Leg circles under the belly teach a horse to move his hind legs freely to the front and side, without the weight of a rider. It will be easier for a horse to do any sort of lateral work as his range of motion increases. Circling the legs relaxes muscles and increases range of motion, teaching him how to move the leg with better coordination and balance.

• *Your horse collapses against the farrier when he tries to lift a back leg?*

Stroke quietly down the front and back of the hind leg with the wand. The next step is to pick up a hind leg just enough so the toe is resting on the ground. Then you can pick it up and make one or two quick small circles keeping it low to the ground, and put the leg down immediately. Feed your horse a little hay during the TTouching so he will begin to relax during the process. Encouraging your horse to *Lower the Head* (p. 163) can also help him remain balanced while holding up a hind leg.

LICK OF THE COW'S TONGUE

The long, smooth strokes of *Lick of the Cow's Tongue* give a horse a stronger sense of connection from belly to back. *Licks* improve flexibility, enabling your horse to bend, collect and perform lateral movements more easily. This versatile TTouch can calm a horse or activate him, depending upon whether you use a flat hand or run your fingertips and slightly curved fingers more vigorously through the hair.

To rejuvenate or activate: Before and after competition, a vigorous stroke with curved fingers sliding through the hair and pressure from the heel of the hand will activate and energize.

To calm: Make the same stroke with the flat of the hand.

Pressure: 1 to 3

Key spots: Barrel, shoulders and across the top of the croup, always stroking obliquely across the lay of the hair.

HOW TO

On the belly and back: Start on the middle of the abdomen just behind the elbows and stroke over the top of the back. Make parallel strokes all the way back to the flanks.

If your horse is spooky, sensitive or won't accept leg contact, you may not be able to use long strokes at first. Instead, start on the belly line with flat-hand *Abalone* circles (p. 171) with a four-inch slide upward, followed by another, until you reach the middle of the spine. It may take several ten-minute sessions over a period of a week to get your horse over any ticklishness or oversensitivity so you can do soothing flat-hand *Licks.*

Photo 1 Stand near the girth area. Place one hand on the back and begin the stroke at the midline of the belly with the other hand. (Another choice is to place both hands flat on the horse's mid-abdominal line for balance, keeping one hand low as the other hand strokes upward.)

Photo 2 Draw your hand toward you across the hair with a long, soft, continuous stroke.

Photo 3 As you start to come to mid-barrel, rotate your hand so your fingers point upward toward the horse's topline.

Photo 4 Continue the stroke smoothly upward until you reach the middle of the topline.

Photo 5 Finish when you cross over the spine. Start the next stroke one hand's width behind the first one. Try different pressures and speeds, and work both sides of the horse.

On the barrel make your strokes about six inches apart so you cover the entire belly-barrel-back from behind the elbows to the flank. Cover the whole barrel like mowing rows of hay.

On the croup: Standing on a stool or bale, place your hands on opposite sides of the croup. With a firm stroking motion—hands slightly curved, using fingertips and heel of the hand—make alternating strokes over the whole croup. This will help a horse engage and activate his hindquarters, whether for cutting, spinning, jumping, dressage or to strengthen him for mountain trails.

What should you do if...

- *Your horse pins his ears, moves away or kicks, or the skin twitches when you start the long strokes?*

Begin with *Belly Lifts* (p. 209) and *Abalone TTouches* (p. 171) all over the belly and barrel. When your horse finds these acceptable, combine *Abalone TTouches* with short strokes between and graduate to long soft strokes with the flat hand. This may take several sessions.

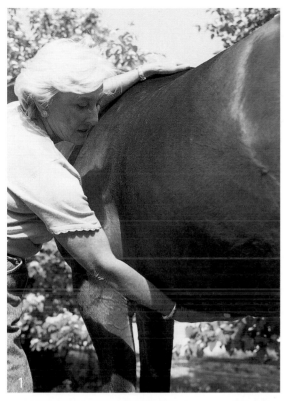

• *Your horse doesn't like to be touched in the udder or sheath area?*

Many people do not pay enough attention to the udder and sheath areas, which need to be cleaned like the rest of the horse. Starting with the wand is safer for you and less threatening to the horse. You can then turn the wand around and use the button end to start TTouching. Then try *Abalone TTouches* using a warm, damp, cotton cloth or glove. Acknowl-edge any concern that the horse shows by pausing momentarily, letting him know that you are indeed listening to him, thereby gaining his trust.

• *If your horse is hot and sweaty after work?*

Place a damp cotton sock or cloth over your hand while you do the long strokes of this TTouch. The damp sock cools the horse while the TTouch helps him recover from exertion more quickly.

The gift of this TTouch came from working with llamas, who are often resistant to being touched on the face. We learned that if we first touched them with the back of our hands and fingers rather than the palm side, they were much more accepting. The back of the hand is less threatening and seems much less invasive.

Over the years, we found this TTouch worked not only for contact-shy llamas but also for horses, and other animals who are nervous, threatened or uncomfortable about being TTouched.

Pressure: 1 to 2

HOW TO

Photos 1 and 2 The face, ears and neck are three favorite places to connect with your horse using *Llama TTouch*. Use the back of your hand to push the skin in a circle with light (number 1 or 2

Key Uses

- Builds confidence in timid, head- or ear-shy horses

- Helps when approaching a horse you don't know for the first time

- Soothes horses nervous about being TTouched

- Encourages horses who are unable to lower the head in response to your request

- Allows you to TTouch horses in sore areas on the neck

pressure) contact. Be sure to hold your hand softly and maintain a connection with your other hand on the neck, crest or halter.

LYING LEOPARD TTOUCH

This relaxing, trust-building TTouch provides a bridge from the soothing warmth of *Abalone* (p. 171) to the more precise focus of *Clouded Leopard* (p. 195). The connection comes from your partially flattened fingers and not from the palm of the hand as in *Abalone*, or the pads of the fingers as in *Clouded Leopard*.

Move the skin in a circle with contact from the first two phalanges of the four fingers. The middle of your palm can be cupped lightly over the body depending upon where you are working. Maintain your contact with the outside of the thumb.

Circles are done primarily with the first and second phalanges, as compared with the whole-hand contact of *Abalone TTouch*.

Pressure: 1 to 3

Keynotes: Focusing, soothing, calming, trust-building.

Key spots: Head, neck, legs, back, barrel.

HOW TO

Photos 1, 2, 3 and 4 I demonstrate some of the typical places to apply *Lying Leopard TTouch*. Steady the head with the opposite hand on the halter. This is especially beneficial for developing trust and a special communication with your horse.

Photo 5 Note the distance between fingers and thumb and contact with the side of the thumb. The contact is clearly with the flattened fingers yet the palm is close enough to give a feeling of security and warmth. The left hand has a light contact on the lead, steadying the head.

Note: Avoid pressing with the heel of your hand as it will stiffen your finger and interfere with the clarity of the circle.

Key Uses

- Improves attention and focus
- Grounds a flighty, fearful or "touchy" horse
- Builds trust and self-confidence
- Reduces pain and prevents swelling in acute injury (number 1 pressure)

MOUTH TTOUCH

Working on your horse's muzzle—mouth, gums and nostrils—can change a multitude of attitudes and emotional responses such as biting, nipping, stubbornness, inflexibility, flightiness, unpredictability and resistance to training. The muzzle has a direct connection to the limbic system, the part of the brain that controls emotions and is the center of learning. Horses who are stubborn or flighty will often resist mouth contact, sometimes to the degree of rearing.

The *Mouth TTouch* may be a new experience for your horse. If he pulls away, use the chain over his nose (see p. 158) to steady his head, and if he throws it up high, fasten the chain lead, or soft Zephyr lead, up the side of the halter. A horse who is difficult to bridle must first learn to keep his head at your level and open his mouth from a thumb inserted softly into the corner of his lips.

Caution: If you are concerned about being bitten, or if you are not experienced with horses, trust your inner voice and stick to working on the outer areas of the mouth and chin.

Pressure: 2 to 3 (Mouth, Tongue and Lips)

1 to 3 (Nostrils)

HOW TO

Mouth

Photo 1 Stand facing in the same direction as your horse and hold the halter firmly with one hand. Begin with a few flat-hand circles—*Lying Leopard TTouches* (p. 181)—around the mouth.

Photo 2 The chin is one of the most valuable spots to work on. Resistant or nervous horses will often tighten their chin. Loosening the chin with circles and gentle kneading will relax your horse and overcome tension.

Key Uses: Mouth, Tongue and Lips

- Prepares for deworming or electrolytes

- Helps horses accept teeth floating and other oral procedures

- Trains young horses to accept the bit

- Teaches endurance horses to accept vet check procedures, or any horse to accept having vital signs such as capillary refill evaluated

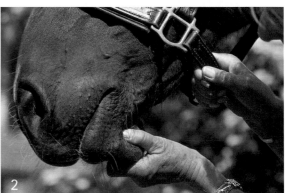

Tongue and Lips

Photos 3, 4 and 5 Note the different handholds for getting in the mouth. In Photo 3, my hand is hooked on the nose, the thumb tapping the roof of the mouth. In Photo 4, the lower lip is kneaded

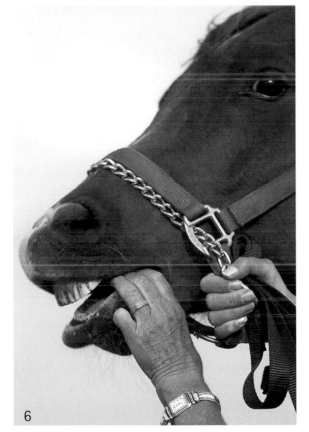

gently before inserting the fingers. In Photo 5, the horse accepts the new sensation of my fingers in his mouth. Just a few minutes of this nonhabitual handling is great preparation for carrying a bit, deworming or dental work.

Photo 6 Slide three fingers into the mouth over the tongue. Use your middle and index fingers to tap the tongue as if you are playing a piano. Many horses will open their mouth wide or toss their head because of the strange sensation, but with a little persistence on your part they soon settle down and accept the contact. Hold your horse's head still with a steady grip on the side of the halter. *Keep your fingers clear of any canine teeth!* The tongue is a strong muscle and could suck your fingers up to the molars where you could be pinched, so stabilize your fingers by holding your thumb firmly in the chin groove. Tapping on the tongue can help resensitize a dull or hard mouth, and a horse with

an oversensitive mouth will get used to this contact and learn to respond more willingly to the bit.

Photo 7 Gently knead the lower lip between your thumb inside the horse's mouth and your fingers hooked behind in the groove of his chin. Start in one corner and work around the lower lip with small, connected circles. A few minutes of TTouches like this can work wonders for a nervous horse.

Photos 8 and 9 Slip your fingers, held close together, under the upper lip, leaving your thumb on the outside of his mouth. Hold the halter firmly with your other hand to keep his head still. The gums should feel moist and slippery. If the gums are dry, dip your hands in the water bucket and slide your hand back and forth four or five times over the gums. Your horse will enjoy this exercise after a few practice sessions. (For a larger picture of this, see p. 170.)

Nostrils

Photos 10 and 11 Working with the nostrils—stretching the edges in every direction, and gently reaching inside and doing little circles as far as your thumb or fingers will reach—can be very beneficial. Because of the mouth and nostril's connection to the limbic system, an ancient part of the brain connected with emotion and learning, I believe accustoming a horse to accepting and enjoying nostril work can influence all sorts of behavior, and is time well spent.

Key Uses: Nostrils

- Makes a resistant horse more accepting of his head handled

- Helps horses with head-shaking or allergies

- Calms and stabilizes the emotions of horses who are overreactive, skittish or "willful"

Photo 12 If your horse tosses his head to evade paste-deworming or electrolyting by oral syringe, try a *Mouth Wrap*. Place a lightweight, cool, damp towel over the nose in this fashion to dissolve his resistance. Insert your thumb in the corner of his mouth, as I am doing here, in order to prepare him for the syringe, which you can see in my left hand.

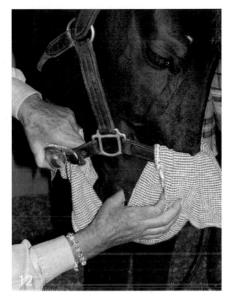

What should you do if...

• *Your horse will not allow you to touch his mouth by rearing or going into a giraffe-like pose with his head beyond reach?*

If your horse rears, there is a solution that has never failed to work. Wring out a wet, thin towel like a dishcloth (see Photo 12), and secure it over the nose by hooking it over the noseband and through the chinstrap. You can then do *Lying Leopard TTouches* through the cloth and slip your hands in the open side near the mouth.

If the problem is the horse is raising the head beyond your reach, begin with *Lowering the Head* (p. 163) with the chain or Zephyr lead up the side of the halter. If you still can't get to the mouth, lift the chin to raise the horse's head even higher than he wants it. Support it there for 20 seconds or so and then slowly lower it. Most horses will maintain a lower head position afterward.

• *Your horse nips or bites?*

Use *Taming the Tiger* (p. 166) for safe control. First, practice *Mouth TTouches* on a friendly horse until you feel confident. Many young horses nip because they were allowed to "mouth" a human when they were foals. Nipping or biting (see p. 42) can also be the result of normal playfulness or just plain boredom. Working the mouth while keeping the head still almost always overcomes these habits.

Caution: If your horse normally accepts you handling his mouth but suddenly won't let you anywhere near it, he could have a problem such as a tooth abscess. Consult your veterinarian.

TAIL TTOUCH

Often overlooked as a behavioral barometer, the tail can provide unique insights into a horse's personality and behavior. *Tail TTouch* is a group of TTouches that are especially beneficial for horses who fear movement or noise behind or around them, or who kick at other horses or in the trailer. Tail work helps relax tight back and neck muscles and stops tail wringing.

You can change a horse's behavior by changing the way he carries his tail. All of the *Tail TTouches* will contribute to a new feeling of confidence, and the *Tail Pull*, in particular, will intensify the connection from poll to tail, completing the circuit from poll to tail. It can even elevate a horse's status in the herd.

A tightly tucked tail often indicates tension held in the body, even in a horse who appears otherwise calm. *Tail TTouches* are an essential step to retraining the high-headed horse, because such horses are usually concerned about movement behind. Such horses will often visibly release tight muscles after the first session of tail work.

Key Uses

- Overcomes fear of movement behind
- Builds confidence
- Prepares a horse for a rectal exam
- Stops muscle tremors in an exhausted or stressed horse
- Teaches a horse to wear a crupper
- Helps a horse accept a thermometer or speculum
- Lowers the head
- Stops kicking
- Readies a mare for breeding

Caution: With young or high-strung horses, be extra cautious or skip tail work until your horse has learned to trust you and is completely safe behind.

HOW TO

Photo 1 Begin by standing safely to one side. Hold the tail in one hand and with your other hand, separate a small clump of hair and stroke slowly to the end of the hair. This has a calming effect and is great for the horse who is afraid of movement behind him. If there's any chance the horse could kick, or he clamps his tail, pull it firmly out of the tail groove to do the slides. This normally inhibits kicking and will enable a tense horse to relax.

Photo 2 Horses who are spooky or nervous will react if squeezed on the point of the buttocks. With one hand on the croup, make number 3 pressure *Raccoon TTouches* (p. 213) all around the area to release fear. This will prepare a nervous or tight-tailed horse for the next steps.

Photo 3 Still standing slightly to the side, place both hands under the sides of the tail and do small circles until your horse releases the tail and lifts it. Be careful not to get your fingers caught under a clamped tail. This is good prep before your veterinarian does a pregnancy check, making the procedure more comfortable for both the vet and your mare.

Photo 4 Lift the tail by grasping a clump of hair and circling it in both directions.

Pearling

Photos 5 and 6 Hold the tail firmly between both hands, tipping the vertebrae back and forth down the tail bone. It's another way to make your horse relax and feel safe behind.

Photo 7 Put one hand under the tail about six inches from the top. Lift the tail. Place the other hand on top of the tail bone a few inches below the first hand. Push the tail inward with your bottom hand as you lift up with your other hand, creating an arch. Maintain the arch as you rotate the tail several times in each direction.

Tail Pulling

Photos 8 and 9 Standing slightly to the side of your horse, hold the raised tail firmly in both hands. Shift your weight from your leading foot to your back foot, applying a steady pull without bending your elbows. Hold the traction for a few seconds and then slowly shift your weight from your back foot to your front foot to release the pull. Repeat two or three times. After several such pulls and releases, most horses turn their heads around to see what feels so good. *Tail Pulls* relax the neck and back, activate cranial-sacral fluid through the spine and create a connection through the entire body. They are also useful to give a horse a kinesthetic sense of his body, to overcome fear of movement behind, or to release tight muscles in the hindquarters.

TROIKA TTOUCH

As you may recall from earlier in this book, it was my grandfather, Will Caywood, who inspired my initial interest in equine bodywork. Although most TTouches are named after animals, I call this one the *Troika TTouch* in honor of my grandfather's Russian connection—a troika being a Russian carriage or sleigh drawn by three horses hitched in a special manner.

While training racehorses in Russia from 1902 to 1905, my grandfather learned a type of horse massage from Russian gypsies. This art of massage was comprised of short, sliding strokes all over the body. In 1905, he was awarded the title of leading trainer at the Moscow Hippodrome Racetrack, an honor he attributed to the fact that every horse in his stable received 30 minutes of bodywork daily. The *Troika TTouch* is an adaptation of this original bodywork that includes a circular, sliding or scratching motion over the hair. Although this TTouch does not have the same long-term effects on learning like the other circular TTouches that move the skin instead of sliding over the hair, it's easy to do, it's great for circulation, and a wonderful TTouch for building trust.

This TTouch has become invaluable at my seven-day *Starting Young Horses* workshop held annually at the Bitterroot Guest Ranch in Dubois, Wyoming. As a first contact, clinic participants quietly mix with the herd of barely handled four-year-olds to gain their interest and trust with the *Troika TTouch*. After a week of Ground Exercises and TTouches, these youngsters are trusting, confident, and ready to ride.

Pressure: 1 to 4

The *Troika TTouch* can be relaxing or invigorating, depending upon your tempo and pressure. For relaxing your horse, use a slow, light (1 to 2) pressure. For a more invigorating effect, use a faster tempo with a 3 to 4 pressure.

Key Uses

- Establishes trust in horses who are fearful or wary of people
- Satisfies your horse's need to scratch hard-to-reach itchy spots
- Bonds with your horse, especially one who doesn't have a chance to socialize with other horses
- Activates circulation

HOW TO

- This TTouch involves a two-part move, using the side of your thumb, and all four fingers opening and closing as they circle over the skin. There are two variations. Both involve moving the thumb and fingers in circles over the hair. One is done with small circles with a scratching motion, and the second form makes larger soothing circles, great for activating circulation.

- Set your hand lightly on the surface of the skin and make rhythmic sliding circles over the surface of the hair with the side of your thumb, and at the same time, make circular movements with all four fingers in an opening and closing pattern. The fingers and thumb meet as you make each circle, creating a light fold in the skin that is stimulating to the horse.

- Begin by finding an itchy spot where your horse likes to be scratched. Good places to start are on the withers and croup where horses naturally groom each other with their teeth. Along the neck and around the base of the tail are other favorites of many horses. Itchy areas that your horse cannot easily reach, like the forehead, chest, mid-belly line and buttocks are other places where you can earn points and gain trust. Explore to see what your horse enjoys. Start lightly and as the horse shows interest, sometimes by sticking out the upper lip, you can apply a little more vigorous contact. Work all over the body, varying the pressures to suit your horse.

Variation 1

For a soothing feeling that stimulates circulation, make the contact with the *finger pads*, moving thumb and fingers in six- to eight-inch circles. This variation is useful with sport horses.

Variation 2

Make small circles and use your *fingernails* of your four fingers in a light, scratching motion that is more stimulating and that most horses love. This variation is what I often use when first approaching a young or wary horse, although most horses enjoy it. Gaining the trust of a young or wary horse I find easiest when the horse is completely free in a stall or paddock, and able to move away at will. This freedom gives your horse the choice of coming to you to ask for more contact—an attitude that can lay the foundation for a wonderful friendship.

Photo This four-year-old Lusitano stallion, Gracil, belongs to Frédéric Pignon and his wife Magali Delgado, the stars and head trainers of Cavalia, the phenomenally successful traveling equine theatre that celebrates the bond between humans and horses. When I first visited Fred and Magali at their home in Southern France, Gracil was shy and distrustful of strangers. Because I was so taken with this lovely young horse, Frédéric invited me to work with him. I TTouched him in his stall without halter or rope, starting with *Troika TTouches* and *Lowering the Head*. During our three, 10-minute sessions together, he became affectionate and trusting, clearly enjoying our new connection as much as I did. He is now one of the star performers in Cavalia, a poignant and profound demonstration of the relationship that is possible between humans and horses.

TTouches for Awareness

TTouches for Awareness continue the process of building trust by enhancing a horse's sense of body awareness in space (called proprioception, see p. 163). This process translates into improved movement, suppleness and balance. It also shifts your horse's emotional response to his environment, which can be very challenging to a horse in today's world. Your horse will remain calmer in the face of traffic, parades, unusual movement overhead (helicopters, hot-air balloons), animals (strange ones like llamas or emus, as well as pigs, cattle, and loose dogs) or close encounters of any kind on the trail or showground.

With awareness comes increased safety, one of the overriding principles of the Tellington Method. All the TTouches, Ground Exercises and Ridden Work have safety benefits. Once your horse develops a better sense of his personal space, he will be less afraid of sounds and objects behind and above him and more secure in his own body. Horses who don't feel secure or aware tend to kick at other horses, bolt, freeze or jump on you or run you over.

Stress, tension and fear restrict learning; TTouches for Awareness prevent or release stressful responses to everyday activities with horses. With these TTouches, you can give your horse a new sense of physical, mental and emotional well-being, helping him feel safe in new situations or unexpected environments.

TTouches for Awareness also help you become a better "detective." You are able to observe much more about your horse, such as how much tension is carried in the back or how tight he is in the body. Such awareness can be the gateway to improving his comfort and movement, reducing stress and enhancing the horse/human relationship.

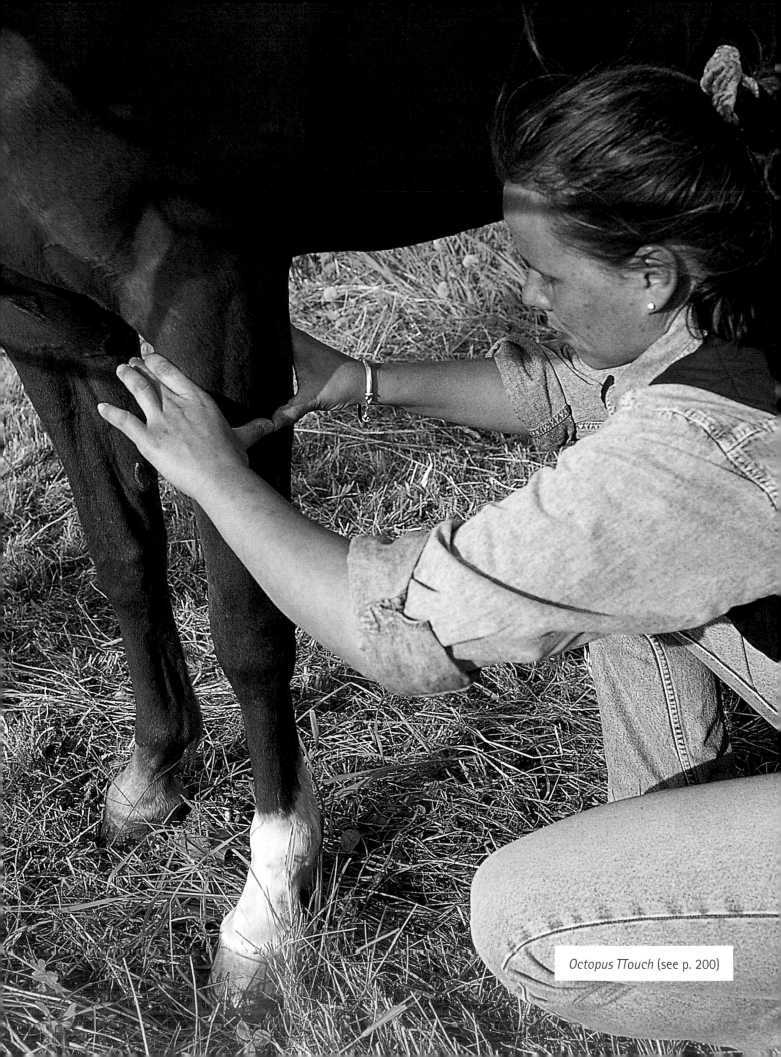

Octopus TTouch (see p. 200)

BACK LIFT

If there were one thing that you could do every day for the good of your horse, it might be to lift the back. The *Back Lift* encourages a horse to contract the abdominal muscles and raise his back from pressure with the fingertips, fingernails or flat hand. By raising the topline, the horse lowers his head and lengthens and relaxes his neck. Hollow areas on the back—behind the withers or in front of the loins—fill out when the back is raised. If your horse is working hard and tends to have stiff or sore muscles, *Back Lifts* can bring relief.

Key Uses

- Lowers the head
- Relaxes sore or stiff back muscles
- Lengthens and relaxes the neck
- Encourages engagement of the hind legs
- Increases suppleness and flexibility
- Improves all-around performance

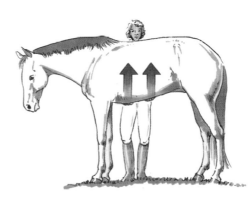

A few minutes of *Back Lifts* before and after riding help improve horses who drop or hollow their back, are ewe-necked, sway-backed, stiff, difficult to engage or collect, and who don't step far enough under their bodies with their hind legs.

Lifting the back changes the relationship of the vertebrae, which allows the horse to lower his head. This is very useful because all horses, particularly nervous ones, will begin to relax as their heads come down.

Pressure: 2 to 5

Begin with three or four *Lying Leopard TTouches* (p. 181) along the midline of the belly to prepare your horse for the fingertip pressure, especially if your horse is ticklish, tense or sensitive in that area.

Some horses, if surprised, will kick when they feel the fingernail pressure. Keep your hand far enough forward so that if he does reflexively kick the first time you ask for a lift, he'll miss your hand.

HOW TO

With your palms up and fingers curved and pressed tightly together to make them stronger, press your fingernails just beside the midline. If your horse tends to be reactive, start out with the fingertips, moving to the fingernails if the back does not raise up. Use a quick press-and-release movement rather than constant pressure. Once your horse is accustomed to the exercise, your flat hand or a raking stroke from the midline with the fingertips spread apart will likely get the same response.

Photo 1 Viewing the underside of the belly, you can clearly see my finger position slightly off the center line. Press and release quickly, moving an inch or so from spot to spot. Generally two or three signals, followed by a firm stroke upward, will be enough for your horse to contract the abdominal muscles and lift the back.

Photo 2 I'm using one hand to hold the wand on the withers and croup to measure the degree of lift.

Photo 3 Here you can see how much the back has raised. You can strengthen the back through a regular program of *Back Lifts.* Measure the distance from the measuring stick to the deepest part of the horse's back and keep a record. If you do a minute or two of *Back Lifts* daily, over a period of several weeks most horses' backs will stay up.

What should you do if…
• *Your horse won't lift his back?*

You may have to use your fingernails the first time or two. If you don't get a response on one spot, move to another place slightly off the midline of the belly. If you are not sure if the topline is lifting, ask a helper to observe for you, because it's often difficult to see the back raise when you are concentrating on the belly. Another option: use *Belly Lifts* or *Pelvic Tilts* first (pp. 209 and 222).

CHIMP TTOUCH

This TTouch works well if your fingers are stiff or inflexible due to injury, weather or arthritis. The name was inspired by the way chimpanzees use their hands when moving about.

If you have difficulty making your circles round when first learning TTouch, try beginning with this easy hand position. *Chimp TTouches* are great for making connected, energizing circles along the neck and back, and they are less threatening to the horse when first approaching sensitive areas.

Pressure: 2 to 3

HOW TO

Photo Hold your hand softly curled, your fingers folded in towards your palm. Use the flat surface on the back of the fingers between the second and third phalange to make the circles.

CLOUDED LEOPARD TTOUCH

This TTouch (the original "TTouch that Teaches") was named after a Clouded Leopard cub I worked on in the Los Angeles Zoo. The TTouch can be as light as a cloud or as strong as a leopard.

The *Clouded Leopard* is the basic TTouch for activating awareness of the horse's mind-body in a way that:

• Expands your horse's intelligence—defined as the ability to adapt to new situations.

• Enhances your horse's willingness and ability to learn.

• Builds trust and confidence in an insecure, flighty or oversensitive horse.

• Releases fear at the cellular level.

• Improves proprioception—the horse's sensory perception of where his limbs are in space and in motion, to improve his coordination and balance.

Pressure: 1 to 4

Key spots: Neck, back, barrel, croup, sole of the hoof.

Key Uses

• Builds confidence and trust

• Deepens the horse/human bond

• Improves willingness and ability to learn

• Enhances coordination and suppleness

• Reduces spookiness

• Eases soreness or stiffness

HOW TO

Holding the hand gently curved, use the pads of your fingers to push the skin in a circle. Keep your fingers together to give your hand stability, allowing more fluidity in the circle and requiring less effort. Be sure to keep the first joints of your fingers rounded—hyperflexing the joints will be uncomfortable for you and to your horse. Place your other hand on the underside of the neck, on the crest, on the back or even on the side of the halter to maintain a connection.

You can intensify the effects of this TTouch by anchoring your thumb, keeping the heel of the hand and your wrist well off the body and your wrist as straight as is comfortable. This will depend on the size of the horse in relationship to the size of the person, as well as where you are working on the horse.

Photo I steady the horse's neck with my left hand on the underside of the neck. This connection between the two hands steadies and balances the mare. Note that my wrist is held well off the body, with the thumb serving as a stabilizing anchor while the softly curved fingers lightly touch each other. Note the uniform curve of each joint.

HOOF TAPPING

Tapping the walls of the hoof, as well as the sole, with the knob end of the wand, can have many beneficial effects.

Pressure: 1 to 4

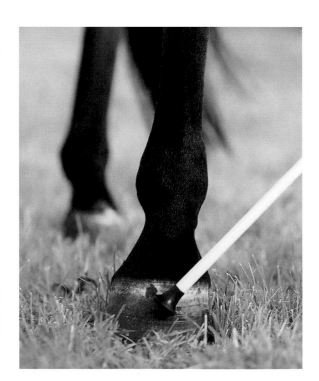

Key Uses

- Makes a skittish horse more connected to the ground
- Helps even up a slightly irregular gait
- Prepares a young horse for showing in hand
- Helps a "stumbly" horse pick up his feet

HOW TO

Photo On the outer wall, tap gently around the perimeter of the hoof wall, making three rows of taps to be sure to cover the whole hoof. Tap firmly enough that the horse feels it but not so hard the horse moves away. Tapping on the sole will "desensitize" a horse who tends to pull the hoof away from the farrier.

INCH WORM

This relaxing, enjoyable TTouch helps to release neck and shoulder tightness. As you work, your horse's head will soon be level with the withers.

Pressure: 2 to 3

HOW TO

Photos 1 and 2 Place your hands on the top of the neck about four inches apart, with the thumbs on one side of the crest and the fingers on the other. Holding the crest firmly, push your hands slowly toward each other without sliding. When your hands are almost together, hold this position for a few seconds and then slowly move your hands apart, allowing the skin to return to the beginning position. Then slide your hands softly apart a few inches.

JELLYFISH JIGGLE

This jiggling, wave-like TTouch is used to soften and loosen muscles.

Pressure: 3 to 4

Key spots: Try *Jellyfish Jiggles* on the soft muscles at the lower part of the shoulder above the forearm, large muscles of the croup and hindquarters, on the mid-back/loin area approximately six to eight inches below the midline.

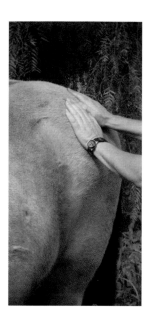

HOW TO

Place both hands over the neck, back or hindquarters. Holding your hands horizontally with your fingertips nearly touching, jiggle the skin upward with your fingers and palm to send a wave of movement upward. On the large muscles of the croup, hold your hands close together and vertical. When working on the neck or shoulder, you may find it easier to use one hand. When you see it demonstrated on a horse's hindquarters, it looks like you are jiggling Jell-O.

Photo *Jellyfish Jiggle* is useful for relaxing the large muscles of the croup. Place your flat hands on the croup as shown and make soft, upward jiggling motions to the muscle under your hands. It can also be used for gentle jiggles along the back, approximately six inches below the top of the spine.

MANE AND FORELOCK SLIDES

Mane Slides are useful preparation for pulling or braiding the mane and particularly helpful for horses who object to mane-pulling. For any horse, they will help relax the neck, shoulders and back. They increase blood flow and circulation through the neck. This is especially useful for horses doing collected work, which can restrict circulation.

Key Uses

- Soothes horses who object to mane pulling
- Relaxes the neck, shoulders and back
- Relieves itching and discomfort in cases of "sweet itch" or summer eczema.

Pressure: 1 to 3

HOW TO

Here are two ways to do *Mane Slides:*

- Take a one-inch section of mane and slide your fingers along the strands from the crest to the end, straight upward. This is especially helpful for horses who are sensitive to or resistant about having their manes pulled (thinned or shortened by pulling out small clumps of hair).

- Separate the mane into one-inch sections. Taking one section at a time, slide your fingers from crest to the end, pulling downward as you tip the crest over slightly. Take one section toward the left and the next section to the right. The neck should be close to level for optimal relaxation. Start where your horse is the most accepting, generally in the middle of the crest.

Tellington Tip

If your horse is sensitive about mane pulling, hold the strands upward instead of down, and pull out the extra hair from this position rather than with the usual downward method. There are also products available that make this chore much easier on both horse and human.

Photo 1 Separate a small section of mane and slide firmly upward, stabilizing with the free hand. We've had reports of horses suffering from "sweet itch" or summer eczema who found relief from circles, slides and lifts on small clumps of mane along the length of the crest.

Forelock Slide

Photo 2 This is one of the most rewarding means of relating to your horse and deepening trust and relationship, at the same time achieving a relaxed, peaceful state in both horse and human.

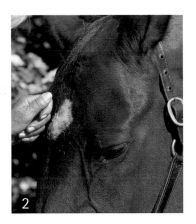

NECK ROCKING

Rocking the neck rhythmically and rapidly back and forth helps to free up the neck and allows the horse to lengthen it.

Pressure: 2 to 4

HOW TO

Photo 1 Begin at the top of the neck and work toward the chest, rocking the crest away from you with one hand while you rock the windpipe toward you. With each move "jump" your hands to the next place down the neck, keeping up a energetic rhythm.

Key Uses

• Frees up and lengthens the neck

Photo 2 This movement requires trust and will be impossible on a high-headed or ewe-necked horse until he has learned *Lowering the Head* (p. 163) and trusts you enough to keep the neck level for *Connected Circles* (p. 173).

NOAH'S MARCH

Noah's March puts the "finishing TTouch" on your horse at the end of a session.

If you think of the basic TTouches as dots on different parts of the body, *Noah's March* "connects the dots" to complete the picture. It gives your horse a connection to the whole body after bringing awareness to individual areas with the variety of TTouches. Noah's March is also an effective way to introduce yourself to a new horse.

Pressure: 1 to 3

Keynotes: Sweeping, connecting, integrating.

Key spots: Upper neck, whole body, or to "finish off" an area you've been working on with another TTouch.

HOW TO

• **As an introductory TTouch:** Before you begin *Body Exploration* (p. 151), make several smooth short strokes on the part of the body you plan to begin working on so you don't surprise your horse with the probing *Bear TTouch* (p. 217).

• **"Finishing off" a TTouch session:** Beginning at the head and neck area, use the entire flat hand to make long, sweeping strokes with the

Key Uses

• Completes a TTouch session

• "Refreshes" in-between TTouches

• Introduces you to a new horse

direction of the hair. Cover all of the body, including the tail and all the way down the legs to the hooves. When done slowly and methodically, this TTouch relaxes and reintegrates.

• **Awakening:** When you want to wake the horse up or revitalize before a competition, make swift long strokes.

Photo My flat, relaxed hand follows the contour over the shoulder.

OCTOPUS TTOUCH

Octopus TTouches, like the amazing underwater creatures they are named for, encircle and envelop your horse's legs in a way like no other. After TTouching a small octopus to reduce the stress of shipping to the Baltimore Aquarium, I became enthralled with these intelligent beings.

That's how the name became a part of TTouch. Some polarity therapists have suggested that the inexplicably powerful effect of this TTouch may be due to the unique figure-eight pattern created by the crossing of the hands in the stroke down the leg which, in their view, creates a balancing of the

Key Uses

- Improves the quality of your horse's gaits
- Brings awareness to the limbs of horses who shy or stumble
- Reduces fatigue in performance horses after an event or long trailer ride
- Grounds anxious or nervous horses
- Lengthens stride
- Reduces joint stiffness or lameness
- Picks up feet for the farrier

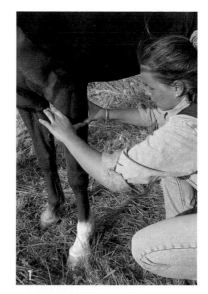
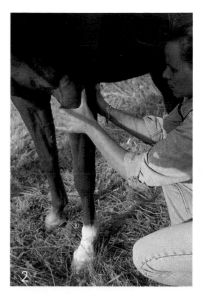
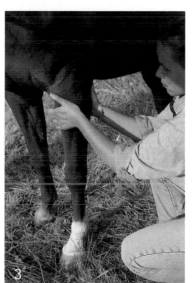
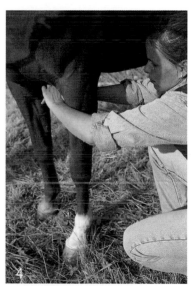
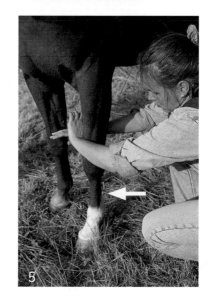
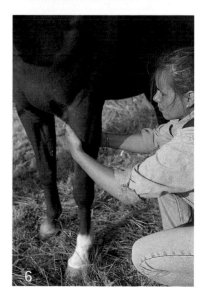

body's polarities. It has the effect of calming and grounding and increasing sure-footedness.

Pressure: 2 to 3

This TTouch, which is much more challenging to describe than to actually do, has many benefits. With a little practice, these flowing movements become a pleasure for both you and your horse.

HOW TO

Phase A

Photo 1 Place both hands a few inches below the elbow. (For a larger picture of this, see p. 192.)

Photo 2 Slide your thumbs upward over the hair to activate circulation.

Photo 3 Continue sliding your hands around the leg...

Photo 4 ...and place one hand lightly on top of the other.

Photo 5 Slide your hands lightly down the inside of the leg to the mid-cannon bone where the arrow stops.

Photo 6 Slide your hands upward against the hair to the top of the inside of the leg.

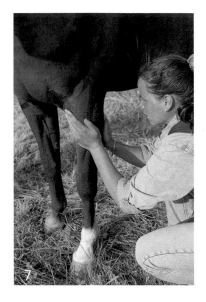  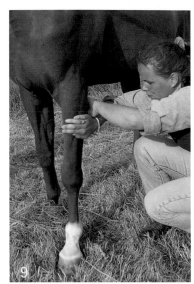

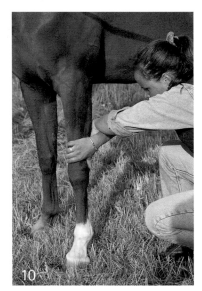 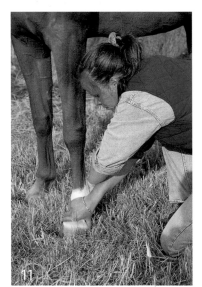

Photo 7 Slide your hands over the hair back to the outside of the forearm.

Photo 8 On the outside of the leg keep both hands turned inward with one placed *above* the other (*not* one hand *on top* of the other) on the horse's leg.

Photo 9 The hands continue to slide around the leg, one hand around the front and the other around the back of the leg.

Photo 10 Your own forearms are now crossed. Slide down the leg until…

Photo 11 …your hands wrap around the front and back of the hoof, actually meeting the ground.

Phase B

Begin the entire process again, this time beginning just above the knee and taking Step 5 down to the fetlock joint on the inside.

Phase C

Begin again, this time in the middle of the outside cannon bone and repeat all steps.

Phase D

Start at the shoulder and come once all the way down the leg to emphasize the connection to the ground.

Repeat on the hind legs starting at the top of the thigh.

SPONGE TTOUCH

This TTouch gives you the feeling of going in between the muscles, as if they were parting.

Pressure: 2 to 3

Key spots: Heavily muscled necks.

HOW TO

• Push the skin in a circle and a quarter with a light pressure, usually a 3, and spiral into the center of the circle as though you were depressing a wet sponge.

• Withdraw your fingers straight out as though the sponge was expanding to follow your fingers.

• Slide an inch or two with a clear connecting line to the next spot to TTouch.

Practice "sponging in" with a *Bear TTouch* or *Raccoon TTouch* (pp. 217 and 213). Pressing directly into the muscles with *Bear* can painful, but if you make a light *Clouded Leopard* circle (p. 195) with your finger pads first, the body is prepared and the muscles seem to open effortlessly. Sponging in lightly and slowly with *Raccoon* (using the fingertips rather than fingernails) can be done on tighter areas where deep pressure would be painful and cause the horse to react.

Use the *Bear TTouch* to "aerate" or relax tight muscles or a *Raccoon* finger position for a soft communicating contact.

Key Uses
• Releases tight neck muscles on performance and sport horses or stallions

Photo 1 My left hand is on the crest pulling it toward my right hand as I make a light circular *Clouded Leopard TTouch* to get the mare's attention and relax the muscles, followed by a *Bear TTouch* with a *Sponge* press-and-release.

Photo 2 Here, I pull the mare's head toward me with the halter as I sponge in with my fingertips after making a preliminary circle and a quarter to prepare the muscle to open.

TARANTULAS PULLING THE PLOW

The unusual name of this TTouch was inspired by a large, gentle, California tarantula who lived in my office for some time. The TTouch itself was inspired by an ancient Mongolian treatment called *chua'ka* used to release fear before battle. Modern *chua'ka* for humans is thought to break habit-

ual emotional patterns of response by releasing skin that had become stuck to muscles due to longstanding holding patterns. It can be painful and invasive. However, we call our version "skin rolling" or *Tarantulas*. It differs in that where the skin is "stuck" or tight, we "walk" the fingertips along, pulling the thumbs like a plow, creating only a small furrow. The TTouch version is pleasant and noninvasive and we find it releases fear and instills confidence.

This TTouch can be stimulating, or soothing and connecting. On horses we use it to calm and connect rather than stimulate.

Keynotes: Rhythmical, connected movement.

Key spots: Long lines on the barrel, running parallel to the spine: from girth to flank; from top of the neck to shoulder; from shoulder point to withers, or downward from; elbow to coronet band and stifle to hoof.

HOW TO

- Begin by placing your hands side by side, with fingers curved, thumbs straight and wrists held upward several inches off the horse's body.

- Practice first with one hand by "walking" the forefinger and middle finger rolling over the finger nail, taking little "steps" about an inch apart. Think of the famous image in the Yellow Pages slogan, "Let your fingers do the walking."

- Once you can walk your two fingers along smoothly with one hand, practice coordinating the same movement with both hands moving along beside each other.

- With the thumbs slightly apart, "walk" the forefingers and middle fingers of both hands forward while allowing the two thumbs to follow behind, pushing a light furrow of skin ahead of them like a plow.

- Go with or across the grain rather than against it. The long lines have the effect of connecting the whole body.

- The fingers activate the neural impulses and the thumbs follow behind, creating a calming effect.

- In areas where the skin is too tight to lift or create a furrow, simply drag the thumbnails along, visualizing a clear connection of the body.

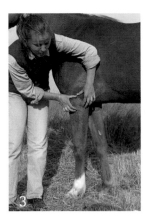   

Photos 1 and 2 On the barrel and neck the skin should be loose, allowing you to roll the skin along in this way. Note the "steps" of the forefinger and middle finger.

Photos 3, 4, 5 and 6 Begin at the top of the leg and "walk" the fingers along, with a steady rhythmical motion, the thumbs following like a plow. Because there is no loose muscle to roll, the thumbs scrape over the surface.

TIGER TTOUCH

Use *Tiger TTouch* for horses who are heavily muscled and sluggish, or dull or unresponsive to the aids. This TTouch also can relieve itching without irritating the nerve endings.

Pressure: 1 to 6

HOW TO

Place your hand on your horse's body in a claw-like position. Keep your wrist off the body by an inch or so and your fingers spread slightly apart. Maintaining a steady connection with your thumb, move your four fingers simultaneously in four clockwise circles. Hold the first joint (fingernails) perpendicular to the body, describing the circles with your nails. As in *Bear TTouch* (p. 217) you need fingernails for this movement.

Photo The *Tiger TTouch*, when applied with a pressure of number 2 or 3, can be useful around "hot spots" to reduce itching. Place your hand on the body with fingers apart and the fingernails at 90

Key Uses

- "Wakes up" heavily muscled areas—use 3 to 5 pressure

- Stimulates areas of dullness or insensitivity—use 2 to 6 pressure

- Provides firmer TTouch for horses who are sensitive about being touched

- Scratches itchy spots—use 1 to 3 pressure

degrees from the body. The thumb holds a steady contact about two inches from the forefinger, while each of the fingers makes a small circle.

ZIG-ZAG TTOUCH

Zig-Zag TTouches provide an enjoyable way of getting acquainted with a horse who doesn't know you or hasn't been handled or groomed much. The sensation is much like mutual grooming, the pleasant withers and back scratching that a fellow equine might provide. It can help your horse enjoy being with you.

Zig-Zags can "break the freeze" when your horse is standing in front of the trailer, blocked and emotionally "shut down." You can also use these TTouches under your saddle blanket for rapid cooling before removing your tack. My sister Robyn also uses it along the belly line as many horses respond by lifting the back, one of the best things you can do for your horse (see p. 193 for more information).

This TTouch consists of diagonal strokes primarily along the back, but can also be used on the neck and croup, or belly as just described.

Pressure: 2 to 3

Key Uses

- Helps you get acquainted with a new horse
- "Reawakens" horses who have emotionally shut down
- Cools down post-workout
- Promotes trust

Note: If your horse does not like *Zig-Zag TTouches,* he may be hypersensitive, tense or sore. So first start with gentle *Abalone* circles (p. 171) or another TTouch that the horse finds acceptable before proceeding.

HOW TO

Photos 1 and 2 *Zig-Zag TTouches* cover about 12 inches up and down per stroke from the midline—as the lines in the photos show.

TTouches for Health

While virtually all the TTouches and Ground Exercises in this book help reduce stress and foster a happier, healthier horse, there are three primary TTouches—used for over 30 years—that can help to alleviate acute health problems, such as colic, shock or trauma. They are *Ear TTouches* and *Belly Lifts* for use on a colicky horse while waiting for your veterinarian to arrive, and *Raccoon TTouches* to alleviate swelling and injury in fresh wounds and bruises.

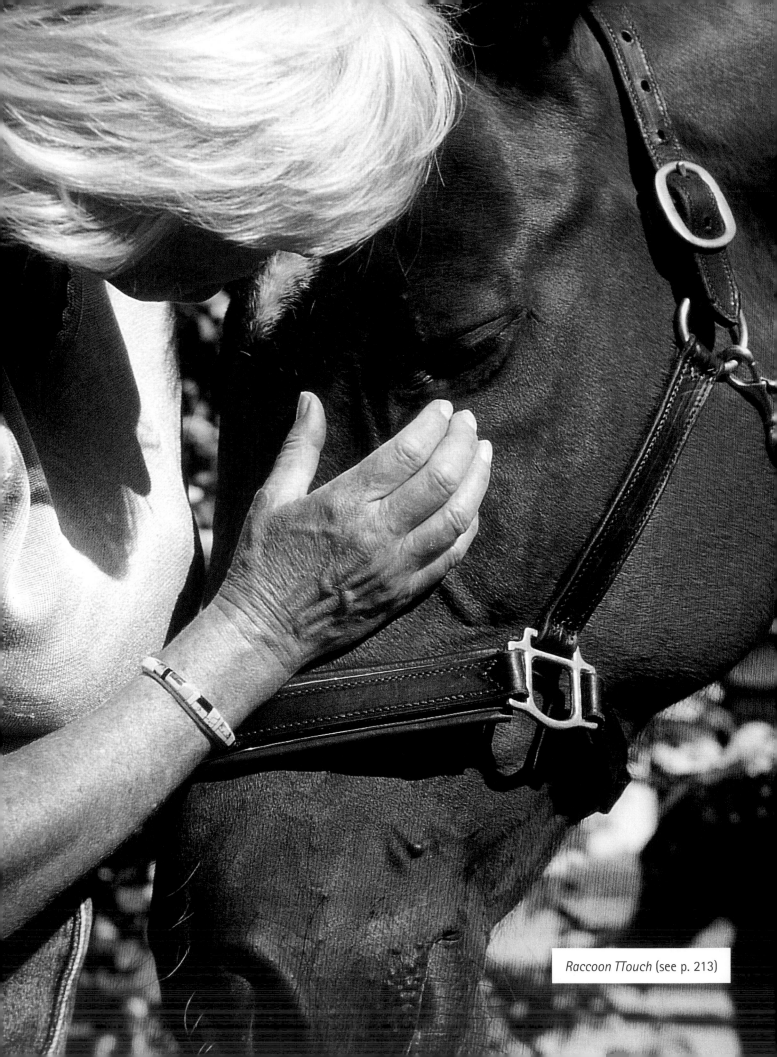

Raccoon TTouch (see p. 213)

BELLY LIFT

We are often asked to explain the difference between *Back Lift* and *Belly Lift*. Both lifts affect belly and back muscles; however, with *Belly Lift*, the intention is to support the belly, taking the downward pressure temporarily off the back. Doing *Back Lift*, you are asking the horse to engage the belly muscles and raise his own back (see *Back Lift*, p. 193).

HOW TO

Belly Lifts can be done in several ways:

- Two people holding hands under the belly
- Using a towel folded to about 6–8" in width
- Using a wide girth or surcingle

When using your hands, allow as much flat surface as possible to lie against the horse's belly (be sure to remove any rings or jewelry that might poke into the belly). A folded towel or surcingle is preferable because the pressure is distributed more evenly and it will be easier on your back.

Starting just behind the front legs, your helper holds the towel steady while you slowly lift it until you can't lift any more. Hold this position for about 10 seconds. Then *slowly* release the pressure—the slow release is of utmost importance in getting the desired effect. It's ideal to make the release twice as long as the lift. If your horse objects, lift less. Now move the towel four to six inches toward the hindquarters and repeat. Continue until you are as close to the flank as the horse allows (some horses are very ticklish in this area). Repeat the cycle three or four times, starting each time at the elbow.

Key Uses

- Eases colic signs by relieving spasm and activating the wavelike action of the gut
- Improves gut sounds
- Relieves downward pressure from the extra weight of the fetus in pregnant mares
- Helps horses who are cinchy, cold-backed, or young learn to accept the girth instead of holding their breath and tensing up
- Introduces young horses to the sensation of a surcingle
- Relaxes back muscles in horses with sore backs
- Helps raise low or sway backs
- Overcomes ticklishness or touchiness on the belly

- In the case of acute colic when your horse is threatening to go down, you may find it more acceptable to do faster movements—four-second lifts, four-second holds and four-second releases.

Photo The optimal way to accomplish a *Belly Lift*: two people holding a long, narrow towel, lifting, holding and slowly releasing the pressure. Begin at a point just behind the elbow and work your way back toward the hindquarters with each lift.

- **When alone:** Use an extra-long bath or beach towel folded lengthwise about six inches wide. Drop it over the back and catch it under the belly, holding one end of the towel a few inches below the middle of the back on your side, and the other end coming up from underneath the belly.

• Lifting with the girth: Put the saddle in place and do the lifts as you would with a towel.

• Or, use your arm from the elbow to the hand to do a one-person belly lift lifting your arm by pushing it up with your hip, instead of lifting with your shoulder.

Caution: Be careful to lift from your pelvis and legs rather than back and shoulders.

Tellington Tip

For very sensitive horses, use a six-inch-wide elastic bandage folded in two. You may see a smoother lift and release and less reaction from such horses.

EAR TTOUCHES (EAR SLIDES)

Stroking a horse's ears for faster recovery after hard work dates back to stagecoach days in England, where it was said that teams arriving at rest stops would drink a draught of beer while grooms would stroke their ears to ready them for the next day's work. By an accident of fate, I stumbled onto ear work when my Arabian endurance mare, Bint Gulida, colicked in 1958. After a four-day impaction (in those days in California there was no possibility of surgery), my veterinarian recommended that we humanely put her down.

Because we were preparing for my first 100-mile-in-one-day endurance ride, measuring pulse, respiration and temperature, and checking the body were part of our daily routine. I found Gulida's temperature to be seriously subnormal and her ears ice-cold. Before succumbing to the vet's edict, I decided to spend a last hour

Key Uses

• Calms a nervous or frightened animal

• Invigorates a tired horse and revives one who is exhausted

• Lowers pulse and respiration, induces relaxation

• Alleviates pain and shock caused by injury or colic while waiting for vet

• Helps boost immune system and regulates temperature

with her. I covered her with dryer-heated blankets and intuitively began stroking her ears to warm them. At the end of the hour, her ears were warm, her temperature had returned to normal and she passed manure. That was the end of the impaction! It was 20 years later when I met Dr. Christine Kruger in Germany that I learned of the ears' connection to the entire nervous system and continued my journey of discovery of the value of ear work.

Now we know that *Ear TTouches* activate the triple heater meridian (an acupressure point that wraps around the ear and runs across the shoulder and down the front leg to the hoof) that positively affects the digestive, respiratory and reproductive systems.

Pressure: 1 to 5

To calm your horse on a windy or cold day before you ride, or at a competition where he is nervous and excited, do five minutes of *Ear TTouches* in the stall. This can save you an hour of warm up time that you would otherwise need to calm him down. It has an added advantage of loosening up a stiff horse before you get on. By stroking the ears outward at an angle perpendicular to the neck, you can relax tight muscles at the poll or upper neck. Ear work is said by craniosacral therapists to assist in the activation of cranial-sacral fluid.

HOW TO

Slide from the middle of the poll over the base of the ear all the way to the very tips, emphasizing contact with the tip as you slide your hand off the ear. If the horse allows, fold the ear together to give him a feeling of the inside of his ears. Some horses enjoy having your finger sliding or circling on the inside of the ear as well as the outside.

Photo 1 Stand in front of your horse and lower his head with one hand on the noseband, and stroke the forelock slowly from roots to tip. This is something lovely you can do for your horse as it is quite relaxing and gains trust (see *Mane and Forelock Slides*, p. 198).

Photo 2 If your horse is sensitive about having his ears touched, do a few *Lying Leopard* or *Abalone TTouches* (pp. 181 and 171) on his forehead. This can be soothing for horses who are moody or perhaps get the equivalent of headaches.

Photo 3 Now stroke from the middle of the poll (over the base of his ear) smoothly over the ear and finish with a little twist between fingers and thumb as you glide off the tip. Once your horse is comfortable

having his ears stroked, slide your thumb along the inside of his ear as you stroke the outside. Try some tiny *Raccoon TTouches* (p. 213) on the insides and outside of the ear. There are acupuncture points throughout the ear that relate to different parts of the body. These points can be stimulated by TTouch to improve general health, and when dealing with specific organ dysfunction, stiffness or arthritis. *Raccoon TTouches* inside the ears help prepare the horse for medication or clipping.

Photos 4A and B Bring the ears straight out to the side (or at a very slight angle forward) and slide your hand from base to tip. Remember to hold the nose-band on the opposite side from this ear so you can balance the slight pull with a little resistance, as well as keep the horse's head straight. Some horses enjoy or tolerate only light, slow strokes unless they are in pain or shock. In this event, you should stroke fast and firmly and keep it up until the horse is comfortable, and his pulse and respiration return to normal ranges, or until your vet arrives. In extreme cases, this may be as much as an hour or more.

Photo 5 Hold the front of the noseband to lower the head and stroke the ear with the back of the hand from forehead to neck.

What should you do if…

• *Your horse doesn't like to be touched on the ears?*

Use *Llama TTouches* (p. 180). Make circles with the back of your hand on the horse's forehead and ears. If your horse is still unsure or worried, use a sheepskin mitt to push the ear back against the neck, or your arm stroking back all the way up to your elbows.

RACCOON TTOUCH

I named this TTouch in honor of raccoons because it reminded me of the tiny, precise movements of their hand-like paws.

Key spots: Swellings anywhere and girth galls.
Pressure: 1 to 3

HOW TO

These tiny, usually light TTouches are done any-

where on the body with the tips of the fingers, avoiding pressure with the fingernails. The heel of the hand and wrist are held well off the body as with the *Clouded Leopard TTouch* (p. 195). You will usually use the four fingers together; however, you will find some areas where emphasis on the forefinger or middle finger will be more effective.

Photo This mare is obviously enjoying the soothing and relaxing effects of a light *Raccoon TTouch* with a 2 pressure. My left hand is on the halter. (For a larger picture of this, see p. 208.)

Tellington Tip
Do these TTouches holding an ice cube in a towel to reduce swelling.

Key Uses

- Reduces heat and swelling
- Stimulates healing around the edges of wounds
- Relaxes clamped tail when used on underside of tail
- Helps clear blocked tear ducts
- Soothes area around the eyes in the case of a blow
- Increases circulation around the coronary band on horses with acute laminitis

Performance Plus in 10 Minutes a Day

There are some TTouches we have found to be particularly effective for sport and competitive horses. Horses who have greater muscular development and a higher level of fitness demand more attention to maintain peak performance and prevent damage to bones, tendons and ligaments.

Combining the new TTouches presented on the following pages with the TTouches for Trust, TTouches for Awareness and TTouches for Health, which I have just given you, will reduce stress and fatigue and help keep your horse fresh, supple and willing.

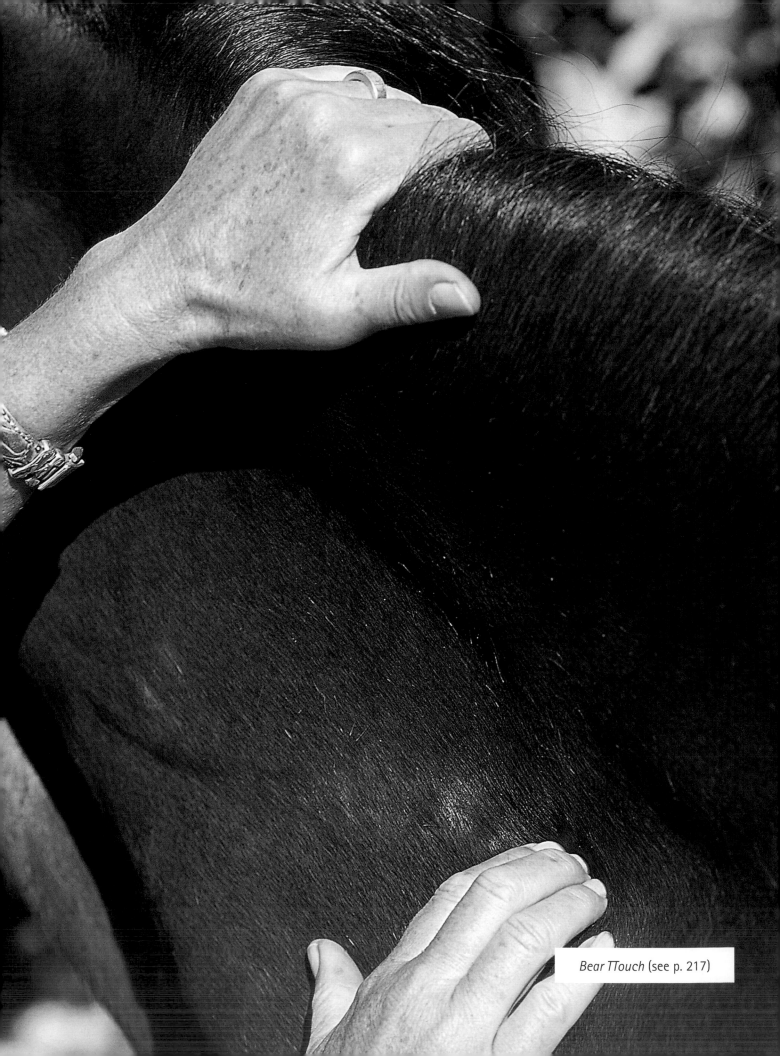

Bear TTouch (see p. 217)

BEAR TTOUCH

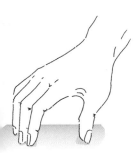

The name was inspired by the use of the fingernails being compared to a bear's claws. *Bear TTouches* use the fingernails to go deeply into heavy muscles. It can also be used very lightly for circles on itchy areas where normal scratching may not be satisfying and can lead to irritation.

Differentiating feature: The *Raccoon TTouch* (p. 213) and *Bear* look similar, but *Raccoon* is applied with the fingertips without the pressure from fingernails, and for *Bear,* the first phalange is placed at a 90-degree angle to the body with the focus on the nail contact.

Pressure: 1 (for sensitive areas) to 8 (on the large muscles like the croup)

Key spots: On heavily muscled areas of the body such as the neck and the coronary band of the foot to activate circulation.

HOW TO

* You will need fingernails that extend slightly beyond the end of your fingers for this TTouch.

* Hold the fingernails at a 90-degree angle to the horse's body, emphasizing contact with the nails. When the fingers curve over, the effect is muffled.

* Think *deep* rather than *hard.*

* Each circle is tiny—imagine the size of the head of a pin.

* Hold your fingers close together and put your attention on the middle finger even though you make the circle with all your fingers. You will find in many cases that the little finger is just along for the ride but will have very little connection.

> ### Key Uses
>
> * Explores the body for areas of tension or soreness
> * Promotes circulation to deep muscles
> * Releases tightness in neck and croup
> * Lengthens the neck and increases range of motion
> * Brings awareness to insensitive areas of the body
> * Activates circulation around the coronary band in horses prone to laminitis

* Hold a firm contact with the thumb a couple of inches from the fingers when using deeper *Bear TTouch.* The lighter the *Bear TTouch,* the less contact with the thumb.

* A 2 pressure can be effective with no thumb contact.

* If you have long fingers and your first joints tend to hyperflex, or if your hands become tired after a few *Bear/Sponge TTouches* (see Photo 2), switch to the *Rhino TTouch* (p. 224) in the neck muscles.

Photo 1 *Bear TTouch* is used to do *Body Exploration* and *Temperament Gauge* (pp. 151 and 156). Note the 90-degree angle of my fingers. I first made a small *Raccoon TTouch* with a 3 pressure to relax the mare and get her attention, and then executed a precise, tiny *Bear TTouch* to bring awareness into this rigid area of the crest.

Photo 2 My left hand stabilizes the head by holding the halter firmly so my fingers can "sponge" (see *Sponge TTouch,* p. 203) straight into the muscle as

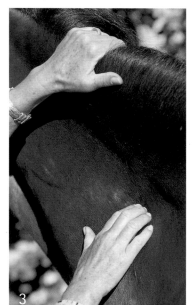

far as the tissue will allow without resistance. This softens and releases tight neck muscles. Use only as much pressure as your horse enjoys. The fingers are pressed firmly together for support as my fingertips "enter" straight into the neck muscles after a 3 pressure *Raccoon TTouch*. Note the upright position of my fingers in relation to the neck.

Photo 3 Limit use of deep pressure *Bear/Sponge TTouch* on the neck. I recommend making one line following the curve of the neck between the crest and the cervical vertebrae as shown, with about six *Bear TTouches*. More than this number of TTouches could make a horse sore rather than releasing tight muscles. If the horse is sensitive on the neck, use *Abalone* (p. 171) with *Coiled Python Lifts* (p. 172) instead. (For a larger picture of this, see p. 216.)

Photo 4 *Bear TTouch* on the coronary band. The nails are used almost like acupuncture needles to bring awareness and activate circulation. Because the hand has to reach down, the first phalange is at less of an angle than it would be on the body, shown in other photos here, although the nails are clearly in contact.

Tellington Tip

To release tight neck muscles in the neck of heavy muscled horses use the Bear TTouch combined with a Sponge TTouch (p. 203). Think of "aerating " the muscles, especially in well-muscled performance horses or heavy-necked stallions.

FLICK OF THE BEAR'S PAW

This TTouch is reminiscent of "strapping"—a traditional British method of slapping a braided mat of hay on a horse to activate circulation and strengthen muscles. It is often useful to begin a session with *Flicks* when your horse is nervous about TTouches and won't stand still. If you've done a few minutes of calming TTouches before a competition, a minute of *Flicks* on each side will wake him up. It's also useful if your horse is too calm or a little tired after already showing in several classes at a show.

Pressure: 1 to 4

HOW TO

The quick flicking motion of this TTouch reminds me of a bear fishing for salmon or a person brushing lint off clothing. The amount of pressure will vary from horse to horse. Some horses enjoy a vigorous movement and contact while others prefer a very light, almost sweeping touch. Use your wrists flexibly as you skip from place to place over the body.

Feathering

A lighter version of *Flick of the Bear's Paw*, called *Feathering* is useful for horses who are supersensitive or hyperactive. Your fingertips make as brief and light a contact as brushing with a feather. Beginning with this lighter TTouch and progressing to the somewhat heavier *Flicks* can give your horse more confidence.

Key Uses

- Helps when approaching horses with initial fear of contact
- Energizes performance horses before an event
- "Wakes up" a feeling in the body without creating nervousness

NECK BENDING

Increase flexibility and suppleness in your horse by teaching him to bend the neck willingly and easily in both directions.

HOW TO

To begin, stand the horse squarely, and ask him to turn the head to the side just a few degrees while keeping the centerline of the nose perpendicular to

Key Uses

- Improves balance
- Enhances lateral flexion
- Releases tight shoulder and back muscles
- Improves straightness

the ground. Start in the direction that's easiest for him, and turn the head only to the degree that he can keep an even distribution of weight over both front feet. If you turn too far, the neck will turn off the centerline, putting more weight over one front leg, causing your horse to move or brace himself. A small movement will achieve more than large movements for releasing the upper neck and prepare him to be able to turn the head back easily.

• Stand to the side of the head, place your fingers in the *Bear TTouch* (p. 217) position between the crest and the bottom of the neck about eight inches behind the ears. Use the noseband or nose bone to turn the head sideways while pressing the right hand into the neck in *Bear TTouch*. Keep the neck as straightforward as possible. Ask for a very small move to the side the first few times and then return the head to the centerline. Do this only two or three times in the easy direction and then ask the other way.

• Make sure that you are standing balanced with your feet hip-width apart, and keep a clear visual image as you "ask" your horse to make this move with a light signal. Your horse may surprise you by turning and looking back toward his tail almost on his own. As long as you are clear and balanced, most horses "get it" within minutes.

• Once the horse has the idea, you can instigate the same movement by touching on the jowl with one hand and the other fingers on the nose. It doesn't take more than a few times bending in each direction for the body to learn how to release those muscles. It's remarkable how much a stiff-necked horse can change in just one session.

• If the neck is extremely tight or your horse is reactive to being touched on the face, begin by *Lowering the Head* (p. 163) and do *Lying Leopard*

TTouches (p. 181) over the entire face until your horse is trusting and comfortable with the contact.

• If you find resistance to *Neck Bending*, first do *Inch Worm* and *Back Lifts* (pp. 197 and 193) to release tight neck muscles, and *Rib Releases* (p. 224) to allow suppleness and flexion throughout the body rather than just in the neck.

Photo Place your fingers in *Bear TTouch* in the middle of the neck about eight inches behind the ears. Press into the neck with one hand as you use the noseband to signal your horse to turn his head back toward you. Begin by asking for a *very small movement* in the direction that's easiest for your horse, then return the head to the centerline. Do this two or three times in the easy direction, then ask in the other direction. Keep the centerline of the nose perpendicular to the ground if you can.

NECK RELEASE

This is a type of neck stretch that increases circulation, induces relaxation and strengthens trust. Trust and relaxation are key words here, because without them, this movement is not possible. When you combine this movement with *Tail TTouches, Pelvic Tilt, Lick of the Cow's Tongue* and *Back Lift* (pp. 185, 222, 177, 193), you can discover ranges of movement and suppleness you may not have thought possible.

To prepare for this exercise, first teach *Lowering the Head* (p. 163) and *Ear TTouches* (p. 210).

HOW TO

Photo 1 Begin by lowering the head.

Key Uses

- Increases circulation
- Induces relaxation
- Strengthens trust

Photo 2 Place one hand on the chin and the other between the ears.

Photo 3 Ask for the neck opening by smoothly lifting the chin toward you while pressing softly on the forehead.

Photo 4 The ultimate trust comes when you can get the neck release with both hands under the chin.

PELVIC TILT

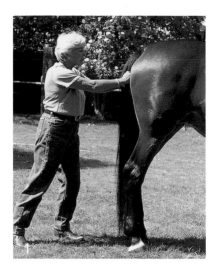

This is a gentle push, hold-and-release movement on a horse's point of buttocks to help release tension and holding patterns in the hindquarters and give the horse a new sense of connection through the pelvis to the back and shoulders.

HOW TO

Photos 1 and 2 Stand behind your horse facing the tail. Place one foot ahead of the other, with your fists resting just below the buttock bones. Pushing off from your feet through your body and arms, make a small movement forward, hold for up to four seconds, then *slowly* release. You may not feel much shift, but the movement can be seen from the side.

Key Uses

- Helps release tension
- Aids connection

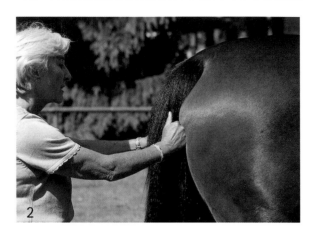

RAINBOW TTOUCH

Bring awareness to and promote circulation in the lower leg with this invigorating, fun TTouch. The name results from the movement of the hands as they make arc-like slides up and down the leg.

Pressure: 3 to 4

HOW TO

To do the *Rainbow TTouch,* move both hands at the same time in opposite directions on the inside and outside of the leg as if you were making a rainbow on each side of the leg. Position your body as shown in the photographs. If the horse raises his leg or steps forward, you can safely move with him or away if necessary.

Key Uses

- Promotes circulation in lower legs
- Makes horse more aware of lower limbs
- Energizes in preparation for performance

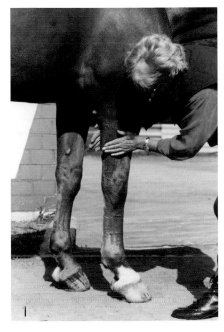
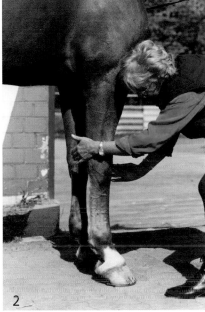
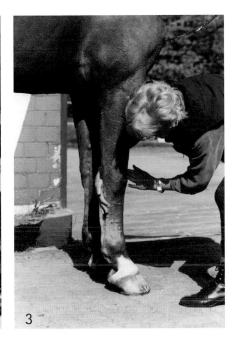

Photos 1, 2 and 3 **Stand facing your horse, slightly off to one side, so you are not in a position to be bumped if the horse stamps or paws. Begin at the top of the leg and work from the elbow down to the fetlock joint on the front legs and the thigh to fetlock on the hind legs.** This movement consists of two arcs or rainbow-like forms. It takes some concentrating in the beginning because one hand does an arc in one direction and the other hand moves at the same time in the opposite arc.

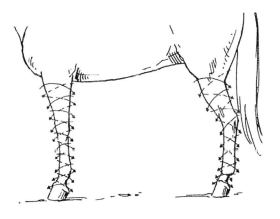

If you begin on a left front leg, stand facing the back, slightly to the side. The left hand makes an arc on the inside of the leg, stroking over the hair from the back of the leg to the front while the other hand makes the arching stroke on the outside from front to back. Once you have the rhythm, make this a fairly fast movement. This is a stimulating, activating sport TTouch to increase circulation and get the horse grounded in a minute or less, just before a performance. It's good to do it right after *Octopus TTouch* (p. 200). Work from the top of the leg to the pastern.

Caution: On the hind legs, do this only if your horse is totally trusting and trustworthy about the work. In this case, stand facing the front, just to the side of the hind leg, and begin with the arm closest to the horse making the rainbow arc from the front of the leg to the back, while the arm farthest away from the horse makes the arc from the back of the leg to the front.

RHINO TTOUCH

When a heavily muscled horse enjoys deep *Bear/Sponge TTouches*, and your hands get tired after three or four of these at a number 8 pressure, shift to *Rhino TTouch*. I don't recommend this TTouch on a lightly muscled horse or one with sore muscles.

Your horse will show you if he likes this TTouch by lowering the head and sometimes half closing the eyes. If a horse is emotionally shut down, he may not enjoy this TTouch.

Pressure: 2 to 10

HOW TO

Photo 1 Snug your thumb tightly against your curled fingers and make a 3 pressure circle and sponge in with the thumbnail.

Photo 2 As you push in with your right hand, pull the crest of the mane toward you or turn the head in a push-pull movement. Your wrist should be straight and the push should come all the way from your feet. This gives you the possibility of deep pressure without stress to your own body. The *Rhino* as well as the deep *Bear TTouch* should only be applied if your horse relaxes and seems to enjoy it.

Key Uses

- Continues effects of *Bear TTouches* (p. 217) when your hands get tired

RIB RELEASE

This movement is a subtle rocking between the two hands, with the intention of creating more flexibility in the rib cage. Combining *Rib Release* with *Neck Bending* (p. 219) can greatly increase a horse's ability to bend evenly in both directions.

Pressure: 3 to 4

Key Uses

- Increases flexibility
- Improves lateral movements
- Enhances quality of gaits and willingness

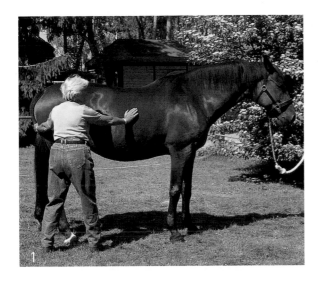

HOW TO

Photo 1 Place one hand on the ribs with the thumb anchored in a groove between two ribs and the other hand holding the tail firmly downward and locked against the inner side of the thigh. Put a subtle pressure between the ribs, creating a light torque between your hands by moving your pelvis and your weight from the back foot to the front. Your hands will be moved by your pelvis rather than emphasizing the push from one hand and the pull from the other.

Photo 2 Begin several ribs ahead of the flank and move as far forward as you can reach. Feel the movement through the release and think of rotating your torso to get the movement. I've seen significant improvements in flexibility and freedom of movement with this TTouch.

SHOULDER RELEASE

Slipping your fingers under the top of the shoulder (scapula) in this way allows a horse to immediately lengthen and lower the neck, increase length of stride and cross the front legs for a greater range of motion for lateral movements. Generally, this is a move that has to be done only a time or two to have a lasting effect.

This is particularly useful when you're dealing with a high-headed horse because it's very possible he won't be able to lower his head below the withers until you have "opened" the shoulders in this way—with the *Shoulder Release.*

Key Uses

- Allows a horse to lower the head and lengthen the neck

- Lengthens stride

- Releases tight shoulder, chest, neck and back muscles

HOW TO

● Turn the horse's neck slightly to the side you're working on. With the tips of your fingers find the ridge of the scapula (see photo) and wiggle your fingers underneath the shoulder blade. As the shoulder opens, slide your hands farther apart until the scapula "pops out," creating a bulge that you can then jiggle. You can't force your way in—you have to find the opening. Some horses are much tighter in this area than others. The whole movement should take a minute or so and can be repeated on both sides. I recommend moving the horse at the walk and trot with a lowered head to allow for a new integration of the unaccustomed movement. Do the two sides once or twice, but not more.

Photo Shoulder releases help a horse release tension through the neck, chest and shoulders. Working uphill or through deep sand can cause these areas to become sore. Curl your fingers lightly and slip them into the groove between the scapula and neck. You may find this easy to do on some horses and more difficult on others, depending upon how heavily muscled the horse is. As you slide your fingers into the groove, your horse will lower his head and stretch it forward. In addition to providing relief for the immediate area, shoulder releases can also help allay wither soreness.

Ground Exercises

Dancing with Your Horse

Take leading to the next level with these special exercises that will inspire you to learn right along with your horse. As you practice these Tai-Chi-like steps with your horse, you will learn to synchronize subtle signals with one hand on the lead while simultaneously giving direction and focus with the wand in the other hand. Coupled with moving your feet in specific ways, you may be amazed to discover a new sense of balance and coordination. This "dance" of horse and handler activates whole-brain learning involving both hemispheres of the brain and spinning up new neural pathways—in effect, enhancing your capacity to learn right along with your equine companion!

Grace of the Cheetah (see p. 240)

BOOMER'S BOUND

Do you dream of a bombproof horse? *Boomer's Bound* is an effective exercise to instill trust in your horse by waving the wand above his head. Named after the huge Australian kangaroos that bound in great leaps across the outback, this is a great way to teach your young horse confidence around the head and over the ears, or for reprogramming horses who are head shy or skittish about movements above or beside their head and neck.

Key Uses

- Retrains horses who duck away or spook when a blanket is put over their head

- Prepares a young horse for movements above him when he is first mounted

- Helps difficult loaders or horses who are claustrophobic in the trailer

HOW TO

Photos 1 and 2 Assuming you are standing on the left side, hold the lead line folded in your left hand while holding the wand in your right hand, close to the button. Move the wand slowly in a large arc from the withers over the area above the horse's ears, down to the tip of the nose as shown in the photos. Once your horse stands quietly, you can practice at the walk. The stop signal is at the end of the movement—with a light touch on his nose, together with a soothing voice command and light signal on the lead line.

What should you do if…

- *Your horse does not like to have his ears touched?*

Attach the lead line up the side of the halter as shown on p. 159. Move the wand slowly above his head while giving him a little feed in a shallow container at chest level. Talk to him quietly while you gently stroke his ears from front to tips with the wand.

- *Your horse is scared by the wand above his head, so*

he throws his head up and pulls back?

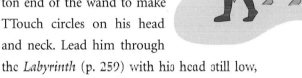

Attach the chain lead (or Zephyr lead) to the side of the halter and ask your horse to *Lower the Head* (p. 163). Use the button end of the wand to make TTouch circles on his head and neck. Lead him through the *Labyrinth* (p. 259) with his head still low, and move the wand slowly above his head.

CHA CHA

This leading exercise describes a rhythmic movement of taking one step back and one step forward, moving diagonal legs—like a dance between horse and handler. This subtle exercise holds a key to improved coordination and is an excellent exercise in preparation to back up. If your horse stops and stands laterally more than diagonally, it can dramatically improve your horse's balance. At the same time, it will help refine your ability to give light, clear signals from the wand and lead.

WHAT YOU NEED

- Chain or Zephyr lead
- Wand

HOW TO

To perform the dance steps of *Cha Cha*, you're going to ask your horse to back up and come forward with diagonal pairs of legs, one step at a time. Notice whether your horse naturally backs with diagonal pairs, which is the ideal situation. If he moves one

ADVANCED DANCE STEPS

One of my students uses *Cha Cha* in the wash rack to remind her Arab mare to come forward and *stay* forward. She reports that it has been an invaluable exercise to teach her *not* to pull back or charge back out of the wash rack. She takes *Cha Cha* one step further by varying the number of steps forward and back—two steps back, one forward, three steps back, two forward, etc., until the mare is completely responsive in the hand and "in the groove." She finds that the random nature of the fore/aft steps really gets her tuned in and paying attention.

Key Uses

- Trains a horse to come forward from a light signal and not pull back
- Prepares a horse to load and unload from the trailer without resistance
- Encourages a horse to back up with ease on cue
- Teaches a horse to stand squarely
- Helps a horse to become lighter and more responsive in hand and under saddle
- Improves coordination and brings your horse into a better state of balance

leg at a time, stroke and tap the diagonal hind leg and then immediately tap the front leg while giving a voice command and light signal on the halter. Another approach: stroke the front and back of the front leg, the belly and then the diagonal hind leg.

Photo 1 I place Serena between two rails to ensure that she steps straight back. She's learned now to move back in balance and...

Photo 2 ...as Serena is stepping in midair, I release the "back" signal from the head and pull downward slightly on the chain, while pushing steadily on Serena's front leg with the wand so she will stop and stay still after only one step. Notice how even and balanced the steps are now.

Photo 3 I immediately tap Serena lightly on the croup with a small circular movement (see also *Dingo*, p. 235).

Photo 4 I plant the wand firmly on the croup with a signal back on the chain so Serena stops and stands perfectly still.

Photos 5 and 6 Here's a closer view of my light ask-and-release signals on the chain close to the halter to take one step back and one step forward.

Note: The direction of the chain signal is downward in Photo 1 so the mare will plant her feet as soon as she has taken one step.

Photo 7 With the lead folded in your left hand as shown, grasp the chain between thumb and forefinger about three inches from the halter ring. With the wand in your other hand, ask your horse to take a step back, starting with the most forward front leg. Then give a light "close-and-release" signal on the chain, at the same tapping the leg with the wand.

Photo 8 Serena doesn't understand, so I raise her head slightly and tap the diagonal hind leg while signaling back on the chain. The chain signal should be light or the horse may twist the head, lose balance and be unable to step back.

Photo 9 The light dawns! Serena understands, and responds by moving her left front and right hind legs back together. Evenly spaced steps with front and hind legs are the hallmark of balance. Horses who are uncoordinated usually take too long a step with a front leg and a short step behind. Even steps are what you're aiming for.

What should you do if….
- *Your horse doesn't respond to your signals?*

Follow the steps in photos 7 to 9.

DANCING COBRA

Many years ago, I discovered that standing in front of a horse with the wand crossed over the lead in front of you is a very effective way to get the attention of an unruly horse—one who has learned to pull or dances around you on a lead line, refusing to walk straight ahead or stop. Sometimes, standing in front of such a horse reminds me of a cobra raising up out of a basket responding to the music of a flute. Hence, the name of this exercise.

This exercise teaches a horse to step forward only one or two steps, and to stop and stand still—from your body language and the movement of the wand crossed in front of you—without any pressure on the halter. It teaches balance, concentration and self-control.

Dancing Cobra is excellent for horses who tend rush ahead of you at the walk, are pushy when being led, have poor self control or who pull back when tied. With this exercise, they learn to step forward instead of pulling back from tension on the halter.

HOW TO

Photo 1 To move forward: Stand about three feet in front of your horse and face him, with your body bent slightly forward. Hold the lead line between both hands with the wand in the hand that's on the end of the lead. Give a light signal and release with the lead stretched while crossing the wand over the lead, sweeping it slowly toward you, and stepping back. For optimum effect, practice this position in the *Labyrinth* as shown here, by first asking the horse to take just two steps forward and stop. Once this is easy, practice three steps forward, and stop. Remember you must keep stepping backward as your horse moves and don't stop stepping back until your horse stops.

Photos 2 and 3 Stopping: Ask for one or two

steps, then stop him by pointing the wand toward his nose and bend slightly toward him. If he doesn't stop, lightly touch him on the nose to bring his head up, shifting his center of gravity back so it will be easier to stop.

What should you do if ...

- *Your horse won't stop?*

  Here are three solutions:

  ❶ Tap the chain of the lead line with the wand.

This will cause your horse to raise his head and shift his center of balance further back, making it easier for him to halt.

❷ Review the *Cueing the Camel* (see below) leading position so your horse is reminded of the connection between tapping his chest and stopping.

❸ Get a helper and have her attach a second lead line on the other side of the halter to reinforce your wand and voice signal.

DINGO and CUEING THE CAMEL

With *Dingo*, you can teach your horse to come forward from a light signal on the lead as you tap the croup with the wand. This exercise is an essential tool for training a horse to stand tied and go forward rather than pull back when he feels any pressure on the head. *Cueing the Camel* can be used in conjunction with *Dingo* to stop your horse.

As your horse learns to respond to clear, precise signals both at his head and on his body, the work will carry over to ridden work. The action of the wand can be used when mounted to clarify "go" and "whoa."

With *Dingo*, slow horses learn to respond faster, and impatient horses learn to wait.

The goal is to teach your horse to respond to the lightest signal. If you find you have to keep tapping your horse to make him move forward, make sure you are not causing the reluctance by holding him back with your hand on the lead line. It takes time for most people to learn to use their hands independently, so practicing this ground exercise will help you with your riding.

Key Uses

- Trains young horses to lead and stop from a light signal

- Encourages a timid horse to walk forward (such as through a narrow opening)

- Teaches any horse to load safely and willingly into a trailer

- Retrains a horse who pulls back when tied

HOW TO

Dingo

There are four steps to *Dingo* executed in the following order, only seconds apart: you **steady** the head, **stroke** the back (two or three times), **signal** with the lead to step forward, and **scoop** or **tap** with the wand on the top of the croup.

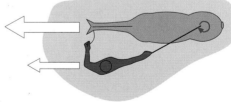

❶ Give a light signal on the chain toward the chest to get the horse's attention. This preliminary motion keeps a horse from moving forward on the

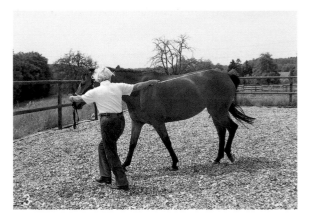

stroke, which some horses will do if they are nervous or sensitive.

❷ Stroke the back firmly to connect the horse from forehand to hindquarters and prepare him for the tap on the croup.

❸ Give a light signal-and-release with the lead to come forward. A scoop or tap (in a circular movement) on the croup reinforces the step-forward command. The *tapping on the croup* is a means to ultimately teach your horse to come forward from the signal on the lead, without the wand.

❹ At the same time, give the clear verbal command, "*and waaalk.*"

We're often asked why we tap on the top of the croup instead of the usual tap on the thigh. We do it because it's more instinctive for horses to step sideways than forward from the tap on the thigh, and they are encouraged to think, rather than just react. The intent of the Tellington Method is to take horses beyond instinct and teach them to think.

Photos 1 and 2 Note that the lead line is held in one hand only and is looped safely. Steadying your horse with light contact on the chain, stroke his back firmly with the wand two or three times from the withers to the croup.

Photo 3 and 4 Give a light, forward signal-and-release on his halter, and a forward-scooping tap, tap, with the wand, on the top of his croup.

Cueing the Camel

To do *Cuing the Camel,* bring the wand to the front of the chest, pointing the soft end down toward the ground as you move it forward. Signal your horse to stop with a "*whoooaaa*" as you give a light signal on the chain and tap on the chest. The tapping encourages him to shift his weight back and stop in balance.

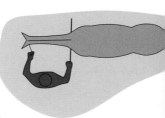

When taking a horse over an obstacle like the *Platform* (p. 269), use *Dingo* leading position. These obstacles are excellent exercises to build your horse's trust in going where you ask him, even when it *seems* threatening. In particular, they prepare your horse to learn to be loaded into a trailer without fuss or apprehension.

What should you do if...

- *Your horse falls onto his forehand as he stops?*

Lift the chain up and slightly backward, to help rebalance him.

- *Your horse is nervous?*

With the lead line, ask him to *Lower his Head* (p. 163) below the withers. Gently tap his croup with the wand and move forward with his head low. Practice walking forward for just two steps, then stop. Give light, clear cues with the wand on the chest and the lead line. Remember to use clear voice signals—for walking forward as well as stopping—to avoid confusing him and adding to his discomfort. This is an excellent exercise to practice with a horse who has a tendency to pull back when tied, and often is used in conjunction with *Taming the Tiger* (p. 166).

ELEGANT ELEPHANT

Elegant Elephant is the most basic and secure leading position used in the Tellington Method. The effortless control this position gives you reminds me of the strength and elegance of an elephant. Imagine the knob of the wand as the tip of an elephant's trunk.

Most of us were taught to lead a horse by standing to the side between the head and the shoulder, so if your horse charged ahead you could put your elbow in his neck and bend your horse around in a circle to slow down or stop. This usually kept the horse from stepping on you.

However, there are two drawbacks to this style of leading. First, your horse tends to pay less attention to you when you're behind the head because *he's leading you!* And second, when you bend your horse around you to slow down or stop, he's pulled off balance, and we spend a lot of time and attention getting our horses *in* balance. There's actually a third drawback to this position behind the head. It commonly teaches a horse to pull and ignore your signals to slow down or stop.

Key Uses

- Reduces a horse's tendency to pull on the lead
- Retrains horses who are difficult to stop in hand or from the saddle
- Prevents horses from running circles around the handler when led

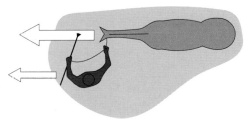

We've discovered over many years that getting out just a little ahead of the head and to the side, and using a chain over the nose combined with the movement of the wand, teaches a horse to watch the movement and listen to our requests. Learning this cooperation on the ground almost always carries over to under-saddle work. Be sure to work from both sides of the horse to activate both hemispheres of the brain.

HOW TO

Basic Position

• Say you are leading from the left side of your horse. Hold the end of the chain lead (or Zephyr lead) and the wand in your left hand. Balance the wand near its midpoint with the knob or button end toward your horse. Your right hand will be lightly on the chain.

• Before you try this position with your horse, it's useful to practice on a fence. Practice the light tug-and-release signal from the chain to go forward and stop. Remember, your horse will respond on the release part of the signal rather than on the tug.

• Hold the lead line in both hands with your right hand on the chain and your left hand on the end of the line.

Photo 1A Tie a knot at the end of the lead and place it across the palm with the knot near the little finger. Note the slight slack in the chain, which should be there unless you are giving a signal to go, slow or stop. We call this slack "being in neutral." In your left hand, you also hold the wand—midway down its length—with the knob ahead of your horse's nose. Your horse will learn to follow the movement of this knob. Having both hands on the lead enables you to quickly shorten or lengthen the lead line if your horse jumps or pulls back.

Photo 1B Take up the slack of the lead line in a loop between your middle and index finger. This avoids the risk of having the line wrap itself around your hand or fingers should your horse move suddenly.

Photos 2A and B To teach your horse to follow the motion of the wand, begin with a soft stroke on the muzzle and a sweep of the wand smoothly forward. Move the knob forward along the path you intend your horse to follow. Following this motion, give the forward signal-and-release on the chain, and a clear voice command to walk. Say "*and waaaaalk*," with drawn out words and toning to smooth the transition and give your horse time to organize the movement.

Photos 3 and 4 Here I am ahead of Dorina and to the side, with the wand slightly lower than nose level because the mare has a tendency to be high-headed and a little high-strung. This lower position of her head helped to calm and settle her.

Photo 5 To stop, give the voice command as a drawn out clear "*and whoaaaa*." Hold the tone and maintain your body position even with the head until your horse comes to a full stop. (This long tone also encourages you to breathe deeply.) Holding the wand about 20 inches from the horse's nose, move it rhythmically up and down three or four inches. Until your horse learns to stop from the voice and movement of the wand ahead of the nose, reinforce the command by tapping your horse's chest with the button end of the wand, and once or twice on the opposite shoulder while you give the signal to stop with the chain signal.

What should you do if…

• *Your horse turns toward you as soon as you ask for a halt?*

Keep moving forward until your horse has stopped. Most people say "*whoa*," and then stop. The horse keeps going and is pulled to the left. Keep walking and keep your horse's head straight, occasionally touching the shoulder with the wand.

1A

1B

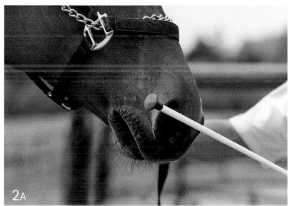

2A

2B

3

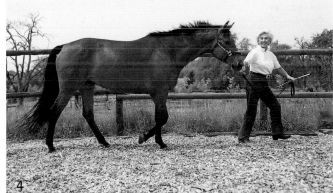

4

5

GRACE OF THE CHEETAH

his leading position invites your horse to follow the movement of the wand ahead of his nose, keeping a distance of approximately four to five feet between you, and stop from a movement of the wand out in front of his nose combined with your quiet voice command. This leading position was named after a cheetah because you have to be as quick and as graceful as one of these elegant big cats to switch the wand from one hand to other while you're walking. Many of my students tell me their coordination improved as they held the image of moving as gracefully as a cheetah as they switched the wand from one hand to the other.

Key Uses

- Teaches your horse to listen in order to follow, stop or stay back from a movement of the wand

- Trains your horse to keep a distance from you and develop independence

- Lengthens the topline and back

- Promotes stopping through the body without pressure from the halter

- Stops your horse from crowding you on the ground

- Instills self-confidence

- Encourages flighty or unfocused horses to pay attention

HOW TO

Photo 1 Here the gelding is moving over the poles in *Joyful Dolphin* (p. 244) position—the lead in the left hand and the wand in the right hand, pointed at the tail to ensure forward momentum.

Photo 2 Now the wand is ahead of the horse's nose in *Grace of the Cheetah*. Switch your wand into your left hand and then slide your right hand about 14 inches up the lead as shown here. You now have the wand and the end of the lead in your left hand. Your horse follows the wand over the poles. This is good preparation for *Freework* (p. 257) where the horse first learns to follow the wand and then your hand. We also use this position to stop a horse, making very small up-and-down motions with the wand about three feet ahead of the nose, followed immediately with two light taps on the chest and the word command "*whoaaa*." (For a larger picture of this, see p. 230.)

JOURNEY OF THE HOMING PIGEON

This leading position requires two people, one on each side, both holding a wand and lead. The name was inspired by the image of the handlers on each side giving a sense of security and reminding me of open wings. Most nervous horses become calmer, bringing an end to the flight reflex as the horse focuses or "homes in" on the wands. Having one person in control, while the other practices switching from one leading position to the other while the horse is moving is a good way to learn the difference between *Elegant Elephant* (p. 237) and *Grace of the Cheetah* (p. 240).

WHAT YOU NEED

- Two people
- One lead line with a chain plus one Zephyr lead or two Zephyr leads (see p. 157)
- Two wands

GETTING STARTED

- Each person holds the lead line in two hands, to be able to easily and quickly shorten or lengthen the lead.

- The end of the line is held in the outside hand. The person on the left holds the wand in the left hand together with the end of lead. The other hand will be on the lead anywhere from close to the halter to several feet away, and can slide closer or farther away from the halter, depending upon whether they are using the *Elegant Elephant* or *Cheetah* leading position.

- Decide who will be in charge. It's important that one person decides the direction and gives the primary commands to stop, go and turn.

Key Uses

- Teaches attentiveness, patience and balance
- Activates both hemispheres of the brain, enhancing learning
- Promotes communication and coordination between two handlers
- Accustoms horse and handler to work from right side
- Gives horse the experience of having two people work around him in a positive situation
- Trains a horse not to crowd you and to be straight
- Reforms horses who are difficult to control, rear, pull or circle around you
- Rebalances horses who have difficulty bending in one direction
- Releases the neck and back

- The person in charge uses the chain (or Zephyr) lead (for clarity and added security) fastened in the usual way over the noseband and up the opposite side (see p. 158). The support person's Zephyr lead loops through the side ring on the opposite side of the halter and is twisted back on itself (see Photos 1A and 1B).

- The goal is to get the horse to rebalance and pay close attention to your aids. When your horse listens willingly in hand, that cooperative attitude will carry over under saddle.

JOYFUL DOLPHIN

This leading exercise teaches your horse to respond to your aids for walk, trot and stop while maintaining a steady four- to six-foot distance from you out at the end of the lead. It gives your horse a certain amount of responsibility to keep the distance. He can watch your body language; he can see you better. As a result, a different relationship develops with a sense of freedom so your horse learns to cooperate and enjoy the work you do together.

To prepare your horse to stay out on the end of a short line while moving forward, we do a preliminary exercise.

The tip of your wand "jumps" softly from point to point over the horse from the croup to the withers to the poll to the nose. I'm reminded of a dolphin leaping through the waves. Once your horse learns to stay out at the end of the line and goes forward easily, no longer needing the flicks with the wand on shoulder, neck and nose, we call this exercise simply *Joyful Dolphin*.

Caution: In these exercises, for safety always stay level with your horse's shoulder. If you get further behind, there is a potential danger of a horse kicking you.

HOW TO

• Begin by walking and trotting your horse in a straight line and then progress to walking a large oval. We longe horses on an oval rather than on a circle, and use a regular lead line and wand so the handler walks with the horse rather than standing still in the middle of a circle. This helps the horse keep his balance and makes him mindful of his distance from the handler and where he is going.

> ### Key Uses
>
> • Prepares a horse for longeing, with the horse close enough to be safely controlled by the voice and a touch of the wand
>
> • Teaches a young horse to listen to your aids in preparation for riding

• Once your horse has mastered this exercise and calmly responds to your voice commands and the movement of the wand, you can graduate to using a longer or longe line. Using a *Body Wrap* (p. 160) helps the horse stay calm and focused.

Photo 1 Start in *Dingo* (p. 235) leading position, the lead line folded in a figure eight in your left hand and the wand's button end in your right. As your horse steps forward, step away from him, sliding out on the lead.

Photo 2 Now I touch Donita with a light flick on top of the croup, walking forward in a straight line with a light slack in the lead so as not to pull her.

Photo 3 Next is a rhythmic tap on the side of the withers so she'll keep going forward and stay out on the line.

Photo 4 A light tap on the top of the neck serves a two-fold purpose: to signal the horse to stay out and at the same time encourage her to calmly accept contact in this area, especially the horse who is overly sensitive or head-shy.

Photo 5 A soft flick on the halter ring or the side of the nose as if you were using a paint brush directs Donita away from me. Notice again the swinging lead. For some horses, this length of chain hanging out of the halter ring would be too heavy and would

pull the horse's head toward the handler. If your horse has a tendency to drift toward you, shorten the chain so that only two to three inches extend from the halter.

Photo 6 To stop, change to the *Grace of the Cheetah* (p. 240) by switching the wand into your left hand (holding it along with the end of the lead) and placing it ahead of the horse, and slide your right hand about 12 inches up the lead line toward your horse's head. Make a short motion with the wand about three feet ahead of your horse and then tap him lightly on the chest, as you say "*whoaaa.*"

What should you do if...

• *Your horse is crowding you?*

The weight of the chain hanging away from the halter may be pulling your horse toward you. It is often helpful to shorten the chain (see *Tellington Tools*, p. 158, Photo 5). You can also keep your horse away from you with *Peacock*—moving the wand like a slow windshield wiper to keep a space between you (p. 247). It's often necessary to tap with the wand lightly on the neck behind the ear or on the side of the nose to ask him to move him away in the very beginning. If he still does not understand, use *Journey of the Homing Pigeon* (p. 241) to give him a clearer idea about keeping his distance.

GLIDE OF THE EAGLE

Once your horse has learned the *Joyful Dolphin* leading position, try this fun exercise that tests your horse's willingness to stay level with you—over poles or in a straight line at a walk or trot. Hold the lead line and the wand in the same hand. Point the wand toward the horse's shoulder. This will enable you to get as far away from your horse as possible and is most useful for an exercise such as trotting over cavalletti.

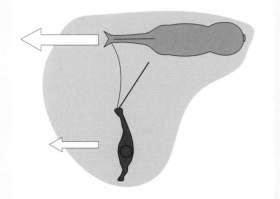

Photo The ultimate test of balance and dancing together, I hold the end of the lead and the wand in my right hand, leaving my left hand free as I walk lightly alongside the horse. The horse doesn't drop back or surge forward, but stays even with my shoulder. This is great practice for presenting your horse in hand. Practice leading from both sides of the horse and on a circle.

PEACOCK

There is a great deal of discussion in the horse world these days about "respect" and having horses "stay in their own space." One popular method of achieving this is to "ripple" or spin the lead line in the horse's face. While this will keep a horse "off you," all too often, I've seen it make horses high-headed and head shy, often with dropped backs, making them tight and stiff in the hindquarters. Such an invasive motion clearly violates the Equine Golden Rule: *Treat your horse as you would like to be treated.*

With the *Peacock* and other Ground Exercises, you can teach your horse not to crowd you and to maintain whatever distance from you that you desire, whether it's one foot, four feet or more.

HOW TO

Photo Hold your horse's lead with your right hand, and with your left hand holding the middle of the wand with the button end up, sweep the wand like a windshield wiper back and forth between you and the horse, slowly and rhythmically.

Key Uses

- Teaches your horse to follow, but not run you over, on a narrow trail

- Helps keep your horse beside you when leading across water so he can't jump on top of you

- Prepares for trotting your horse in hand for the judge, allowing him to fly elegantly beside you on a loose lead (see *Glide of the Eagle*, left)

- Stops a horse from crowding you in hand

THE STATUE

This enjoyable exercise teaches patience and obedience. Your horse will learn to stand like a statue and wait for your signals. He will stand still without being tied while you groom him, tack up, set up obstacles, or turn from him to talk with people. (I do recommend, though, that you keep him in sight, if only out of the corner of your eye.)

Before you begin, be sure your horse is totally confident while you stroke the legs with the wand and that he responds well to *Elegant Elephant, Dingo and Cueing the Camel* and *Cha Cha* (pp. 237, 235, and 232), all of which will teach him to pay attention to placement of feet, balance and signals from the wand, lead (chain or Zephyr) and voice.

The mutual trust developed during such in-hand training will carry over to under-saddle work, and your relationship with your horse will become one of trust and kindness.

HOW TO

•   To teach your horse *The Statue*, start by standing him in his halter and lead. Back slowly away until you've reached the end of the lead. If he's learned his lessons mentioned above, he'll know he's not supposed to move until you signal to him with your voice, the lead or a tap with the wand.

•   While he's still, move yourself slowly to the right and stand still, then to the left side and again stand quietly, then return to the front. Keep your arm and wand stretched out toward your horse, and maintain a distance of five to six feet. If you move too fast or breathe unevenly or quickly, your horse won't stand still. If you really concentrate, though, your breathing and body posture will have an almost hypnotic effect on him.

•   Should your horse take a step in any direction, move him quietly back to the same spot he was

standing. With practice, he'll move back to his original spot when you hold the wand in front of his nose or tap his chest with it. Eventually he will stand absolutely still with your quiet command, "*Stand.*" This needs to be said at just the right moment—just before your horse is about to move.

•   Horses learn the meanings of various gestures and words just as well as dogs. Of course, whatever signal you give for your horse to stand is going to work better when you can react before his first inclination to move. Do it quietly and patiently. Remember, if you aren't concentrating and alert, you are not going to be able to react fast enough and will have to start the exercise over.

Photo 1   Robyn Hood demonstrates with an Icelandic horse, Odin, who is learning *The Statue* for the first time. Robyn stands approximately six feet in front of Odin so he focuses on the wand and learns to watch her body language.

Photo 2   Robyn moves smoothly to the right side, keeping the wand at waist height between her body and Odin. Saying the word "stand" in soothing tones can help keep your horse's attention.

Photo 3   Robyn steps smoothly and slowly to the opposite side with the wand still at waist height. Odin follows her with his head but keeps his feet perfectly

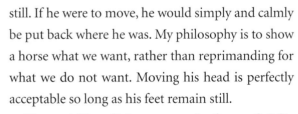

still. If he were to move, he would simply and calmly be put back where he was. My philosophy is to show a horse what we want, rather than reprimanding for what we do not want. Moving his head is perfectly acceptable so long as his feet remain still.

Photo 4 Here Robyn moves in front of Odin again, this time about 12 feet away, and he remains quietly focused.

Playground for Higher Learning®

TRAINING ADVENTURES FOR
HORSE AND HUMAN

The Playground for Higher Learning is reminiscent of training courses used by European cavalries in centuries past. In such venues, six or more horses worked together in an arena with cannons going off, bugles blowing and fires burning.

Our updated "playground" prepares the horse for myriad modern-day challenges—horses sharing trails with all-terrain vehicles, mountain bikes and hikers; motorized traffic of all sorts; llamas and other unexpected encounters. Working your horse through these exercises can reduce many of the risks encountered by the modern equestrian.

Most of us grew up with the idea that horses only learn through repetition—and lots of it. But in our experience, this approach dulls the mind and tires the body, leaving the horse confused and challenged to figure out what you want. Attempting to force a horse or punishing him only reinforces his initial fear and resistance.

The Playground for Higher Learning gives you a positive alternative to teaching your horse by repetition and pressure. The approach is revolutionary in that it recognizes the horse's ability to learn quickly when he is given clear information.

Our playground helps take horses beyond their instinctive fears by making them confident about the ground beneath their feet and the space around and above their bodies. In this section, I'll show you how to set up the obstacles and "chunk" the steps down so that your horse can be successful, obedient and confident.

Invite your friends over, team up and have fun working your horses together. You will see rapid results on two tracks: First, you will notice an almost instant "upgrading" of your horse's athletic capacity; and at the same time, enjoy a safer, more confident and responsive equine partner, both at home and on the trail.

Platform (see p. 269)

BARRELS

Barrels have multiple uses as you build your playground. Fifty-gallon barrels are best, but smaller ones come in handy, too. You can use them to support your rails to train your horse to go through narrow places, to hold up plastic sheets, and to put grain on as reward stations around the arena.

Teaching your horse to trust the sound that the grain on the barrel makes as he takes some nibbles off the top is an excellent lesson in de-spooking. If your horse is nervous to begin with, place a small throw rug on top of the barrel to muffle the sound of the grain. The rubberized side up will also keep the grain from flying around.

HOW TO

Photo 1 In the *Elegant Elephant* (p. 237) leading position, I'm preparing to bring the young horse onto the platform by first inviting her to investigate and nibble some grain sitting on top of the barrels. This will encourage her to relax and think.

Photo 2 The mare stands quietly, confidently exploring the boundaries of the platform and barrels. This type of exercise will help make a horse feel safe in tight quarters or new situations.

Key Uses
• Prepares for trailer loading and crossing bridges

THE FAN, CAVALLETTI AND PICK-UP STICKS

The *Fan, Cavalletti* and *Pick-Up Sticks* are a trio of exercises that bring multiple benefits to you and your horse.

If your horse has been described as clumsy, lazy or disinterested, these exercises will amaze you with their power to transform movement. And, if your horse is already a top-notch mover, they will take him to new heights.

The exercises teach a horse to pay attention to where he places his feet, and to learn to shorten or lengthen his stride. Performing them all improves *proprioception*—a horse's awareness of where his feet are in space. This is especially beneficial for jumpers, marathon driving and endurance horses, and makes your trail horse safer and more sure-footed over every type of terrain.

Key Uses

- Transforms your horse's athletic ability
- Reduces stumbling
- Supples and relaxes the back
- Develops coordination, communication and cooperation
- Hones your horse's ability to judge distance and footing (temporal-spatial awareness)

If your horse has a tendency to bump or trip on the poles, stop and take a few minutes to systematically tap around the hoof wall with the button end of the wand to make your horse aware of his feet. First tap both front feet and make several rounds over the obstacles; then tap the back feet. You'll usually see an immediate shift in your horse's ability to make "clean rounds."

WHAT YOU NEED

To cover all needs: Buy 10 poles, 12 feet long, and four inches in diameter so that you have enough poles to set up any two obstacles at the same time, including the *Labyrinth* (p. 259). These poles can be made of wood or high-impact, shatterproof plastic. Individual obstacles need:

- *The Fan:* Four poles and a hub: tires; a bale of hay; straw or shavings; a simple cavalletti pole with a base; or any other small object to set one end of the poles on. If your rails are only 10 feet long, your hub will need to be lower.

- *Cavalletti:* Four to six poles.

- *Pick-Up Sticks:* Four poles, stabilized on one end with a cupped pole-holder.

In addition, special cups are needed to stabilize the poles and prevent them from rolling.

The Fan

As you guide your horse with the wand and chain on a curved path through the poles, he must bend and lift the feet at the same time, increasing range of motion of the hips, back and shoulders. This can be both therapeutic and gymnastic.

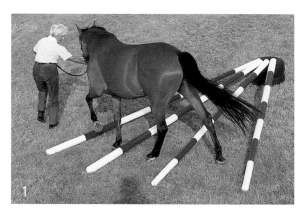

Photo 1 Direct the head of your horse and accentuate the arc of a circle as you step over the poles. With each pass, choose a different height. With the poles the distance apart shown here, there are three choices. Over the red-painted section, where the poles are about seven inches high, you get a slight bend and medium length of step. Over the outer edge of the poles over the white section, you achieve less bend but the longest stride. Moving from the outer white sections toward the inside where Ravina is now stepping in this photo, shortens the stride and increases the height of the step.

Photo 2　Here are three challenges: the first and third poles are lying on the ground and the second and fourth are raised, and the distance is purposefully uneven. This variation will activate the horse's hoof-eye coordination and is excellent practice for stretching and contracting muscles. I stay ahead of Ravina and lift my leg to an exaggerated height. It looks a little strange, but often a horse will mirror the movement of the handler.

Cavalletti

A wonderful lesson that a horse learns from trotting over ground poles—an exercise known as cavalletti—is to really pay attention to the handler's subtle signals of the voice and wand. When you walk or run along the outside of the poles, your horse learns to stay beside you, rating his speed. This benefits not just the gymnastic aspects of training but also enriches the horse's mind, as he tunes in to watching your body language and listens for direction. Your horse will be moving along on a four-foot line really listening to you, not charging forward or hanging back. This exercise is useful for energizing the lazy horse or for settling the "chargey" horse.

Photo 3　The gelding Jodin walks quietly through the ground poles, keeping his distance from Kirsten, who aims the wand at his shoulder and is leading in a leading position we call *Glide of the Eagle* (p. 246). This leaves her left arm free for balance.

Photo 4　With her wand in the right hand in *Joyful Dolphin* (p. 244), Kirsten keeps Jodin moving briskly at the trot, side by side with Kirsten, not charging forward or hanging back.

Photo 5　Kirsten switches her wand to the left hand—*Grace of the Cheetah* (p. 240)—and holds it slightly ahead of the horse to slow him down a little.

Photo 6　Raising the poles on one end is the next step.

Photo 7 The poles are still set at the walking distance, a bit too close together for the trot, and Jodin steps over two poles instead of taking a stride in between. Spacing is most important. For the average-size, 15-hand horse at a relaxed trot in hand, three feet is okay, but as the impulsion increases so must the distance between poles. Under saddle, four feet is a normal stride.

Photo 8 Kirsten and Jodin come back through the poles in the opposite direction. This time Jodin lifts his legs carefully, and with the poles just slightly farther apart, he steps correctly between them.

Pick-Up Sticks

This random placing of ground poles is like a puzzle, offering many variations of spacing. This exercise is particularly useful for trail and endurance horses and also fun to ride through.

Caution: Use the stabilizing cups to prevent the poles from rolling if you are on smooth ground where it might happen.

Many horses in this day and age haven't had the advantage of learning about varying terrain, and gaining the experience of being cautious on rough ground. They simply aren't aware that they have to pay attention. With *Pick-Up Sticks,* you can recreate this experience. It's remarkable how quickly horses recapture their innate sense of sure-footedness with only a few sessions.

Large, rapidly growing horses often have poor coordination and reflexes, so they simply don't know where their feet are. These horses benefit not only from *Hoof Tapping* (p. 196) but also need focused *Coiled Python Lifts* and *Octopus TTouches* (pp. 172 and 200). This is also true of horses who are spooky and high-headed.

Photos 9 and 10 With lowered head and full concentration, Serena picks her way carefully. Notice the loose lead, giving the mare the space and opportunity to learn.

Photo 11 *Pick-Up Sticks* is a great exercise that simulates uneven ground—in the safety of your own arena.

FREEWORK

Once you have mastered *Dancing Cobra* (p. 234) with a lead line, try it with your horse loose in a fenced-in area. Start in the *Labyrinth* (p. 259) with just a piece of string around your horse's neck. Using the wand and your body language for emphasis, indicate how you want him to respond. Once he is listening well, you can remove the string and try the exercise with him completely free. Now you can have some fun!

Freework—also called *Liberty Work*—is working with your horse through the obstacles of the Play ground for Higher Learning. It develops cooperation and a special relationship with your horse. The feeling of your horse following you without a halter or rope is as precious as riding without a bridle. Most horsewomen and men don't think it's possible so they don't try it, yet it's one of the most fun and inspiring activities.

One of my most memorable images is of four horses working at liberty with their handlers at the Reken, Germany, test center in a study I conducted in 1978. All the horses in the study were brought there because they were considered unmanageable, and in some cases, dangerous. After three weeks, these horses were able to negotiate—even "dance through"—the obstacles at liberty, quietly and confidently.

There are a variety of methods to achieve this work at liberty. The Tellington Method is enjoyable and interesting for both horse and rider.

Key Uses

- Builds horse and human confidence and trust
- Develops cooperation and balance
- Is fun for horse and partner

HOW TO

- I like to begin in the stall, TTouching and grooming without a halter, so my horse begins to get the idea of listening to my hand signals and enjoying my company. Next, practice *The Statue* (p. 248) exercise where your horse stands still while you walk slowly around and away from him. Begin the exercise with a halter and then with only a light rope around the neck.

- Now you can lead him through the *Labyrinth* in *Elegant Elephant* (p. 237) and *Dancing Cobra* using a light rope around the neck and signaling come and stop with your voice, wand and body language. Finally, replace the rope with a light twine around the neck.

Photo 1 Kirsten stops Serena in *Dancing Cobra*, beginning with a light rope around her neck instead of a halter.

Photos 2A and B Kirsten uses her hands and wand to signal forward.

Photo 3 The mare stops from Kirsten's body language and verbal "*whoaaa.*"

Photo 4 Carry a little grain in your pocket as incentive and reward.

Photos 5A and B Working with the *Platform* (p. 269) and *Teeter-Totter* (p. 273) in a variety of ways is fun for you both.

LABYRINTH

Many books have been published in recent years about the meditative, peaceful and calming effects people experience when negotiating a circular labyrinth. There's an unexplainable effect created by the boundaries of this configuration. Leading a horse mindfully through our special arrangement of ground poles has a similar effect on horses. This was one of the first Ground Exercises that we developed back in the early 1980s, and it's my favorite way to teach a horse to be attentive, relaxed and balanced.

Biofeedback studies of horses being led through the *Labyrinth* may help unlock the mysteries of this ancient phenomenon. The studies revealed that when horses took the precise steps required to negotiate the turns in balance, beta brainwaves associated with logical thinking in people were activated. This may provide an intriguing explanation for one of the unusual benefits we consistently see from this exercise: Horses worked in the *Labyrinth* literally learn how to learn.

Keynote: The key exercise for promoting focus, attention, and balance.

The *Labyrinth* is a unique experience with many ways for you to "lead the dance." Here are several approaches to try with your equine friends:

❶ Lead in the basic *Elegant Elephant* (p. 237) position to teach your horse to take two or three steps at a time and bend smoothly around corners.

❷ Work your horse "between two hands" in the *Dingo* (p. 235) for perfect stops and starts.

❸ In *Dancing Cobra* (p. 234), walk backward and stop every two steps.

❹ Grab a friend and lead through in *Homing Pigeon* (p. 241), with your friend on the outside in *Cheetah* (p. 240), and you directing the dance in *Elegant Elephant.*

Key Uses

- Helps a horse focus and pay attention to your signals
- Slows down a horse who is challenging to control
- Improves balance, patience and self-control
- Encourages reactive, high-headed horses to come "down to earth"

❺ Practice the *Half-Walk* (p. 280) for ultimate balance. Lower your horse's head, and invite him forward, taking slow, shortened steps. This takes a little experimenting and you'll probably have to practice in *Dingo* until your horse responds to very light signals on the chain to step forward in balance.

❻ Back through the *Labyrinth*, using the boundaries to focus your horse while practicing the "one step forward, one step back" movements of *Cha Cha* (p. 232).

❼ *Freework:* Guide your horse through the maze without a halter or tack. It's the icing on the cake! The refinements of movement attained with the use of the wand and chain will pay off here. With the slightest help from the wand and your body language, you and your horse can play "circus" and have the reward of a special communication. (For *Freework,* see p. 257.)

WHAT YOU NEED

- Wand, chain lead or Zephyr lead and halter, fitted as shown on p. 158.

- Six poles, 12 feet long, arranged in the pattern shown here, or, in a pinch, you can use rope. Start

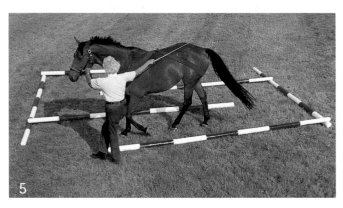

with a distance of about four feet between rails. If your horse is tall or stiff and has difficulty bending around the corners or staying within the boundaries, or is nervous about entering the *Labyrinth*, make the pathways wider.

• When you're working with a difficult horse who tends to rush forward, it is useful to have a helper on the other side with a lead line attached, and holding the wand in the *Grace of the Cheetah* position to move the horse through the maze in *Journey of the Homing Pigeon* position.

HOW TO

Photo 1 Lead your horse into the *Labyrinth* in the *Elegant Elephant* position from the left side. Hold your right hand on the end of the chain with the end of the nylon lead in your left hand along with the wand, held in the middle with the button end toward your horse. Your horse will learn to watch the wand and follow it.

Photos 2, 3 and 4 Stop and stand for a few seconds in the middle of the first "aisle." Then continue around the corner and stop again in the middle second aisle. Your goal is to have your horse stop straight and walk forward readily when you give a light signal on the chain and a forward movement with the wand, drawing your horse forward. Stop briefly and stand every one or two steps.

Benchmark of Success

Your horse stays in balance around the curves in both directions. That's when the hind feet follow on the same arc as the front feet. Once you've accomplished this, your horse will be well on the way to good balance and coordination.

Photo 5 In *Dingo,* signal forward with the lead and reinforce with the wand on the back and croup. Enter the *Labyrinth* holding the lead with the left hand and tapping your horse forward with the wand on the croup after stroking the back. Take two steps, and stop with a tap on the chest (*Cueing the Camel,* p. 235) and signal on the chain. Continue this all the way through and switch back to *Elegant Elephant* to exit.

Photo 6 *Dancing Cobra* is one of the best exercises we have found for developing equine self-control. Standing in front of a horse seems like a strange thing to do if you've never tried it, but it's one of the most effective ways of getting your horse's attention and teaching self-control. You stand in front, the lead line in both hands and the wand held crossways in front of your horse. Take only one or two steps backward at a time. The value of this exercise lies in the fact that there is nothing holding the horse back. He has to watch you and stop from a movement from the wand, rather than a signal on the lead. He has to be well balanced to take only one or two steps forward and stop.

Tellington Tip

Lead your horse through the Labyrinth with the head and neck at two levels: the normal relaxed position; and with the head low and neck lengthened in Photo 5. This is an excellent exercise for spooky horses and for Western Pleasure horses to get that required low head carriage. If your horse is very laid back or tends to fall on the forehand, raise the head to shift the center of gravity back, allowing your horse to step under with the hind legs.

NECKLINE AND GROUND DRIVING

Over 40 years ago, I began *Ground Driving* young horses in preparation for riding so that a horse learns to turn, stop and listen to signals before he's ever mounted. However, it takes a great deal of experience to become proficient in *Ground Driving.* By working with an assistant, you can achieve the benefits of *Ground Driving* without years of practice.

Because many people who come to our Starting Young Horses clinics have no previous experience Ground Driving, in 1978, I introduced a new exercise: I have one person lead the horse while a second person drives him, and instead of starting with the driving lines attached to a bit we begin with them attached to the halter. This prevents a horse from becoming overbent or behind the bit or high-headed, which is often seen with "normal" ground driving.

Neckline Driving soon became another step in "chunking down" the training (and retraining) process. I remember the moment we got the idea: it

Key Uses

- Teaches your horse to trust you
- Calms horses who are spooky, "chargey," jiggy, or nervous about movement and things behind or above them
- Improves the posture of horses who are strung-out, above the bit, behind the bit (overbent) or ewe-necked
- Helps the horse become more responsive, lighter and more balanced
- Encourages high-headed and hollow-backed horses to "round up"
- Changes the behavior of claustrophobic horses who rush through narrow spaces
- Betters the attitude of horses who kick at other horses
- Trains horses to quietly cross water and walk through ditches without jumping
- Teaches horses to shift weight back to halt
- Prepares young horses for under-saddle training

was with a high-headed Arabian gelding who came to a weeklong session. He was spooky about any movement behind him. The lightest contact with his mouth sent his nose straight up in the air. In a true "aha" moment, I put the neckline on him and he dropped his head, giving him a new sense of awareness and safety in his body.

Neckline and Ground Driving is also excellent preparation for riding with a *Balance Rein* (p. 279), teaching a horse to shift his weight back, turn or stop without you "getting in his mouth."

NON-SLIP KNOT

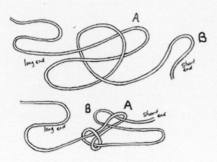

Here is a simple non-slip knot you can use to fasten the lines around the neck so they don't tighten or loosen while you are driving your horse. Be sure to pull the knot snugly so it doesn't slip.

Attach the two lines around the neck together so there is an equal pressure on both sides of the neck. Do this by leaving about eight inches of extra line hanging from each knot and then wrapping it around the other line a couple times to secure it.

WHAT YOU NEED

- A flat nylon or leather halter
- Wand
- Chain or Zephyr lead
- Two or four 21-foot driving lines, 7 to 9 mm in diameter

HOW TO

Photo 1 *Neckline and Ground Driving* requires two people—one at the horse's head and the other holding the lines. Have your helper stand at the horse's head holding the lead and wand. Attach the rope around the neck with the special non-slip knot shown in the sidebar (p. 262). Then, holding the end of the rope in one hand, take a couple of wraps of the rope on the end of the wand. Stroke the horse along the back with the wand to accustom her to the rope touching her sides. Press firmly enough to avoid tickling. You can see this three-year-old Quarter Horse mare is concerned with the initial strokes—that's why we do the first steps standing rather than moving.

We begin here with this "pigtail" exercise to accustom her to the lines along her sides before proceeding with *Neckline Driving*.

Photo 2 Encourage your horse to look back as the mare is doing here, so she learns self-control and to stand when something makes her nervous—such as the wand stroking her barrel. You can see from the raised head and cock of her ear that she is not sure.

Note: When you're retraining a skittish horse, give him a bit of grain when he turns back. This will override the flight reflex and teach him to trust you. A little grain keeps him breathing, activates the parasympathetic nervous system and replaces something he is concerned about with a pleasant experience. It is difficult to hold the breath and chew at the same time!

Photo 3 Here she has relaxed as the wand strokes her hind leg. Teaching a horse to stand quietly when anything touches the hind legs is cheap insurance. From this lesson she will learn not to panic if she's ever caught up in brush or wire.

Photo 4 Here the mare walks off quietly and confidently. Repeat the walk and halt sequence several times; then change sides and repeat from the right. This few minutes of preparation really helps overcome fear. Repeat this process on the off side before attaching two lines.

Photo 5   Here is the next step in preparation for *Neckline Driving*. We have added a second set of lines and an elastic *Body Wrap* (p. 160) and I'm simply following along slightly to the side so the mare can see me. Note that the lines are crossed over the back. My handler is in control slightly ahead of the mare and to her side. The *Body Wrap* gives a connection through the body and helps her accept the lines touching the hind legs. This is especially useful for a spooky, young or green horse.

Photo 6   The lines are now against the sides. I'm still positioned to the side where the mare can see me. I can now give the voice commands and line signals to stop and go. However, with the lines attached to her neck, I cannot turn. This phase is just to overcome fear of the lines touching her sides and any movement from behind.

Photo 7   This is the final step—driving with two sets of lines. One set is attached to the halter so I can signal left and right turns, and the other still on the chest. It is called "double-line" driving. This makes stopping in balance easy and prevents a horse from getting above or behind the bit. It takes practice to handle two sets of lines, but the results are worth it.

Variations

As the driver, remember it's your job to give the person leading the horse clear direction about where you want to go and enough time to execute the plan. Some horses take a moment or two to respond to the signal from behind.

Once you, your horse and your helper are functioning smoothly, you can drive your horse around the arena and try some other Playground for Higher Learning exercises to keep your horse interested and thinking. Use various pole configurations—*Labyrinth* (p. 259) and *The Fan* (p. 253)—as you are driving to give the horse something familiar, a focal point and a parameter.

Photo A A key step in the education of a young horse is the introduction to the girth with a surcingle. By adding a fleece-lined chest piece as shown in this photo, you can diffuse the restrictive feeling of the girth. The chest piece also holds the surcingle forward when the girth is loose, preventing the surcingle from sliding back. Here we weave the lines around the breast piece instead of using the nonslip knot around the neck as shown on p. 262. The person leading at the head is in control, and the driver gives the signals for whoa and go.

Photo B *Ground Driving* your young horse a few times with a saddle is helpful before riding. Attach the ropes to the halter and run them through the stirrups as shown in this photo. If you don't have a chest band, you can use a rope around the chest attached to the billet straps (if you are using a heavier Western saddle, use a standard leather breast collar). This keeps the saddle from slipping so the girth can be a hole or two looser than it needs to be with a rider. We've discovered that this slightly snug rope or chestpiece distributes the attention of young horses so they aren't concerned about the girth in the beginning. Note that we have tied the stirrups up so the lines run straight from the halter through the stirrups to the driver's hands.

WORK WITH PLASTIC SHEETS

Working your horse with plastic sheets is excellent preparation for riding outside on trails and at horse shows where "foreign" objects, unfamiliar noises, and flapping tents or flags, are likely to appear. Your horse will overcome his fear of noisy, moving things; items above him, like you on his back or the roof of a trailer; and trash such as plastic bags caught in trees or blowing across the trail. He will become confident about going through

Key Uses

- Reduces shying and spooking
- Prepares for first mounting
- Readies for going through water
- Promotes acceptance of overhead blankets
- Makes the starting gate procedure safer

narrow spaces or stepping on something unusual or unpredictable. Like the other Playground obstacle exercises, this one builds great trust between horse and handler.

Working with plastic in a variety of non-threatening ways is one of the most effective exercises for teaching a horse to override the flight reflex and think about it instead. We have found that when your horse conquers fear in one situation, anxiety in general is reduced and your horse becomes more confident.

When your horse becomes really comfortable working with plastic, you can do three exercises together: walk over the *Platform*, under plastic and down an aisle between plastic "walls." This is great preparation for trailer loading.

WHAT YOU NEED

- Three strips of thick, opaque plastic sheeting, 12 by 6 feet

- Two stands, such as hay bales or step stools

- Two or more helpers

We set up plastic sheets in three ways: on the ground, as a corridor between poles and overhead.

❶ Walking between strips of plastic **on the ground,** a horse learns to trust his footing and override fear.

❷ Working **between poles** is especially useful for preventing or overcoming claustrophobia and teaching confidence in narrow places like trailers and starting gates.

❸ Going **under plastic** gives a horse the confidence to be unafraid of movement of objects above—the trailer's ceiling, a rider mounting for the first time, spectators in grandstands. Teaching your horse to walk quietly under plastic without fear (dropping the back and scooting forward, or refusing and sucking back) is one of the best insurance policies you can have. Forcing a frightened horse will only

intensify the fear. We've found that this exercise can quickly override a horse's tendency for spookiness.

In the first lesson, it is not necessary for your horse to step directly onto the plastic. Give your horse some time to think about it. You might be surprised at the progress after a couple of days of processing the new information. (Studies at the University of Pennsylvania showed that horses "digest" new learning for up to three days.)

HOW TO

Plastic Sheets on the Ground

Photo 1 Start with two strips of plastic (see above), laid on the ground in a "V" shape. Position the "bottom" narrow end of the "V" six feet apart, and the open end a comfortable eight feet apart to make it more inviting. Lead your horse in the *Elegant Elephant* position (p. 237).

Photo 2 If your horse snorts or blows at the plastic, offer him a bit of grain directly from the plastic or from a flat pan placed just off the edge. The grain is not intended to coax the horse to the plastic but rather to calm him—chewing activates the parasympathetic nervous system, overriding the flight response. I've let the lead slip through my hand so the mare is standing upright, allowing her the freedom to eat.

Photo 3 If the plastic is clear, rolling it up a little as shown here makes it more visible. Walk through several times, narrowing the space as your horse becomes confident. Encourage her to stop and sniff (and eat a nibble of grain on the plastic) from time to time. In this way she will learn to stop, look and listen to you whenever a scary situation arises.

Photo 4 The ends of the plastic sheets are now pulled together. I use the wand to tap the neck gently so the mare keeps her distance and steps freely over the plastic.

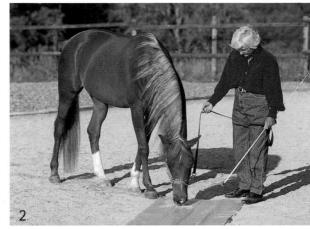

Photo 5 The mare is fully confident now, and stepping onto the plastic is no longer an issue. This rolled plastic also teaches a horse to be careful and unafraid in strange footing.

Work between Poles

Photo 6 Hang the sheets of plastic over two rails, making an aisle, and walk the horse through. You can walk him on the ground or on a *Platform* (p. 269). Here, Kirsten sets a small amount of grain on the barrel. (These plastic barrels have the advantage of being less noisy than metal barrels.)

Photos 7 and 8 The mare checks out the plastic carefully and walks quietly through. She is still a little uncertain, as indicated by her left ear looking at the blowing plastic, but she has learned to trust her

handler. If you have any concerns about your horse going safely through, make the lane wider until he is calm.

Work under Plastic

Work under Wands

We developed this bridging step to prepare a horse for the under-plastic work. This work with wands we playfully call the "West Point March." You will need two helpers, stands (hay bales work nicely) and two wands (or you can substitute colorful plastic "pool noodles," which are lightweight and easy for the horse to see).

Photo 9 I walk the mare forward in *Elegant Elephant*, occasionally stroking her neck with *Cheetah* (p. 240) whenever she shows concern—note the high head and laid-back ears. Kirsten strokes her neck with the wand from the off side.

Photo 10 After several passes through, and having had a few nibbles from Kirsten's hand, the mare's ears are forward and her head is lowered, indicating that she is relaxing. Now the wands can be held upright.

Photo 11 Both helpers stand higher on the tubs and hold the wands together. This is a key step for preparing an unridden horse to be unafraid of the first mounting, or for any spooky horse to get over fear. The mare is a little concerned but does not rush or hollow her back.

Photos 12 and 13 The last step is to ask your horse to go underneath plastic held overhead. Your two helpers stand on tubs, bales or stools and hold the plastic sheet in the air as shown.

If your horse rushes through at first, make sure you stay ahead of him, give him a loose line, and don't try to hold him back. He will be quieter the next time after he has realized he had no reason to be concerned.

Photo 14 By the time your horse passes quietly and confidently under the plastic you are well on your way to having a safe, confident, brave horse.

Water on the Plastic

When your horse has become comfortable walking on plastic, but is afraid of walking through water, add some water to the plastic sheet on the ground and incorporate this new obstacle into your program. Many horses are frightened of water and this is a most useful exercise to get them used to it.

PLATFORM

Working on a *Platform* is one of the best preparations for trailer loading and unloading and crossing bridges or any unusual surface.

A nervous horse is often uncertain about stepping onto a surface he senses is not quite solid. Once you have encouraged him, and all goes well, his trust in you will grow. Overriding his insecurities in this fashion greatly benefits your daily routine. In this exercise, the hollow sound of stepping on the wood as well as the boards "giving" slightly underfoot provide a new experience.

Key Uses

- Trains trailer loading and backing out
- Prepares for standing in stocks and wash racks
- Helps ready for walking onto a weight scale
- Teaches how to cross bridges
- Improves balance

WHAT YOU NEED

Heavy Duty Platform

- For one that can double as a *Teeter-Totter* (p. 273), you need three, 2 by 12 inch boards, 10 feet long.

- Nail these boards together with six, 2 by 6 boards, three feet long underneath. To make the *Teeter-Totter*, nail the two middle boards underneath just wide enough apart so you can stabilize it with a beam or post to serve as a fulcrum. This can be approximately six inches across and as wide as your *Teeter-Totter* (see photos on p. 273).

- Use another 2 by 12 inch board, 10 feet long, as a "V" border on the ground when introducing your horse to stepping (and hearing the noise) on the *Platform* (see Photo 21 on p. 302)

Lightweight Options

If you are training just one horse, or don't want to move a heavy platform, here is a good substitute.

Note: This plywood option does not work for making a *Teeter-Totter*.

- A 4 by 8 foot sheet of plywood, one inch thick.

- Four square beams, four feet long, 4 by 4 inches, positioned widthwise under the plywood. Doing this creates a step up, and walking on the raised plywood makes more of a hollow sound than when it is flat on the ground.

- A 2 by 12 board, eight feet long to make the "V" border on the ground (as above).

Substitute for Wood

- Quickly created alternatives for the platform are a pair of large, flattened cardboard boxes or a piece of carpet. Sometimes horses show as much fear of stepping on these as the boards (see Photo 38 on p. 306); in these cases, make the "V" out of the same material or use a ground pole.

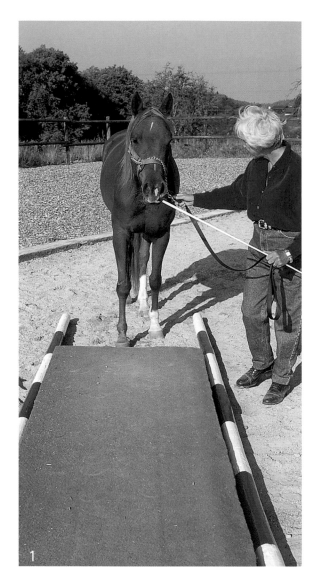

HOW TO

Photo 1 Stop and stand in front of the *Platform*, giving your horse a few moments to think. Notice the poles along the sides of it to give a boundary to keep the horse in the center.

Photo 2 Kirsten sets out a little grain to give the mare a reason to investigate. I point to the food with my wand. (For a larger picture of this, see p. 252.)

Photo 3A Standing partially on the *Platform* in the *Dingo* (p. 235) position, I keep the mare's head in the middle with my left hand and quietly tap her

forward with the wand. Slightly unsure, the mare pops her shoulder a little to the left. (Another option might be to lead her *across* the width of the *Platform* a few times rather than down it lengthwise.)

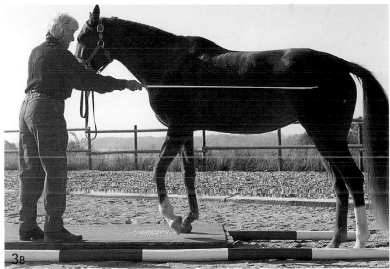

Photo 3B I step fully onto the platform to encourage the mare to come on and straighten her by tapping her along her side with the wand.

Photo 4 Fully on the *Platform* now, I switch to *Elegant Elephant* (p. 237) and the mare stands quietly. The first few times you do this exercise, don't attempt to stop. Simply walk forward and off the platform until your horse becomes accustomed to the hollow sound of the plywood beneath her feet. This may take a little practice until your horse gains the confidence and understanding to stand still as I am doing here.

Photo 5 As soon as your horse will stand quietly, ask her to back off the *Platform*—excellent practice for unloading from a trailer. Here, I give a signal with my hand only a few inches from the halter ring and tap the mare lightly on the chest to take a step back.

Photo 6 To take that first step down off the *Platform*, I give a light signal on the point of the shoulder with my thumb (*Rhino TTouch*, p. 224); otherwise, many horses have a tendency to step forward again when the ground drops out from under their hind feet. This small step can save you the grief of having a horse refuse to back out of a step-in trailer because he got scared once. If this is the case, you can teach him to do this on the ground first, then back off the *Platform*.

A useful exercise to practice on the *Platform* is *Cha Cha* (p. 232): Using *Dingo* and *Cueing the Camel* (p. 235), bring the horse forward one step, then back one step by tapping the wand on his front legs (the forward front leg first), and using a light chain action in a backward motion on the halter. Repeat the step forward and step back.

What should you do if...

- *Your horse refuses to step onto the platform?*

Place a little feed on the wood. The chewing will help him breathe and relax, and he will also lower his head. After he takes another step, stop and feed him again. You may also find that *Dingo* will encourage him to step forward. As I've mentioned before, when a horse is afraid of any exercise, the use of food is an excellent idea; when a horse eats, the parasympathetic nervous system is activated, helping to override the sympathetic nervous system that instigates the fight-or-flight response (see p. 25).

TEETER-TOTTER

Once your horse is comfortable walking over the *Platform*, you can progress to the *Teeter-Totter*. This exercise will improve your horse's confidence *and* sense of balance—and it will be fun for both of you.

WHAT YOU NEED

See the *Platform* (p. 269) for required materials.

HOW TO

I suggest walking your horse all the way over the *Teeter-Totter* with a pause in the middle the first few times before asking the horse to rock back and forth.

Photos 1 and 2 In *Elegant Elephant* (p. 237), the mare steps onto the platform, rocks the *Teeter-Totter* forward and stands quietly. All she has to do is raise her head and take one step back to tip the *Teeter-Totter* back. Your horse will quickly learn to enjoy this forward-backward rocking game. Once your horse has mastered the low *Teeter-Totter*, you can raise it higher with a bigger fulcrum.

Photo 3 The ultimate partnership! I'm riding over the *Teeter-Totter* bareback, bridleless, guiding my mount with only a *Liberty Neck Ring* (p. 282).

TIRES

Teaching your horse to step into *Tires* has a dual purpose. It will make him sure-footed while at the same time preparing him to pick his way carefully over rough ground. Once your horse learns to step into tires, he'll have no trouble placing his foot in a bucket for soaking, or standing still for an X ray or ultrasound.

Place the tires in various patterns and at different distances so your horse learns to be comfortable with a variety of footing.

HOW TO

Photo 1 These tires are cut in half like bagels, a safe way to begin until your horse is confident, and you don't take a chance on a horse catching a fetlock on the edge of the tire, panicking and pulling back. Another option is to place regular tires slightly apart to make "holes" in between them. This will still give the horse a sense of stepping into spaces without the chance of catching a shoe or hoof.

Key Uses

- Promotes sure-footedness
- Prepares for rough ground
- Teaches to stand still for foot soaking, X rays, and ultrasounds

Photo 2 Here I am picking up the foot and placing it in the tire so the horse learns to step into the tire rather than around it.

Photo 3 Spread the tires apart slightly so that your horse learns to look down and walk between them. This will encourage him to be more confident stepping in them.

Ridden Work

The Joy of Riding

Most people come to riding because they love the sense of freedom associated with horses. The idea of galloping across a mountain meadow is a dream that many people hold dear. All too often, however, the reality of riding may not actually jibe with the vision we hold, and the horse we thought would be our dream horse can give us nightmares.

Although riding can be a joy when you feel safe and secure, it is often said that it takes years of riding to become proficient. One often hears the statement, "You've got to be the boss or your horse will take advantage of you." The Tellington Method can change these age-old precepts by giving your horse a foundation for trust with TTouch and a desire to cooperate with the Ground Exercises. Together they can be your springboard to a higher level of confidence and capability in the saddle.

All three components of the Tellington Method—TTouches, Ground Exercises and Ridden Work—can put you on a fast track to success in the saddle. The Tellington riding equipment will give you effective tools to find balance and harmony during Ridden Work that can lead to the intimate relationship and rewarding friendship with horses that riders dream about. And by discovering the joy of *Bridleless Riding*, you can achieve the ultimate centaur-like experience: melding as one with your horse.

Liberty Neck Ring and Bridleless Riding (see p. 282)

BALANCE REIN

The *Balance Rein* is like a "necklace" used as a second rein around the base of the neck to rebalance a horse. It is used in combination with any bit for horses who have a tendency to go above the bit or behind the vertical. The *Balance Rein* also invites horses to bring their back up, and lengthen and round the neck by activating the "seeking reflex."

Many years ago, paleontologist Deb Bennett, Ph.D., observed the immediate changes in a normally high-headed, skittish Paso Fino I was riding. She theorized that the contact of the *Balance Rein* at the base of the neck was causing the horse to activate the muscles that run between the front legs and lift the back. As a result, the gelding was able to relax and was much more supple and responsive.

Key Uses

- Balances a horse
- Overcomes the habit of coming above or behind the bit
- Slows down a horse
- Steadies a spooky horse
- Helps a horse lengthen the neck
- Smooths out a rough trot
- Keeps a horse on the track with nose bent to the inside
- Steadies a rider's hand

WHAT YOU NEED

A 21-foot long, 7 mm rope (like a colorful, patterned climbing rope). You can make the rope wider with a chain stitch (similar to crochet—see photos). Or, you can order a *Balance Rein* from Tellington TTouch Training (see *Resources,* p. 311). It is made of braided nylon and beta Biothane, and has an adjustable buckle.

HOW TO

- While trail riding or schooling a horse with English tack or riding a young Western horse with two hands, you can hold the *Balance Rein* in the outside hand along with your bridle rein. If you are collecting a horse for competition, you may find it most effective to hold the *Balance Rein* in both hands along with your bridle reins.

For best results, take slightly more contact with the *Balance Rein.* We generally recommend 55 percent of the contact on the *Balance Rein* and 45 percent on the bridle reins. If you're riding Western with the reins in one hand, you may want to let the *Balance Rein* lie on the neck, ready to pick it up if your horse gets excited. In this case it's best to attach the *Balance Rein* with a short latigo string to your saddle so it won't slip forward if your horse puts his head down to drink or graze.

Photos 1 and 2 This mare came to my clinic because of her habit of "boring" into the bit and coming behind the vertical with her nose on her chest. She was too fast at the walk and trot and when her rider attempted to rate her, she brought her nose to her chest. With a combination of the *Balance Rein* and *Half-Walk* (p. 280), she was able to rebalance, and as

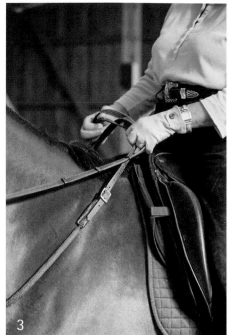

a result, she began to accept the bit and was able to respond to my rein aids and slow down when asked, without coming behind the bit with her nose tucked to her chest.

Photo 3 This is the Tellington *Balance Rein*, an attractive piece of equipment. You can hold it in two hands along with your reins as shown in Photos 1 and 2, or you can hold it only in one hand with the outside rein as shown in this photo. I'm using about 50 percent of contact on the *Balance Rein* and 50 percent on the bridle reins, with the *Balance Rein* held with the outside rein.

HALF-WALK

The exercise we call the *Half-Walk* teaches your horse to take short, precise steps, slow down and listen to the lightest signals from your hands and seat. It can be taught under saddle or from the ground. The result will be improved balance and a more rhythmical stride.

I intuitively stumbled upon this concept while giving a seminar to a select group of trainers from the Spanish Riding School in 1982. The venue was the training stable of one of the teachers just outside Vienna, and I chose a difficult horse just recently brought in for training. This was a 12-year-old French Thoroughbred, recently purchased by a client as a jumper—without the approval of the trainer, I must add. The horse had been ridden too fast over fences and was skittish under saddle.

Key Uses

- Teaches concentration, balance and response to light aids
- Lengthens stride by first shortening it; adds more "gears" to your horse's repertoire
- Lowers the head and lengthens the body
- Settles a "jiggy" horse to walk calmly
- Teaches a cutting horse to walk slowly into a herd

When I mounted, I discovered the gelding would only jig instead of walk and tended to a high head-carriage and tight back. This was early in the development of the Tellington Method and years before I came up with the *Balance Rein*. If I gave this same demonstration on a jiggy horse today, I would either use a *Balance Rein*, or dismount and do assorted TTouches and *Labyrinth* with the horse. And, I would certainly check the fit of the saddle!

However, I was already in the saddle, so I intuitively raised my hands and brought the horse's head higher with rhythmical "half-halt" signals on the reins, asking for shortened steps. This settled the gelding, and after a very few minutes I slowly lengthened the reins—and much to everyone's surprise he lowered his head and settled into a walk. Out of the blue, one of the retired trainers remarked in German, "Interesting, that walk was formerly known in the Spanish Riding School as the 'third walk' but hasn't been used in decades."

I was just as surprised by the effect as the rest of the observers that day, and have since integrated the movement we call *Half-Walk* into the training of all horses, and not just for problems.

HOW TO

Ground Exercise

To achieve the *Half-Walk* from the ground, bend slightly forward, take small steps, give subtle sig-

nals on the chain between your thumb and forefinger, and make small up-and-down movements of the wand several feet ahead of the horse's nose. Once your horse gets the idea, the payoff will be a heightened level of focus, concentration, coordination and balance. From the ground the *Half-Walk* can be readily achieved with the head lowered, and from the saddle the head is raised to get the same result of shortened step.

Photo 1 I lead Dorina into the *Labyrinth* (p. 259) with lowered head and very light signals to take careful slow steps. At the same time, I bend over a little and slow my steps so the mare will mirror me. The chain is up the side rather than over the nose. This exercise was particularly useful for Dorina. She was high-headed, high-strung and had a strong tendency to rear under saddle or if she felt pressure on her head.

Photo 2 Dorina, now in a *Body Wrap* (p. 160), negotiates the corner, responding to a light ask-and-release signal on the chain and steady "painting the pathway" with the wand. The hind step is a little long, but she manages to bend nicely, keep her head low and maintain her balance around the corner. Once you've mastered the lowered head, graduate to asking for the same shortened movement with the head up.

Ridden Work

You can easily teach the shortened, slightly hesitant step of *Half-Walk* from the saddle. Raise your horse's head to shift the center of gravity toward the hindquarters and take the weight off the forehand. At the same time, lighten your seat slightly by pressing down and putting a little more weight in the stirrups. Ask your horse to take short steps by applying slight "squeeze and release" movements of your fingers on the reins. Ask for only five or six of these shortened steps and then allow the reins to slip through your fingers so your horse will lower the head, stretch the neck out, release the back and lengthen the stride.

Photo 3 Note my lightened seat, raised hands and weight more in the stirrups. This mare rushed at the walk and was a serious puller in a snaffle. By adding the *Lindell Sidepull* (p. 286) and *Balance Rein* (p. 279) and giving her a chance to rebalance, she relaxed and was able to respond nicely to leg, seat and hands.

Photo 4 Here we see the lengthened neck and relaxed walk. Repeat the exercise by shifting from the *Half-Walk* to the lengthened stride only three

or four consecutive times during each riding session. You may be surprised how quickly your horse can learn this.

LIBERTY NECK RING AND BRIDLELESS RIDING

Riding with only the neck ring can reawaken the joy of riding and put a new "handle" on your equine partner.

As a child, you may have taken pleasure in riding bareback with just a rope around your horse's neck. It was part of the fun and sense of freedom of riding. For more than three decades, riding with a neck ring or just a rope around the neck—often with nothing on the horse's head—has been one of the foundation exercises of the Tellington Method. Riding without a bridle, or with your reins hanging free on the neck, gives me a feeling that I'm riding Pegasus, the winged horse!

Riding without a bridle isn't new nor is it a gimmick. Nearly 30 years ago, while based at our Pacific Coast School of Horsemanship, I toured the US giving demonstrations of bridleless drill-team jumping with students riding Hungarian stallions, one

Key Uses

- Gives you and your horse a new sense of trust and partnership
- Develops your confidence in your seat
- Helps you balance without relying upon the reins
- Improves your horse's balance and general performance with a bridle
- Teaches a horse to neck-rein
- Revives a sour or stiff horse
- Despooks a nervous horse
- Slows down a jumper who rushes fences

mare and a gelding. This display of riding inspired people with a sense of wonder at the ability to ride a horse with seemingly so little control.

In 1975, I introduced *Bridleless Riding* to Europe at Equitana in Germany. Four of us jumped a course bareback and bridleless. Europeans were incredulous, and a major German equestrian magazine published an article stating how impossible and dangerous this was, adding that there must be a special secret. However, in the ensuing two decades, thousands of riders in Europe and North America have discovered the joy and advantages of deepening their relationship with their horse through riding without a bridle.

In certain instances, you may not feel comfortable "taking it all off." Perhaps you are starting a young horse, insurance at your stable will not allow it, or you simply do not feel that it would be a safe thing to do. Can using the *Neck Ring* with a bridle still have benefit? Absolutely! You needn't ever take off the bridle completely to get the benefits of riding with a neck lariat. Simply laying the reins on your horse's neck and using the *Neck Ring* to turn, slow down and stop can bring much joy to you and freedom for your horse.

WHAT YOU NEED

We normally use a stiff, adjustable ring made of lariat rope that the horse can feel readily (see *Resources*, p. 311). The stiffness also makes it easy for the rider to reach the top of the neck for turning. You could use a normal lead rope, but it's not as easy to use nor as effective for turning.

HOW TO

Holding the Liberty Neck Ring: Start with whatever bridle you are already using. Don't be afraid to experiment with different ways of holding the reins and *Neck Ring*. You can hold the *Neck Ring* in both hands, or try holding the reins in one hand and the *Neck Ring* in the other. Or you may find it easier in the beginning to pick up the reins when you signal with the *Neck Ring* to turn or stop. You should quickly find that using the *Neck Ring* will reduce your dependency on the reins and give you a new sense of balance.

Using the Liberty Neck Ring: If you ride Western, it may be easier for stopping and turning to hold the reins in one hand and the *Neck Ring* in the other. If you ride English, give a light signal on the turning rein at the same time that you signal the turn with the *Neck Ring*.

To give the signal to stop, pick up the *Neck Ring* to make a light signal-and-release contact about two-thirds of the way up the horse's neck while using a long, toned, verbal "*whoaaa.*" Let the lariat follow the angle of the shoulder rather than pulling straight back. In the beginning, you may have to use your rein along with the *Neck Ring* to reinforce the signal as you and your horse learn these new dance steps. Signal and release two or three times to accomplish a complete halt while closing your inner thigh.

Remember, the horse will actually respond on the "release" rather than the pull—if you constantly pull on the ring, many horses will simply lean into it. Be aware, too, that you are pulling against the sensitive windpipe. So, give only a light contact and release to turn or stop and avoid pulling. Even if you choose not to remove the bridle, riding with the lariat neck ring is a great tool for both you and your horse. If you have as much fun and success with it as we think you will, add a *Liberty Neck Ring* to your tool kit.

Photo 1 Beginning with the reins tied, and with both hands on the *Neck Ring* placed halfway up the neck, I'm giving the signal to turn and stop. (If you find it necessary you can pick up the reins.) Getting to the stage where your horse stops and turns easily may take only a matter of minutes.

___

Tellington Tip

In addition to the signal on the Neck Ring, use your legs to stop and turn. To stop, close your thighs slightly and be sure to keep your lower leg off your horse. To turn in balance, close your inner calf against your horse and put your outer leg slightly back behind the girth. Although I prefer to keep my horse in balance with the leg aids just described, some riders enjoy signaling the turn with a shift of their body weight in the direction they are turning.

___

Photo 2 Now you can take the bridle off. For safety and a sense of security, we recommend using a helper on the ground when you first leave the bridle hanging on the fence post. We use a 20-foot rope fastened around the neck at the throat, with a non-slip knot. Put a double half hitch over the horse's nose in the beginning. (You place one loop around the nose and hang a second loop over it so the rope does not slip down the nose.) You can use a bowline knot or the easy-to-tie knot as shown on p. 262. Your helper should stay about 10 feet out from you. It's up to you to tell your helper where you want to go; it's fun to ride through some of the ground obstacles at this point.

Note: Be sure your horse is unafraid of ropes before you do this because a spooky horse could shy at the long rope!

Photo 3 Kirsten has dropped the half hitches off the nose, and you can see how much the gelding has lowered his head. If your horse tends to be high-headed, this lowering of the head and accompanying relaxation may be a welcome surprise.

Photo 4 You can use the wand to gently tap the side of the ring (or sometimes the nose) to turn, or tap on the chest to reinforce the stop. Ride in an enclosed area unless you feel fully confident.

Photo 5 Hold the ring off the neck when you are not giving a signal to turn or stop. Off I go bareback at the trot. The sense of freedom for horse and rider is difficult to describe. I've worked with many sour show horses and stiff older horses who come alive once you free up their heads. And, it gives you a special feeling of connection with your horse. (For a larger picture of this, see p. 278.)

Photos 6 and 7 You'll feel as I do that you've sprouted wings as you trot over cavalletti and sail over a jump.

- **Encourages collection:** There is a passive reflex at the base of a horse's neck, often mentioned by Dr. Deb Bennett, called the "seeking" reflex. When this is triggered, which can be encouraged with the *Balance Rein* or *Neck Ring* set at the base of the neck, the horse's withers rise and the neck rounds from withers to poll. The horse's belly muscles engage and the back comes up, making a horse more supple and able to engage the back and hindquarters. We use the ring with a bridle for this effect.

- **Teaches a horse to back up:** Pick up the *Neck Ring* and use it in combination with your reins. It encourages the horse to back in balance, without dropping the withers and hollowing his back.

- **Improves gaited horses:** We have found the *Neck Ring* helps a horse pick up his neck from the withers to improve the gait with Icelandics, Peruvian Pasos, Tennessee Walkers, Paso Finos and other gaited breeds. It is important to use a light touch-and-release signal about two-thirds of the way up the horse's neck and avoid pulling.

- **Teaches a horse to neck-rein:** Making turns with the *Neck Ring* is a great way to start a horse neck-reining. The outside of the *Neck Ring* touches the horse's neck about six inches behind the ear, and the inside of the *Neck Ring* touches just in front of the shoulder. Use a touch-and-release signal rather than holding the pressure.

- **Calms horses on the trail:** Horses who rush or jig when they turn back toward the barn can be steadied by using the *Neck Ring* low on the neck along with your reins. If you ride one-handed, pick up the lariat with your free hand and use the touch-and-release signal just above the base of your horse's neck. If you ride two-handed, hold the lariat with your middle fingers and the reins between the ring and middle fingers. This technique also can be used for spooky horses. Pick up the *Neck Ring* as needed and allow it to rest on the horse's neck when not needed.

  I tie the *Neck Ring* to the front of the saddle with a short piece of leather so I can drop it on the neck when I don't need it, then there is no danger of it sliding over my horse's head if he lowers his head.

- **Slows horses who rush jumps:** Using the *Neck Ring* along with the reins can help to steady a horse who tends to rush in front of a jump. Engage the *Neck Ring* from the base of the neck to about halfway up it.

LINDELL SIDEPULL

The *Lindell Sidepull* is a type of bitless bridle with a stiff noseband (often made from lariat rope) that has the reins attached to rings on the sides. The side rings make it easier to turn than the bosal hackamore reins that attach under the horse's chin. We cover the rope nosepiece with a latex wrap to prevent chafing.

This *Lindell Sidepull* has a very different effect than a standard rawhide bosal where the reins are attached to the knob of the bosal underneath the

jaw. A bosal often causes a horse to raise his head and "ewe" his neck when he feels the pressure of the rawhide on the sensitive part of his jaw.

With the *Lindell* I made some changes to a regular sidepull by moving the cheekpieces away from the eye, and replacing the need for a throatlatch with a jowl strap. This strap can be fastened snugly so that the nosepiece can be left loose.

Starting Young Horses

Start young horses—three- or four-year-olds—in this type of bridle without a bit. It helps to teach them balance without a disruptive "chunk of iron" in their mouth while they learn to carry a rider. Then combine the *Lindell* with a snaffle bit, both with a set of reins.

Note: I have used a *Lindell* successfully on some "pullers" who were really hard to hold in a snaffle, and they quit pulling when ridden alone.

HOW TO

Photo 1 Fitting the *Lindell*: place the nosepiece approximately four fingers below the protruding cheekbone for English riding and a couple of inches

lower if the horse goes with a lower head carriage, as in Western disciplines. Fit the jowl strap snugly (but not tightly) so it does not slide around, allowing the nosepiece to be loose. This *Lindell* is shown here *without* the latex wrap so you can see the stiff rope nosepiece. To see the wrapped *Lindell* in its preferred configuration with the latex, see Photo 3 on page 288.

Photo 2 Combination of a *Lindell* fitted under a snaffle bit bridle. We removed the browband on the *Lindell*, and the rein fits over the outside of the bridle cheekpiece.

Photo 3 Whether used on an English horse, as shown here, or Western, the *Lindell* encourages a horse to relax and lengthen and gives him a break from carrying a bit or traveling in a collected frame. The combination of the snaffle and *Lindell* is useful for a horse who has a tendency to pull or get behind the bit.

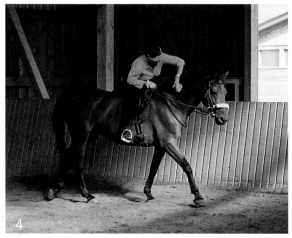

Photo 4 Success! I reach forward to TTouch this mare, who responded beautifully to a combination of *Lindell Sidepull*, snaffle, and *Balance Rein* (p. 279).

PROMISE WRAP and PROMISE ROPE

The *Promise Wrap*—an elastic band (usually four inches wide), and the *Promise Rope*—a half-inch rope, fasten to the saddle and fit around the hindquarters of the horse.

They are called a *Promise Wrap* and *Promise Rope* because they encourage engagement (as in an engagement ring!) The elastic band is normally best for a nervous or spooky horse, and the rope is my first choice to encourage a faster or longer stride or to prevent a horse from kicking at another. Since it is impossible to predict which will have the best effect, I usually try the elastic version first.

WHAT YOU NEED

• Ace bandages hold their elasticity well, and I really like colored leg wraps because of their visual interest, but only if they are long enough (Ace bandages are usually longer). It's important not to have the elastic too tight, so for very large horses, you may well need two leg wraps tied together.

• A rope about half an inch in diameter, long enough to fit as shown in Photo 4, p. 290.

• The *Promise Wrap* should sit just below the point of buttocks (see Photo 1, p. 289).

Key Uses

- Gives spooky horses a feeling of containment

- Helps horses with a dropped back or ewe-neck

- Encourages lazy or short-strided horses to move out

- Reassures horses who spin and bolt under saddle

- Relaxes horses who kick at others while ridden

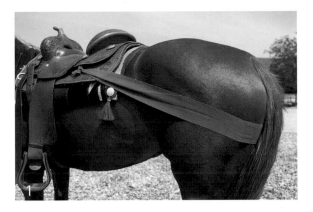

- The *Promise Rope* sits lower—in the deepest part of the curve of the gaskin, about eight to 12 inches above the hocks (see Photo 4). Be careful it is not too loose so that your horse doesn't try to kick at it or get his leg over the rope. Take the time necessary to prepare your horse to accept the sensation of the rope against his legs.

- How tight should the wrap be? Just snug enough that it doesn't slip. Too tight can be counterproductive—especially for horses who are sore or have loose stifles.

Note: Before mounting, walk and trot the horse in hand so the feeling around the hindquarters will not surprise him.

HOW TO

Photo 1 On a Western saddle, attach the ends of the *Promise Wrap* to the rear cinch rings. On an English saddle, attach the wrap to the top of the stirrup billet under the saddle flap.

Photo 2 This formerly balky horse rounds nicely and shows the difference a *Promise Wrap* can make.

Photo 3 Riding in the *Promise Wrap* delivers the "promise" for engagement as this lovely gray

demonstrates. Note that I've also added a *Tellington Training Bit* (p. 290) and *Balance Rein* (p. 279) to further improve self-carriage and balance, and reduce the horse's fear of things behind, which will make him more confident. This Tellington "triple" is also useful for a horse who is concerned or kicks at horses coming up behind him on the trail. The *Promise Wrap* can also be used over the saddle during warm-up.

Photo 4 Here I am riding with a *Promise Rope* around the hindquarters. This half-inch rope is attached to the billet straps under my leg on each side of the saddle. Note how the rope sits about 10 inches above the hocks, in the deepest part of the curve of the gaskin. Notice the relaxed gait and softness through the body as this horse trots in front of a crowd at a training demonstration in Reken, Germany.

VARIATION

You can ride, longe or do Ground Exercises with an elastic *Body Wrap*—two stretchy leg wraps connected around the chest (three for a large horse), over the saddle and around the hindquarters. This is especially useful for a nervous horse to increase confidence by giving a feeling of connection from chest to hindquarters. For more about using the *Body Wrap*, see p. 160.

TELLINGTON TRAINING BIT

The *Tellington Training Bit* is made of stainless steel with a copper roller set up in the port, and curved, loose shanks. We use it with two sets of lightweight, narrow reins. Used in this manner, it acts somewhat like a Pelham, but the copper roller and higher port offer tongue relief and are the keys to its success. Even a few sessions of longeing with the bit will encourage a rounder frame. In contrast, a straight-shanked bit has a tendency to induce stiffness through the jaw and poll.

While some people are horrified at the thought of putting anything more than a snaffle into their horse's mouth, recent research about bitting has

Key Uses

- Improves transitions, carriage, balance and engagement in any horse
- Reshapes ewe-necked, hollow-backed or strung-out horses
- Softens the back and encourages flexion at the poll
- Calms and controls over-competitive or spooky horses

given us a new understanding about how bits affect the mouth. It begins with an awareness that when one part of the body becomes tight, the tension extends to the rest of the body.

Like the stops connecting a subway route, all of the points—from tongue to jaw to sternum to shoulder—must be free of tension in order for your horse to move freely and comfortably. Constrict any one of those points and you've jammed the system, manifesting as behavioral and performance "issues" ranging from balkiness and short-striding to sourness and head-tossing. Standard single-jointed snaffle bits, with their nutcracker, "pinch and restrict" action, exert downward force on the tongue, preventing the horse from swallowing or being comfortable.

We find that the *Tellington Training Bit* consistently softens the horse along these key points as well as the back.

HOW TO

Fitting the Bit

- Be sure there is at least one-quarter inch clearance between the top of the shank (where the headstall attaches) and the horse's cheek. The mouthpiece comes in five-inch and five-and-a-half-inch sizes and fits most horses. There is a narrower version for small-muzzled Arabian horses.

- Adjust the bit so there is a good wrinkle in the corner of the horse's mouth, then open the mouth and check to be sure that the sides of the port are not touching the first molars.

- The headstall and curb chain (a flat chain with a leather strap at each end is my preferred type, see Photo 1, p. 292), attach to the uppermost ring of the bit. I sometimes see the curb chain incorrectly fastened to the upper rein slot. Adjust the curb chain so that when you pull the lower rein tight, the curb chain comes in contact with the chin when the bot-

tom of the shank has reached a 45-degree angle from the line of the mouth. If it's too loose, the port of the mouthpiece will hit the upper palate before there is any contact with the curb chain, a necessary action to create flexion at the poll. If the chain is too tight, it will make your horse move stiffly.

- Use a cavesson (noseband) adjusted to about three fingers' width below the cheekbone—loose enough for you to place one or two fingers sideways between the noseband and the jawbone.

- It is easiest to use reins of different sizes. We suggest half an inch for the top rein and three-eighths of an inch for the bottom. The top rein fits into the slit that is even with the mouthpiece, and the bottom rein fastens into the opening at the bottom of the shank.

Introducing the Bit

- It is not uncommon for the horse to actively play with the roller, especially when the bit is first introduced, but the horse should quiet the mouth within 10 minutes.

- Before you ride, allow your horse to carry the bit for 10 to 15 minutes with the reins tied up for safety (but loose enough to allow the horse to extend and lower the head and neck). Attach the longe line to the side ring of the halter rather than the bit. Longeing with the *Tellington Training Bit* and *Body Wrap* (p. 160) rather than side reins helps improve transitions, posture, balance and engagement, especially with horses who are strung out behind.

Riding with the Bit

- If you're used to riding on contact, lighten up.

- Steady and balance your horse primarily with the top rein.

- Be sure to keep the lower rein loose or "draped"—not tight!

1

2A

2B

- The curb (bottom) rein softens the poll and will correct a high head or ewe-neck and raise a dropped back.

- Combine the *Tellington Training Bit*, *Promise Wrap* and *Balance Rein* (pp. 288 and 279) for optimal results during training. Once your horse gets the idea of balance, you can usually go back to a snaffle, or alternate between a snaffle and *Tellington Training Bit*.

Photo 1 A correctly fitted curb chain.

Photo 2A An ideal angle of shank to line of mouth. When the curb rein is pulled tight, the angle of the shank is 45 degrees from the line of the mouth.

Photo 2B Here the curb chain is too loose, which places the shank at a steeper angle to the line of the mouth and causing a horse to open his mouth.

Photo 3 The cavesson should be fit so that your fingers can slip underneath it easily.

Photo 4 To hold the reins, place your little finger between them with the top rein on the outside of the little finger. It is challenging to ride with two sets of reins in the beginning but the rewards in your horse's performance and behavior will be worth the effort.

Photo 5 This mare is typically strung out and has a tendency to be balky and refuse to go forward. Here we had just put on the *Tellington Training Bit*. The mare balked and wouldn't go forward.

Photo 6 We added a *Promise Wrap*, and shortly her balance and carriage changed. Within 20 minutes, she was going forward willingly and rider and horse were comfortable and happy.

Case Study: The Story of Thor

Overcoming Fear of the Trailer

This is the story of the yearling warmblood gelding, Thor. As a weanling he had a trailer accident while unloading that scared him so badly he would not even approach a trailer again. The incident happened while he was at summer pasture with a group of other colts. Apparently he panicked while unloading and tried to back out under the rump bar, breaking his withers.

While doing the photo shoot for this book, my friend Gabriele Boiselle asked me if we could work with Thor to get him over his fear, since he had to be loaded to return to summer pasture the following year. His story illustrates how Tellington Ground Exercises and TTouches can be creatively combined to shift behavior and make a lasting difference.

Here is the story of Thor:

Photo 1 To make a connection with Thor, I TTouch his face and cup my hand over his eye—a gesture that induces trust and friendship. Note *the chain up the side* so I can teach Thor to *Lower his Head* and come forward without putting pressure on his nose.

Photo 2 My husband, Roland Kleger, takes Thor on the other side in *Journey of the Homing Pigeon* to give him a sense of boundaries and security. By activating both sides of a horse's brain, learning is accelerated. Thor is literally learning how to learn. We want him to understand each step in preparation for riding in a trailer, not simply to respond to conditioned responses or coercion. I stroke Thor's front legs to ground him.

Photo 3 Leading in *Homing Pigeon* with a person on each side of the horse with wands to stroke and calm, teaches attentiveness, patience and balance. The *Zephyr lead* is attached to the upper back corner of the off-side halter ring and the chain is now over the nose so he will learn to listen to a gentle, light signal. Roland balances Thor from the off

side in *Grace of the Cheetah* (the wand held full length like the long tail of a cheetah) being sure to stay at least three feet out on the line so as not to give a feeling of claustrophobia. With my hand closer to his head, and the wand held the middle to shorten it, I take responsibility for guiding Thor in *Elegant Elephant*.

Photo 4A Thor's first introduction to the *Labyrinth*. I bend forward to encourage him to lower his head and examine the poles. Roland is holding his wand full length in the *Grace of the Cheetah* position to give the colt a feeling of space and allow him to figure out this new exercise. My wand is held in the middle (*Elegant Elephant* position) with the knob lowered to further encourage Thor to check out the poles.

Photo 4B Bending around the corners of the *Labyrinth*, Thor learns to slow down, focus and listen to our signals. In the confines of the *Labyrinth* he also learns to accept input from both handlers, teaching him self-control, patience and balance.

Photo 5 We walk Thor across the poles of the *Labyrinth*, this time to encourage him to pay attention to where he places his feet.

Photo 6A As we approach the plastic tarps, you can see from the set of Thor's ears that he is a little uncertain. (There is much talk in the horse world about "horse whispering." However, we feel it's equally important to listen to the whispers of your *horse* before he has to shout to get your attention. When Thor hesitated, he was saying, "Wait a minute! What's this all about? Is it safe?")

Photo 6B Because of his reaction, I take Thor alone for reasons of safety. If he felt really hemmed in, he could have panicked, reared or leaped to the side, putting my helper on the off side at risk. Once a horse becomes accustomed to the feeling of protective boundaries from being lead from two sides, the *Homing Pigeon* gives a feeling of confidence and enhances learning.

Photo 7 I keep the two leads on the halter so I can switch easily back to *Homing Pigeon* when Thor again settles. In addition, the second lead helps me balance Thor and keep him straight. He cautiously takes some grain from the corner of the tarp. I hold my wand full length so I can easily stroke his legs to reassure him.

Photo 8 I ask Thor to stop and stand quietly before coming between the plastic sheets, positioned well apart for his comfort and my safety. I hold the wand to the side in the *Peacock* position to teach him

not to crowd me. With these exercises, he will learn to stand quietly and wait patiently until I ask him to come forward. *Work with Plastic Sheets* on the ground establishes trust between horse and handler.

Photo 9 He comes forward between the plastic and eats grain again from a corner and this time he is more relaxed. When a horse is nervous, the sympathetic nervous system is activated in preparation for flight or fight. Eating overrides the flight reflex by activating the calming parasympathetic nervous system.

Photo 10 I take him through the plastic a second time, slowly. It would take another session or two to teach him to walk quietly *over* the plastic, but it's not as important for him to actually walk on the plastic for loading as it is to get accustomed to the particular sound and feel of a ramp and trailer floor.

Photo 11 Next comes the exercise *between* plastic sheets to accustom Thor to the idea of standing in the narrow confines of the trailer, an experience that can be claustrophobic for some horses. We pause before entering, and he takes a little grain from the person on the left corner. You may not have four friends to help you at home, so lay your plastic over poles and raise them on bales of straw or hay. Be sure the plastic strips are far enough apart that your horse cannot swing around and hit the plastic if he suddenly loses his nerve.

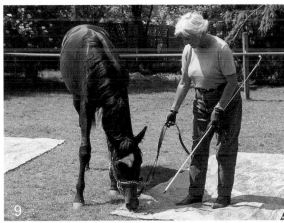

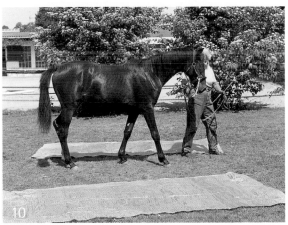

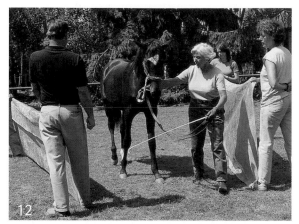

crowding me—a habit that is not safe for the handler. The third time through he comes willingly without crowding or hesitation.

Photo 13 Next step: preparation to accept the trailer roof overhead. To give a sense of height of the trailer roof, two helpers stand on chairs and arch the wands overhead. Although nervous and high headed, Thor is willing to come forward. I stretch my arm out and move the wand back and forth along his neck with *Peacock* to keep him from crowding into me for security.

Photo 14 To help overcome his concern about the presence of the helpers above his head, we invite Thor to stretch his neck out to nibble a bit of grain.

Photo 15 We've made the exercise easier by standing down from the chairs. I bend over slightly to encourage the colt to come forward and keep his head

Photo 12 We stop again in the middle for a few moments to give Thor time to process his new learning. I stroke his legs to calm and reassure him. The wand works like an extension of my arm to keep him connected to me. Notice I am slightly ahead of his nose with my arm outstretched to prevent him from

low. Why low? High-headed goes hand in hand with high-strung. When the flight instinct is activated, the head goes up. *Lowering the Head* helps overcome fear and desire to flee and opens the way to trust.

Photo 16 Thor strides confidently under the wands on a loose line with no hint of crowding or rushing. He's ready to move on to the next exercise.

Photos 17 and 18 Horses often refuse to enter a trailer because they are unaccustomed to a low roof over their head. Here, Thor carefully takes grain from the hand and then scoots under the plastic. With the increased challenge of the exercise, I again keep my arm outstretched with a close hold near the halter, to ensure that Thor stays on his own track so he doesn't crowd me.

Photo 19 The second time under the plastic, he passes the next benchmark by walking calmly under the canopy while staying on his own track.

Photo 20 And now to the ramp! Before loading, get your horse accustomed to the hollow sound of hooves on the trailer ramp. I believe many a horse has refused to load because of that very sound. We take Thor again in the *Homing Pigeon,* and this time both of us have our wands held full length in *Cheetah,* giving the colt enough space to check out the *Platform.*

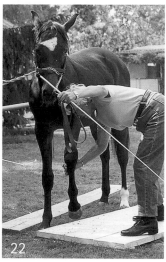

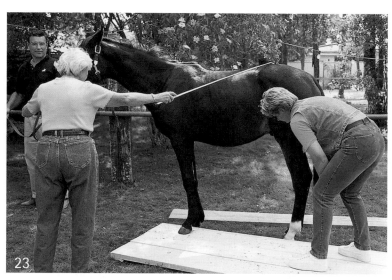

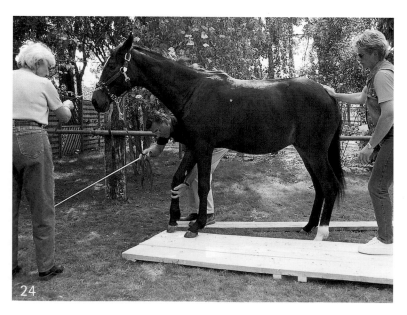

Photo 21 Because Thor is reluctant to step on the *Platform*, we make this exercise easy by adding another board to form a "V" and then walk him through the narrow open space to teach him to come forward, even when he's a little uncertain.

Photo 22 The second time through I quietly place Thor's foot on the ramp.

Photo 23 I steady Thor with the wand pressing on the croup in *Dingo* while helper Zinta Lace quietly strokes a hind leg. We want Thor to get a brief sense of the hollow-sounding boards under his feet before stepping quickly across the corner.

Photo 24 Roland places Thor's other front foot on the platform while Zinta steadies him on the hip.

Photo 25 Next step: We lay poles alongside the *Platform* to create a visual boundary, and Thor gingerly places a foot on the boards while we steady him in *Homing Pigeon*. This gives him confidence.

Photo 26 Reluctant to step onto the platform with his back feet, Thor stretches far forward to reach the grain.

Photo 27 Stroking his legs encourages Thor to step onto the *Platform*, but the sound surprises him and he balances precariously on tiptoes, not daring to put his back feet down firmly. This is particularly significant because when a horse is in a state of fear, the nervous system sends a signal to inhibit the flow of blood and sensory impulses to the lower limbs. So, it's no wonder that some horses lose their balance in trailers and have difficulty backing out.

Photo 28 Our homework has paid off! Thor quickly regains his trust and settles enough to eat.

Photos 29 and 30 Now it's time to take him alone. I stand on the *Platform* instead of off to the side, making it easier to control his head and to show him it's safe. Thor comes forward willingly, and I ask him to slow down and think as he places each foot on the *Platform*. I then switch the wand to my other hand, take both leads in my left hand about six inches from the halter, and ask him to come forward in *Dingo*.

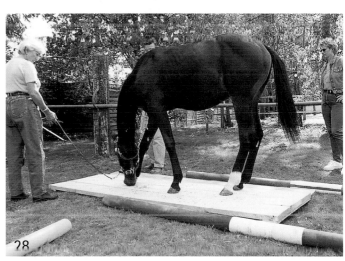

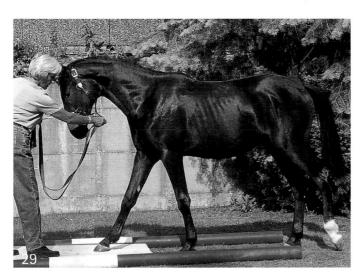

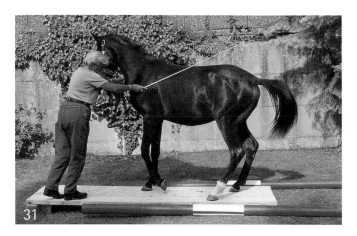

Photo 31 Although willing to come onto the *Platform*, Thor again becomes panicky when his back feet step onto the boards. I'm able to steady him between the wand and chain lead and keep him straight. So he doesn't step off the side, I walk him promptly off the *Platform*.

Photo 32 We put him back in the *Homing Pigeon*, which by now has given him the confidence of feeling supported from both sides. He walks readily on, with lowered head and confident steps.

Photo 33 Learning to back off a trailer is an important lesson. Here we bring Thor from the opposite direction and this time I stop him with his front feet on the *Platform*. I ask him to back off the boards with a light signal on the halter and a light touch on the point of his shoulder. I've known many horses who learn to load into a trailer but are afraid to back off. This simple lesson of backing off the *Platform* takes only minutes and will prepare a horse for future trailering success and safe transport.

Photo 34 Minutes later he stands quietly and confidently on the *Platform* with ears up, a trusting look in his eye, and all four feet squarely on the boards. I touch him lightly on his shoulder to continue building his confidence while Roland maintains off-side support and balance with wand and

lead. If Roland wasn't there at this early stage of experience, Thor would be much more likely to fidget, move around or push toward me for support.

This preparation for loading, which took about an hour, would normally have been done over several sessions until a horse goes through all the steps of the Playground for Higher Learning, but since we had only this one day, we went through the most important steps of *Dingo*, *Work with Plastic Sheets*, and the *Platform* to lay the foundation for trust.

Photo 35 Now we were ready to approach the trailer. Thor is reluctant to come near the ramp, and his back feet are planted as far back as possible.

Photo 36 Many folks believe that offering grain in such situations is nothing more than a bribe. However, research shows that chewing activates the parasympathetic nervous system, as hormones associated with calming are released in saliva. It also encourages him to lower his head and helps override his cellular memory of pain linked to his first trailering experience. This also replaces past trauma with a positive reward.

Photo 37 Now we take him around the side to eat grain off the fender to show Thor another view of the trailer. I find this often helps to further take the edge off fear.

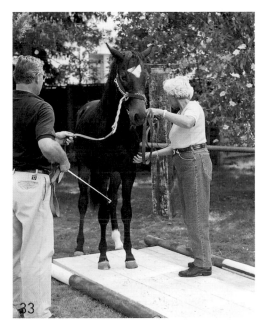

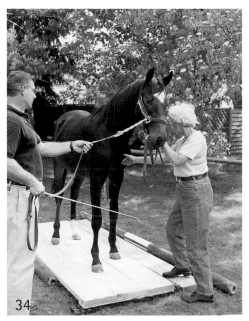

38

39

and attempts to escape the situation. Although some might interpret this behavior as stubborn or dominant, I believe we need to recognize and respect that this is his way of expressing his deep-seated fear of the trailer. Roland and I are both careful to give Thor his head so as not to trigger his fight-or-flight reflex or pull him off balance, causing him to fall and possibly injure himself.

Photo 39 I do a few minutes of *Ear TTouches* to quiet Thor, regain his trust and reestablish his focus.

It's important to note that we would never have taken him this far if it had not been his only chance to load. It's intriguing how much horses can learn if you chunk down these lessons over a few days. The thinking time usually allows them to release much fear if they haven't been punished.

Photo 40 I go back into *Dingo* to ask Thor to come forward. At this point I simply ask him to stand quietly while I breathe deeply, quiet my mind for a few moments and visualize him coming forward over the carpet. I put no pressure on him to come forward. Instead I simply ask him to stand straight, figure out what is being asked and give him an opportunity to come forward on his own. It's important that Roland, standing on the off side, not attempt to signal Thor forward by pulling on the lead but rather remain a calm presence with just enough contact to keep Thor between the poles.

One of the goals of trailer loading using the Tellington Method is to have a horse who not only goes in the trailer readily and without stress, but because of the exercises learns to respond to light signals on the lead and wand with trust and understanding.

Photo 41 Thor is not quite ready to trust this strange surface! A lovely, controlled levade, without any sign of panic, is his solution to get to the other side!

One of the interesting aspects of putting a horse through so many different experiences is an unex-

Photo 38 I've discovered over many years that lining up the *Platform* to the back of the trailer ramp is often an easier way to load a reluctant horse once he has negotiated the *Platform* quietly away from the trailer. I've also used two flattened cardboard boxes to teach a horse to come forward over a strange surface close to the trailer before loading. Because we don't have any cardboard available, I decide to try something new and lay out a piece of carpet to give Thor a new sensation under his feet before entering the hollow-sounding trailer.

Upon seeing the carpet so close to the trailer, Thor decides this is not a safe place to be—he rears

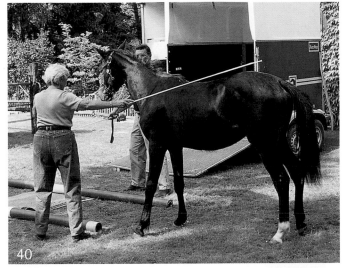

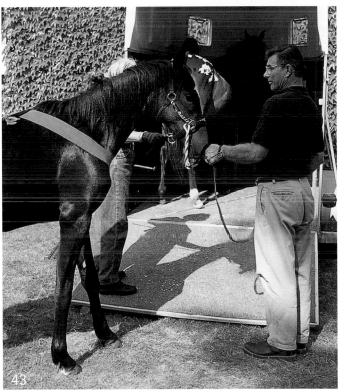

pected gift. Once a horse loses his fear in one area, he will often become more courageous in other dimensions, including work under saddle. Although you would think doing a levade over the carpet would be traumatizing, Thor actually gained confidence from the experience. Even though he didn't step onto the carpet I felt he was ready to move on to the trailer.

Photo 42 This time, as we approach the ramp, Thor reaches for the grain with confidence.

Photo 43 We've loaded Thor's pasture buddy into the trailer and taken the middle partition out since this is the way they normally travel to summer pasture. Thor touches Roland's hand as though for reassurance. We've put an elastic *Body Wrap* on Thor to give him a feeling of containment and confidence.

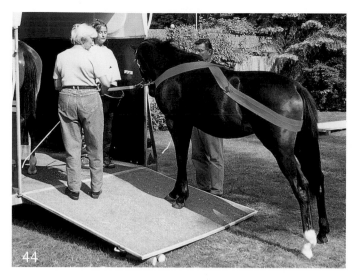

Photo 44 The colt walks quietly on the ramp and stands still with his hind legs still stretched out. We pick up his back feet one at a time to move them forward (not shown here).

Photo 45 Mission accomplished! Thor walks in without hesitation to join his Appy buddy and stands quietly munching hay without being tied. We continue stroking him with the wands and TTouching him on the point of buttock for several minutes to provide continuing reassurance and support.

Photo 46 We ask Thor to back out partially and then allow him to turn so he comes down the ramp facing out the first time.

Photo 47 With horses who are nervous about trailer loading or unloading, I find that encouraging them to turn and walk out forward a few times helps build their confidence and prepares them later to back out quietly.

Photo 48 To finish the exercise, we load Thor a second time without his friend in the trailer. He walks in without hesitation as Roland strokes him quietly on the croup.

Photo 49 We head quietly and confidently back to the pasture (p. 310). Thor has processed and integrated a great deal of new information. He's learned not just how to load, but also to:

- Come forward to specific signals from wand and lead

- Stop and stand patiently

- Override the fight or flight reflex

- Override the bracing patterns that made him appear "stubborn" and resistant

- Be more confident and brave in new and unfamiliar situations

- Become more balanced physically, mentally and emotionally

- Develop a new level of trust in people he doesn't know

- Accept movement overhead and strange sensations underfoot

In a single session not only did Thor learn to load safely and without trauma, but this education has laid the groundwork to prepare him to develop into a confident, willing, responsive and safe partner under saddle.

One month later Thor loaded without hesitation to head for summer pasture, and at the time of the printing of this book, he has matured into a perfect loader.

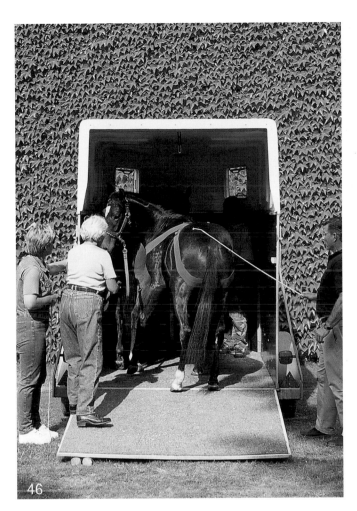

49

Resources

Recommended Reading

Cummings, Peggy. *Connected Groundwork I: Exercises for Developing and Maintaining Freedom of Movement and Self-Carriage.* Boise, ID: Connected Riding Enterprises, 2004.

Cummings, Peggy. *Connected Riding—An Introduction: Synchronizing Movements of Horse and Rider for Ease.* Gaithersburg, MD: PRIMEDIA Equine Group, 1999.

Harman, Joyce. *The Horse's Pain-Free Back and Saddle-Fit Book.* North Pomfret, VT: Trafalgar Square Publishing, 2004.

Murdoch, Wendy. *Simplify Your Riding: Step-by-Step Techniques to Improve Your Riding Skills.* Middleton, NH: Carriage House Publishing, 2004.

Pert, Candace B., Ph.D. *Molecules of Emotion.* New York, NY: Scribner, 1997.

Swift, Sally. *Centered Riding.* North Pomfret, VT: Trafalgar Square Publishing, 1985.

Swift, Sally. *Centered Riding 2: Further Exploration.* North Pomfret, VT: Trafalgar Square Publishing, 2002.

Suhr, Julie. *Ten Feet Tall, Still.* Scotts Valley, CA: Marinera Publishing, 2002.

Wanless, Mary. *For the Good of the Horse.* North Pomfret, VT: Trafalgar Square Publishing, 1997.

Wise, Anna. *The High Performance Mind.* New York: Tarcher, Putnam Publishing Group, 1996.

Recommended Equipment, Supplies and Contacts

Flexible, Treeless and User-Adjustable Saddles

Balance International
Westcott Venture Park
Westcott
Aylesbury
Bucks HP18 0XB
United Kingdom
USA: 888-612-7393
UK: 01296 658333
From outside of the UK/USA:
International Code + 44 1296 658333
www.balanceinternational.com

Bob Marshall Treeless Saddles
HorseWorks
254 Spears Lane
Vienna, IL 62995
618-658-5507
www.endurance.net/horseworks/

Free 'N' Easy Saddles
10675 Elizabeth Way
Colorado Springs, CO 80908
719-439-2472
www.mossrockendurance.com

ReactorPanel Saddle Company
414 Lesser Street
Oakland, CA 94601
510-698-6272 or 888-771-4402
www.reactorpanel.com

Specialized Saddles
8267 Bosque Rd.
Canutillo, TX 79835
505-882-3342
www.specializedsaddles.com

Saddle Pads

Cloud Nine Saddle Pads
PO Box 67
White Post, VA 22663
866-425-6839
E-mail: joyceridescloud9@cs.com

Dixie Midnight No-Sweat Vent Pad
PO Box 1012
Lithia, FL 33547
888-287-6716
www.dixiemidnight.com

Skito Equalizer Pad
Slypner Gear
150 Sullivan St.
Claremont, NH 03743
800-759-7637
www.slypnergear.com

Other Equipment

Blocker (Aussie) Tie Ring
Blocker Ranch, Inc.
21111 S. Springwater Rd.
Estacada, OR 97023
877-503-9255
www.blockerranch.com

Easyboot Epics/Easyboot Bares
Old Macs
Hoof Boots
EasyCare, Inc.
2300 E. Vistoso Commerce Loop Rd.
Tucson, AZ 85755
800-447-8836 or 520-297-1900
www.easycareinc.com

Epona Lavender Calming Rinse
JMS Sheepskin Products
Long Riders Gear
PO Box 2525
Pismo Beach, CA 93448
888-420-GEAR
www.longridersgear.com

Grazing Muzzles/Safety Halters
Best Friend Equine Supply, Inc.
145 Cappshire Rd.
Fairfield Glade, TN 38558
931-484-8590 or 866-MUZZLES
800-681-2495
www.bestfriendequine.com

Grooma® Brush
800-531-9632
www.grooma.com

Miracle Collar
Weaver Leather, Inc.
7540 CR 201
PO Box 68
Mt. Hope, OH 44660
800-932-8371
www.miraclecollar.com

Trail-Rite Magical Ointment/Cooling Blankets
Trail-Rite Ranch & Products
18171 Lost Creek Road
Saugus, CA 91350
661-513-9269
www.trail-rite.com

V-Max Heart-Rate Monitors
Equine Performance Technology
6361 Old Natchez Trace
Santa Fe, TN 38482
913-682-2158 or 888-216-6602
www.vmaxept.com

Herbal Supplements and Suppliers

Essence of Nature
Anaflora Flower Essences for Animals
PO Box 1056
Mt. Shasta, CA 96067
530-926-6424
www.anaflora.com

Rescue Remedy
Directly from Nature
1128 Pico Blvd.
Santa Monica, CA 90405
800-214-2850
www.bachflower.com

Vitex (and other herbal blends)
Hilton Herbs, Ltd.
Down Close Farm
North Perrott
Crewkerne
Somerset TA18 7SH
United Kingdom
+44 1460 270700
www.hiltonherbs.com

Wendals USA
2780 Richville Dr. SE
Massillon, OH 44646
800-321-0235
www.wendalsusa.com

Holistic Veterinarians and Practitioners

The American Academy of Veterinary Acupuncture (AAVA)
100 Roscommon Dr., Suite 320
Middletown, CT 06457
860-635-6300
www.aava.org

American Holistic Veterinary Medical Association (AHVMA)
2218 Old Emmorton Rd.
Bel Air, MD 21015
410-569-0795
www.ahvma.org

American Veterinary Chiropractic Association (AVCA)
442154 E 140 Rd.
Bluejacket, OK 74333
978-784-2231
www.avcadoctors.com or
www.animalchiropractic.org

Feldenkrais Educational Foundation of North America (FEFNA)
3611 SW Hood Ave., Suite 100
Portland, OR 97239
866-333-6248 or 503-221-6612
www.feldenkrais.com

To Learn More about the Tellington Method:

Tellington TTouch Training
PO Box 3793
Santa Fe, NM 87501
866-4-TTOUCH
info@TTouch.com
www.ttouch.com

Sarah Fisher
Tilley Farm
Timsbury Road
Farmborough, Bath
Somerset BA2 0AB
United Kingdom
01761 471182
info@tteam.co.uk
www.ttouchtteam.co.uk

Canada office and subscriptions to TTEAM Connections (quarterly newsletter)
5435 Rochdell Rd.
Vernon, BC
Canada V1B 3E8
800-255-2336
ttouch@shaw.ca

Find a TTouch Practitioner near you at http://www.ttouch.com/pracDirectory.shtml.

To purchase the Balance Rein, Liberty Neck Rein, Lindell Sidepull, Wand and other TTEAM equipment, call 1-866-4-TTOUCH or visit us on the Web at http://www.ttouch.com/productsEquipment.shtml#horses.

Research and Studies on TTEAM® and TTouch®

(For further information, see http://www.lindatellington-jones.com/researchStudies.shtml)

Papers/Articles

Evans, Julie. n.d. The effects of TTouch on dog behavior. Master's thesis, United Kingdom.

Mühlhausen, Relana, and Nickle, Caroline. 2003. TTEAM as an intervention in the therapy of patients with dementia and chronic alcoholism. German Sports University, Cologne.

Roeder, Marie. 2004. The effects of TTouch on horses as measured by an electroencephalogram (EEG). Master's thesis, Homboldt University, Berlin.

Wendler, M. Cecelia, RN, Ph.D., CC. 2003. Effects of Tellington TTouch in healthy adults awaiting venipuncture. *Research in Nursing and Health* 26:40–52.

Research Studies/Programs

The effects on the socialization of teenage girls doing TTEAM on horses. Relana Mühlhausen, German Sports University, Cologne, 2004.

TTouch research and education program: a cooperative effort between the University of Minnesota and the Center for Spirituality and Healing, 2002–.

Loading stress in the horse: behavioural and physiological measurement of the effectiveness of non-aversive raining (TTEAM) for horses with trailer loading resistance. Stephanie Shanahan.University of Ontario Veterinary School, Guelph, Ontario, 2001.

Therapeutic program for youth at risk. Maureen Frederickson and Horses and Companion Animals, Animal Systems, Buffalo, New York, 2001.

Therapy for emotionally and behaviorally disabled youth: MN LYNC (Minnesota Linking Youth, Nature and Critters) integrating TTEAM and TTouch for youth at risk, 2000.

TTEAM as a complement in the rehabilitation of horses with neurological deficits. Initiated by Mark Mendelson, DVM, and TTouch instructor Carol Lang, 1999.

Study of TTouch with Anna Wise, Boulder Institute of Biofeedback, Boulder, Colorado, 1987.

Study of the Effects of TTouch for reduction of stress, N. Khanzhina, DVM, and V. Akivis, Bitsa Olympic Center, Moscow, 1985.

Five-week study of 20 horses with health and behavior issues. Reken Test Center, Germany, 1976. (Linda's first book, *The Tellington-Jones Equine Awareness Method: the TTEAM Approach to Problem-free Training*, with Ursula Bruns, resulted from this study.)

Acknowledgments

This book was actually conceived in 1984, shortly after *EQUUS* magazine published the first series on my work, "The Touch That Teaches." Bobbie Lieberman wrote those three articles, and there was so much interest that she and I decided that we would write a book together. It's hard to believe it's taken all these years to come to fruition, but here it is and we wish to thank all the people who have contributed to the effort.

First, I want to thank Bobbie for the countless hours we have spent together honing the fine details. We worked together on the phone, by computer, and for many weeks at my home in Hawaii and her home in California. The fact that Bobbie has written dozens of articles on the Tellington Method over the years, and has used the Tellington Method for so long on her own endurance horses, has been invaluable.

There are really no words to adequately thank my sister, Robyn Hood, for the contributions she has made to the development, dissemination and teaching of the work for more than two decades. Robyn refined and added many details to the solutions and lessons in this book, and her husband, Phil Pretty, did the initial editing of the entire book, for which I am very grateful.

Bobbie and I are convinced that our publisher Caroline Robbins is, without a doubt, the most thorough and skilled editor in the business. After all the rewrites we initially made, she took her trusty pencil to the manuscript and we spent at least 50 additional hours fine-tuning the text under her direction. Thank you, thank you, Caroline. Many thanks also to Martha Cook of Trafalgar Square Publishing, for her support and assistance with the production of this book and all my others she has helped bring to readers, and to assistant editor Rebecca Didier, whose perseverance and attention to detail have been an invaluable contribution.

I am so grateful that Gabriele Boiselle agreed to take the photographs for this book. We have been friends for many years and have done countless photo shoots in exotic corners of the world. The photos were taken in two locations: one series with Gabriele's own horses at her stable in Speyer, Germany, and one venue at Doris Suess's Mascot Arabian Farm in southern Switzerland. Many thanks to Doris for hosting this shoot and for organizing dozens of horse and dog trainings for me over the past 25 years.

My thanks go also to Beth Preston for her charming and informative drawings.

My deep appreciation goes to Kirsten Henry, who for more than 10 years has organized the venues, horses and people for my photo shoots. As usual, she did a wonderful job of planning, coordinating and helping to choose the photos for the book, and checking the translation from English to German.

My husband, Roland Kleger, deserves special accolades for always coming up with a word that eluded me, and was ever patient no matter how many hours I sat at the computer or spent on the phone with Bobbie.

Bobbie had some excellent assistance with photo selection and organization. Our thanks to Gary Lyons, Scott Graham and Allen Temple for their participation. Thanks as well to Karl Phaler for giving feedback about the descriptions of the TTouches from the point of view of a horseman without previous exposure to my method.

I am thankful to Susan Harding for writing the Introduction. We have been friends for almost 20 years, and Susan is a longtime member of my advisory board. As the director of four major horse magazines she has a unique and valuable overview of the horse world.

Thank you to John Lyons, who was kind enough to write the Foreword.

I also want to thank all the teachers of my work who are sharing their knowledge with horse lovers around the globe.

And last, but certainly not least, I give thanks for all the horses over the years who have taught me so much, and all the horses I've never met whose problems have caused their riders to seek solutions using the Tellington Method. Without them this book would not have been written.

Linda Tellington-Jones
Kailua Kona, Hawaii, October 2006

Linda Tellington-Jones

A young Canadian girl riding her pony to a rural school on the Alberta plains near Edmonton...

An internationally acclaimed authority on the behavior, training and healing of horses and other animals...

Between these two bookends, the life of Linda Tellington-Jones unfolds. She began teaching riding at the age of 13, achieved her first of six Tevis Cup completions in 1960, and owned and operated the Pacific Coast School of Horsemanship—an international nine-month residential school in Badger, California—with her then-husband Wentworth Tellington. Linda has an unusually varied equestrian background. She wrote a pioneering book about endurance riding, was a US Pony Club instructor, an American Horse Show Association judge and a founding member of the California Dressage Society in the 1960s. She has taught riders and trained horses on five continents while competing in 100-mile endurance, dressage and combined training events.

Linda created the Tellington Method three decades ago as a system of training and healing horses that deepens mutual trust, overrides common resistances, and strengthens the horse-human bond. Her techniques include a unique form of bodywork, ground exercises and ridden work to improve a horse's behavior, performance and health while increasing his willingness and ability to learn in a supportive and trusting environment.

Pioneering the concept of equine adult education, in the early 1970s, Linda taught a series of eight-week evening classes for adult riders at the University of California-Santa Cruz. When she began teaching adult beginners in Germany in 1975, she realized the need to compress the learning into a weekend experience, and the first Tellington trainings (then known as TTEAM or Tellington Equine Awareness Method) were born.

Linda has given hundreds of presentations and demonstrations worldwide at veterinary conferences,

universities, equestrian expositions, therapeutic riding associations, Olympic training centers, American Association of Riding Instructors, wildlife rehabilitation conferences and zoos, including the North American Handicapped Riding Association and the Delta Society world conferences.

Her work has been featured over the past 18 years on North American, European, UK, Russian, South African and Australian television and in dozens of international publications, including *EQUUS, Practical Horseman, Modern Horse Breeding, Horseman, Arabian Horse World, Trail Blazer, Horse Illustrated* and *Horse and Rider.*

Linda's awards include Horsewoman of the Year (North American Horsemen's Association, 1994); Lifetime Achievement Award (American Riding Instructors Association, 1992); and the Award for Creative Citizenship (State of California, 1969).

She has written 11 books about TTouch and the Tellington Method, which have been printed in 12 languages, and has released 18 videos. At present, over 1,300 certified TTouch practitioners (of horses, companion animals and humans) work in 26 countries and on six continents, as well as Tellington Training Centers in Canada, Germany, Austria, Switzerland, South Africa, the UK and US, to make the Tellington Method accessible around the world.

For more information on the Tellington Method, a list of upcoming clinics and a directory of practitioners, visit Linda's Web site at www.ttouch.com.

BOBBIE LIEBERMAN is an award-winning writer, editor and journalist. She is a former senior editor of *EQUUS* magazine and editor and publisher of *Modern Horse Breeding*. She has served as a sports editor, newsletter editor, literary agent and ghostwriter. She wrote one of the first series of articles about Linda Tellington-Jones, "The Touch That Teaches," for *EQUUS* magazine, in 1983. She was also editor of *TTEAM Up with Your Horse*, named Best Newsletter by American Horse Publications in 1999. When not editing or writing, Bobbie enjoys riding her Arabians and Tennessee Walking Horses in endurance rides throughout the Southwest. She lives in Southern California.

GABRIELE BOISELLE is an equestrian photographer and editor of many books and calendars about horses. See her Web site www.editionboiselle.com to learn more about her outstanding photography and her publications. About her collaboration with Linda, Gabriele says, "Linda and I have been friends for 15 years and have traveled extensively together to many countries. I have never seen Linda pass by a horse who was calling for help. I have found us treating horses in the middle of the night, me dead tired and Linda radiating energy and light while working in a cold, dark stable. Because I share in Linda's mission of helping horses (and all animals), I did my utmost to follow her instructions to get the best possible photographs of her TTouches and other exercises, and am thankful for the opportunity to share in her work. The photos were mainly taken in Switzerland, but also at Speyer in Germany, where I live with my horses and dogs."

As far as **BETH PRESTON** can remember, she has always been fascinated by horses, but didn't have much chance to ride until 13, when her completely "unhorsey" parents decided that a girl who spent hours every day just sitting on the pasture fence talking to the neighbor's horses deserved riding lessons. That began her association with the Perkins family, who, in 1964, moved to Huntington Farm in South Strafford, Vermont, and developed one of the first eventing facilities in the area. Over the next 15 years, she dropped in and out of college, married, had children, and completed her professional nursing degree. A sideline drawing portraits, mostly of horses and dogs, first led to the opportunity to illustrate Jane Savoie's now best-selling *That Winning Feeling!* and *It's Not Just About the Ribbons*, published by Trafalgar Square. She still lives in Strafford and divides her time between nursing, farming, riding, drawing, and trying to keep up with seven grandchildren.

Index

Page numbers in *italic* indicate photographs or illustrations.

*A*balone *TTouch*
    Flat Hand Exploration using, 150, 151
    how to, 149, 150, 171, *171*
Abdomen, *Body Exploration,* 153
Above the bit. *See* High-headed
Accident-prone, 33
    See also Balance or coordination issues
Acknowledging fear, 24
"Aerating" the muscles, 149, 203, 218
Aggressive horses, getting after (myth), 14
Aggressive to other horses, *34,* 34–35
    See also Low on pecking order
"Aha moments," xvii–xviii, xix, 22, 262
"Alpha" horse, 34
American Saddlebreds, 35
Animal Behavior, Cognition and Welfare Group
        (Lincolnshire School of Agriculture), 126
Arabians, 35, 70, 107
Asymmetry in horses, 81–82
Attitude impact on personality, 21–22
Auditory learning modality, 24
Aussie (Blocker), 94
"Awakened Mind State," xvii
Awareness. *See* TTouches for Awareness

*B*ach Flower Rescue Remedy, 73, 76
Back and loins, *Body Exploration,* 153, *154,* 155
Backing up (rein back), *36,* 36–37
Back Lift (TTouch), 149, 153, 193–194, *193–194,* 209
Back problems (long, hollow, stiff, dropped, sore), *35,* 35–36
Balance or coordination issues, *37,* 37–39
    See also Accident-prone
Balance Rein (Ridden Work), 278–280, *279–280*
"Balky" (refusal to move forward), *39,* 39–41
    See also Walk, too slow
Barn sour, 41–42
    See also Herdbound; Rearing
Barrels (Ground Exercise), 253, *253*
Basic Circle (TTouch), *147,* 147–151
    breath awareness (your), 123, 150–151
    circle direction, 149, 150
    clockwise, 149, 150
    connecting circles, 147–148
    conscious breathing (your), 150–151
    counter clockwise, 149, 150
    direction of circle, 149, 150
    distal inter phalange (DIP), 149, 150
    face of clock, visualizing, 145, 147, 150
    feedback from horse, 150, 152, 153, *154,* 155
    finger movements, refining, 147, *147,* 149–150
    left-handed, 149
    medial inter phalange (MIP), 149, 150
    "one and one-quarter circle," 147, 148
    one-second circle, 150
    phalanges of fingers, 149–150
    pressure scale, 145, 148–149, 150

proximal inter phalange (PIP), 149, 150
    right-handed, 149
    tempo, 145, 150
    three-second circle, 150
    two-second circle, 150
    visualizing face of clock, 145, 147, 150
    See also Tellington TTouches
Bear TTouch
    Fingertip Exploration using, 151–157, *154–156,* 217
    how to, 148–149, 153, 217–218, *217–218*
Beckett, Tom (DVM), 23
Beet pulp vs. grain, 13
Behavior and training issues, 30–126
    accident-prone, 33. *See also* Balance or coordination issues
    aggressive to other horses, *34,* 34–35. *See also* Low on pecking order
    backing up (rein back), *36,* 36–37
    back problems (long, hollow, stiff, dropped, sore), *35,* 35–36
    balance or coordination issues, *37,* 37–39. *See also* Accident-prone
    "balky" (refusal to move forward), *39,* 39–41. *See also* Walk, too slow
    barn sour, 41–42. *See also* Herdbound; Rearing
    biting, nipping, "lipping," snapping the air, *42,* 42–44. *See also* Grooming sensitivity
    bridling, difficulty with (won't accept bit), *44,* 44–45. *See also* Ear shy
    bucking, *46,* 46–48
    cinchy/girthy, *48,* 48–50, *154,* 155. *See also* Biting
    claustrophobia, *50,* 50–52
    "clipper-phobic" (fear of clipping), *52,* 52–53. *See also* Grooming sensitivity
    "cold-backed," 54, *54. See also* Cinchy/girthy
    cribbing (windsucking), 55
    cross-cantering (cross-firing), 55–56
    crowding/pulling, *57,* 57–59. *See also* Balance or coordination issues
    ear shy, *59–60,* 59–61
    ewe-neck, 55, 61–62
    fear of movement or objects behind, 62–63. *See also* High-headed; Shying ("spooky"); Tail clamping
    feet, won't pick up/leave down, snatches away, *63–64,* 63–65
    gaits, too fast, 65, 65–67
    grooming sensitivity, *67,* 67–68. *See also* Biting; Hard to catch
    hard to catch, *69,* 69. *See also* Grooming sensitivity
    head-tossing/flinging, *70,* 70–71
    heavy on the forehand, *71,* 71–72
    herdbound (reluctant to leave companion), *72,* 72–74
    high-headed, *74,* 74–75. *See also* Back problems; Ewe-neck; Shying ("spooky")
    injury, difficulty treating, 76
    jiggy/joggy, 76–77, *77. See also* Ewe-neck; Overcompetitive

kicking, 16, *78,* 78–80. *See also* Fear of movement or objects behind
    lazy, *80,* 80–81. *See also* Stubborn
    leads, favors one, 81–83. *See also* Balance or coordination issues
    longeing/lungeing problems, 16, 83–84
    low on pecking order, *84,* 84–85. *See also* Aggressive to other horses; Claustrophobia
    mare, moody ("mareish"), 86, 156
    mounting, won't stand while, 49, *87,* 87–88
    overcollected/overbent (behind the bit/behind the vertical), *88,* 88–89
    overcompetitive, 74, *90,* 90–91. *See also* Bucking
    overreaching/forging, 91
    paste deworming, resistance to, *92, 92*
    pawing, *93, 93*
    pulling back when tied, *94,* 94–96
    rearing, 96–98, *97*
    resistant to the leg, 99–100
    ring sour, *100,* 100–101
    "rooting"/snatching at the bit, *101,* 101–102
    rough-gaited, 102
    rubbing against handler, 103, *103*
    running away and bolting, *103,* 103–105
    short-striding (not tracking up), 105–106
    shying ("spooky"), *107,* 107–109
    "spray phobic," *109,* 109–110
    stallion behavior, inappropriate ("studdy"), 43–44, *110,* 110–111, 125
    stiff laterally (doesn't bend in one direction), 112–113
    stubborn, *113,* 113–115
    stumbling, 115–116
    tail, carrying to one side, 119–120
    tail clamping, *116,* 116–118. *See also* Fear of movement or objects behind
    tailgating, 120–121. *See also* Herdbound; Overcompetitive
    tail switching/wringing, 118–119
    tongue biting, sucking, or "lolling," *121,* 121–122
    vet, scared of the, *122,* 122–123
    walk, too slow, 124–125. *See also* Lazy; Stumbling
    weaving, pacing, stall-walking, 16, *125,* 125–126
    See also Roots of unwanted behavior; Tellington Method
Behavior impact on performance, 21
Behind the bit/vertical. *See* Overcollected/overbent
Belly Lift (TTouch), 153, 209–210, *209–210*
Belly muscles *(rectus abdominus),* 35
Bennett, Deb (Ph.D.), 62, 279, 286
Bint Gulida, 130, 210
Biofeedback Institute of Boulder (CO), xviii, 145
Biting, always a biter (myth), 15, 43
Biting, nipping, "lipping," snapping the air, *42,* 42–44
    See also Grooming sensitivity
Bitsa Olympic Equestrian Center (Russia), xix
Bitsa Veterinary Center (Russia), xix
Bitterroot Guest Ranch (Dubois, WY), 188
"Blocked" reaction, 152
Blocker (Aussie), 94

how to, 149, 156, 210–212, *210–212*
Elegant Elephant (Ground Exercise)
  Case Study (Thor: Trailer Loading), 296, *297*
  how to, *237*, 237–239, *239*
Emotional "transmitters," 17
Endocrine anomalies, 13, 15, 22, 86
Endorphins, 55
Entrainment process, xix
Environment and behavior, 16–17
EPM, 16, 22, 33, 39, 46, 115, 124, 134
EquiMeasure, 36
Equine dentists/nutritionists, 12–13
Erhorn, Claus, 89
Essence of Nature, 126
Estrus. *See* Hormonal havoc; Mare, moody
Evolution of Tellington Method, xvii, 145
Ewe-neck, 55, 61–62
Exercise practices, 16, 22
Exertional rhabdomyolysis (tying up syndrome), 13, 137
Exhaustion, 131–133
  See also Colic; Shock; Tying up syndrome
Eyesight, 17

*F*ace of clock (visualizing), TTouch, 145, 147, 150
Faint instinct, 22–23
Fan, The (Ground Exercise), 24, 253–255, *254*
Farriers, 64, *64*
  See also Feet; Hoof issues
Fear, acknowledging, 24
Fear of movement or objects behind, 62–63
  See also High-headed; Shying ("spooky"); Tail clamping
Fear of trailer. *See* Case Study (Thor: Trailer Loading)
Feathering, *Flick of the Bear's Paw* (TTouch), 219
Feedback, listening to, 150, 152, 153, *154*, 155
Feet, won't pick up/leave down, snatches away, *63–64*, 63–65
Feldenkrais, Moshe (Dr.), xvii, xviii, 14, 37
Fidgeting instinct, 23
Fighting with a horse (myth), 14, 23
Fight instinct, 22, 23, 24, 25
Fillis, James, 112
Finger movements (refining), TTouch, 147, *147*, 149–150
Fingernails for *Body Exploration*, 152
Fingertip Exploration, *Body Exploration*, 151–157, *154–156*, 217
"Five Fs" (instinctive behaviors), 22–23
Flat Hand Exploration, *Body Exploration*, 151
Flick of the Bear's Paw (TTouch), 149, 219, *219*
Flight instinct, 22, 23, 24, 25, 107
Flighty. *See* Gaits
Floating teeth, 12
Flower essences for weavers, 126
Foals
  Body Wrap and Body Rope (TTouch), 160
  nipping, 43
  teaching to tie, 96
  See also Young Horses
Follows too closely. *See* Tailgating
Food allergies, 13
Fooling around instinct, 23
Forage as foundation of diet, 13
Forelock Slides. See Mane and Forelock Slides (TTouch)

Forging. *See* Overreaching
Founder, 16
Four modalities of learning, 24
Freework (Ground Exercise), 257–258, *258*
Freeze instinct, 22, 23, 24
French Olympic Committee, 133
Fresh feeling and bucking, 48
Front Leg Circles (TTouch), 156, 174–175, *174–175*

*G*aits, too fast, *65*, 65–67
Gaskin and forearm muscles, *Body Exploration*, 153, *154*, 155
Gastric ulcers, 133–134
  See also Colic
GastroGard, 134
Gel pads caution, 36
German Reken Equine Test Center, xix, 257
Girthy. *See* Cinchy/girthy
Glide of the Eagle (Ground Exercise), 246, *246*
  See also *Joyful Dolphin* (Ground Exercise)
Golden Rule of Horsemanship, 7, 247
Goldstern, 36
"Goosey" horses, 101
Grace of the Cheetah (Ground Exercise)
  Case Study (Thor: Trailer Loading), 296, *297*, 301, *301*
  how to, 240, *240*
Grain-based diets, 13
Grooma brushes, 68, 95
Grooming sensitivity, *67*, 67–68
  See also Biting; Hard to catch
Ground driving. *See* Neckline and Ground Driving (Ground Exercise)
Ground Exercises, xvi, 25, 140
  See also Case Study (Thor: Trailer Loading); Dancing with Your Horse; Playground for Higher Learning; Tellington Method
Group situations for learning, 7
Gut sounds, vital sign, 130, 132

"*H*alf cross-tie" *Taming the Tiger* (TTouch), 163, 166–167, *167*
Half-Walk (Ridden Work), 156, 280–282, *281–282*
Hard to catch, 69, *69*
  See also Grooming sensitivity
Harman, Joyce (DVM, MRCVS), 36
Head shy. *See* Ear shy
Head-tossing/flinging, *70*, 70–71
Health. *See* TTouches for Health
Health issues, 127–137
  choke, 129
  colic, 13, 16, 130–131. *See also* Shock
  exhaustion, 131–133. *See also* Colic; Shock; Tying up
  gastric ulcers, 133–134. *See also* Colic
  neurological dysfunction, 134–135
  shock, 135–136
  stress: pre- and post-surgical care, 136
  tying up syndrome, 13, 137
  See also Tellington Method
Heart rate, vital sign, 132
Heavy on the forehand, *71*, 71–72
Henry, Kirsten, 112
Herdbound (reluctant to leave companion), *72*, 72–74
Herpesvirus, 16, 22, 46, 134
High-headed, *74*, 74–75

See also Back problems; Ewe-neck; Shying ("spooky")
Highly reactive horses, *Body Exploration*, 156, 156–157
High-strung. *See* Gaits
Hilton Herbs, 86
Hind Leg Circles (TTouch), 156, 175–177, *177*
Hippodrome Racetrack (Moscow), xvii, 188
Hologram vs. linear, Tellington Method, 7
Homo sapiens transformation from horses, 5
Hood, Robyn, xviii, 5, 74, 84–85, 148, 248–249, *249*
Hoof issues, 11–12, 115, 156
Hoof Tapping (TTouch), 149, 196, *196*
Hormonal havoc, 13, 15, 22, 86
Horse industry, changes in, 5
Horse's Pain-Free Back and Saddle-Fit Book, The (Harman), 36
"Horse whisperers," 5, 298
"Hot spots," 12, 82, 205
Howard, Charles, 22
Human-animal bond, xvi, xviii, 17, 21
Humanistic Psychology Institute (San Francisco, CA), xvii
Hydration, vital sign, 132
Hypermotile (overactive) gut sounds, 130

*I*nch Worm (TTouch), 149, 197, *197*
Individuality of horses, 5, 7
Injury, difficulty treating, 76
Instinct vs. learning, 22–23
Intelligence, defined, 15
Introduction to the Tellington Equine Awareness Method, An (Tellington-Jones), xix
Intuitive part of brain, TTouch, 145
Irregular canter. *See* Cross-cantering
Irregular gaits. *See* Rough-gaited

*J*ackson, M. J., 91
Jellyfish Jiggle (TTouch), 149, 153, 197–198, *198*
Jelly scrubbers, 68
Jiggy/joggy, 76–77, *77*
  See also Ewe-neck; Overcompetitive
Journey of the Homing Pigeon (Ground Exercise)
  Case Study (Thor: Trailer Loading), 296, *297*, 298, *298*, 301, *301*, 304, *304*
  how to, *241*, 241–243, *243*
Joyful Dolphin (Ground Exercise), 244–246, *244–246*
Joy of Riding. *See* Ridden Work
Justin Thyme, 89

*K*icking, 16, *78*, 78–80
  See also Fear of movement or objects behind
Kinesthetic learning modality, 24
Kleger, Roland, 296
Knot, non-slip, 262, *262*, 263
Kruger, Christine (Dr.), 210–211

*L*abyrinth (Ground Exercise), xix
  Case Study (Thor: Trailer Loading), 296, *297*
  how to, 259–261, *260*
Lace, Zinta, 302
Language of horse, learning to read, 17
Lazy, *80*, 80–81
  See also Stubborn
Leading problems. *See* Crowding/pulling
Leads, favors one, 81–83
  See also Balance or coordination issues